RUNNING ON EMPTY

RUNNING ON EMPTY

The Rise and Fall of Southampton College, 1963–2005

John A. Strong

excelsior editions

An imprint of State University of New York Press

Published by
State University of New York Press, Albany

Printed in the United States of America

Excelsior Editions
is an imprint of State University of New York Press

For information, contact State University of New York Press, Albany, NY
www.sunypress.edu

Production, Laurie D. Searl
Marketing, Kate McDonnell

Library of Congress Cataloging-in-Publication Data

Strong, John A., 1935–
Running on empty : the rise and fall of Southampton College, 1963–2005 / John A. Strong.
p. cm. — (Excelsior editions)
Includes bibliographical references and index.
ISBN 978-1-4384-4697-4 (hardcover : alk. paper) —
ISBN 978-1-4384-4696-7 (pbk. : alk. paper)
1. Southampton College—History. 2. Long Island University—History.
I. Title.
LD3844.S87 2013
378.747'25—dc23 2012025926

10 9 8 7 6 5 4 3 2 1

Contents

List of Figures vii

Preface xi

Chapter One
Long Island University: Beginnings, Bankruptcy, and Bad Decisions 1

Chapter Two
Southampton: A Magical Place 15

Chapter Three
Getting Started, 1963–1970 31

Chapter Four
LIU in Crisis: The Administration of R. Gordon Hoxie, 1964–1968 53

Chapter Five
Drift and Uncertainty, 1968–1972 75

Chapter Six
Great Potential amid Continuing Deficits: The Marmion Administration, 1972–1978 95

Chapter Seven
High Hopes and Hard Realities:
Donald Wilson and the Merger, 1979–1985 129

Chapter Eight
A Decade to Build: The Bishop Steinberg Era Begins 157

Chapter Nine
A Decade of Treading Water, 1993–2002 173

Chapter Ten
Inventing a New College, 2002–2003 203

Chapter Eleven
The Final Days, 2003–2004 225

Chapter Twelve
The Long Goodbye, 2004–2005 249

Chapter Thirteen
Epilogue 265

Notes 281

References 291

Index 299

Figures

1.1. Mary Lai (Center), vice president for finance, and Vincent Aloia (right), academic dean of Southampton College. Photo circa 1966 — 7

3.1. Edward C. Glanz, Southampton College provost 1963–1971, and Richard Bergman, dean of students, in 1963 — 32

3.2. The interdisciplinary faculty poker game — 35

3.3. Professor Ral Welker at his retirement in 1993 — 39

4.1. Long Island University chancellor Gordon Hoxie and Dean Fairbrother, president of the student government — 56

4.2. First Southampton College graduation in May 1967 — 61

5.1. Gordell Wright, Southampton College alumnus from the Shinnecock Nation — 86

6.1. Harry Marmion, president 1972–1978 — 96

6.2. Guatemala Field Trip 1974 — 99

6.3. William Burke, academic dean 1973–1980 — 100

6.4. Signing the first LIU Southampton College Federation of Teacher's agreement, April 2, 1975 — 103

6.5. Faculty union representatives in first labor action ca. 1977 — 103

6.6. Jeff Coderre, the first Fulbright recipient, in 1975 — 106

6.7. Seamester ship Harvey Gamage — 109

6.8. Doug Hardy and Professor Richard Weber with Seamester students 110

6.9. President Steinberg visiting with Seamester students 110

6.10. Helen Smith, director of the HEOP program, Walter Jones, academic vice president, and Eric Posmentier, Natural Science division 115

7.1. Mary Topping, Pat Dzintarnieks, and Dorothy Clarke 133

7.2. Donald Wilson, president of Southampton College, Robert Pattison, union president, and Chancellor Bush Brown, signing labor agreement in 1982 146

7.3. President Donald Wilson and Jenifer Auger at 1982 commencement 147

7.4. Jon Frazier, Buffalo T (Terry) Jones, and Angier Biddle Duke in December 1986 155

8.1. Friends World students at the 1997 World Conference on the Southampton campus. Photo ca. 2012 166

9.1. Tim Bishop, Mary Welker, Robert Sillerman, and President David Steinberg 174

9.2. Robert DeLuca, president of Group for the East End, Provost Tim Bishop, New York State Assemblyman Fred Thiele (class of 1976), New York State Senator Kenneth LaValle, and Southampton student Michele Koestner 179

9.3. Dan Gearon and George Harney at the campus farewell party in 2005 183

9.4. Professor Sandra Shumway and the author in Spring 1998 190

9.5. John Neill and Psychobiology student 191

9.6. Dean Maggie Madden (1999–2000) and Lawrence McCann 194

9.7. Yoshi Higa, "The Pedaling Professor" 195

9.8. Students in the Amazon rainforest in 2001 201

10.1. Faculty representing Southampton College in the Sag Harborfest boat race 207

10.2. Phyllis Kudder Sullivan with student Jackie Sherman Smith 217

10.3. Interdisciplinary seminar on prehistoric culture and ceramics 218

10.4. Dean Charles Hitchcock 224

12.1. Southampton "orphans" protesting at the campus gate 257

12.2. Poster announcing the Orphans of LIU demonstration 258

12.3. Joanne Douglas, '05, wearing her sentiments about LIU on her graduation cap 262

12.4. Chancellor Robert Sillerman at the last graduation 263

13.1. Professor Scott Carlin, Elisha Gibson, Peter Saltanis, and Kasey Jacobs with the "Veggie Car" 266

13.2. Official opening of Stony Brook Southampton 270

13.3. A Tradition Continues: Annual Christmas Windmill lighting 272

13.4. Algonquian Language Revitalization Project 274

13.5. Deserted western section of Southampton campus 279

Preface

I JOINED THE FACULTY OF SOUTHAMPTON COLLEGE in 1965, two years after it opened, and retired in 1998, seven years before it closed at the end of the spring 2005 semester. Long Island University, founded in 1926 by a successful Brooklyn entrepreneur, Ralph Jonas, had expanded to Long Island where it founded the C. W. Post Campus in 1953 and Southampton College a decade later. When I retired, Southampton College provost Tim Bishop urged me to write a brief history of the Southampton campus. He wanted a narrative history of the campus to serve as a reference for use in writing grants and for the preparation of reports to the Middle States Association and the New York State Department of Education. I agreed with the understanding that it would be a serious history project and not a public relations monograph. I was in a good position to take on the project because I had been an active participant in campus affairs over the years, serving as chair of the History department, director of the Social Science division, chair of the Faculty Council as well as sitting on most of the major faculty committees. I also benefited from an excellent doctoral thesis on the history of Long Island University by Elliot Gatner "Long Island University: The History of a Relevant and Responsible University, 1926–1968" (1974), and, more recently from the historical narrative by Maren Carden and Susan Dinan, "Struggle for Access," published in *Long Island University: Seventy Five Years: Access and Excellence* (2001) commemorating the seventy-fifth anniversary of the university. Although my assessment differs somewhat, their research informed my account of the early years of the university.

I was not able to get started until I returned from a Fulbright appointment to teach Native American history and culture at the University of Miskolc in Hungary. There were more interruptions from time to time when

I had to put the college history aside to work on research and writing in my own field of ethnohistory. These interruptions came more frequently and often lasted longer than expected.

By the spring of 2004, I had worked out a preliminary outline and had begun interviewing faculty, students, administrators, staff members, and building and grounds personnel. I was also in the process of preparing an extensive file, consisting of faculty minutes, union records, Middle States and New York State Department of Education reports, campus newspapers, and media clippings. The nature of my project changed abruptly on June 17, 2004, when Long Island University president David Steinberg announced that the Southampton campus would be closed at the end of the 2005 spring semester. My first thought was to box up the records and materials and go home. There was no longer a need for an institutional history. There would be no more Middle States reviews and no more administrators looking for information about the evolution of existing policies or programs.

The week following Steinberg's announcement, my project took on a new life in a very different direction. Many in the campus community urged me to continue my work because they wanted to preserve the story of what they believed was a unique small college in a very special place. The campus on the eastern end of Long Island overlooks Shinnecock Bay with a spectacular view of the Atlantic Ocean. It was this attractive environment that brought prominent artists and writers to Southampton, East Hampton, and Montauk, beginning in the later decades of the nineteenth century. The setting was so engaging that many students never left the area. This sense of place shaped a social bond that evolved over the years, shared by the students, faculty, administrators, and staff from the provost to the custodial personnel. This feeling of belonging to a special small community was expressed frequently in campus publications and in surveys over the years. It was this shared memory they wanted to preserve in a historical record.

Another less benign interest quickly emerged. Questions soon were raised about the abrupt decision to close the campus by former provost Tim Bishop, New York State Senator Kenneth Lavelle (R), State Assemblyman Fred Thiele (I), and Southampton town supervisor "Skip" Heaney (R). Three of these officials had a long and close connection with the college. Bishop had come to the college as an administrator in 1973 and was appointed provost in 1986, a position he held until he retired to run as the Democratic candidate for congress in 2002. He is currently in his sixth term, representing the first congressional district of New York. Thiele and Heaney were among the college's distinguished alumni. Thiele has held his assembly seat since 1995. These men were influential leaders who did not like such surprises in their home districts.

The decision by the Long Island University Board of Trustees to close the campus was surprising to many others as well because the outward signs indicated a bright future for the college. The college had a nationally recognized Marine Science program and Southampton students, mostly from that major, had earned a disproportionately high number of prestigious Fulbright awards. A widely acclaimed Master of Fine Arts in Creative Writing headed by Robert Reeves and Roger Rosenblatt was flourishing. The university had opened Chancellors Hall, a long awaited new administrative and classroom building in 1998 and had announced that a new "green" library would open in the fall. A $60 million capital campaign had been launched in 2003 with plans for extensive campus renovations. The faculty had just completed a new, innovative, interdisciplinary curriculum touted by Southampton College chancellor Robert Sillerman to be the first step in a pioneering educational reform, destined to become a model for higher education throughout the country. The college had frequently been referred to by President Steinberg as "the jewel in the Long Island University crown." After the campus closed he was heard to say that the "albatross" was finally off our neck. Almost overnight the jewel in the crown had become a dead bird burdening the university.

One college administrator voiced a rhetorical question shared by many on Eastern Long Island. As she looked out her office window at the idyllic panorama, she shook her head and said to herself, "what a great place, what potential, how could anyone screw this up?" There were, not surprisingly, many explanations offered that summer and speculation continues to this day. Some of Steinberg's harshest critics were faculty members and students from Southampton College. The faculty passed a vote of no confidence in Steinberg's leadership, followed a few months later by a call for him to resign, citing incompetence, gross mismanagement, and lack of vision. Alumni and student protests echoed the charges made by the faculty. The alumni organization "Save the College at Southampton," and a student group calling themselves "Orphans of LIU," mounted angry protests and petitioned the New York State Department of Education, asking them to launch an investigation into Long Island University's financial affairs.

In his defense, Steinberg argued that the college failed because of factors external to the university over which he and the board of trustees had no control. Among these factors, said Steinberg, were national patterns of declining enrollments in private colleges and universities and steadily increasing costs. One such cost, he said, was directly related to the competition from Marine Science programs established in colleges and universities along the Atlantic coast beginning in the 1990s. These institutions had the resources to develop "state of the art" programs and to grant generous scholarships. Another factor, continued Steinberg, was the failure of the Southampton College alumni and the wealthy residents of the Hamptons to provide financial support. The annual deficit grew steadily to an estimated $10 million in 2004–05, raising the total debt to nearly $77 million by the end of 2005. According to Steinberg, the college had been carried on the backs of the other two major university centers at C. W. Post and Brooklyn. "We could no longer, in good conscience, drain funds from them. We had no choice but to close."

There was no disputing the factors outlined by Steinberg. Warnings about the perilous future of private colleges with insufficient endowments had been sounded in the *Chronicle of Higher Education* in 1967, shortly after the founding of Southampton College. Several other studies came to similar conclusions, citing problems posed by declining enrollments and donor gifts. Small private colleges without sufficient endowments were particularly vulnerable to these developments (Gwathney 1967, 1; see also Bowen 1968, Hans and Wynn 1970). Nearly a decade later studies based on Higher Education General Information Survey files (HEGIS) noted that the situation remained unchanged (Bowen and Minter 1975; El Kawas 1976, 16). Another study concluded that in underfunded private colleges "financial distress may give way to quality distress" (Wynn 1974). A more recent study by John Thelin (2004, 336–38) noted those public and private institutions with endowments drew potential students from the struggling colleges by offering new dorms in place of cinder block structures built in the 1960s, new gyms with health and fitness centers, career planning, and an array of other student services.

Southampton College was a case study of the "struggling colleges" with cinder block dormitories described by Thelin. A rather shabby physical plant suffering from years of "delayed maintenance" made it increasingly difficult to attract and to retain students. Fewer than half of the freshmen students remained for four years and graduated with their class. In contrast, the more successful college and universities became concerned when their graduation rate fell below 75 percent (Thelin 2004, 329). A significant factor related to the high attrition rate was the open enrollment policy necessitated by the dependence on tuition income each fall. Unprepared and poorly motivated students were among the first to drop out. Southampton College, it could be said, was born in stressful times and lived on in great stress until it finally died four decades later, still under stress. Given these realities, argued Steinberg, it was quite an accomplishment for the college to have survived as long as it did.

This line of argument did little to quiet his critics who pressed the LIU officials with more questions. Why, for example, was LIU unable to raise the necessary funds? Why were local residents and alumni unwilling to donate funds? Why had there been no planning in reaction to the steadily spiraling annual deficits? Why had there been no consultations with the local college administrators and Southampton alumni? Why was the Long Island Board of Trustees caught by surprise? How closely had the board been involved in the growing problems that finally caused the college to close? Why had the Board of Trustees been reluctant to make significant donations to support the college?

There were most certainly many external factors limiting the options available to Long Island University officials over the years, but as some critics pointed out, there were also many opportunities lost by questionable decisions, poor management and lack of vision. David Paul, for example, noted in his account of the near collapse and subsequent turnabout of Drexel University (2008, 190) that external factors often become an excuse for failures in management. This narrative will, I believe, help the readers come to their own conclusions about the failure of Southampton College.

Although this history can be read as a cautionary tale about small private colleges, it is, more importantly, the celebration of a small campus community comprised of students, faculty, and staff who shared a strong bond with each other and with a very special place on the far eastern end of Long Island.

This project would not have been possible without the help of many people in the Southampton College community. The largest debt is owed to Tim Bishop who supported the project from the beginning, providing me with a computer and office space. His support continued after he left the college to serve in congress. He was always available by phone to answer questions that frequently arose as I went through the college archives. I recall one occasion when he took my call while he was in his limo rushing to the airport en route to his office in Washington. He was always candid, even with questions that were often critical of the college administration.

The college library staff provided me with invaluable information and insights as they guided me through the archival collections. Robert Gerbereux, director of the Southampton College library, William Roberson, the head reference librarian, Robert Battenfeld, the reference librarian, Pam Greinke, the department secretary, and Mary Pat O. Takis, who prepared a finding aid for the Southampton College Archives, all gave graciously of their time until the college closed in May 2005. Conrad Schaeffling, head of special collections at the B. Davis Schwartz Memorial Library on C. W. Post campus, and his assistant Jarron Jewel guided me through the relevant materials and the documents that had been transferred from Southampton into their collections after 2005. Janet Marks, the Brooklyn Center archivist, was also most helpful in locating documents related to the early years of the university.

An important contribution to the preservation of Southampton College history was made by Southampton town officials. Sundy Schermeyer, the

Southampton town clerk, provided space in the town archives for a special collection of materials related to the history of Southampton College. Zachary Studenroth, the Southampton town historian, and his assistant, Lynnette Pintauro, organized a special collection of documents and photographs given to me during the spring and summer of 2005. The collection is now located permanently in the Southampton Town Clerk's office, in Southampton Town Hall, Southampton, New York.

I owe a great debt to the faculty, students, and staff who agreed to be interviewed either informally or on videotape. They patiently sat for videotaped sessions that sometimes lasted as long as two hours. Casual conversations over the years since 2005 with members of the campus community also gave me unexpected insights into the more personal aspects of institutional operations. Three students, Daniela Gregory, Derek Barbanti, and John Shortle, made important contributions to my research. Gregory, who chose to write her honors thesis on the history of student environmental organizations at Southampton, was active in the environmental movement during her undergraduate years at Southampton. Her research and her own experiences as a participant provided me with significant insights into the evolution of this movement. Barbanti and Shortle filmed my interviews and put them on a DVD format.

I am also indebted to the following members of the college community who read the manuscript and responded with corrections, criticisms, and insightful comments: Donald Baker (Social Science), Robert Danziger (Natural Science), Howard Reisman (Natural Science), Joe Warren (Marine Science), Carol Gilbert (director of alumni relations), Jenifer Auger (class of 1982), and Sandra Shumway (Natural Science). Auger, who went on to earn her MA in English at the University of Massachusetts and is now an assistant professor in English/Communications at Massachusetts College of Liberal Arts, gave me detailed comments about grammar, punctuation, and style.

Invaluable insights came from members of the administration. Rory Shaffer-Walsh, the director of admissions when the college closed, provided me with a broader perspective based on her successful experience in college admissions before and after her time at Southampton. Daniel Rodas, Southampton College's last provost who is now the director of development and human services for the university, helped me to put the history of Southampton College into the broader context of higher education. During the spring of 2005, as the college was gradually closing down, his office door was always open to unannounced visitors. We had many lengthy discussions about the state of higher education in what amounted to a valuable tutoring session for me.

One of the most perceptive sources of information about the history and culture of Long Island University was Mary Lai. Her astounding memory, her insightful analysis, and her openness played a crucial role in my research. She made herself available for an extensive taped interview and for numerous follow-up questions over the phone. Kenneth Mensing, Web project manager and C. W. Post campus historian, helped me to better understand the early history of the Post campus and, in particular, the role of R. Gordon Hoxie.

Two scholars familiar with local college histories shared their knowledge and insights with me. Comparisons with the history of Southampton College's primary competitor, Dowling College, were based largely on the research and publications of Leroy Douglas, who helped me understand the significance of the evolution of Adelphi-Suffolk into Dowling College for my analysis of the early history of Southampton College. Natalie Naylor, professor emeritus from Hofstra University and former director of the Long Island Studies Institute, gave me much appreciated advice and thoughtful criticism, which enriched the manuscript.

My strongest supporter and severest critic was my wife, Jane, who patiently read each chapter with an eagle eye. She played a crucial role in editing and reshaping the final draft.

Chapter One

Long Island University

Beginnings, Bankruptcy, and Bad Decisions

> The university has continued to exist in limbo, teetering between tragedy and comedy.
>
> —Elliott Gatner, 1974

From Beginnings to Bankruptcy, 1926–1946

Soon after Southampton College closed in 2004, the State University of New York at Stony Brook took over Southampton's nationally recognized Marine Science program and began negotiations to purchase the campus. There was a general consensus that it would be in the best interests of all parties for the state to establish a four-year center at Southampton. There is some small irony in this because Long Island University (LIU) was founded in the midst of a controversy between those who advocated a publicly supported university and those who wanted a private institution in Brooklyn. The borough had been growing steadily following World War I and the number of young people who wanted a college education was rising even faster (Clark, Leslie, and O'Brien 2010, 16–17). Some advocates argued that the college should be an extension of the City College (CCNY) rather than a private institution (Gatner 1974, 49). CCNY, founded in 1847, had expanded rapidly by the 1930s, but it was having financial difficulties and had begun raising admissions standards to limit enrollment. For public institutions, in contrast to private colleges that were ever seeking prospective students, additional students led to increased costs.

Students from Brooklyn made up more than one-third of the City College enrollment in 1923, but Brooklyn residents wanted an independent branch established in their own borough. The movement for an independent public college was led by Brooklyn borough president Joseph Guider, who wanted to establish a campus in Prospect Park (Gatner 1974, 53). The movement for a public institution soon became embroiled in controversy over questions of organization, site location, financial control, and concerns about the costs for additional students (ibid., 53–63). In November 1925, Ralph Jonas, a wealthy Brooklyn financier who had recently been elected president of the Brooklyn Chamber of Commerce, worked with Guider to negotiate a settlement. Jonas believed that the only way to resolve the debate was to establish two universities in Brooklyn, one public and one private. Support for a private university came from a small circle of local businessmen. These were flush times on Wall Street. Enormous sums of money flowed in and out of financiers' portfolios. It seemed like a good climate for philanthropic endeavors.

In 1926 Jonas put up $500,000 to establish an endowment fund for a private university while continuing his support for his "two university" proposal. New York mayor Jimmy Walker, and James H. Post, a wealthy industrialist, agreed with Jonas about the feasibility of a private university. Post, who served as president of the Adelphi College Board of Trustees, gave a gift of $50,000 to Jonas's endowment fund. The Adelphi trustees welcomed the development of a four-year coed center because Adelphi, at that time, was a women's college (ibid., 52). At the same time Brooklyn public officials continued pressing for a public university. In the late spring the New York State legislature gave its approval for the creation of a public university in Brooklyn.

Now that a publicly funded university was approved and in the planning stages, Post, Jonas, and their supporters pressed their efforts in the private sector. The fundraising drive continued throughout the spring and summer of 1926. By the late fall nearly $5 million in pledges and cash had been raised (Gatner 1974, 526). Another historic irony for LIU is that the institution was never again to have such immediate success in raising money for its endowment. The large endowment fund, however, certainly impressed the New York State Board of Regents. On December 9, 1926, the New York State Board of Regents approved a provisional charter to a group of educators and entrepreneurs led by Ralph Jonas and James Post.

One of the concerns that motivated Jonas was his deeply felt commitment to the ideal of an open system of higher education that would not discriminate on the basis of race, class, or religion. In a time when many colleges and universities had quotas for Jews and other minorities, Long Island University opened its doors to all. Nicholas Murray Butler, president of Columbia University, for example, went to considerable effort to establish a strict quota system on Jewish applicants. He was not alone. Shortly after World War I, a similar quota system was put in place in Cornell, Union College, Colgate, Syracuse, and St Lawrence (Clark et al. 2010, 18–30).[1] Although the Long Island University policy was to keep no record of race, ethnicity, or religion, the rosters reviewed by historian Elliott Gatner indicate that 210 of the first entering class of 278 were probably Jewish (Gatner

1974, 103). The Brooklyn campus continues to this day to admirably serve the needs of the diverse local community, which now includes large numbers of African Americans and Hispanics.

The new Board of Trustees appointed George Robert Hardie, a former professor of Latin at St. Lawrence University, to be dean of the College of Arts and Sciences. Hardie had also served as an official with the New York State Department of Education. Dean Hardie, pretty much on his own, designed the curriculum and hired the first faculty in less than six months. Wasting no time agonizing over the university's statement of purpose, a task that often daunts faculty and administrative committees, Hardie simply copied the mission statement from his alma mater, St. Lawrence University, where he had served as a professor and administrative officer for twenty-five years (Gatner 1974, 79–83). The problem with his rather imperious approach, however, was that it alienated the faculty and students who resented being left out of the process. To make matters worse, Hardie's personality was ill suited to the role of a university leader who must continually negotiate with faculty, administrators, and trustees. He was described as being "headstrong, unpredictable, dour, imperious, obstinate and authoritarian" (ibid., 84).

The aim of Long Island University, said Hardie, was to prepare students for life by providing them with a "broad outlook on the field of knowledge" and specific training in one chosen subject. More specifically, the emphasis would be on developing intellectual discipline, "reasoned self control," an appreciation for the "finer aspects of life, heightened enjoyment of spiritual satisfactions, well balanced judgment, and a quickened sense of obligation to serve the general good." Most of the subsequent statements made by LIU for accrediting bodies over the years have been a series of footnotes to the St. Lawrence formulation.

The first four years were very difficult. Predictably, Hardie's authoritarian manner soon alienated faculty and students, but the first serious crisis was caused by elements over which Hardie had no control. Two years after the university opened its doors, the stock market collapsed and many of the donors were unable to make good on their pledges (Carden and Dinan 2001, 60). The endowment was wiped out. Ralph Jonas himself lost $93 million in a single afternoon (Gatner 1974, 78n). This was a defining moment for LIU. The institution never fully recovered from this loss. Without an adequate endowment the university was forced to survive primarily on the tuition that came in each September. Under these circumstances the best of leaders would have had difficulty achieving significant improvements in facilities or in the quality of faculty, administrators, and students.

In spite of these problems, the university survived as the enrollment grew to 1,575. The admissions office accepted nearly everyone who applied, drawing from those who couldn't get into Columbia, St. Johns, New York University, or Fordham (Rice 1965, 63–64). LIU offered a second chance for "late bloomers" and for first-generation college students from immigrant families. These were, of course, high risk students, many of whom never "bloomed" at all. The attrition rates were probably very high. Unfortunately, the admissions office kept no records nor statistics and had no formal admissions policy until after a reorganization in 1955 (ibid., 77). The attrition rate for 1954–58 was nearly 74 percent, about 24 percent higher than the national average. The attrition may have been even higher in the 1930s.

Although the attrition rates were high, the New York State Board of Regents replaced the provisional charter with a permanent charter on February 19, 1931. The next goal was to have the university accredited by the Middle States Association. This accreditation was very important because it opened the door to much-needed financial support from foundations and government agencies. Hardie was advised that the university should withdraw its application because it had no hope of accreditation (Gatner 1974, 583). Two of the reasons, undoubtedly, were the tenuous fiscal condition of the university and the unprofessional operating conditions of the admissions office (Rice 1965, 218–20). Without an endowment, Hardie had difficulty covering operating expenses. In desperation he had begun borrowing from banks against future tuition, a policy that would soon lead to a major economic crisis for the university.

Under a cloud of uncertainty about the survival of the institution, the university held its first commencement on June 11, 1931. The ceremony was held in the auditorium of the Brooklyn Academy of Music. The somber celebration was marked with an incident that historian Elliott Gatner thought was a foreshadowing of the university's subsequent history. The stage curtain fell down on the United States Secretary of the Interior, Ray Lyman Wilbur, as he was giving the commencement address, covering him and the faculty sitting on the stage. Gatner commented, "perhaps, somehow, this was an omen. The University has continued to exist in limbo, teetering between tragedy and comedy" (Gatner 1974, 130).

Rumors of tragedy soon were heard. Student and faculty disaffection with Dean Hardie's imperious style along with the university's growing debt gave rise to a rumor that the Board of Trustees was going to close the institution. Enrollment had dropped below nine hundred (Carden and Dinan 2001, 60). The rumor of a closing, a familiar theme later in the history of Southampton College, was not so far from the truth. The trustees had given Hardie responsibility to manage the university's fiscal affairs, but his experience at St. Lawrence, a university with a large, stable endowment, was of no use to him in Brooklyn. In the spring of 1932 the university had been able to pay the faculty only a portion of their full salaries. By June 1932 there was only $3,738 left in the university bank account (Gatner 1974, 530).

Jonas, the acting chairman of the board, wasted no time. He appointed five new board members and did not renew Hardie's contract. In Elliott

Gatner's words, Hardie's departure was "unwept, unhonored, and unsung" (Gatner 1974, 137). Jonas then hired Tristram Walker Metcalfe, an old high school friend, first to serve as the chief financial officer, and later as president of the university. Metcalfe, a self-taught accountant with a gift for grasping the intricacies of financial statistics, did not have a college degree, but he did have some experience as an advisor to the mayor of New York on educational policy.[2] Metcalf quickly stanched the hemorrhaging with a fiscal reorganization plan, which included extensive reductions in all areas of the budget and an end to borrowing against future tuition. The university survived the immediate crisis, but was unable to improve the quality of its facilities and academic programs. The trustees had survived financial distress by implementing a policy that led to "quality distress." A study of forty-eight liberal arts colleges and universities by the Center for Higher Education defined "quality distress" as the outcome of an operating mode that focuses on institutional survival from one year to the next. "Faced with financial problems they survive by cutting into one of their last reserves, their quality" (Wynn 1974, 16–17, 28).

In 1935 Metcalfe made a second attempt to win Middle States approval and was turned down once more. An unaccredited institution with a small endowment can, under the best of administrations, make very little progress in any direction. Forced to rely primarily on tuition for survival, LIU could not afford to be at all selective in its admission policy. Middle States may also have looked askance at a university whose president did not have a college degree, no matter how astute he was at financial matters. Four years later, Metcalfe again applied to Middle States, with the same result. The evaluation team noted the lack of an adequate endowment, low admissions standards, and a questionable athletic scholarship policy in its rejection of Metcalfe's application (Gatner 1974, 583). The scholarship issue cast a shadow on one of the university's most celebrated accomplishments during the prewar period. The LIU basketball team, the "Blackbirds," won national attention when they went to the finals in the first two National Invitation Tournaments (NIT) in 1938 and 1939. In 1939 they were undefeated and won the national title. Their victory was tarnished by the suspicion that their coach, Claire Bee, had bent the rules for his players. Rule bending, unfortunately, was widely condoned by many of the college basketball powers at the time. This practice led to a major scandal in the early 1950s that would have a devastating impact on LIU's reputation.

It was the lack of an endowment, however, that was the more serious of the problems noted by the Middle States evaluators. The university had no choice but to operate on a hand-to-mouth fiscal basis, making it vulnerable to outside forces over which it had no control. In 1942, when the military draft drastically reduced enrollment, the university again came close to closing. Faced with the grim choice between selling its assets and closing or going into bankruptcy, Metcalfe chose the latter (Carden and Dinan 2001, 63). The bankruptcy option required the university to restructure its financial affairs under the supervision of Judge Matthew T. Abruzzo. President Metcalfe worked with the judge to guide the university through the crisis. In 1943, Ralph Jonas resigned and was replaced on the board by William Zeckendorf, a wealthy real estate investor. What saved the university, of course, was the return of the veterans whose education was paid for through the G.I. Bill. Enrollment jumped from 636 students in 1943 to 4,216 in 1948.

The G.I Bonanza and the Move to Brookville, 1946–1953

In 1946 Metcalfe hired Mary Lai, who had graduated from LIU in 1942, to serve as bursar. It turned out to be one of the best hires in the history of the university.

Mary Lai, who retired in 2004, is a bright, energetic, and pragmatic woman who outshined and outlived most of the university leaders under whom she served. She soon became an indispensable member of the university administration. Lai worked tirelessly on the documents required by the bankruptcy court until 1947 when the university was declared solvent. Another important development was the election of Zeckendorf to serve as chairman in 1947. He continued in that office for the next two decades, providing a stable continuity of leadership. Zeckendorf's financial success and his growing influence with financial and political leaders in the New York area were important assets to the young university.

The sudden increase in enrollment ended the financial crisis, but created problems of staffing and space. The understaffed faculty were teaching fifteen-hour loads each semester, whereas most four-year colleges based faculty salaries on a twelve-hour requirement. Many LIU instructors were also teaching an additional six hours of overload. These faculty loads raised serious questions about the quality of education during these early years. The instructors were overworked, underqualified, and underpaid. Only a small number of them held doctorates, and they were still being paid at 1927 levels (Gatner 1974, 258). The facilities were cramped. In some cases, four faculty had to share the same desk. The university had to rent space in nearby office buildings, which was often not suitable for a college campus. The library, for example, had to place a major part of its collection in a rat-infested storage area. The result was disastrous, as the rodents destroyed most of the materials.

Another problem was the unique difficulties faced by the returning veterans. Many lacked the experience and skills required for college-level work. They also had pressing practical needs such as housing, part-time employment, medical needs, and help with the bureaucratic maze in the Federal Veterans Administration. The university appointed a veterans' counselor to

FIGURE 1.1. Mary Lai (center), Vice President for Finance. Ms. Lai joined the LIU administration in 1946 and retired in 2003. Southampton College Academic Dean Vincent Aloia (right). Photo circa 1966. *Courtesy of Southampton Town Historian.*

serve as an "ombudsman," who was an intermediary linking the veterans, the federal Veterans Administration and the university (Gatner 1974, 262–63). The administration did little, however, to help the veterans and the other students who needed remedial assistance. This undoubtedly played a significant role in the unusually high attrition rates that plagued the university.

Instead of consolidating the postwar gains and responding to the concerns of the Middle States critique, Metcalfe went shopping for a place in the country. There appears to have been no consultation with the faculty or staff about this important decision and no evidence that an alternative policy that would place more funds into a university endowment was even considered. This is another example of policy decisions made from the top without benefit of consultation and without consideration of long-range consequences. Metcalfe became convinced that when the veterans graduated, LIU would need to find a new recruiting area. "Long Island," he told the trustees, "is a fertile area" (Gatner, 269). The influx of new tuition dollars, therefore, was not used to build up an endowment, but Metcalfe was certainly right about the potential for student recruiting in Nassau County.

Metcalfe's search brought him to the estate of Marjorie Merriweather Post Davies, whose father, Charles William Post, founded the C. W. Post breakfast cereal company (J. Murphy 1989, 29–36). The property, located in the town of Oyster Bay on the fashionable "Gold Coast" of Nassau County, was in marked contrast to the urban environment of downtown Brooklyn. In May 1947, Metcalfe negotiated the purchase of the Post estate for $260,000. It was a bargain even in those times because the estate, which included twenty landscaped acres and several buildings, was valued by the tax assessor at more than a million dollars (Gatner 1974, 256). Marjorie Davies apparently felt that the property was becoming too expensive to maintain. There was, however, an important proviso requiring that an exemption from the residential zoning laws be obtained before the purchase could be completed.

Frustrated by these delays, Metcalfe decided to establish a base near Brookville for an evening extension program. When Carrol Newsom, the associate commissioner of education, learned of these plans, he wrote a sharp rebuke to Metcalfe in January 1951 telling him that the courses offered in Brookville were not registered and, therefore could not be given college credit (LIUABCL, RG 2:6, Newsom to Walker January 15, 1951). The following spring, Metcalfe established evening extension courses in Hicksville, ignoring the warning from the state education department. In the fall, he opened classes on the Davies estate even though the zoning issue had not been resolved.

Metcalfe's actions undoubtedly further provoked the landowners in Brookville. Alarmed at the prospect of a university disturbing their quiet, rustic environment, they organized a well-financed legal action to oppose any change in the zoning law. Although they would have opposed any university, they were particularly agitated by the nature of LIU's student body, which included so many "Negroes, Jews, or Italians" from Brooklyn (Gatner 1974, 281). On February 20, 1951, the *New York Times* headlines reinforced negative perceptions of the university. Three LIU basketball players had been arrested in the point-shaving scheme that soon became a national scandal. This was much more serious than the minor infraction attributed to Coach Clair Bee in the late 1930s, but it suggests that a climate of overlooking such behavior may have played a role in the devastating scandal that engulfed the university in 1951.

Four more LIU players and twenty-five others from six major universities across the country were eventually charged (Rosen 1978, 113–17; 141–46). It was a public relations disaster, which reinforced the negative perceptions of Long Island University. Ironically, Coach Bee and his team had taken a principled stand in 1936 when they were invited to play in the Olympics, which were held that year in Hitler's Germany. They were told that the Jewish players could not accompany the team. Coach Bee, at the urging of his team, turned down the opportunity to play on the international stage (Carden and Dinan 2001, 63). Bee also refused to play games in any of the segregated states in the United States. This principled stand, unfortunately, was overshadowed by the basketball scandal. It could be argued that the widespread publicity about the scandal solidified a negative public perception of LIU that it was never able to counter.

Fundraising had always been a major challenge for the university because donors were reluctant to give funds to an institution with a reputation for academic mediocrity and fiscal instability. The university's problems, compounded now by their involvement in one of the worst sports scandals in American history, undoubtedly influenced the Middle States Association to postpone yet another application for accreditation. In December 1951, Metcalf was told to reschedule an inspection by the Middle States commission in 1953. Unfortunately, Metcalfe did not live to see his beloved university achieve accreditation. In February 1952, President Metcalfe, whose health had been failing for a year, died of cancer.

The board appointed William M. Hudson as acting president to replace Metcalfe. Hudson, described as "an uncertain and pusillanimous leader" by historian Elliott Gatner, faced some very difficult challenges. Hudson had a Yale masters degree and a law degree from Brooklyn but he was cautious and hesitant to take the sort of risks that excited Metcalfe. The Board of Trustees, buffeted by scandals, falling tuition revenues, and rising operation costs, was having second thoughts about opening a campus in Brookville (Gatner 1974, 293). The point-shaving scandal, in particular, fueled opposition to the expansion into Nassau County. The legal battle waged over the zoning regulation by the wealthy landowners who lived near the proposed campus site dragged on for six years. Hudson decided that it would be best to abandon the attempt to establish a base in Nassau County for the immediate future. Students would have to finish their degrees at the Brooklyn Center and receive a diploma from there.

In an interesting footnote, particularly in the light of the Southampton closure, one of the students enrolled in the Hicksville program threatened to sue on the grounds that the university was bound by law to grant him a diploma from Hicksville, not from Brooklyn. Alvin Bahnsen, a history professor at C. W. Post, recalled the incident. He said that he remembered "most vividly" a meeting called by Hudson at the Hicksville High School with the students enrolled in the university's evening program there. One student, he said, angrily refused to accept the closure and "challenged the right of the university to close the extension, on the grounds that the letter of acceptance to the extension program assured him that would receive his degree through the Extension Program at Brookville . . . it was enough to force the Acting President to reconsider his action" ("Celebrating the 25th Anniversary of C.W. Post," 1979). The student's assertion that the admission acceptance was a binding legal contract raised the possibility of expensive legal actions which the university could ill afford.

The Admiral and the Struggle for Accreditation, 1953–55

Hudson's fears about the expansion were abated in October 1953, when the court ruled in favor of LIU. One month later, the LIU Board of Trustees announced the appointment of retired admiral Richard Lansing Conolly to replace acting president Hudson, somewhat allaying the fears of the Old Brookville elites. Zeckendorf, in his autobiography, proudly claimed sole credit for recruiting Conolly (Zeckendorf and McCreary 1970). This was the way things had always been done at LIU. There was no search committee with participation from faculty, administrators, or students. Conolly, a four star admiral who had served as president of the Naval War College, gave the university instant recognition and an enhanced status. His right wing political views also helped in developing good relations with the Gold Coast elites.[3] One of Conolly's favorite speeches for local organizations and school commencements was titled "Soviet Imperialism: A Threat to Freedom Everywhere" (LIUABCL, RG 2:6, Conolly File May 10, 1952). He also warned about the dangers of increasing the availability of public-supported higher education, a trend, he said, that was "undesirable in a democracy" (LIUABCL, RG 2:6, Charter Day Address March 8, 1955).

Conolly endorsed the move to expand the university and his presence assured the wealthy Brookville neighbors that the new university campus would be governed by a firm, conservative hand. During his eight and one-half years as president, the university enrollment grew from 2,000 to 10,000. To his credit, he increased faculty salaries from a level far below accepted standards to a level only slightly below average. Conolly, however, adopted Metcalfe's imperious leadership style, paying little attention to the faculty's voice in policy matters.

Conolly now moved aggressively to obtain Middle States accreditation. Several accounts credit Conolly's personal qualities, so dramatically expressed in his military career, with the successful campaign to obtain accreditation. He appointed R. Gordon Hoxie to serve as the dean of the College of Arts and Sciences at the Brooklyn center in the spring of 1954 and asked him to oversee the accreditation process. Hoxie came to LIU with a distinguished resume which included a PhD from Columbia University and three years of experience as assistant to the chancellor at the University of Denver. Hoxie was an easy choice for Conolly because the two men had similar political views and administrative styles. When Middle States finally granted LIU accreditation in 1955, Hoxie was quick to claim full credit for the success. In an article Hoxie wrote for the *Oyster Bay Guardian* in 1969, which was reprinted in a pamphlet prepared for the twenty-fifth anniversary of C. W. Post, he gave his own account of the accreditation campaign. His recollection reveals a great deal about the leadership styles of both men:

> The Admiral had applied for accreditation and he promised a comprehensive report by September first. A committee had been at work on the report for several months . . . but he deemed their report completely unacceptable. My orders: start all over and finish it in thirty days. That is how I got in the habit of a seven day week, 14 hours per day schedule. . . . At 3:00 A.M., September first this report was completed. We got accredited.

This account, however, is sharply disputed by Mary Lai, who worked closely with the faculty and staff committees during the preparation of the report (pers. comm. Dec. 23, 2005). She said that the report was completed by the committees in the spring, but Conolly believed that it was often too critical and needed to be more "positive." Hoxie, said Lai, edited it with puffed-up prose and gave it a more positive spin. In fact, she continued, he complicated the process at the last minute when the committee was reviewing the final printed draft. "He came into the room all excited and insisted that the organizational chart for the university officers be changed because he was listed as Ralph G. Hoxie instead of R. Gordon Hoxie." The committee had to remove the page and make the change. Hoxie's account in the Oyster Bay newspaper was misleading in another way as well. Middle States did not grant LIU accreditation in the fall of 1954 as Hoxie implied. The evaluating team delayed approval for another year.

The Middle States team visited the university and issued a preliminary evaluation in October 1954 (Gatner, 1974, 585–86; LIUABCL R.G. 3:2, Middle States Evaluation Oct. 10–13, 1954). The commission noted with concern that there was a high faculty turnover and low morale. The faculties at Brooklyn and Post, they reported, were not included in the development of university policy and felt somewhat alienated from the administration. The Middle States investigators noted that the courses tended to be descriptive rather than analytical. Another concern, of course, was the lack of an endowment.

The commission raised serious questions about the admissions office, which was still below established standards. "The admissions officers," said the report, "are pleasant people, but it is not clear how much actual training they have had in their field. It was noticeable that although the evaluators were informed that the admissions standards had been recently raised, the officers carrying out the admissions policy did not seem to be aware of this fact" (quoted in Rice 1965, 75). The university had, in fact, never changed its open admissions policy and had never made a serious effort to bring its admissions office up to a minimum level of professional standards. The Middle States commission again noted that there was little evidence of university coordination of curricula and programs. The faculty tended to identify primarily with their own centers rather than with LIU as an institution (Gatner 1974, 592–93). In spite of these reservations, the Middle States report noted that LIU was meeting the needs of Brooklyn-area students whose "standing in high school was in the lower middle range of achievement" (quoted by Gatner, 587).

Hoxie's efforts at "spin" didn't work as well as claimed in his account. Middle States accreditation commission chairman Ewald Nyquist wrote to Admiral Conolly on December 2, 1954, telling him that the commission had decided to withhold approval for another year. At that time the commission wanted to see evidence that progress had been made in six areas listed in the letter (Rice 1965, Appendix C). The areas of concern included financial resources for the university, the reluctance of Conolly to delegate authority, the high number of adjunct (part time) instructors, the lack of faculty participation in the policymaking activities of the university, and the need for a "realistic educational plan for the development of the entire institution over the next few years, with particular attention to the development of the Brookville (C. W. Post) branch." This setback undoubtedly contributed to a souring of the relationship between Conolly and Hoxie. Another factor was the deteriorating relationship between Hoxie and the faculty at Brooklyn. His imperious leadership style alienated both students and faculty. Finally, in the spring of 1955, Conolly removed Hoxie from Brooklyn and named him president of the new C. W. Post center. Rumors circulated that Conolly actually wanted to fire Hoxie but feared that it might alienate Marjorie Merriweather Post Davies and some of the wealthy Gold Coast donors who liked Hoxie. Hoxie had also cultivated support among the LIU trustees.

In the fall of 1955, Nyquist wrote to Conolly telling him that the Middle States Commission had voted to accredit LIU, but warned that they were still concerned about the university finances, the admissions practices, and the problems posed by the admission of the "bottom ranking students." The endorsement was rather weak, but it was a major threshold for the university. The commission recommended that immediate attention be paid to a review of unified institutional goals and related programs for the centers and required a provisional report in five years documenting efforts to address all of their concerns.

Ignoring the concerns in the report for a more centralized university structure, the trustees further confused the matter by giving the new campus a name that encouraged an independent identity. They decided to name the campus after Mrs. Davies's father in an attempt, said historian Elliott Gatner, "to present a more genteel image of the college and to de-emphasize the connection with the 'hustling, bustling,' entrepreneurs and 'dirt clogged streets of Brooklyn.' It was also an 'obvious move to flatter Mrs. Post [*sic*], one of America's wealthiest women, and to encourage her financial support" (Gatner 1974, 303; Carden and Dinan 2001, 68). Although she did give about $5 million over a fifteen-year period, Hoxie eventually alienated her and her family with constant badgering for more money. He had blatantly stressed his relationship with the Post family to bolster his support from the Board of Trustees. The Post family finally broke off all contact with LIU, refusing to respond to correspondence from the development office (Kenneth Mensing, pers. comm. May 2006).

The decision to name the campus after the Post family also set in motion an "identity crisis" that has never been resolved and, many believe, hurt both fund raising and student recruitment. The name of a college often has a significant impact on the public perception of the institution (*New York Times* Aug 20, 2005). Mary Lai addressed this issue in an analysis she wrote in 1970. She noted that some university officials had discussed the confusion created by the C. W. Post name in 1963, about the time that Southampton College was founded. Many thought that it was an independent college, and others were uncertain as to where it was located. A treasurer's report in 1963 stated that "[t]he obvious solution for clarifying these ambiguities is to name each center of the university by its location. Thus we would have: LIU Brooklyn, LIU Brookville, and LIU Southampton" (Lai 1970, 12). Lai agreed with this proposal, pointing out that these designations put the university name at the forefront. In response the LIU Board of Trustees ordered that letterheads, programs, and newspaper advertising place the LIU name in prominence, but it did not change the name of the Post campus.

In spite of the changes ordered by the board, the public perception of LIU and its various parts remained rather vague. Susan Ulrich, who worked in the Southampton College admissions office for many years, spoke of her frustrations when she went to high school college day fairs: "Organizers as well as prospective students weren't sure if we were a branch of the state university, an independent college, or a part of LIU. Our public image seemed to be blurred and poorly understood" (pers. comm. July 2005). There were, of course, other factors at work here. Many of the students and faculty at Post and Southampton preferred to identify with their own centers because of Long Island University's negative image.

The Post campus, however, was an immediate success. The estate buildings were transformed into campus facilities to accommodate the rapid growth in the student population. From the two hundred students enrolled in 1955, the student body grew to include seven thousand undergraduate and 3,500 graduate students by the mid-1970s. Demands for teacher education programs led to the creation of extension centers in Hauppauge, Brentwood, and Westhampton Beach. This experience with extension programs may have encouraged President Conolly and the trustees to consider a more extensive expansion onto eastern Long Island. The president wrote a confidential letter to Edward Fearon, the president of the Southampton Chamber of Commerce, on May 10, 1961, telling him that the university had decided to "establish a co-educational four-year liberal arts college in Southampton for commuting students in the fall of 1962, provided that suitable physical facilities are provided by the local community." In a postscript, he asked that Fearon not mention this decision until "our joint project is further developed." (LIUABCL R.G. 2:6, Box 1, Conolly to Fearon).

A few months later, the Middle States committee returned to LIU to determine the progress made by the university in addressing the concerns raised in 1954 (LIUABCL R.G. 3:2, Middle States Evaluation of LIU Oct. 22–25, 1961, 69–70). There were impressive improvements, noted the committee, but there was still a concern about the financial organization and the identity of the university. The committee noted that the university had not restructured the fiscal organization. It was still a federation of campuses, each with its own budget supported primarily by its own tuition. This structure contributed to a continuing "identity problem" for the university. The faculty also tended to identify with their own campus rather than with LIU. A priority, stated the Middle States committee, should be to establish a university-wide set of goals and purposes.

Another concern that had not been addressed was the tendency of the administrators to ignore the faculty when they formulated university policies. This alienated many of the faculty and contributed to a pattern of poor relations between them and the administration (Gatner 1974, 594). Faculty morale remained low. The faculty were still concerned about the excessive workloads and complained that university personnel policies were "generally inadequate." These problems contributed to the emergence of an aggressive union movement in the 1970s.

One key recommendation that had particular significance for the establishment of Southampton College called upon the university to defer all new expansion until they consolidated the gains made at C. W. Post (Gatner 1974, 593). This advice from Middle States, which came in October 1961, in the midst of Conolly's negotiations with local Southampton citizens, was ignored. There was very little thought given to the potential problems posed by the lack of sufficient capital to adequately fund the development of the new center. Many board members were very enthusiastic about the move and raised few objections. According to Mary Lai, one trustee was heard to exclaim, "Southampton, the name is magic!" (Lai, pers. comm. Oct. 25, 2005).

Chapter Two

Southampton

A Magical Place

> What a great place, what potential, how could anyone screw this up?
>
> —Anonymous administrator reflecting on the college closing, June 2005

Adelphi Considers a Southampton Campus, 1953–1960

There had been some discussion about establishing a college in eastern Suffolk during the early postwar years. Adelphi College, which had moved to Garden City from Brooklyn in 1929, and had become coeducational after World War II, began offering extension courses in Suffolk County in 1953 for the staff at Pilgrim State Hospital. The following year, the Long Island Association of businesses began to discuss the advantages of a four-year college on eastern Long Island. The New York State Department of Education reported that about half of Long Island high school students wanted to continue their education after graduation. There was particular interest in a teacher's college for Suffolk County (Douglas 2006, 92–95). The state developed tentative plans in 1955–56, but in spite of the Brookhaven town government's enthusiastic endorsement, political squabbles involving Robert Moses and the local leaders in the Democratic and Republican parties doomed the proposal. In the summer of 1956, Adelphi went ahead on its own and opened a very successful business program in the Port Jefferson high school, and then began to develop plans for a four-year college in Stony Brook.

In sharp contrast to the LIU administration's move into Suffolk County, Adelphi carefully prepared a plan for the prospective college, which included market research and proposals for fundraising. Anticipating a student body equally divided between dormitory residents and commuters, the plans called for dormitories to be constructed along with classrooms and an athletic field. The proposed location was changed abruptly in the fall of 1956 when

New York State decided to open a four-year university center in Stony Brook. Adelphi turned its attention to potential locations in Sayville and Southampton. In 1958, three years before Conolly's confidential letter to Fearon, Adephi began working with Southampton mayor Harold DuFrane and local civic leaders such as Angier Biddle Duke and William B. Platt on plans for a college in Southampton (Douglas 2007, 88–89; *Southampton Press* June 5, 1958).

In the summer of 1958, the Adelphi trustees began negotiating for the purchase of the Chisholm Estate on a hundred-acre tract in Southampton overlooking West Neck Harbor on Peconic Bay. William Platt formed a committee to raise funds to purchase the property and to finance the construction of dormitories and other campus facilities. If Platt's committee was successful, Adelphi planned to have the campus ready for the first class in the fall of 1960. The Southampton location appealed to the Adelphi administrators because it offered an opportunity to develop relationships with some of the well-known artists and writers who spent their summers in the Hamptons (Douglas 2007, 89). In October 1958, Dr. Paul Eddy, president of Adelphi, addressed the Southampton Chamber of Commerce at a meeting that attracted more than one hundred people. He praised William Platt for his fundraising efforts and went on to announce that "we are on the verge of the contract signing for the Chisholm Estate" (*Southampton Press* Oct. 2, 1958). He spoke with great enthusiasm about the plans for developing a liberal arts college which would eventually enroll a thousand students, but he added in a note of caution that the local people would have "to provide the money for our home here."

Although enthusiastic about the prospects for a Southampton campus in the idyllic setting on Peconic Bay, the trustees moved cautiously. They had been warned by Chester Blakelock, the secretary of the Long Island State Park Commission, that Southampton was too far east of the population center in Suffolk County to attract commuter students (Douglas 2007, 88). There was also a concern about the time needed for constructing new buildings and renovating the existing structures. Within six months after Dr. Eddy's address, the excitement over a Southampton campus had begun to fade. The anticipated donations never materialized. Many of the wealthy Southampton summer residents who could have given significant contributions had little interest in a local college without a national reputation. Some of them were openly hostile to the whole idea. It was a lesson that the Long Island University administrators ignored over the decades as they fruitlessly pursued the illusion of a pot of gold somewhere in the estates along the Atlantic shore. Adelphi, however, wisely paid attention to these potential problems and turned its attention to Sayville, in the town of Islip, which was located much closer to a denser population base. As a result, the anticipated 1960 opening of Adelphi-Suffolk College took place there rather than in Southampton. In 2004, when LIU closed the Southampton campus, Adelphi-Suffolk, now called Dowling College and located on the former Vanderbilt estate in Oakdale, enrolled 7,300 full and part-time students.

Support from The Grassroots: The Southampton College Committee, 1961–63

The efforts to bring a college to Southampton continued in spite of the disappointing experience with Adelphi. It was the East End Guidance Association, however, that took the first initiative. Members of the association approached the LIU Board of Trustees about the possibility of establishing a branch on the East End. Long Island University, flush from the success of their expansion to the C. W. Post campus in Brookville, responded positively, but said that a community group would have to provide the property with buildings suitable for a college facility. They wanted to be able to open up the new campus with as little delay as possible. In February 1961, the guidance association approached Ed Fearon and asked for his support. In March, the new Southampton village mayor, Edward Brennan, established a committee made up of representatives from interested community groups to raise funds for a college. Many parents, local businessmen, and civic leaders also saw the advantages of a local college.

There was widespread agreement among the permanent residents about the advantages of a local college. The newly established Southampton Village College Committee began exploring possible sites for a campus. They inquired about the sixteen-acre Merrill estate on Hill Street in the village, which was owned by Amherst College. The property was valued at $225,000 and there was an adjacent twenty-five-acre parcel available for $96,000. According to Mayor Brennan, the title to the property would revert back to the village if the Long Island University campus failed. The village, said Brennan, could then sell it to another educational institution.

The mayor proposed to raise the funds from the eighty thousand residents living in eastern Suffolk at that time. This approach, he believed, would placate the summer colony who had voiced opposition to the college plan. He was wrong. Southampton and the neighboring town of East Hampton had become fashionable summer resorts for wealthy New Yorkers by the beginning of the twentieth century. These summer residents wanted privacy and high-quality medical care. Craigh Leonard, chairman of the hospital fundraising committee, argued that Brennan's proposal would compete with the hospital's campaign. Leonard spoke for many of the wealthy summer residents, who wanted the assurance of a good medical facility while they were so far away from their own Manhattan doctors. The summer colony had little interest in an educational institution that might disturb their bucolic retreat from urban life. In addition to the mayor's miscalculation about the summer people, other parts of his proposal were also quite naive. He had no idea what it would cost to establish and maintain a four-college campus, and he was far too optimistic about raising funds from the full-time middle-class residents in the Hamptons.

The college committee organized a public meeting on September 29, 1961, in the Parrish Art Museum auditorium to present the plans for the college and to allow for an open discussion of the proposal. President Conolly and members of his staff attended to answer questions from the audience. The committee was somewhat taken aback by the response to their presentation. The press reported that the meeting was marked by "bitterness, wrangling, petty politics and poor taste." Representatives from the summer colony threatened "serious decay" in their relations with the village if the college plans went forward. Some said they would look elsewhere for a summer retreat (*Southampton Press* Oct. 5, 1961).

One of the village trustees who opposed the college plan read telegrams from Mrs. Rodney Wanamaker and other influential summer residents denouncing the mayor's proposal. Strident voices from the opposition argued that the college would bring "undesirables" into the community and wondered "what kind of people these professors and students would be." They did not want an "invasion" of young people. The Southampton Village Improvement Association charged that "a large influx of strangers is not desirable," and predicted that it would drive away the wealthy summer residents. The only change the summer colony supported was an improved hospital with more medical services for the elderly. Some argued that fundraising for the hospital would be more difficult because of competition with the college campaign to finance the purchase of land. They also questioned the need for a college here because the State University of New York had just opened a campus at Stony Brook. They might have added that Adelphi-Suffolk was just beginning its second year in Sayville. Both of these potential competitors were better located in areas of fairly dense and growing populations.

President Conolly tried his best to strike a positive note. He told the audience that the university would be a benefit to the community because it was a private, independent institution and would not be "a drain on the public purse." The opposition, however, brushed his comments aside and continued to voice their vigorous objections. The tone of the opposition shook Conolly and the mayor. The next day the Long Island University trustees issued a statement to the press saying that as a result of the meeting, they would form a committee and give the matter further study. The board members may also have been influenced by the Middle States admonitions about overextending the university resources. There was a concern as well that they not repeat the long and costly court battle that the university had experienced with the Post expansion. It may have been at this time that Conolly decided it would not be feasible to open the college in the fall of 1962. The village mayor was now wary about committing more support to the college campaign. Fearing that his participation would cost him the support of the influential summer residents, Mayor Brennan resigned from the college committee.

In spite of these setbacks, the college committee continued its work. The committee broadened the organization to include representatives from the towns of Southampton, East Hampton, Shelter Island, Southold, Riverhead, and Brookhaven. The expanded committee changed its name to the College Committee of Eastern Long Island (Gatner 1974, 325). Support from the permanent residents of the local communities now began to grow. The Southampton Teachers' Association unanimously voted to endorse the establishment of a Long Island University campus here. A few days later, Edward Fearon, announced that the Chamber of Commerce also enthusiastically endorsed the work of the college committee. The Southampton school board offered the use of its facilities to the new college until a location for the campus was found. In November and December support for the college grew rapidly. The local press ridiculed the reference to "undesirables" made by the summer colony opposition, repeating it frequently with great sarcasm. Perhaps these summer people, said one editor, fear that students at their books will—cast a pall of gloom on cocktail parties and resort socializing" (*Southampton Press* Oct. 26, 1961).

Teachers' associations and parent-teachers associations from neighboring school districts, the East End Guidance Association, the Lions Clubs, the Rotary, the American Association of University Women (AAUW) of East Hampton, and the American Legion all issued public statements supporting the college. Encouraged by this widespread show of support, the committee reconstituted itself, dropping the term *village* and broadening its base to the eastern Suffolk area. J. Wilbert Jones, the superintendent of the Southampton School District, took over as temporary chairman of the college committee and immediately pressed the search for a campus. The Long Island University board told Jones that they were now ready to act as soon as the committee could purchase a site. The Merrill estate was no longer available because Amherst had sold it to the Nyack Boys School. The committee looked at several sites and finally agreed on the Tucker Mill Inn property in the Shinnecock Hills for the new campus, a sixty-acre parcel ideally located on the old Montauk Highway overlooking Shinnecock Bay.

The property, one of the first to be developed after the Shinnecock Hills, had been taken from the Shinnecock Indians under controversial circumstances in 1859. William S. Hoyt and his wife, Janet, came to Southampton from New York in 1878 and moved to Shinnecock Hills in 1886 where they built a cottage on a ridge overlooking Shinnecock Bay and the Atlantic Ocean beyond (Goddard 2011, 55–56). The foundation of the cottage, which burned down a few years later, can still be discerned today.

The unusual oval shaped design of the house provided a panoramic southern view of Shinnecock Bay and beyond to the Atlantic Ocean from a long front porch. From the northern side of the oval one could see the rolling hills of what is now the Shinnecock Hills golf course and Peconic Bay. In 1888, Janet Hoyt learned that a one-hundred-seventy-year-old windmill in Southampton village was to be torn down and replaced with a barn. She moved quickly to rescue what she realized was a historic treasure and moved it to a spot near her new cottage. Fortunately, the windmill was not damaged when the Hoyt cottage burned.

In the 1890s, Arthur B. Claflin, who had made his fortune in textiles, purchased the tract and engaged Grosvenor Atterbury to draw up a plan for a thirty-room "cottage." Claflin told Atterbury that he wanted a Spanish design, which the architect thought was totally inappropriate. Although Atterbury told everyone later that he hated the building, he complied with Claflin's wishes (Wettereau 1991, 40–41). Claflin imported pieces of furniture and a huge, hand-carved fireplace mantle that he purchased, it was said, from a castle in Europe. He added a carriage house a short distance to the east of the "cottage."

Claflin was forced to abandon the estate when he lost his fortune in the Depression. He sold it to an owner who never lived in it and allowed it to deteriorate. After World War II, Thomas Tucker Swartz, who made a fortune in plastics, purchased the estate for $19,000 and turned it into a seasonal hotel for wealthy guests. Swartz and his wife Florence renovated the building and charged $2,000 for the season. In 1954, Swartz, with the help of Shedrick Smith, a versatile groundskeeper with carpentering skills, renovated the windmill to accommodate guests. The interior of the windmill was converted into a three-story apartment with a large window on the second floor affording a view of Shinnecock Bay and the ocean. Unsubstantiated rumors told of a summer stay by Tennessee Williams, who "clacked away at his old portable typewriter." Swartz added several small cottages on the terraces east of the main house for summer guests. After Swartz's's sudden death in 1962, his widow decided to sell the estate for $350,000, a considerable profit considering the purchase price. Smith remained as a groundskeeper and general overseer for the college until his death in 1970. "Smitty," as he was affectionately known, received an honorary bachelor's degree in 1969.

The availability of the Swartz estate soon attracted the members of the college committee. In January 1962, Jones, along with committee members Neil MacNeil, James Osborne, and Edward Fearon, and their attorney, Philip Mathews, presented a check for $5,000 to Florence Swartz with the understanding that the remainder would be paid by December 31, 1962. Mrs. Swartz was to continue operating the Tucker Mill Inn over the summer. The committee estimated that they would need an additional $50,000 for the necessary renovations.

President Conolly's enthusiasm for the expansion to Southampton, however, had been tempered by the negative reactions voiced the previous fall. He wanted clear evidence that there was a market and a positive climate for the college. To this end he hired Research and Action Associated, a market consultant agency, to do a comprehensive market study. The study director, Rhetta M. Arter, and a team of four associates began work early in February 1962, visiting local high schools and interviewing students, administrators, elected officials, and others identified as "opinion molders" (LIUABCL R.G. 2:6). Mary Lai, on her own, traveled out to the East End to visit local high schools. She reported widespread enthusiasm for a local college.

The consultants submitted the completed survey on March 30, a remarkably short time for such a project. The results were encouraging. Suffolk County had a rapidly growing population of fifteen to twenty-four-year-olds and an increasing number of them wanted a college education. Many of the high school seniors on the South Fork said that they preferred to attend a college close to home and 90 percent of the students enrolled in Suffolk Community College indicated that they would like to complete their four-year education on eastern Long Island. Arter and her team also reported widespread support from high school administrators, community groups, and elected officials. There was no mention of the concerns stressed by Chester Blakelock, the executive secretary of the Long Island State Park Commission, and *Suffolk County News* editor Joseph Jahn about the location so far east of the pool of potential students, nor of Adelphi's failure to raise the anticipated donations from the wealthy Southampton residents. Arter's report also made no mention of Adelphi's abortive attempt to establish a campus in Southampton. The LIU administration accepted Arter's assessment and did little additional research. Mary Lai later acknowledged that no one at LIU had been aware of Adelphi's negative experience (pers. comm. Mary Lai Sept. 20, 2007).

There were also some concerns about the need for a new college in eastern Suffolk. Some of those interviewed felt that the State University of New York (SUNY) center at Stony Brook, which was scheduled to open in the fall of 1962, and Adelphi-Suffolk College at Oakdale, which had been successfully recruiting students from Suffolk County since 1959, could meet the educational needs on the East End. One person added that the state university would cost about one-third of the LIU tuition. These reservations were also raised in a letter a woman from Hampton Bays wrote to committee chair J. Wilbert Jones on January 29, 1962 (SCC Archive B I, Box 1B, Dewey to Jones). Mrs. Lloyd Dewey's letter proved to be prophetic. She asked why the college committee had not approached the state university system. "I see no future," she wrote, "for private schools other than those with huge endowments."

President Conolly never read the report, because he and his wife were killed in a plane crash at Idlewild (now Kennedy) Airport in March. John

H. G. Pell, a member of the Board of Trustees, took over as chancellor. Pell, a member of one of America's distinguished families, with a pedigree that went back to the founding of New England, was an estate manager and Wall Street investor with no experience in educational administration. Pell had attended Harvard, but he did not have an earned doctorate. He was a strong supporter of the university's expansion program, but he had given little thought to the long-range problems facing a new university center. He did realize that the university did not have the necessary funds to purchase the property for the campus. He repeated Conolly's message that the college committee would have to purchase the property themselves. Beyond the concern for funds, Pell and retired admiral Chester Wood, the LIU vice president for business and development, apparently ignored other concerns.

As soon as the option on the Tucker Mill property was signed, the committee began a well-organized fundraising campaign, which included subcommittees in twenty-three neighboring communities. The college committee members realized that they needed to have a prominent leader for the campaign ahead. They chose Dr. William Agar, a retired geologist who had been educated at Princeton and had served as a faculty member at Yale. His two vice chairmen were well-known members of the Southampton community. Samuel Herrick, the owner of a hardware store that had been established by his grandfather in 1870, and Arthur Hull, who owned a car dealership in the village, had close ties with the local business community. Each community selected civic-minded people who volunteered their time and talent to the campaign for a local college. James Osborne took over the responsibility for the campaign in the village of Southampton; William Cooper chaired the Montauk group; Dorothea Hendrickson, a local school teacher, organized the Bridgehampton committee; and Dr. Russell Smyth led the campaign in Sag Harbor.

From May to October 1962, the committee worked feverishly on a grassroots campaign. Chase Atwood wrote weekly reports to Admiral Wood with details about the activities of the local committees (SCC Archive B I Box 1B, College Committee for Eastern Long Island, Atwood to Wood). By the middle of August 1962, the college committee announced that they had raised $50,000. The surviving committee records include nineteen pages listing donors who gave small amounts ranging from ten to two hundred dollars. There were also some larger gifts ranging from $1,000 to $5,000. The widespread response indicated the sincere interest in the college, but it also demonstrated a touching naiveté about the costs of founding and maintaining a private college.

Although many members of the wealthy summer colony were hostile to the college proposal, some did help with the fundraising. In August, Mrs. Reginald Fincke held a meeting at her home and invited the wives of prominent summer residents. It was these women who were most likely to be active in community affairs. The husbands usually came out on weekends and spent their time at the golf courses or at the beach. Mrs. Fincke said that she was enthusiastic about the college and pledged to raise an additional $100,000 in the following three months. She gave a significant donation to support the construction of a fine arts theater building that would also house the Humanities department. The building was named in her honor and her portrait was placed just inside the door of the auditorium. The family, ironically, had been honored with a silent immortality because the building, not surprisingly, was seldom referred to as the "Fincke Theater."

Mrs. Fincke organized several meetings of summer residents in different homes. At one of these meetings, Chester Wood told them that based on the success of the C. W. Post College, the Southampton branch would thrive and "LIU would not be back asking the community for more funds and more help." These words would later haunt the fundraising campaigns in the future. They also indicate how little understanding Wood had about the financial challenges facing most private universities.

In the late summer of 1962, James Osborne told the *Southampton Press* (Aug. 23, 1962) that they still hoped to have the $325,000 raised by the December deadline, but that the bank would take what they had by December and continue to accept pledges for an additional three years. Osborne said that he would send his committee members and volunteers door to door in an all-out effort to meet the deadline. In October, the committee reported that they had raised $100,000 in cash and pledges. This money came from an impressive range of donors. Francis Sullivan, a social studies teacher in Hampton Bays, organized a door-to-door solicitation. The Lions Club of East Hampton held a cocktail party to raise funds. The Southampton Elks club gave $250. The largest contributors, however, were the local businesses. One hundred and two of the 306 businesses raised a total of $80,000 (*Southampton Press* Nov. 29, 1962).

Some individuals, such as William Swan of Quogue, who gave $2,500, made their own independent donations, but one of the more memorable contributions came from the Southampton seventh grade. The students donated the five-dollar prize that they won in the Halloween Float parade to the college fund. They had constructed a model of the college windmill to draw attention to the fundraising campaign. After the parade, the students took the float to the front steps of the Chamber of Commerce office and parked it there. They also designed a wishing well and placed it by the float, inviting the public to drop in donations (*Southampton Press* Nov. 8, 1962). Another example of a remarkable community effort was the Junior Founder Program. Parents were invited to make a contribution of $100 or more in the names of their children. The children would then be honored as Junior Founders and have their names inscribed in a Junior Founders Record Book. Forty-seven families contributed to the fund.

Although the wealthy summer residents did not respond as generously as the committee had hoped, Mrs. Fincke did meet her quota of $50,000. In December, Mrs. Ailsa Mellon Bruce, founder of the Avalon Foundation and prominent summer resident, announced that her foundation was giving $15,000 to the college committee. If this donation was included in Mrs. Fincke's figures, it would mean that the rest of the summer colony made a relatively modest contribution. It is clear from the public statements made as the campaign progressed that the summer residents did not respond as enthusiastically as Mrs. Fincke expected. Perhaps the husbands dampened their wives' civic enthusiasms. The lack of support from the wealthy summer residents was to prove a major disappointment to Long Island University fundraisers over the years.

In October, the committee announced that they had raised $110,000. The fact that the hospital committee raised $953,247 in the same time period indicated where the wealthy summer residents placed their priorities. By November, the college committee had $150,000 and were discussing the possibility of a mortgage. On December 6, a desperate call went out reminding people that all donations were tax deductible. Harry Frank, a local store owner, chaired a drive that raised another $15,000 from the business community. The Riverhead Savings Bank gave $5,000, but most of the donations came in small amounts from civic organizations with very limited resources: the Shinnecock Indian Reservation gave $360; the North Sea Fire Department, gave $600; the Hampton Bays Board of Trade and Village Improvement gave $200, the Dune Post Veterans of Foreign Wars gave $183.61, the Elks Club gave $100, the Southampton Music Society gave $25, and the Southampton Horticultural Society gave $50 (*Southampton Press* June 12,1962).

The local media helped to publicize the campaign by celebrating each contribution. Representatives from the civic organizations were often photographed handing checks to members of the college committee. Unusual contributions received good press as well. The *Southampton Press* and the *Bridgehampton News* both gave headline treatment to the story of "A donation from Ethiopia" (*Southampton Press* Jan. 10, 1963; *Bridgehampton News* Jan. 18, 1963). The campaign, said the papers, has reached all the way to the "ancient Kingdom of Ethiopia." Arthur W. Tunnell, a summer resident working for the USAID program in Ethiopia, had sent a check for an undisclosed amount to the committee.

Mrs. Cary Potter, another summer resident, gave a donation in the form of a scholarship for "a young man from the Shinnecock Reservation." She said that it was in honor of her ancestor, John Eliot, the Massachusetts missionary who had learned to speak an Algonquian language from a Long Island Indian named Cockenoe. Although there is no documented connection between Cockenoe and John Eliot, William Wallace Tooker, a local amateur ethnographer, made the claim in his brief biography of Cockenoe, and it became a part of Long Island folklore. Unfortunately, there is no record of the recipient, nor does it appear the scholarship was continued after 1963.

By the end of December, the fundraisers had $176,000, a little over half of the purchase price. In spite of the shortfall, the Long Island University Board of Trustees approved a resolution on December 17, 1962, stating that the Southampton campus would open on September 1963. The college committee used this news to reinvigorate their fundraising campaign.

By March 1963, however, they were still $185,000 short of the goal. The Long Island University Board of Trustees negotiated a mortgage for the remainder of the sale price and purchased two more small parcels totaling fifteen acres prior to the opening of the campus in September 1963. The college appeared to be off to a good beginning. There was support from nearly all segments of the East End communities. Business people, summer residents, educators, civic associations, cultural organizations, and even the Shinnecock Nation endorsed the need for a college.

The Uniqueness of the Hamptons: How the Cultural and Geographical Setting Informed the College Mission

Chancellor Pell recruited Dr. Edward Glanz to serve as the first provost of the new college. Glanz had been chairman of the Psychology department in the College of Basic Studies at Boston University. The two-year Basic Studies program was designed to help students improve their basic study skills in preparation for full matriculation into the university curriculum in their junior year. The program had a creative two-year interdisciplinary curriculum, which organized students into cohorts that take required core courses. The instructors in the various disciplines worked closely together as they monitored the students in their cohort. Each cohort had its own set of instructors from the disciplines of Natural Science, Social Science, Humanities, and Rhetoric and an academic advisor.

The basic studies concept developed, in part, as a response to the challenges of the World War II veterans who came in under the G.I. Bill. Many lacked the necessary skills and study habits for a college curriculum. The innovative program undoubtedly played a role in reducing the high attrition rate, which had also plagued LIU during that same period. Although Boston University later changed the name to the College of General Studies in 1992, the basic approach has changed very little. The success of this program had convinced Glanz that the interdisciplinary approach could be applied to a regular four-year college program. He came to Southampton in December 1962 to begin planning for the new college. His immediate concern was to shape a long range mission statement. Glanz determined that the focus should be on the culture and geography of the Southampton area. He recognized the advantages presented by the marine environment on the south fork of eastern Long Island. From the roof of the Claflin estate, which had been renovated to serve as the administration building, one could look north and see Peconic Bay and then turn to the south and enjoy a spectacular view of Shinnecock Bay and, beyond, the Atlantic Ocean. Glanz hired Jay Barton to direct the Natural Science division and to develop an interdisciplinary Marine Science major. Barton, a biologist with a PhD from Purdue, had served as the director of a summer institute for the Natural Science Foundation.

Tomas Haresign, who was being interviewed to teach genetics in the spring of 1964, recalled Glanz's enthusiasm for the Marine Science program. Instead of asking about Haresign's academic training and experience, he pressed him with questions about a marine science facility. "Almost the first words out of his mouth after we were introduced," recalled Haresign, "were to solicit my views on where we could build, how we could build, what we could build, as a marine station" (Haresign, pers. comm. Jan. 18, 2001) Glanz's enthusiasm for the potential of Southampton was infectious.

The social, historical, and cultural context of the East End was also unique. The campus was located on the eastern edge of the Shinnecock Hills, an area of low rolling hills that extended about four miles eastward from the Shinnecock Canal. The hills were centered in the rich cultural environment of the Hamptons. Artists and writers had established a flourishing colony here in the nineteenth century, which continues to distinguish the area today.[1] Glanz recognized the potential of the local artists and writers for the college. He hired Dr. John Willoughby to direct the Humanities division and to develop a curriculum that would build on these cultural resources. Willoughby, a Rhodes scholar with graduate degrees from Oxford and the University of Rochester, had been doing some teaching and minor administrative work at the University of Chicago when he was invited to join the new faculty at Southampton. "I came," he said in a 1973 remembrance, "without really expecting to make more than a brief visit out of curiosity, but I ended up staying for an enjoyable decade so far" (Handler 1973, 18–19). Willoughby was excited about the prospect of developing an interdisciplinary humanities program in the Hamptons where so many nationally known artists and writers were available.

The summer visitors helped to create a romantic myth about the East End, which soon drew New York elites from the business community.[2] Janet Hoyt entertained many of these people who, no doubt enjoyed the spectacular views from her cottage porch. She also played an indirect role in another important theme in the college history. She was an amateur artist who had studied art by visiting the great museums of Europe. It was Janet who raised funds and invited William Merritt Chase to found an art school at Shinnecock. When Chase was a guest at her summer home in 1890, she convinced him to establish an art school where students could take advantage of the summer sun and the magnificent landscape (Harrison and Denne 2002, 47–48). It may well have been Janet Hoyt who approached Samuel Parrish (1849–1932), a wealthy patron of the arts who lived in Southampton Village, to support the art school. She shared his enthusiasm for civic endeavors, and both were involved in the establishment of the Shinnecock Hills Golf Club.[3]

Parrish certainly understood and appreciated the works of such contemporary artists as William Merritt Chase. He gave his full support to the establishment of Chase's art school. Chase built a studio and several small cottages for his students on the parcel provided by Parrish. In 1892, Chase opened the Shinnecock Summer School of Art. This cluster of cottages, which soon became known as "Art Village," attracted hundreds of artists over the years, many of whom settled permanently on the south fork. Although the school lasted only a little more than a decade, it played an important role in establishing an artistic tradition on the south fork of Long Island.

By the beginning of the twentieth century a younger generation of artists had followed Thomas and Mary Nimmo Moran, Winslow Homer, and Chase. The best known among them was Frederick Childe Hassan who came to East Hampton after he had established a reputation in Manhattan painting urban scenes. From 1919 until his death in 1935, Hassan spent the months from May to November in East Hampton. In the 1920s Ring Lardner, Grantland Rice, and Irving S. Cobb bought cottages near East Hampton. Sara and Gerald Murphy, who had shared the glamorous life of American expatriates in France with Ernest Hemmingway and F. Scott Fitzgerald, lived briefly in East Hampton.

After World War II, a third generation of artists and writers settled in the Hampton for the summers. One of the first in this group was Jackson Pollock, who bought a farmhouse in the small community of Springs, near East Hampton in 1945 (Long 2005, 45–87). Shortly afterward, Pollock and Lee Krasner helped Alfonso Ossorio find a house near them. The existence of this artistic community played a significant role in the development of the new college. The humanities and fine arts programs sought to take full advantage of this rich local resource. It is interesting to note that the historic meeting between Janet Hoyt and William Merritt Chase in 1890 actually took place on what is now the college campus. The rich history of the area certainly made the location a very attractive setting for a liberal arts college.

The third focus was on interaction with the diverse cultures of the East End. Glanz wanted to engage the college in social programs that reached out to African American, Native American, and working-class members of the community. He recruited Donald Baker, who had directed the Political

Science department at Skidmore College and was at the time serving as an evaluator for the newly established Peace Corps. This emphasis was a response to another important aspect of the East End environment. A significant presence on the cultural landscape is the Shinnecock Indian Nation, whose reservation is located less than a mile to the east of the campus. When the white settlers arrived in 1640 and established the first English settlement on Eastern Long Island, they purchased the right to live here from the Shinnecock Indians.

The English continued to press for more and more land. By the end of the seventeenth century all the Shinnecock lands had been taken by the English settlers. This posed a problem because now the Shinnecocks had no place to live. The town resolved the issue in 1703 by granting the Shinnecocks a thousand-year lease to a large parcel of land which extended from the western boundary of the village on westward to Canoe Place, approximately where the Shinnecock Canal is located today. This large parcel included the site where the college would later be located.

In 1859, under circumstances that remain disputed today, the Shinnecocks agreed to void the thousand-year lease, in exchange for an absolute deed in fee simple to the neck of land where the reservation is now located. The Shinnecocks were sharply divided over the offer, but the proprietors managed to convince twenty-one members of the tribe to sign a petition asking the New York State Legislature to allow them to break the lease. Another petition signed by twelve tribal members asserted that the first petition was invalid because some of the signatures were forged. The legislature ignored this accusation and approved the land transfer.

The loss of the Shinnecock Hills in this deal has become a very sensitive part of Shinnecock history that has cast a long shadow on the relations between the tribe and the town of Southampton. Although the college was not involved in the land transaction, the experience of 1859 often made it difficult to overcome Shinnecocks' suspicions about the good intentions of the college. Few of the people involved in the founding of the college, of course, were aware of this history. The issue came full circle in June 2005 when the Shinnecocks brought suit in federal court, claiming ownership of the Shinnecock Hills. Long Island University was among the large property owners named in the suit. Unfortunately for the Shinnecock, the court ruled that the tribe had waited too long to make their land claim and dismissed the suit (*The Shinnecock Nation v. New York State* [2006]).

As the brief survey of Long Island University's history indicates, many of the patterns that hampered the growth and development of Southampton College were well established before the college was founded. The tendency to deal with financial distress by implementing policies which led to "quality distress" began with Tristram Metcalfe. In fairness to Metcalfe, given his inexperience in educational administration and the absence of an endowment, he had little room to maneuver. The public perception that LIU was, at best, a mediocre, fiscally unstable institution severely hampered the fundraising necessary to establish an endowment. There were other problems as well that plagued the university throughout its history. Shifts from policies designed to strengthen central control to policies designed to provide local autonomy and then back again led to confusion and much wasted time and energy. A lack of a clear sense of university identity hampered recruiting and fund raising. One result of the "identity" problem was that the main branches, Brooklyn, C. W. Post, and later Southampton, were always suspicious of the administrators at University Center. The climate of suspicion encouraged strong provincial perspectives in the centers where even the wildest rumors of nefarious acts by the university administration were quickly accepted by some as gospel and spread.

The lack of an endowment and the absence of any serious campaign to create one during the early years led to a constant "crisis" mode of administrative decision making. Even the best of administrators were often forced to make quick decisions without the time to fully evaluate the outcomes. These hasty decisions, often made in desperate circumstances, frequently led to disastrous consequences. Dean Hardie's attempt to borrow on future tuition, for example, foreshadowed similar ill-advised decisions from that time until the closing of the Southampton campus in 2004.

In spite of this uncertain history, Southampton's founding was marked with many encouraging signs. The story of the local citizens who spent so much time and energy raising funds for the college is truly inspiring. There was undoubtedly a wide base of support for Southampton College on the East End of Long Island. Edward Glanz clearly understood the potential of a college that was firmly connected to the local communities, to the natural environment, and to the unique history of the area. He developed a curriculum in consultation with the faculty that was designed to build on these assets. Unfortunately, the "magical place" rested upon an uncertain foundation.

Chapter Three

Getting Started, 1963–1970

Would that a few words could express the excitement, the confusion, the fellowship, the irritation, the joy, the exhaustion, and the stimulation of the birth of this college.

—Sandy McIntosh, quoted in Handler, *Windmill,* 1973

When the college opened in the fall of 1963 with twelve faculty and a freshman class of about three hundred full time students,[1] the country was going through a transition from the quiet, complacent postwar period to a time of political and social upheaval. Each fall, a new freshman class was added to the student body. By the time the fourth cohort arrived in the fall of 1966, the student culture had undergone a significant "sea change." The generation of students who came to colleges and universities during these years were beginning to raise very serious questions about existing institutions and cultural folkways. They challenged conventional wisdom about race, war, and social class. They were not, of course, homogeneous, some still held to the traditional values of the past, but the decade of the sixties was marked by those who wanted change. A few were too impatient to accept a slower pace of change. They often chose to disrupt the existing order and take a riskier path, which brought them into angry confrontations with authorities.

Southampton provost Edward Glanz, along with many of his contemporary college leaders across the country, was completely unprepared for this generation of students. Faculty and students regarded him as a decent, honest man with a sincere commitment to help young people develop good learning skills and the highest moral values. This was to be admired, but, unfortunately, his goals were seen by many students as an attempt to bring them into a general acceptance of the status quo. Glanz saw the traditional New England college as his model, and the trouble began almost from the day the first class arrived on campus.

FIGURE 3.1. Edward C. Glanz (left), Southampton College Provost, 1963–1971, and Richard Bergman (right), Dean of Students, in 1963. *Courtesy of Southampton Town Historian.*

PATTERNS EMERGE: THE INAUGURAL YEAR, 1963–64

Many of the patterns and problems that came to characterize the college were well established at LIU. The first pattern was the tendency to jump into an initiative without sufficient planning and adequate funds. LIU chancellor Pell, who was pressed into service from his position on the Board of Trustees, lacked both experience and enthusiasm for the job. His leadership could be described at best as laissez-faire. Although there was considerable evidence that the postwar population spurt on Long Island created an expanding demand for college seats, Pell and vice chancellor Chester Wood planned for a small first-year class at Southampton of about 150 commuting students. They saw no need to delay until dormitories could be financed and constructed. When more than twice that many were accepted, 165 of whom needed housing, Provost Glanz and his small staff were faced with an unexpected challenge. In addition to this problem, the renovations on Claflin Hall were still in progress in late July. The building was to house the cafeteria, the provost's office, and several classrooms located on the second floor.

The second pattern, on a more positive note, is closely related to the first. The new faculty and staff responded to the challenges with creative imagination and energetic initiative. Richard Bergman, the dean of students, and his assistant, John Luongo, were responsible for student housing as well as student financial aid and scholarships that first year. Bergman recalled arriving on campus in July 1963 "to find an old estate house, a carriage house, three small motel units built by the Tuckers, a small swimming pool with minor cracks, and a windmill." The old Claflin estate house was renamed Southampton Hall. The Abney Peak Lodge was acquired in the fall, but it was not ready for use until the spring of 1964. Bergman wrote the following recollections for a special edition of the campus newspaper, the *Windmill:*

> Working on unsteady bridge tables in an old estate house swarming with construction workers . . . helping them to paint and lay floor tiles, not only to return their many favors but also so that we could use the completed rooms . . . waiting for a turn to use one of the two available telephones—trying to figure out where to house all the prospective resident students on a campus being developed for commuters . . . running a bus service to the off campus motels leased at the last minute as dormitories. (Handler 1973, 4–6)

Bergman also remembered a similar response on the part of other staff members to the difficulties caused by inadequate planning and insufficient funds. David Lees, the first manager of the building and grounds, said Bergman, struggled to keep a "jury-rigged" physical plant together. Repairs had to be made "on the cheap," a pattern that Daniel Gearon, the building and grounds supervisor in 2005 noted was still the case in spite of a mantra from his predecessors that in the long run these stopgap measures and deferred maintenance proved to be very expensive. The result was that the physical plant ended up being both shabby and expensive.

Another example of inadequate planning and preparation for the college was the lack of basic recreational facilities. In the spring of 1967, Glanz had architects prepare a draft design for a gym that conformed to the Georgian style of the other campus buildings. The plans included a basketball court, handball and squash courts, a wrestling room, classrooms, and a larger multipurpose room. Glanz had set the gym as one of his highest priorities for the campus, but Chancellor Hoxie ignored him and used funds earmarked for the gym to purchase the Simonson estate, a thirty-acre plot on the eastern boundary of the campus. When Glanz protested the decision, Hoxie dismissed his concerns telling him that he would use the money from a federal grant to construct the gym. The grant money, however, was used to construct the Fine Arts Center. It is unclear whether Hoxie deliberately lied to Glanz in his characteristic rush to expand the campus or whether it was one more example of poor planning and bad decision making at the University Center. The consequences of the Simonson purchase will be discussed in a later chapter.

Kenneth Hunter, the athletic director, had to be resourceful in response to an unusual challenge for a college basketball coach. Coach Hunter had to have teams practice and to play basketball games in the Southampton middle school gym. In spite of this disadvantage, he managed to coach his teams to outstanding records during the first years of the college. The 1963–64 team led by Roland Stansbury and Jim Friesman won seven out of ten games. The next year 6'6" Marvin Lewis joined the team to begin a decade-long average of fifteen wins a year. The basketball games were one of the student activities in the early years that served to develop a bond and a campus identity.

The small faculty often socialized across disciplinary lines. The faculty "Governor's Club" met for cocktails every Friday afternoon at four o'clock in the Windmill. The club later met in the more spacious Ocean View Lounge in Southampton Hall. An interdisciplinary poker game began in these early years and is still going today, having survived several retirements and even the closing of the college. The membership has changed from time to time around a core of four who were there at the beginning. The game reflects a collegiality across disciplinary lines which became a part of the Southampton campus experience. The current members include Joe Warren (Marine Science), Dan Duberman (Emeritus, Biology), C. W. Post dean Paul Forestell (Psychobiology), Bob Danziger (Chemistry), James Dailey (Business), Julio Gonzalez (Education), Elizabeth Granitz (Economics), Jack Kenneally (Emeritus, English), and the author (History/Anthropology).

The students also developed a sense of community. They acted to protest and to advance their interests. Students, for example, expressed concerns about the facilities on campus. From 1964 to 1967, new buildings were hastily constructed to meet the needs of a rapidly growing student population. When the college opened in the previous fall, there had been a panic caused by the unexpected numbers of residential students. The administration was particularly concerned about the problems that might arise from placing female students in scattered motel locations where there would be very little supervision. The challenges facing the new college were compounded by a hiatus in effective leadership at LIU under Chancellor Pell from 1962 to

FIGURE 3.2. The interdisciplinary faculty poker game 2004. (Left to right) Joe Warren, Dan Duberman, Paul Forestell, Bob Danziger, Jim Dailey, Julio Gonzalez, Liz Granitz, and Jack Kenneally. *Photo by author.*

1964 (Gatner 1974, 423). Pell had allowed administrative affairs to drift and provided little help to the new campus when it opened in 1963. There was no money in the university budget to finance dormitories at Southampton.

In this case, a member of the university administration came to the rescue. Mary Lai once again rose to the occasion. She did some research and discovered a subsidiary of the C.I.T Financial Corporation that would construct dormitory buildings on a "pay as you go" arrangement. Under this arrangement the costs of construction would be shifted to the students, whose room fees would be passed along to the C.I.T corporation on a semi annual basis over the next twelve years (*New York Times* March 22, 1964). The first set of three dormitory buildings, the "Peconic Complex," was constructed in the spring of 1964 on a plot of land donated to the college by William B. Platt, who had taken an active role in the fundraising for the purchase of the campus. The property, located on the northwest boundary of the original purchase, was valued at $30,000 at the time.

Under the arrangement with C.I.T., the construction had to be done as cheaply as possible. The two-story buildings, constructed of cinder block masonry and wall board, each placed on a cement slab, were designed to accommodate a total of 150 female students. There was no basement. All the heating pipes and electrical wiring were encased under the slab, making repairs extremely expensive. Long cracks and mold soon began to appear and students complained about the lapses in heat and hot water. The following year four more buildings were added to the campus: a Natural Science center, a library, a dining hall, and a dormitory complex consisting of six two-story buildings. The university again used the C.I.T. Financing Corporation, along with federal and state funding. The design and construction of the new dorm complex, named Montauk, were the same as those employed in the Peconic dorms. Provost Glanz opposed the architectural design because he wanted a style more in harmony with the environment, but Hoxie simply dismissed his objections.

In the academic areas there were similar "hands-on" initiatives by the faculty. Jay Barton, the Natural Science division director, had to supervise the transformation of the estate carriage house into a science laboratory. John Willoughby, director of the Humanities division, began immediately to cultivate local artists and bring them into contact with the students. He organized an exhibit of Ilya Bolotowsky's abstract paintings on the second floor of Southampton Hall and arranged for him to give several guest lectures. Bolotowsky continued his contact with the college for several years. In 2005, when Tim Bishop reflected on his thirty years working at all levels of the college administration from the admissions office to provost, he emphasized the importance of individual faculty and staff initiatives. One of the main reasons the college survived as long as it did, said Bishop, "was the dedication, energy, resourcefulness, and selfless commitment of the Southampton College people: the faculty, the staff and the administrators. These factors offset the problems posed by the lack of funds and a poorly designed campus built on the cheap" (pers. comm. May 15, 2005).

A third pattern that emerged in this first year was the student profile. The young people who came to Southampton that first year were excited about participating in the founding of a college. Many were also surprised that they were even admitted. Most came from the bottom three-fifths of their high school classes, and half ranked in the lowest two-fifths (SCC, Archives A, I-K, Four Year Progress Report 1967, 31–38). Some had checkered careers in two or more military or prep schools, and some wanted to stay close to home in a small college atmosphere. It was quite a mix of late bloomers, rebels, and serious students. Some never bloomed, some never stopped rebelling, but many took advantage of the opportunities they found at Southampton to develop as individuals and later enjoyed productive careers (SCC Archives A, I-K, Alumni Survey 2002).

Three of the students interviewed for this study, Alan Braveman, Richard Brown, and John Bolog, had attended two or more high schools before coming to Southampton. They had flunked out, dropped out, or been expelled from various public, private, and military schools, and were uncertain about their prospects for a college education. "I went to several schools," said Brown, "so I didn't have a very good record. I came to visit the Southampton campus and had an interview with Chase Atwood, the dean of admissions and to my surprise, he admitted me on the spot." Bolog's grades in military school were so poor that he almost abandoned any thought of college and made some plans, after reading Jack Kerouac's *On the Road*, to hitchhike around the country. Braveman graduated from Valley Forge Military Academy and then traveled around in Europe for nearly two years:

> I left with a crew cut carrying two suitcases, and several rolls of toilet paper and came back with a pony tail, a beard, a set of bongos, my camera and about a hundred rolls of film. I worked for a while and took a few courses at Adelphi, but then I decided to go full time and get my BA degree. I went for an interview at Post because it was close to my home but my grades were not very good and the Valley Forge military school transcript didn't impress anyone. The admissions officer at Post took one look at my hair and gave me a very cold reception. He was most unimpressed with my records and told me that I should apply out at Southampton where they were taking anyone. I think that he was really turned off by my "hippie" appearance. So I came out here and, sure enough, they took me! (It. 54)

All three of these young men went through many changes as a result of their experiences at Southampton, graduated, and went on to have rewarding careers: Braveman in photography, Brown in education, and Bolog in business.

Some students, however, came with more impressive credentials. John Willoughby welcomed Joan Brill, a talented young student who came as a transfer from the Julliard School of Music and invited her to give recitals as a part of the Humanities lecture presentations. Others were average students such as John LaSpina, ('71) a business major, who identified himself as a "late bloomer" in a recent conversation with the author (pers. comm. March 12, 2012). After graduation he established five family recreational complexes from Brooklyn to Coram on eastern Long Island, all centered around bowling. According to *Newsday*, the estimated revenue of his corporation, Maple Family Bowling, was over $11 million. He married his classmate Anita Lombardi, who also had a successful career. She majored in education and went on to earn her master's from SUNY Geneseo in Library Science. She was named Librarian of the Year by the *New York Times* in 2002. Both felt that the close interaction with faculty in small classes at Southampton was very important to their educational and social development. "You gave us our wings," said John (pers. comm. March 15, 2012).

Many made contributions to the local communities in the area. Thomas De Mayo, for example, graduated from the Southampton College and went on to earn his law degree from Hofstra University. De Mayo served as a Southampton town justice from 1978 to 1986 and again from 2000 to 2008.

Robert Martin (1968) was a "classic" late bloomer. He graduated from Port Jefferson High School with a 67 percent average and was rejected on first try by the Southampton College admissions office. His brother, a student at C. W. Post, appealed on his behalf and he finally was accepted. Robert recalled his good fortune in meeting Mel Beville, a faculty member in the business department, who took a special interest in him, raising his self-confidence. He later won a student award in the business department and went on after graduation to a very successful career in management with Colgate Palmolive Corporation (pers. comm. Oct. 10, 2006).

Some students came to Southampton a few years after high school. Bruce Ringer (1970) graduated from New York Military Academy and attended Georgia Tech as an aeronautical engineering major, hoping to enter the space program as a pilot. When an injury disqualified him from the space program, he took a semester off and visited a friend who was a student at Southampton College. Bruce was immediately struck by the contrast between Georgia Tech where, as he put it, "I was only a digit," and the friendly, informal atmosphere on the Southampton campus. After an interview with Professor Ral Welker, the founder of the Marine Science program, he was hooked. Following graduation he worked for the New York State Department of Environmental Conservation and later for a marine electronics installation company. He resumed his relationship with Southampton College in 1986 when began a career as the captain of the college research vessel, *Shinnecock.* Ringer soon became a popular mentor to the students, many of whom addressed him as "Captain Dad." "This was the beginning of fifteen wonderful years of my life," said Ringer. I enjoyed working closely with good friends, colleagues, and students who called me 'Captain Dad.' His relationship with the students and faculty closed the circle that began with Ral Welker's friendly welcome to the campus. Most of the faculty interviewed for this book expressed similar feelings about their experience at the college.

Ironically, both the first class to attend Southampton and the last class who graduated in 2005 began their college experiences in the context of a national tragedy. The Kennedy assassination and the attack on the Twin Towers bracketed the history of Southampton College. John Bolog recalled his shocked response to the news that John F. Kennedy had been assassinated in Dallas:

> I was in my English class in Claflin [Southampton] Hall when I looked out the window and saw the flag being lowered to half mast. The teacher dismissed the class and we spent the rest of the day in front of a small black and white television set. We saw Oswald get shot on live TV. I felt the need for spiritual guidance so I went to the synagogue in East Hampton. (It. 10)

FIGURE 3.3. Professor Ral Welker at his retirement ceremony in 1993. *Courtesy of Southampton Town Historian.*

Other students recalled huddling together watching on a television set in the basement of Southampton Hall, some in shock and some in tears and some speculating on various conspiracy scenarios.

Although many of the students were poorly prepared for college-level academics, some proved to be bright "self-starters" with enthusiasm and creative initiative. The students quickly began to organize themselves with very little assistance or guidance from the administration. Tisha Remkis recalled that

> when the college was first founded . . . there existed little if any form of a Student Activities Office or Student Union. Practically all of the school's functions were sponsored by novice clubs or groups . . . credit and recognition must be given to the fraternities and sororities of Southampton. . . . Besides social events . . . the fraters brought increased contact and communication with the surrounding community through their charities and fundraising campaigns. (quoted in Handler, *Windmill* 1973, 18–19)

These activities ranged from such frivolous endeavors as rolling a keg of beer from the Schaefer Beer pavilion at the World's Fair Grounds in Flushing to the Southampton campus on a handcart, to the establishment of *The Windmill*, a campus newspaper that won several prizes over the years (SCC Archives B, V, B-2, Special Collection).

A Sea Change in Student Culture

In its "Man of the Year" issue for 1967, *Time* magazine celebrated the new generation calling it, "not just a new generation, but a new kind of generation . . . more deeply committed to the fundamental Western ethos—decency, tolerance, brotherhood—than almost any generation since the age of chivalry." Although someone said that on the night Allan Ginsberg recited his poem *Howl* in a gallery in San Francisco, the fifties flipped into the sixties, the shift in youth culture did not happen quite so suddenly. The first two classes to arrive on the Southampton campus had made only mild protest against the curfews and the dress codes. They found ways to get around the rules without confronting the campus authorities. Andy Zak (1969), for example, recalled a popular strategy employed by the male students who lived off campus to deal with the "shirt and tie" requirement for dinner. At that time, students were not allowed to have cars on campus. They didn't want to have to walk back to the motels after class nor did they want to wear the ties all day, so they cut off the collar of a white shirt, and put it in their pocket or backpack along with a tie and wore it under a high necked sweater when they went to dinner (pers. comm.).

With the arrival of the third class in the fall of 1965 there was a "sea change" in student culture. They no longer relied on subterfuge to avoid such regulations; they began to openly challenge the rules. Richard Brown described the emergence of these changes as he saw them:

> In my first year (1964) it was a continuation of the nineteen-fifties. The second year the new class of freshman looked different. They had longer hair, they wore more casual clothes and they questioned everything from the dress code and curfews to racial discrimination, drug laws, and U.S. policies in Vietnam. At first the class who were now juniors didn't know what to make of them but before long more and more of the older students adopted the more casual style and some began to experiment with pot. The campus just looked and felt different. (It. 55)

Sandy McIntosh (1970), who went on to earn an MA in creative writing at Columbia and author six books, recalled that "I was one of ten hippies [in 1966], everyone else, outwardly anyway, was straight, restricted, and anal retentive." By the 1970s, he continued, "the college was made up entirely of freaks, with, perhaps, ten straight people" (*Windmill*, Oct. 14,

1972). Allowing, of course, for Sandy's exaggerated estimates, his comments certainly reflected a common perception of the cultural changes taking place on the campus in the late sixties

By the fall of 1966, the new patterns which came to define the sixties were becoming dominant on campus. Kenneth (Kenny) Haar, an outspoken student who came that fall, said, "Our class spent the whole four years challenging all forms of *in loco parentis*" (It. 27). Provost Glanz tried in vain to resist these changes. Glanz envisioned a small, selective college in Southampton, modeled after a New England school in the 1950s where students wore saddle shoes or white bucks and came to dinner neatly dressed in skirts and ties and jackets. The college would prepare them for the professions and send them out into society well schooled in manners and social graces. Accordingly, Glanz established a dress code, requiring male students to wear a tie and jacket and female students to wear skirts for dinner in the cafeteria. Women were also required to wear skirts to class unless the weather was too cold. As Joan Tutt (1969) recalled, "It's hard to believe now, but the dean of women would put up a red flag on the flag pole in front of the Montauk dormitory on cold or rainy days signaling that it was okay to wear slacks" (It. 63).

In keeping with their policy of *in loco parentis*, the administration imposed rigid curfews on the female students living in the campus dormitories. On week nights the women had to be in their rooms by nine-thirty. If they signed in after that time, the number of minutes late was recorded. If their weekly total of "late minutes" reached a certain number, they could be "grounded" for the weekend. When they signed out for an evening, they had to specify that they were going to an authorized place. A visit to the male dormitory, of course, was prohibited. Kenny Haar, who delighted in provoking the administration at every opportunity, referred to the women's dormitories as "female prisons" and the dean of women as a "warden." One weekend, Haar organized a "tent city" protest (It. 27). William Burke, a natural science professor who later served as dean of the college, described the scene:

> Kenny Haar was president of the Student Government Association and he and some friends, I remember Tom Wassener in particular, set up some tents in a lovely area just below Abney Peak (a female dorm at the time). And it turned out there weren't any rules about girls signing out to tents. . . . They'd have marshmallows and pass around wine or punch and someone, usually Tom, would play the guitar and everyone would sing. It was really nice. (Burke, "Remembrance" in Handler 1973, 23–24)

The dean of women, however, did not agree with Burke's assessment of tent city, but it was clear that these were not the students of the 1950s. It was also clear that the younger faculty supported the students' call for change.

Early in the spring of 1966, the pattern of individual resistance developed into a well-organized challenge to the administration. The student judiciary board met informally and discussed the grievances that were being voiced in the dorms and around campus. The students decided to publish a list of complaints in the campus newspaper. Peter Phillip and Kenny Haar's older sister Susan wrote an open letter in *The Windmill* to Provost Glanz, signed by the presidents of several campus clubs and Les Goodman, the student council president. The letter complained that academic advising, scheduling, and catalogue listings needed reform and attacked the policy of *in loco parentis*. "The college administration," they wrote, "is under the misconception that the student body is composed of boys and girls who lack any sense of responsibility and who must be governed by a paternalistic administration with a psychological system of reward and punishment." They went on to object to letters of censure placed in their files in their personal files without their knowledge, to the dress code, to the prices in the campus bookstore, and to the ban on student cars. They asked that the letter be given "immediate attention" by the administration. Some, including Armand LaMacchia and Peter Bradshaw, the sophomore class president, called for a student strike unless their complaints were addressed. In a campus meeting following the publication of the letter, Bob VanDerzee, president of the senior class, and the primary authors of the letter, Sue Haar and Peter Phillip, convinced the students to give the administration two weeks to respond.

Glanz met with the students and agreed to some changes, but many students remained unsatisfied. The dress code, for example, was changed to allow "neat dungarees," but warned that "inappropriate dungarees," work clothes, and sweatshirts should "be avoided." Shorts were prohibited at all times in classes, and women were to use their own judgment about slacks, but "should recognize the right of their instructors to challenge their judgment in such cases." Clearly, *in loco parentis* still lived, but the dress code and the curfews were under attack and their days were numbered.

For Glanz, a more unsettling aspect of the changes in student culture was the widespread experimenting with drugs in the late 1960s. The drug problem had been openly identified by Dean Richard Bergman in 1966. "We've got a problem," he wrote in the *Windmill*, "some students are involved in the use of Marijuana" (*Windmill*, Dec. 8, 1966). It was a bit of an understatement, but it was undoubtedly a positive thing to bring the issue into a public campus forum. Bergman's announcement reflected the sea change noted by Richard Brown and others. The dean promised an investigation into the matter, but noted that experimentation with drugs was a national phenomenon on campuses. He reported that two students had been arrested in a dormitory room with "over an ounce of pot." Alumni who were interviewed in 2004 recalled that pot was easy to get if you wanted it, but that the number of students who used it was never as many as the media of the times would have you believe. Mickey Director, a basketball player, said, "I never did any pot because I didn't want it to interfere with my playing, but it was all around" (pers. comm. 2005). Others told of growing pot in the windowboxes of their rooms. Many alumni from the sixties and seventies acknowledged experimenting briefly with marijuana but most said they never became regular users. Bergman's investigation undoubtedly revealed little more than what everybody knew. The next spring in a predawn raid on the campus dorms, eight students were arrested on charges of possessing and selling marijuana, LSD, and assorted pills (*Windmill* April 13, 1967). The press, of course, gave the event front page coverage, much to the dismay of the administration and the students. The Student Government Association drafted a letter to *Newsday*, the Associated Press, and local papers objecting to what they felt was "yellow journalism" and denying the implication that Southampton was "haven for pot heads." The student government issued a statement stating that the use of marijuana and LSD was "detrimental to the individual." Over the next few months, student letters and surveys in the *Windmill* reflected a variety of opinions about drug use. Walter Doyle, a *Windmill* staff member, defended marijuana use defiantly. He accused the adult generation of hypocrisy for using alcohol and tobacco while condemning pot (*Windmill* May 4, 1967). "Its our world now," he said and finished with the Dylan quote, "Get out of the new road if you can't lend a hand." Most students, however, agreed with the comments made by the alumni during interviews in 2005. The drugs were easy to get, but majority of the students either abstained or experimented briefly with marijuana. The drug scene on campus does not appear to have been much different than it was on campuses across the country.

The Curriculum Evolves, 1963–1970

Provost Glanz developed the general outline of a core curriculum in consultation with John Willoughby (Humanities) and Jay Barton (Natural Science) in the spring and summer of 1963. When Donald Baker (Social Science) joined the faculty in the fall of 1964, he became a part of the planning group. The curriculum was molded around a common core of courses designed to give all the students a shared academic experience. With this basic understanding of the liberal arts as a beginning, the students would then focus on a specific major of their choice. There was very little flexibility in this four-year program. Students were required to take sixty-eight hours in the core and thirty to forty hours for their major, twelve to eighteen hours for a minor, and six to twelve hours of a foreign language. There were, of course, choices of courses within the major, but these were limited by the small number of available faculty. This left only six to twelve hours of electives in the total of 128 required for graduation. The Bachelor of Science degree required an additional six hours of mathematics in the freshman year (SCC Archives B, V, B-3, College Bulletin 1963–64).

The core seminars in each of the major divisions were interdisciplinary within those areas, but selected written assignments were coordinated across division lines. The five credit Humanities (1 and 2) courses included an introduction to Literature, Art, Philosophy, Music, and Composition. The sophomore Humanities (3 and 4) core focused on Philosophy and Art. The coordinated written work included topics that were determined by the core faculty each semester. The Natural Science 1 and 2 core was an interdisciplinary introduction to Biology, Zoology, and Botany. The sophomore courses (3 and 4) introduced the students to the physical sciences, including Chemistry, Astronomy, Meteorology, and Oceanography. Social Science 1 and 2 was an interdisciplinary introduction to the social sciences: Psychology, Sociology, and Anthropology. The sophomore courses (3 and 4) focused on social organization: History, Economics, and Political Science. In the junior year Civilization (101–102), which traced the evolution of world civilizations, was a joint offering of the Social Science and the Humanities departments. In the senior year, representatives from all of the divisions taught the American Heritage (191–192) course.

Although the April 5, 1967, progress report submitted to the New York State Department of Education did not mention any faculty or student concerns about the core, criticism was growing. The following fall Larry Sartor, the associate dean of students, received a grant to do "a student profile for use in the evaluation of needs and programming at Southampton College" (SCC Archives A, I, K-3, Sartor 1968). The study, done during the 1967–68 school year, noted that while most students and faculty agreed that the core philosophy was an innovative and well-intended approach to the liberal arts, some students resented being required to take the core courses. The Natural Science students, in particular, resisted taking courses that were not directly related to their majors. For others, the requirements represented a loss of freedom at a time when "student power" was beginning to be celebrated in popular culture. These students were more outspoken and certainly more influential than those who supported the core. There were undoubtedly many who had had no strong feelings about the issue as well. Another factor, according to Donald Baker, who was the director of the Social Science division at the time, was the military draft. Many male students feared that the more demanding core courses might lower their grade point average and cost them their student draft deferment. The foreign language and science requirements also caused particular concern among these students.

Some faculty became frustrated with the core because they preferred to teach more upper-level courses in their own disciplines. On occasion, they expressed this frustration to the students, giving weight to the negative perceptions about the core. According to the 1967–68 student profile study, students believed that some faculty were turned off by the core and frequently did not prepare adequately for the weekly lectures. Some students sympathized with those faculty, saying that they understood how difficult it must be to have to face a hostile classroom full of students who resented being "forced" to take the course.

Another problem was that personality and philosophical differences sometimes emerged among the faculty on the core teams. On occasion some team members sat in the back of the lecture hall and made critical, often mean-spirited, comments to each other about the lecturer. Some of these conflicts were related to the antiwar protests. Students quickly became aware of these tensions. The morale declined steadily. At one point, Kenneth (Kenny) Haar, the president of the Student Government Association (SGA), urged students to boycott the core courses until changes were made.

A study of the campus financial problems by Arnold Weinstein, an economist in the Social Science department, concluded that the college must offer unique programs that would attract students. The report stated that the liberal arts core was not unique and would not attract students who wanted a more focused concentration of pre-professional courses. Proposals for curriculum reform came from several sources. Some came from individual faculty members such as Thomas Haresign, who had replaced Jay Barton, as director of the Natural Science Division. Haresign was a strong supporter of the liberal arts, but he did not think that the core was effective. He suggested that students take courses of their own choice in areas outside their majors. Haresign also proposed limitations on the number of courses required in the majors. "No student," he said, "should take more than fifty percent of their courses in their major." This became an issue later as the Marine Science major in his own department expanded its course requirement to more than eighty credits out of the 128 required for graduation.

By 1970 the core was gone, replaced by a liberal arts distribution requirement that called for three one-semester courses from each of the major divisions, two semesters of English composition, four semesters of a foreign language, and four "discrete" areas of physical education. This requirement allowed the students to include the three-course requirement in their own division as a part of their major. There remained, however, sixty-six hours of required courses, which included six to twelve hours of a foreign language. Many students and some enrollment service staff members still considered these new requirements too burdensome. The following year, the faculty reduced the distribution requirement to two courses from each division and two semesters of English composition. They also eliminated the foreign language and the physical education requirements. This liberal arts distribution requirement underwent minor fine tuning, but the basic format remained in place until the fall of 2004, when a curriculum and faculty reorganization was implemented in a desperate attempt to save the college. Ironically, there were many aspects of the "new innovations" that were quite similar to the original core.

The Vietnam Protests

The conflict in Vietnam, which began to intensify with the troop buildup and the bombing campaign in 1965, had become a matter of increasing concern across the country. That spring the students and faculty at the University of Michigan held the "first teach-in," and Mario Savio launched the Free Speech Movement at the Berkeley campus of the University of California. In April, more than twenty thousand protesters gathered in Washington, D.C., to voice their opposition to President Johnson's Vietnam policy. In October, young men began burning their draft cards. The following year the Black Power movement emerged, splitting the civil rights movement between the militant and moderate supporters, and Secretary of Defense Robert McNamara predicted that the Vietnam War would be over in 1967.

The Southampton students reflected this national pattern of unrest about the war. A small number became active in the antiwar movement, writing letters in the *Windmill*, organizing local demonstrations, and participating in national protests in New York City and Washington, D.C. A larger number were more passive in their opposition, occasionally coming to the demonstrations and marches or signing antiwar petitions. There were also a number of students who supported the war. The Centurion Club, organized in 1967 to support the returning Vietnam veterans, spoke out in favor of the war, but never engaged in demonstrations. They adopted a nine-year-old Vietnamese boy whose father worked for the U.S. troops and sent a basket of fruit to veterans in the U.S. Naval hospital in St. Albans, New York. Individual students, such as Chris Hunter, wrote occasional letters and opinion pieces in the *Windmill* (May 4, 1967) supporting American foreign policy. There were, of course, many who took little interest in matters outside of their immediate personal interests.

Student concerns about the war became much more focused following the enactment of the Military Selective Service Act in June 1967. The law required all males from eighteen to twenty-six to register with their local draft boards, but allowed exemptions for full-time students in good standing. Two months later, President Johnson announced that he was calling up an additional 55,000 troops. Not surprisingly, freshmen enrollments at Southampton increased by nearly two hundred over the previous year, and climbed to an all-time high of 1,600 the following year. In the fall, student voices against the war began appearing in the *Windmill*. Wayne Spitzer organized "The Society For Progressive Political Action," and wrote an editorial sharply criticizing the Vietnam War (*Windmill* Nov. 20, 1967).

Several faculty members led by Robert Cooke (Social Science) and Alvin Siegel and Bill Burke (Natural Science) joined with students Jane Pierth, Wayne Spitzer, and Jim Langhauser to sponsor an ad in the *Windmill* calling for participation in the October 21 March on Washington to protest the war (*Windmill* Oct. 16, 1967).

Jane Pierth wrote an article in the *Windmill* about her experiences.

> We left early in AM from the Nat Science center where we had coffee and were greeted by Jay Barton [Dean of the College], who did not agree with our position, but supported our right to express our opinions about the war. He did not oppose us or make us feel uncomfortable about our action. [Glanz who remained "neutral," sent his regards for a safe trip.] Traffic on the New Jersey Turnpike was fairly heavy, since most were headed for Washington also. Waving and sign greetings were exchanged as we passed and were passed by people . . . akin in spirit. . . . The crowd was enormous. I have never seen so many people in one place at one time. . . . There were hippies, veterans, university professors, clergy, nuns, middle-aged housewives by the hundreds, elderly couples, and many, many students like ourselves. . . . We helped to prove . . . that the opinion of opposition to the present war in Vietnam was held, in the majority, by regular, responsible, sincerely concerned people. (*Windmill* Dec. 11, 1967)

When the students returned the following spring, the news from Vietnam continued to dominate the media. Ironically it was a U.S. victory that eroded American support for the war. The Tet offensive on April 4, 1968, was successfully repulsed by the U.S. troops, but the ferocity of the attack convinced many Americans that the war was not going as well as McNamara and the president had led them to believe. Support for war dropped from 74 percent approval to 54 percent. The day after the reports of the Tet offensive reached the United States, the *Windmill* reported that William Burke, chair of the Natural Science department, had announced his candidacy for the First Congressional District in New York. Burke went to the Coalition for a Democratic Alternative convention at Selden, N.Y., and won their support. "I have become a candidate," he said," because of my unalterable opposition to the war in Vietnam and to the Johnson administration and its supporters in the federal government." Burke's decision to take action against U.S. foreign policy within the system reflected the position held by nearly all of the Southampton community who opposed the war. Their response was, with a few exceptions, quite similar to the campus antiwar protests across the country.

The Johnson administration and some of the mass media nevertheless convinced many in the general public that the college communities were on a dangerous course, which threatened to escalate into chaos. Johnson's response to the Central Intelligence Agency's study of the campus protests demonstrates the gap between perception and reality. On September 4, 1968, Richard Helms, the director of the CIA, told the Johnson cabinet that, in fact, the majority of students were either apathetic or narrowly focused on preparing for their careers. Johnson, probably for political reasons, chose to rely on the more hysterical anecdotal reports about radical student activities and communist influence (DeBenedetti 1990, 231–32). Abbie Hoffman satirized these fears by telling reporters many times that he was influenced by all of the "Marxes" Chico, Harpo, Groucho, and Karl!

The brief history of the Southampton chapter of the Students for a Democratic Society (SDS) provides an important insight into the nature of the antiwar movement on the campus. The SDS emerged at the beginning of the 1960s and declined sharply as a result of internal dissentions that surfaced after the "Days of Rage" at the 1968 Democratic Party Convention in Chicago. Their reputation for radical actions had grown since the 1964 convention where they adopted a more militant policy of resistance (Sale 1973, 479ff.). This reputation was a cause for concern when a small group of students led by Andrew Zak, Ronald Stanchfield, John Macella, David Bromberger, Gretchen Berger, and John Litchman organized a chapter of the SDS on campus. Soon afterward Sandy McIntosh, the *Windmill* editor, received an unsigned letter expressing some of the more emotional fears about the organization. The brief letter attacked the SDS, charging that it would bring to the campus "quacks, queers, and communists," who would "damage the college" (*Windmill* Oct. 11, 1968). McIntosh, who did not agree with the sentiments in the letter, printed it on the front page to provoke a discussion. In an accompanying editorial he said he supported the formation of an SDS chapter on campus because he believed there was a need for an open dialogue with all views represented. McIntosh and the other editors during the Vietnam years prided themselves with their objective coverage of the student views about the war.

Terry Victor, a freshman, responded to McIntosh's invitation to voice his opinion about the SDS. He was concerned, he said, about the SDS, fearing that it would be a disruptive force, and pointed to the seizure of buildings at Columbia University as an example. Victor, however, did not argue that the SDS should not be allowed on campus. He urged students to work through their own SGA to voice their opposition to the war. Joining the SDS, he said, would be a waste of time and energy (*Windmill* Oct. 18, 1968). Van Camberis, John Handler, Kevin Braun, and Mark Meyers wrote letters or articles which, in general, agreed with McIntosh's view of the SDS. Camberis said that although he would not join the group, he supported their right to organize on campus (*Windmill* Nov. 16, 1968). Provost Glanz, in a carefully worded statement, said that he supported "creative protest," but not the sort of confrontation that led to the seizure of buildings or the disruption of the campus.

The primary issue of concern that fall was the scheduled presence of military recruiters on campus. John Handler wrote an editorial reminding the SDS that one of their major goals was an open society and criticizing them for opposing military recruiting on campus. He urged them not to take any overt actions against the recruiters (*Windmill* Oct. 25, 1968). Andrew Zak, when asked in 2006 about his recollections of the SDS chapter, chuckled a bit, and said that "it was a very short-lived chapter, pretty much gone by the spring of 1969 . . . we had a few meetings and lots of talk over lunch in the cafeteria, but we never, as I recall, ever did much of anything" (pers. comm. July 29, 2006). Mark Meyers, a reporter for the *Windmill*, attended a meeting of the SDS chapter where they voted to have three "interdependent chairmen instead of a president and vice president," and concluded that the group was benign (*Windmill* Nov. 16, 1968). When the military recruiters set up a table outside the student cafeteria, the SDS put their own table next to them and passed out antiwar literature and flowers. The fate of the Southampton chapter of the SDS was similar to that of the SDS across the country. By the summer of 1970, according to Kirkpatrick Sale's comprehensive history of the movement, the SDS had all but disappeared on university campuses. A small number of alienated radicals on the fringe of the SDS, calling themselves the "Weathermen," went underground and engaged in random acts of violence, but their actions violated all the basic political principles of the SDS (Sale 1973, 651–57).

National opposition to the war became more emotional following Nixon's election in 1968. As the Paris peace talks dragged on, many in the Weathermen and others on the radical fringe of the antiwar movement became embittered and gave up on the democratic process. On the San Francisco State campus, faculty and students boycotted classes for more than four months and held protests that resulted in seven hundred arrests. At Cornell, a black student in a group that seized a building waved a gun and called for blacks to arm themselves in self-defense. The pattern of nonviolent protest within the established institutions, however, continued at Southampton. In the spring of 1969, John LaSpina, a third-year student, invited Eugene McCarthy to speak on campus, but he was unable to come. Ralph Abernathy, who had succeeded Martin Luther King as president of the Southern Christian Leadership Conference (SCLC) did come, and gave the 1969 commencement speech.

In the following fall, the Southampton students participated in the Washington Peace March and a national campus moratorium against the war. At a special meeting of the faculty on October 1, two weeks before the scheduled day of protest, the faculty discussed an administration proposal for dealing with the protest. Glanz opposed canceling classes, but would allow a class to be rescheduled if the instructor and a majority of the class agreed (SCC Archive B, IV, e, Faculty Minutes Oct. 1, 1969). In response,

Professor Robert Cooke presented a motion calling for a statement endorsing the aims of the October Moratorium and a policy that permitted all students and faculty to engage in protests without penalty. After lengthy debate, the faculty passed Cooke's motion.

John Poley, the vice president of the SGA, took the lead in organizing the trip to Washington. Poley had at one time considered a more radical personal action. He and another Southampton student went to Canada to explore the option of going into exile there. After talking with several of the American expatriates they both decided to return home and work within the political system to end the war. Poley's decision is representative of the antiwar sentiment at Southampton. They chose to protest within the existing political institutions. Poley wrote about his experience on the Washington march for a local newspaper:

> Southampton College sent an official delegation of 60 students to the March on Washington, and more than a hundred went on their own. All the way to Washington we picked up the greatest feeling of rapport from the thousands of students traveling to Washington. At each rest stop, peace was the sign. Food was shared and a sense of purpose was radiated to everyone. (*East Hampton Star* Nov. 27, 1969)

Barry Kamison, a freshman, stayed on campus to organize a demonstration, which featured comments by faculty and students opposed to the war. The faculty passed a resolution calling for all troops to be removed by September 1, 1970. Glanz, who felt uncomfortable with the outspoken criticism of the war and fearing a possible backlash from the town, tried to distance his administration from the strong message being sent to the public by the students and faculty. In a statement to the press, he made it clear that the college was not taking an "official position" on the war and described (with considerable relief) the demonstration as "low key, but sincere." This unconvincing and rather transparent strategy irritated people on both sides of the issue.

Glanz's model of a quiet small college where a relatively homogenous community of students and faculty reasoned together without rancor was continually at odds with the realities of the 1960s. He felt much more comfortable with his friends in the local Chamber of Commerce than he did with the students and the younger faculty. Adding to these stresses was the uncertainty about the future of the university and the growing campus debt. The university was in the midst of a transition, which will be discussed in the following chapter. Under the new organizational structure each center was given more autonomy, but this meant little as long as the university finances remained limited. The university changed the title of the three center administrators from provost to president, emphasizing the shift to a decentralized structure, but the "new" President Glanz had no more real power or authority than the "old" Provost Glanz. These frustrations were beginning to wear down President Glanz.

The following spring, another, more disruptive protest rocked the campus. In April, President Nixon ordered the invasion of Cambodia in an attempt to stop the flow of men and supplies down the Ho Chi Minh Trail into South Vietnam. Nearly a million and a half students across the country boycotted classes and 100,000 protesters marched on Washington to express their outrage (Debenedetti 1990, 280). On May 4, the Ohio State Guard killed four student demonstrators at Kent State. The Southampton students barricaded the front entrance to the college and the SGA called for the closing of the campus. Andrew Bales presented a petition signed by 498 of his fellow students to the Faculty Assembly on May 6 stating that "[w]e the undersigned do vehemently oppose the American action in Southeast Asia and call for an immediate boycott of all classes, for the remainder of the spring, 1970 semester." Another student, Michael Granat, submitted a minority petition signed by thirty-one students who were also against the war but did not agree with the boycott. They urged students to find other ways to express their opposition to the war. More than two hundred students, however, agreed with Bales and boycotted classes as the campus demonstrations spread throughout Long Island (Howlett 1995, 66).

The faculty discussed the petitions and found common ground between the two student petitions. They passed a resolution permitting any member of the college community to attend the Washington march or engage in any related protest activity without penalty. SGA president Joe Ratti, a decorated Vietnam veteran who now opposed the war, agreed with the compromise wording (SCC Archive B, IV-e, Faculty Assembly Minutes May 9, 1970). This time President Glanz gave his full support to the resolution, congratulated the faculty, and said that he had sent a telegram to President Nixon with copies to senators Javits and Goodall and to Congressman Pike criticizing the escalation of the war. He agreed to send another telegram to Washington describing actions taken by the college. He would compose this, he said, after consultation with Joseph Ratti, Dean Aloia, and faculty chairman Frank Gambacorta. The following year the Faculty-Student Assembly passed a similar motion in the memory of the students that were killed at Kent State and at Jackson State protesting the war.

The last major demonstration against the war came in the spring of 1972. On April 24, nearly a half-million protesters gathered in Washington, and local demonstrations were held across the country (Debenedetti 1990, 327–28). Joseph Ratti spoke passionately about his opposition to the war and planned to attend the march in New York with Vam Maggipinto. In Southampton the students gathered in the student union (the "Ratskeller") where they listened to rock bands, heard speeches, and planned a spontaneous march into the village of Southampton. The *Windmill* called it the "Biggest Rally in Two Years," but the town police prevented them from holding a demonstration in the village square at Agawam Park because they had not filed for a permit two weeks in advance. They were allowed to march through the village and make their statement (*Windmill* May 12, 1972). This last antiwar demonstration symbolized the student protest at Southampton. They were engaged enough to actively participate in antiwar actions, but they never seized buildings or used violent means to express their opposition to the war.

Chapter Four

LIU in Crisis

The Administration of R. Gordon Hoxie, 1964–1968

"We Never Thought of Ourselves as LIU Students": Identity and the Tuition Protest

The university had survived a financial crisis, a major sports scandal, and negative reports from the Middle States commission, but R. Gordon Hoxie's disastrous administration either set in motion or exacerbated many of the patterns that finally forced the closing of the Southampton campus. With the death of Admiral Conolly, Hoxie's influence and status in the university improved somewhat. When Conolly's ineffectual successor, Chancellor John G. Pell, resigned after two and one-half years, the board offered the position to Hoxie.[1] The search process for a new chancellor, as had been the case in the past at LIU, did not involve the faculty, the students, or the campus administrators. Hoxie, who was inaugurated in July 1964, came into office at a time when student unrest was beginning to emerge in campuses across the country. Students and faculty were now demanding a voice in the selection of university deans and presidents and in major policy decisions. In the fall of 1966 this new mood was expressed at LIU in a university-wide protest against a proposed tuition increase.

The protest also revealed one of the problems that had emerged when LIU expanded to widely separated satellite centers. Each center soon developed its own identity, which was at odds with a sense of loyalty to the university as a whole. This feeling was exacerbated when University Center was established in February 1966 at Brookville. The fifteen-acre estate with three buildings had been the residence of William Bottomly, a prominent American architect. The chancellor and the university administrators moved into what appeared to many in the campus centers to be an isolated fortress where decisions were made in secret. Student newspapers portrayed Hoxie as an imperious autocrat, who entertained his friends with lavish dinner parties in "Hoxie's Palace."

Alumni from classes beginning with the first class of 1967 to the last class of 2004 all had a similar response when asked if they identified with Southampton, with LIU, or with both. "We never thought of ourselves as LIU students," said Richard Brown, "from the beginning we were suspicious of anything that came from Brookville." Alan Braveman agreed with this comment. "LIU had such a negative reputation," said Braveman. "When people asked where we went to college we would say Southampton College and never mention LIU."

Another factor here was the personality and leadership style of R. Gordon Hoxie. He never related well with students and faculty. Mary Lai, who was now the university treasurer, had worked closely with Hoxie during his tenure as chancellor. Lai, a polite and gracious woman who seldom has a negative word to say about anyone, would only say that "Hoxie was a difficult person to like." Indeed he was. Many of the faculty and students saw him as pompous and arrogant. Hoxie loved the pomp and ceremony that went with titles. When he was appointed chancellor in 1964, he insisted on keeping his title as President of C. W. Post. "He liked to be called president," said Mary Lai (pers. comm. July, 2005).

The students and faculty at Southampton had little interaction with LIU officials during the inaugural year when Pell was chancellor. Hoxie's appearances were imperious and dramatic. One time he came by helicopter, landing in front of Southampton Hall, where the local press waited to photograph the event.[2] The visit, however, that did the most to shape his image at Southampton occurred on March 2, 1966. Hoxie had just returned from a visit to South Korea where he had developed a "sister" relationship with Chung-ang University in Seoul. He wore a tweed suit made in Korea, a Korean silk shirt and tie, and Korean topaz cuff links. He gave a slide presentation designed to impress the students and faculty with the international reach of the university. His affected mannerisms, his effete speaking voice, and his Korean attire undermined his message. The students found him an easy target for humor and ridicule. In particular, the students found it hard to reconcile Hoxie's university-funded international travel and private helicopter rides with the news about a tuition increase.

Word reached the Southampton Student Government Association early in November that LIU was planning to raise tuition beginning in the fall of 1967. This was the third increase in the four years since the opening of the college, and the news was not well received by the students. The tuition, which had been $960 in 1963, would be raised to $1,664. When the Brooklyn student government representative had met with Chancellor

Hoxie on November 2, 1966, the students charged that the financial problems faced by the university were caused by incompetence. Dean Fairbrother, the Southampton SGA president called a meeting on the Southampton campus to inform the students about events at Brooklyn. Leigh Harrison, the *Windmill* editor, urged the students to join with the Brooklyn students and make a stand. He repeated the accusations about Hoxie's lavish dinners at the newly established University Center in Brookville (*Windmill Special Edition* Nov. 7, 1966).

Hoxie's proposed tuition increase drew sharp opposition from William M. Birenbaum, the provost at Brooklyn, who argued that tuition was already too high for students from the urban housing in Brooklyn. Birenbaum, a liberal committed to serving the diverse, multicultural community of Brooklyn and popular with faculty and students, was the polar opposite of Hoxie. The two men clashed repeatedly over university policy. The Brooklyn provost opposed the continuing expansion of the university, calling for the consolidation and strengthening of existing programs. He warned that the tuition increase might be used by Hoxie to finance a reckless program of poorly planned expansion which would endanger the future of the university.

Hoxie planned a series of meetings on the three major campuses in an attempt to quiet the unrest. The fact that tuition increases had been accepted before and many times after this increase suggests that Hoxie's personal unpopularity was a major factor in the protest. This was certainly the case at Southampton. Shortly before Hoxie's appearance in the library lecture hall at Southampton, some students met in a dorm room and hatched a prank to disrupt the meeting. Four hours before Hoxie's scheduled appearance, they called the campus security and reported that someone was planning to assassinate Hoxie. In a panic Frank Murphy, the chief of campus security, assigned four guards to the meeting and alerted the Suffolk County police, who stationed five detectives at the entrances to the library. The presence of what appeared to be a "royal guard" for Hoxie set a negative tone before the chancellor took the podium (*Windmill* Nov. 7, 1966).

The meeting was one of the largest turnouts in the short history of the college. Dean Fairbrother chaired the meeting and called on Hoxie to give a short introductory comment before he opened the floor for questions from the faculty and students.[3] Hoxie began by telling the students that many colleges on Long Island were also raising their tuitions because they faced a nationwide problem of increasing costs for higher education. He then repeated a theme which he had voiced earlier in his inaugural speech when he had become chancellor. Our country, he said, faced a crisis because private higher education was in danger of being completely eclipsed by government-sponsored public institutions. American freedom and democracy, he warned, were in danger, and he urged the students to see the tuition increase as necessary to save private colleges across the country, as a small

Figure 4.1. Long Island University Chancellor Gordon Hoxie and Dean Fairbrother, President of the Student Government. *Courtesy of Southampton Town Historian.*

sacrifice to pay for such a noble cause. His rather long leap of logic from Southampton tuition to his "noble cause" was not convincing to many in the room.

The students pressed Hoxie with pointed questions that revealed the underlying suspicions about the Brookville administration. The first questioner asked Hoxie for assurance that the tuition increase would be used on this campus to improve the dormitory and athletic facilities. He charged that the students at Southampton were not getting their money's worth, suggesting that LIU was taking from the Southampton tuition revenues to fund improvements on other campuses. Although the evidence clearly indicated that, in fact, the Southampton campus was being subsidized from funds generated by the C. W. Post and Brooklyn campuses, the student expressed a commonly held belief at Southampton. When Hoxie responded that LIU had put millions into Southampton and that he had pledged to the students at the other centers that their tuition would not be used to subsidize Southampton, he was disrupted by catcalls and shouts from the audience. The student marshals restored order, but the audience remained hostile.

The next question, by student government representative Peter Philip, reflected another pattern that continued throughout the history of the college. He asked Hoxie why there had been no consultation with the Southampton students and faculty about the tuition increase. The chancellor dismissed the question, saying only that he had never seen an institution where there was "so much information and misinformation" floating around. Several of the previous Middle States reports had criticized the university for failing to engage the faculty in important policy decisions. This pattern continued throughout the history of the college, ending with the abrupt decision, made without consultation, to close Southampton in 2004.

It was a question and comment by Brady Tyson, a member of the Political Science department, however, that stung Hoxie. Tyson challenged Hoxie's assertion that public higher education was less "free" than private education. "I do not think," said Tyson, "that gifts from large givers leaves us more free than funds from taxpayers who represent all of the people." Tyson's comment was loudly applauded by the students, angering Hoxie, who never fully regained his composure. Picking up on Tyson's comment, Charles Isaacs, the president of the Brooklyn Student Government Association, who had come to the meeting in a show of student unity, pointed out that Hoxie and the LIU board had operated behind closed doors. Isaacs asserted that this contradicted Hoxie's implication that private universities preserved freedom. Hoxie began to answer, but as he searched for words another student asked what the chances were for Southampton to break away from LIU and become an independent private college. Hoxie retorted sharply that he wouldn't dignify that question with an answer. Before he could regain his composure, Robert Lenti, a student from the audience, asked how Hoxie would feel about Southampton becoming a part of the State University of New York. There was more applause and some foot stamping and laughter. Hoxie objected to the applause and said the question was "a most tragic manifestation . . . a tragic answer to our free society." It seems, he continued, "that there are those that feel that the answer for everything is to be taken over by the government." He returned to his point that private education requires some sacrifice to preserve itself in the face of the threat of government takeover. He deplored the fact that the student energy and organization in the tuition protest had not been "brought to focus on what the real basic challenge is. And it is the future of private higher education."

The students were no longer listening. Hoxie had lost their respect. The next question came from John Kanas, who became a very successful banker after graduation and later served on the LIU Board of Trustees. Kanas attacked Hoxie directly, suggesting that the meeting was a charade to pacify the students and make them more amenable to a decision that had already been made by the board in secret. Hoxie denied this charge, and after a brief exchange with Kanas, said, "I shall never forget this meeting," and ended as gracefully as he could under the circumstances by thanking the students for inviting him. The *Windmill* staff had the last word in the edition following the meeting. Robert Kraus made an accusation that continued to plague the relationship between LIU and Southampton throughout the history of the college. He charged that the answer to the university's financial problems was to correct the ineptitude in the central administration, not to raise tuition. Although this accusation was not always the accurate explanation for a given problem over the years, there was always that lingering suspicion at Southampton. In the end, of course, tuition was raised and continued to increase over the years. The depth of Hoxie's commitment to the cause of private higher education was soon to be revealed in a much more dramatic confrontation that erupted three month later.

Hoxie's "Day of Infamy"

Birenbaum's fears about Hoxie's plans for expansion were realized in February 1967 when the university released its Ten Year Development Plan, "Preface to the Future" (LIUABCL RG 3). The 168-page booklet financed by a grant from the United States Steel Foundation called for a $138 million expansion program, which would be financed by projected income from government grants and private gifts.[4] The ambitious plans proposed a law school and a health center at C. W. Post and a science and engineering facility at Brooklyn, but gave few specifics. Two outside consultants who reviewed the plan were highly critical of the proposed expansion and the overly optimistic estimates of funding sources. These criticisms may explain why the board paid Heald Hobson and Associates, an accounting firm that specialized in university finances, $100,000 to make a thorough study of the university's operations and development plans. The evaluators were to focus on the university's educational programs, its administrative structure, and its long-range plans. They were also to examine the capacity of the university financial resources to carry out the objectives in the Ten Year Plan. The preliminary report was to be given in July 1967.

Hoxie, fearing more criticisms would come in the report and beleaguered by student and faculty opposition, decided to remove Birenbaum before the Heald commission arrived on campus. The chancellor pressured Birenbaum to submit his resignation on March 13, 1967. If Hoxie thought that his action would end his difficulties, he badly miscalculated. Three days later, angry voices of students, faculty, administrators, and department chairs at Brooklyn protested Birenbaum's dismissal (*Newsday* March 16, 1967). Students gathered two thousand signatures supporting Birenbaum and gave him a standing ovation when he addressed them (*Newsday* March 17, 1967).

The Brooklyn faculty passed a resolution, by a vote of 145 to 38, requesting that Hoxie rescind his acceptance of Birenbaum's resignation (*N.Y. Times* March 21, 1967). When Hoxie came to Brooklyn in an attempt to defend his decision, he was met by 1,500 students carrying picket signs, chanting support for Birenbaum (*Newsday* March 21, 1967). Hoxie was jostled by the crowd, which blocked him from entering his office. The chancellor lost his composure, telling the press angrily that this was "a day of infamy in the life of the student body." The next day he followed with a charge that he was the target of a conspiracy by those who wanted to seize power. These students, he continued, "were the pawns of immoral adults" (*Newsday* March 22, 1967). The press delighted in highlighting Hoxie's emotional outbursts.

Members of the Board of Trustees poured fuel on the fire with intemperate comments that were picked up in the local press. When a contingent of student representatives met with the board to ask about the decision to oust Birenbaum, one trustee, Rear Admiral John Bergen (Ret.) curtly told them, "It is none of your business what the Board of Trustees does." Clinton Blume, another trustee, said that he was not used to criticism at his place of business and would not take it as a trustee (Friedheim 1967). A continuing problem with the wealthy businessmen and retired military officers who served on the board was that they had no experience in educational administration and little patience with students.

The widespread public outcry did not move the chancellor, nor did it influence the Board of Trustees. They voted seventeen to one with five members not voting to support Birenbaum's immediate dismissal. On March 27, Hoxie announced that Birenbaum was asked to resign because of his "seeming inability to carry out nominal administrative relationships," and added that he had sought his ouster since the fall of 1965 after Birenbaum's first year at Brooklyn (*Newsday* March 28). Birenbaum responded by saying that LIU confused dissent with disloyalty. Henry Heald and his evaluators began their work in the midst of all this turmoil.

The next week, Brooklyn students went on strike, and the faculty refused to cross the picket lines. The faculty followed with a vote of no confidence in Hoxie by 168–32 (*Newsday* April 3, 1967; Gatner, 477). Hoxie and the board were surprised by the strength of the opposition. The Brooklyn strike lasted for two weeks. The students went so far as to hang Hoxie in effigy (*Windmill* April. 20, 1967). The protest quickly spread to Southampton where the students held a one-day strike, carrying signs with angry messages: "Dump the Dictator," "Hoxie must Go," and the irreverent "Huck Foxie." Alan Braveman accused LIU of practicing a depressing policy of paternalism (*The Long Island Press* April 10, 1967). The Southampton faculty approved a request for Hoxie to resign, by a wide margin (Gatner, 477–78). Donald Baker, chair of the Social Science division, said that the resignation was necessary for the good of the university, noting that he was having trouble recruiting prospective faculty because they did not want to work in a university under Hoxie's leadership.

The conflict received press coverage, which further damaged the public image of Long Island University. The tarnish from the history of financial problems, low admissions standards, and basketball scandals was further darkened by the turmoil at Brooklyn. Articles in *Newsday*, the *New Republic*, the *New York Post*, and the *New York Times* raised serious questions about the operations of the Board of Trustees and the competence of the chancellor. *Newsday* followed the day-to-day developments with headlines that usually supported Birenbaum and Hoxie's critics among the students and faculty. *The New York Post* ran an editorial on April 12, 1967, entitled "Debacle at LIU":

> In their bullying, bungling attempts to deal with the Birenbaum case and the explosive student and faculty protests to which it gave rise, the administration and most of the trustees of LIU have followed a steady, senseless, progression. . . . [T]hey have mistaken authoritarianism for authority—in fact they have sought to substitute a dismal despotism for academic freedom and they have, in the process, discredited themselves and the university.

In the April 15 issue of the *New Republic*, James Ridgeway accused two LIU board members, chairman William Zeckendorf and John P. McGrath, the chairman of a bank that did business with the university, of having serious conflicts of interest. A *New York Times* editorial, reprinted in full in the *Windmill* (April 27, 1967), argued that controversy was a result of the university's poor planning and "hazy sense of direction." The *Times* praised Birenbaum for his sound educational and civic aims, but faulted him for his lack of diplomacy in dealing with Hoxie. Their sharpest criticism, however, was directed at Hoxie and the Board of Trustees. The central administration and governing board had "vacillated between autocracy and indecision, often substituting platitudes for policies." This was not a new critique; the same point had been made in similar language in previous reports by the Middle States evaluators.

Chairman Zeckendorf negotiated a settlement with the students, promising to set up a standing committee of students, faculty, and administrators to examine all of the university's problems and report back by June 1. Any unresolved differences would be settled by an impartial mediator. The board, however, refused to rescind Birenbaum's dismissal. Although they continued to support Hoxie, Zeckendorf's intervention suggested that the chairman and some board members were losing confidence in Chancellor Hoxie.

Charles Isaacs believed that the agreement with the university established a model of "participatory democracy in the educational process," but he was soon to be disappointed (Gatner, 479). With the enthusiastic endorsement from Chancellor Hoxie, the Board of Trustees ignored the negotiated settlement with the Brooklyn faculty and students and set in motion a more radical solution: they would solve the problems at Brooklyn by dumping the center.

In the midst of all the turmoil over the affairs in Brooklyn, Southampton College prepared for its first graduation. Robert VanDerzee ('67), the chairman of the student-faculty planning committee, welcomed parents and guests noting that "this is an important day for all the people on Eastern Long Island." One hundred and thirty-one seniors received their degrees on June 8, 1967, at a ceremony in front of Southampton Hall.

Campus for Sale

When the fall semester opened, the returning students and faculty were shocked to learn that Hoxie was negotiating the sale of the Brooklyn center with the chancellor of the City University of New York (CUNY). The

Figure 4.2. First Southampton College Graduation, May 1967. *Courtesy of Southampton Town Historian.*

executive committee of the Board of Trustees had met on September 19 and resolved to sell the Brooklyn center (*Windmill* Oct. 9, 1967). There had been no consultation with the faculty or students in Brooklyn. The university worked, as it often did, in secret behind closed doors. The immediate response from the Brooklyn students and faculty was outrage. They were convinced that this was Hoxie's attempt to punish the Brooklyn center for the protests of the previous spring. Once again, the negative perception of Hoxie's personality played a role in the controversy. Most of the parties involved were quick to assume the worst about Hoxie's intentions.

The initial impetus for this shift in policy actually came from the preliminary oral report submitted by the Heald Hobson Associates' report in July. The report was also highly critical of the LIU leadership, but the full text was not released to the public for another year. Hoxie did acknowledge that Heald's critique was "replete with hostility towards the trustees . . ." (*Windmill* Dec. 18, 1967, 3). Hoxie, however, selectively seized upon Heald's recommendation about selling off the Brooklyn center with all its urban challenges even though it ran against his oft-repeated statements about his deep commitment to private higher education. His dislike of Birenbaum and his discomfort with Brooklyn's urban challenges trumped his "noble cause" of private higher education.

In late September, Hoxie and the board released a brief quotation from Heald's report recommending that "the Trustees of Long Island University give consideration to selling the Brooklyn site and consolidating its programs on its Long Island Campuses" (*Windmill* Oct. 2, 1967, 3). That press release did not come until after negotiations with the City University of New York were well under way. The final written report, which was not issued until a year later when the controversy over the sale of the center had been resolved, may have been a factor in Zeckendorf's decision, announced in the same month, to resign as chairman of the Board of Trustees, effective the following October. There were, of course, other factors besides Hoxie's personal vendetta involved in the decision to sell Brooklyn. The deal worked out by Zeckendorf would bring a sale price of $32 million for the center (Gatner, 480). While the value of the dollar was quite different in 2005 when LIU sold Southampton to the state university, it is somewhat ironic that the sale price was $35 million.

Although caught by surprise, the Brooklyn SGA, faculty, and alumni moved quickly. They organized a "Save LIU Brooklyn Committee," and passed out flyers asking for contributions and general support. The flyers called on students and alumni to meet at the office of the New York City Board of Education and demonstrate their concerns. Recognizing that there was little hope of changing the trustees' decision through the existing channels inside the university, they took the issue outside to the streets and to the relevant government agencies. They asked the New York State Joint

Legislative Committee on Higher Education to investigate the sale. The committee held several public hearings where they heard a great majority of witnesses oppose the sale. The Long Island University representatives included Zeckendorf, Heald, Hoxie, and Mary Lai. They, of course, supported the sale, as did the representatives from CUNY.

The opposition came from local elected officials: labor unions, faculty, deans from the Brooklyn center, and student organizations. These opposition groups raised many serious questions about the sale. The students noted that CUNY could only take in about three thousand of the seven thousand Brooklyn students who would be displaced by the proposed sale. Transfer to Post was limited to those students who could afford to live in the Post dormitories. Harold Charles, a member of the black students' organization, testified that most of the black students came from Brooklyn and lived at home. These students, worried Charles, would lose their student deferments and end up in Vietnam.

The Southampton students were concerned about the implications for their campus. Alan Braveman, the editor of the *Windmill*, and Ted Kratovil, the newly elected president of the student government, went to a mass meeting at Brooklyn to get more information. The students loudly jeered Hoxie and one faculty member vilified him during a raucous question and answer session. When Braveman returned to Southampton, he wondered in his next editorial what the fate of Southampton would be, given its own financial problems (*Windmill* Oct. 2, 1967, 2). Braveman noted that the 1967 ten-year report released in February (1967) had a glowing account of the university's prospects. Why didn't they have a clue, he asked, about the financial problems or address them before the crisis? In fact, the 1967 report did have critical comments by two outside consultants which were published in the appendix. Hoxie and the board simply ignored these warnings about the dangers of moving ahead with expensive new programs rather than solidifying and improving the ones already in place (see note 4).

The Southampton Student Government Association (SGA) came out in solid support of the Brooklyn Center. In a front page article in the *Windmill* (Oct. 9, 1967), the SGA accused the LIU administration of misrepresentations, bad faith, secretive dealings, and autocratic decision making. They also raised questions about the fate of their own campus. In a resolution that had ironic significance for events four decades later, the SGA demanded that "if Southampton College is to be sold to the state system of education, all members of the Southampton College community should be incorporated into the decision to sell Southampton College." Unfortunately, when the decision came to sell Southampton nearly forty years later, the LIU administration acted pretty much the same way as it had in 1967.

The faculty at Southampton were also concerned about the impact of the sale. Donald Baker was one of the fifty witnesses who testified before the New York Legislative Committee (SCC Archives B, I Box #1B, Baker 1967). He voiced the concerns of many faculty, students and administrators not only at Southampton, but throughout the university:

> It is this cumulative set of circumstances and situations that appear so strange, almost Kafkaesque-like in their overtones. The secretiveness with which the entire Brooklyn affair has been conducted, the flimsiness of the reasons given for the Center's sale, the total disregard of the public, the blundering manner in which administrative affairs have been conducted—all tend to lend credence to those faculty and student groups which much earlier voted no confidence in the present LIU administration. And the Board of Trustees must bear some of the responsibility for not having listened to those voices. (Baker 1967, 12)

The coalition opposing the sale was not content to rely on the official channels of resistance. They organized a dramatic march of four thousand student demonstrators to cross the Brooklyn Bridge to protest at City Hall, where they demanded that Mayor Lindsey and the city council investigate the sale. Mayor Lindsey came out against the sale, as did the members of the city council and Brooklyn's representatives in Washington and Albany. This did not deter Hoxie and the trustees, although it may have caused Zeckendorf and a few of the trustees to begin having more doubts about Hoxie's leadership. When Zeckendorf announced in July that he would step down as chairman of the board the following October, he may have assumed that the sale would be completed by then. Instead, he departed in the middle of a confused and raucous controversy that put the university in a very bad light.

The Board of Trustees elected John P. McGrath, the president of the East New York Savings Bank, to succeed Zeckendorf as chairman. Zeckendorf, however, remained as a voting member of the board. This change in leadership may have made Hoxie a bit nervous because McGrath was reputed to be unimpressed with the chancellor (*Windmill* Oct. 16, 1967, 4). Arthur T. Roth, the chairman of the Franklin National Bank, who became the vice chairman of the board, however, was one of Hoxie's staunch allies. The chancellor kept close watch on these changes in the board and influenced them as much as he could. Hoxie, according to Mary Lai, was always maneuvering to keep a majority of the trustees on his side. Whatever his feelings might have been about Hoxie, McGrath remained committed, pursuing the sale of the Brooklyn center in spite of the increasing pressure from the legislative committee.

LIU raised the stakes by placing a freeze on the Brooklyn admissions office and announcing that they would close the center even if the sale did not go through (*Windmill* Oct. 23, 1967, 1). This placed more pressure on the faculty and students, and it alarmed the remaining centers. Donald Baker and William Burke, chair of the Natural Science division, worried about the problems they would face at Southampton if they had to absorb the tenured professors from Brooklyn. Many of their nontenured faculty would very likely lose their jobs. The Southampton deans and faculty representatives issued a memorandum stating that, "[m]orale of students and faculty of Southampton College of LIU is once again this year being undermined." There were also rumors that Southampton provost Edward Glanz would be demoted in a move designed to give Hoxie more authority over campus affairs. Many at Southampton believed that Hoxie was angry at Glanz for not speaking up more forcefully on the chancellor's behalf during the tuition protests the year before. In a thinly veiled warning to Hoxie, the Southampton advisory council issued a statement affirming its support for Provost Glanz and for the individual goals of the separate colleges of the university (*Windmill* Nov. 14, 1967, 1).

Many members of the legislative committee, particularly those from Manhattan and Brooklyn, were convinced that the decision to abandon Brooklyn was driven by a desire to leave behind the urban problems and shift resources to the suburban middle-class campuses at Post and Southampton. Many others had raised the same concern, arguing that the financial stress cited by Hoxie was a red herring. They wanted more detailed information about university finances. Rather than comply with this request, the university stonewalled. When the committee issued a subpoena to Hoxie requesting that he answer more questions about the university's financial records, the chancellor refused to appear, saying curtly that he had said all that he had to say about the finances in his first appearance before the committee.

State Assemblyman Joseph Kotter, who had ordered the subpoena, said that Hoxie's former presentation had been inadequate and that his defiance was inhibiting the investigation (*Windmill* Oct. 30, 1967, 1). The university's refusal to fully cooperate with the committee led to a flurry of telegrams to James Allen, the state commissioner of education, demanding that the New York Board of Regents intervene and suspend the LIU Board of Trustees. A week earlier the Brooklyn faculty had voted 123 to 13 in support of a similar resolution calling for the same action by the regents. Allen agreed to bring the issue to the regents.

The New York City and Long Island newspapers closely followed the chaotic events in Brooklyn. In November, the barrage of bad publicity continued with a sharp critique by Murray Kempton in the *New York Post* (reprinted in *The Windmill* Nov. 14, 1967). There is nothing wrong with LIU, said Kempton, that a new board and chancellor wouldn't fix. "In the last six months, these trustees have lied to their students, their teachers, and to the U.S Steel Foundation, which they induced to pay for the mendacities in the fund-raising brochure that promised so much to the Brooklyn campus from which they were proposing to lam not six months later."

A month after LIU announced the freeze on Brooklyn admissions, Hoxie reversed the university policy saying that the Board of Trustees, out of a sense of responsibility, "to make certain that there was an uninterrupted educational opportunity at the Brooklyn Center site" reopened the admissions office (*Windmill* Nov. 20, 1967, 1). The change in policy came because it was now clear that the sale would not be completed as expected by December 1, 1967. The reason for the delay, said Hoxie, was that the university wanted the Board of Regents "to study the matter without undue haste." It was a transparent attempt to put a positive spin on the decision of the regents to intervene. In response to the questions raised about the university finances, Hoxie said that the university would need an annual increase of two and one-half million dollars in gifts and grants to resolve its financial problems.

When the faculty representatives asked Hoxie why the university did not employ a professional fundraiser to address this problem, his answer revealed the degree to which the university was out of touch with well-established patterns in other private universities. "We already have a highly competent professional person on the LIU staff in John Bairdi [the Brooklyn provost]" (*Windmill* Dec. 18, 1967). What Hoxie did not add was that in response to a recommendation from the Middle States Association, the trustees had authorized the preparation of a proposal for a major fundraising campaign in 1965. With the help of Dr. Deane W. Malott, a consultant who was president emeritus of Cornell University, a plan had been prepared and presented to the public at LIU Charter Day in February 1967 as a part of the ten-year development plan. Many of the trustees, however, were unenthusiastic because they did not want to be put on the spot for large donations. Zeckendorf often reminded his fellow trustees that only a few of the trustees had over the years "carried the weight of which they were capable" (Gatner 1974, 572). This pattern has never changed. Consequently, as soon as the $32 million offer from CUNY was placed on the table, the trustees quickly shelved the highly touted fundraising campaign.

This cavalier attitude toward fundraising ignored the many warnings in the professional journals in the mid-sixties about the financial difficulties facing private college and universities with small endowments. Projected declines in enrollments and public giving could no longer be offset with tuition increases (Hammond 1984, 367; Wynn 1974, 43–44). Major universities, warned H. R. Bowen (1968, 3–4), will not necessarily disappear, but they will stagnate and fall behind public institutions. It is possible, of course, that the best professional fundraisers available would have had trouble convincing donors to give money to a university with LIU's reputation for chaos and questionable leadership. LIU now had the added problem of a continuing public relations disaster caused by the Brooklyn controversy, which was aired almost weekly in the press.

Soon after the spring semester of 1968 began, the regents announced their findings. They ignored the advice of Commissioner James Allen and ruled that LIU had a legal right to sell the campus and that CUNY had a similar right to purchase it (*New York Times* Feb. 24, 1968, 1:2; Gatner 1974, 490). This was a major victory for LIU, but the coalition against the sale now increased their pressure on the elected state and local officials. The Brooklyn students, alumni, and faculty carried on the lobbying efforts in New York and Albany. One primary target of the lobbying campaign was Mayor Lindsey's office.

LIU inadvertently hurt their cause when members of the Board of Trustees issued statements in the press that showed a complete lack of sensitivity. They argued that CUNY "could be more responsive to minority students than a private institution," suggesting that private schools were somehow unable to deal effectively with minority issues (Gatner 1974, 491). One board member, when pressed about the obligations of LIU to serve the poor urban community around the Brooklyn campus, remarked dismissively that it was not their primary responsibility to provide education for students who couldn't afford the cost of tuition.

LIU's bad press, the visits from student and faculty delegations, and the pressure from the Brooklyn and Manhattan political leaders finally moved Mayor Lindsey to take a public stand against the proposed sale (*New York Times* April 17, 1968, 1:5; Gatner 1974, 491). The LIU board, however, continued to press their case, but the New York City Board of Higher Education took its cue from the mayor and officially declined LIU's offer (*New York Times* April 28, 1968 73, 1; Gatner, 492). Thus ended an unsavory episode that had been a major public relations disaster, but there was more to come!

The Heald Hobson Report 1968: "The future of Long Island University as a private institution is not assured"

Zeckendorf and some of the board were now disillusioned with Hoxie's leadership. Some board members had little sympathy with student and faculty complaints, but they faulted Hoxie for bungling the sale of Brooklyn. When Henry Heald submitted the final text of his report in August 1968, it confirmed many of the assessments made by Hoxie's critics. The report concluded that the university's priorities for future development were not realistic, agreeing in essence with William Birenbaum's critique of Hoxie's plans for rapid expansion. Specifically, Heald found that the plans for financing a law school, a school of social work, an institute of public administration, an institute of advanced scientific studies, and five new doctoral programs were unrealistic. "It hardly seems wise to contemplate establishing additional professional schools when those presently established are all unaccredited" (SCC RG 1, Heald Hobson, 5) In an embarrassing assessment of the university's goal of becoming a "high quality private university," the report stated that there were "too many present deficiencies and an unlikely prospect of securing the volume of private support which would be necessary to build quality on the scale necessary to achieve that status" (ibid., 3). "The university," continued the report, "does no regular and detailed short and long term financial planning. The ten-year plan is basically promotional. Its projections in terms of academic programs, sources of income, and enrollment projections are not realistic and are based on inadequate data" (ibid., 20). The critique was very similar to the ones voiced by Birenbaum and by Deane Malott.

The report supported the perception held by many students and faculty that Hoxie was "a dictator" who governed without consultation. "It is a matter of serious concern and for immediate action," said Heald, that "so much authority is centered in the Chancellor's office" (SCC RG 1, Heald Hobson, 6). A related problem was the absence of organizational charts and job descriptions, resulting in confusion about accountability and the limits of authority. The Board of Trustees was faulted for a "lack of expertise in terms of higher educational developments, university programs, and university administration" (ibid., 15).

Turning to Southampton, the report noted that it was obvious "that neither careful and detailed planning nor concomitant financial resources went into the creation of this unit," and it called for a thorough evaluation of all aspects of the center (SCC RG 1, Heald Hobson, 31). Heald noted that, in sharp contrast to LIU, when Hampshire College was established the founders raised $14 million before they began operations (ibid.,43). The administrative failures of the university leadership, acknowledged Heald, had, "of course complicated and frustrated the development efforts of this unit" (ibid., 32). These frustrations were reflected in the low faculty morale among those interviewed. The faculty was particularly concerned about Hoxie's leadership and about the lack of funds for basic classroom equipment, scholarships, and travel expenses for research and professional conferences. A larger concern was the failure to raise admissions requirements, as had been envisioned when the center opened. President Glanz, when he interviewed the new faculty during the first years of the center, had held out the hope that he could soon develop a more selective admissions policy. Unfortunately, the continued dependence on the yearly income from tuition to meet operating expenses and pay off the burden of debt, which the university passed along to the fledgling center, made it impossible to become more exclusive. An analysis of freshmen class profiles showed that the quality of the classes had not improved markedly since the first class entered in 1963. More than 50 percent still came from the bottom fourth and fifth of their high school classes (ibid., 37).

Southampton's problems should have been no surprise. The report, however, came to an ominous conclusion about the whole university. Heald remarked pointedly that "the future of Long Island University as a private institution is not assured. It has practically no endowment, an uncertain reputation, and significant deficiencies" (SCC RG 1, Heald Hobson, 75). The report echoed many of the criticisms in the evaluations of the Middle States in 1961 and in the 1964 evaluations by Middle States and the New York State Education Department, criticisms which LIU had ignored. The 1961 report noted that "the rapid expansion and lack of sufficient planning . . . [resulted] in a fragmentation of the university and a blurring of its vision of itself" (LIUABCL, RG Group 2, Subgroup 2:6. LIU Condensation Summary 1961 Middle States 1962, 2). C. W. Post, in particular, had no effective planning. The faculty had been ignored during the period of rapid growth. There had been very little direct involvement, for example, in curriculum development. The 1964 Middle States evaluation raised questions about the concentration of decision making in the chancellor's office and the "insufficient know-how at the top" level of the administration. The New York State evaluators called for the university to address the failures of the university-wide administrative leadership, the inadequate facilities, and the insufficient library holdings. The administration under Chancellor Pell was deemed to be "deficient in planning and in exercising unifying control" (Gatner 1974, 618). When Chancellor Hoxie took over in the fall of 1964, he ignored most of these evaluations and no one on the Board of Trustees objected. With all of these unaddressed problems at the university level it was naive to expect that Southampton could become an elite private institution.

Hoxie's Untidy Exit: More Bad Press

Zeckendorf was having troubles of his own in August 1968. His firm went into bankruptcy, leaving him little time to devote to LIU's problems. In his autobiography he describes his financial maneuverings that summer in great detail but never once mentions anything about the problems at LIU (Zeckendorf and McCreary 1970). When the Board of Trustees discussed the implications of the aborted sale of Brooklyn and the Heald Hobson report for Hoxie's future, an acrimonious split emerged in the board between Hoxie's critics, led by Zeckendorf, and Hoxie's supporters, led by Arthur T. Roth. The squabble became public when Roth told reporters that Zeckendorf was leading an unauthorized campaign on the board to fire Hoxie. He further charged that Zeckendorf's recent plunge into bankruptcy not only raised serious questions about his decision-making ability but also disqualified him from membership on the Board of Trustees. Zeckendorf, said Roth, was pressuring the board into a bad decision. Zeckendorf responded angrily that he "would not get down to that level of diatribe." Hoxie seemed mystified by this turn of events. "I can't quite comprehend what is going on," he told reporters; "the University was going so beautifully this year, then, wow, this thing." Then he warned that the controversy "has stirred such bitterness that it could irreparably damage the university" (*New York Times* September 24, 1968, 42). Hoxie may have been right about the damage, but he failed to comprehend that he was primarily responsible for it.

The day before, Hoxie had turned his attention to matters that were more to his liking; he gave out the trophy for the "best in show" at the Westbury Kennel Club. This was his world, far removed from the teeming streets of Brooklyn and its urban problems. Perhaps it helps to explain how he could be oblivious to his role in the collapse of the Brooklyn sale, the votes of no confidence on all three LIU centers, and the scathing critique in the Heald Hobson report. Hoxie's distance from reality was best exemplified by a letter he sent on September 24 to all the faculty members in LIU, asking them to appeal to the Board of Trustees in his behalf. "We got the letters," said Donald Baker, "with our paychecks" (pers. comm. 2010).

Baker responded with a letter to the board that probably expressed the reaction of a majority of the faculty. He said that he was deeply concerned with the erosion in confidence and the persistent internal conflicts that have undermined the university in recent years (pers. comm.). He pointed out that Hoxie seemed unable to acknowledge or realize that his own actions had led to the controversies which engulfed him. For the good of the university, argued Baker, Hoxie should resign or be removed by the board. In desperation, Hoxie requested a meeting with all the presidents of the AAUP chapters on the university campuses where he made a personal appeal for support (Haresign, It. 26). It was, of course, all in vain. At a Southampton faculty meeting called to discuss a vote of no confidence in Hoxie, Alvin Siegel, who later served as academic dean, spoke unequivocally for the great majority of his colleagues. He rose to address those few who still counseled moderation, saying, rather forcefully, "The time to drive the stake into a vampire is when you have him." The faculty responded with a nearly unanimous resolution stating that it was "in the best interest of Long Island University for the present chancellor to be replaced as soon as possible" (It. 45) The surprising thing, given similar votes on the other campuses, was that Hoxie even thought that it was possible to find support from the faculty members.

The meeting to determine Hoxie's fate was scheduled for September 30, 1968. Hoxie was desperate to save his job. He warned the board that his ouster would be viewed as a triumph for Birenbaum, who had been "actively undermining my position" in his "striving for power." This was, said Hoxie, "mischief"; he had not been asked to resign, and he continued, "I am not considering it" (*Windmill* Sept. 27, 1968). He did admit, however, that there were rumors of a move by some members of the board to fire him. It was not a rumor. Zeckendorf convinced a majority of the trustees that Hoxie could not lead a university that included the Brooklyn center, nor could he address the issues raised in the Heald Hobson support without the support of the faculty and students. Hoxie emerged from the meeting a shaken man, despondent and on the verge of tears (*New York Times* Sept. 30, 1968, 24; Oct. 1, 1968, 1:2). He was never to hold a position of leadership in a university again.[5]

The chaotic events that marked Hoxie's downfall had a lasting effect on the university. Fundraising was now an even greater challenge because of the negative public image, and the three centers became even more alienated from the central administration. At Southampton, the lack of funds for developing the campus facilities and programs was a continuing frustration. As a result, the students, faculty, and administration turned their backs on Brookville and searched for local solutions to the challenges of a young institution.

The Gym Campaign, 1968–1970

The gym campaign is one example of the focus on local solutions. The first class graduated without a gym. This became an issue with the students during the protests over the tuition increase. The success of the basketball team, which had to play the home games in the village public school gym, increased and continually reminded the students of the inadequate campus facilities. "We have talked about the gym so many times that we are getting sick of it," wrote Alan Braveman in his *Windmill* editorial (Feb. 19, 1968). He reminded his readers that in the previous spring Provost Glanz had promised that the construction of a 32,000 square foot gym with a seating capacity of 2,200 was to begin soon. The students formed a gym planning committee, led by Elliott Sommer, a freshman, Van Camberis, the president of the SGA, and Alan Braveman to help Coach Ken Hunter and Provost Glanz in their efforts to negotiate with the LIU trustees. The campaign drew the generous support of two prominent local businessmen, Arthur Hull, who owned the Chevrolet dealership, and Harry Frank, owner of a clothing store. Both men had played important roles in bringing the college to Southampton. In the spring of 1968, the students marched from the campus to the Hull Chevrolet office in Southampton to celebrate the start of a student sponsored fundraising campaign for the gym. Hull donated $1,500 to the fund.

The constant pressure from the students and their supporters in the administration and on the faculty finally resulted in the construction of a gym. It was a lengthy and frustrating struggle, which further alienated the Southampton campus community from the LIU University Center administration. Although the student campaign fell short of the necessary funds, the LIU administration led the students to believe that construction of the gym would take place in the fall of 1968. A groundbreaking ceremony was held in October. Elliot Sommer shared the ceremonial shovel with Coach Kenneth Hunter and Provost Glanz (*Windmill* Oct. 18, 1968). Provost Glanz described the celebration as "an important event in the life of the five-year old college, a rite of passage." Arthur Hull, the chairman of the Southampton College Council, and one of the more generous supporters of the college, congratulated the students on their efforts and assured the students that the gym would be constructed that fall as promised.

Glanz, Hull, and the students were bitterly disappointed when the university backed out of its commitment. Provost Glanz did the best he could to mask his disappointment with the trustees. He issued a report to the campus about the confusion, "the misunderstandings of fact, and distortions of information." He said that the board had approved the groundbreaking at their meeting in the summer of 1968. The reason given for the unexpected delay was that the Suffolk County Health Department approval was "uncertain" and that the schedule of construction could not be set until the "architectural and engineering decisions have been made" (*Windmill* Nov. 8, 1968). The board of health wanted assurances that the campus would install a sewage disposal system before they would give approval for the gym. Glanz did not explain why the LIU Board of Trustees approved the ceremony before these matters had been resolved. The sewage problem continued to be an issue until the college closed, because LIU installed a system of septic tanks that was barely adequate. Once again the Southampton College community readily believed the worst of LIU. Was it a question of devious manipulation or gross incompetence? Take your pick. Arthur Hull resigned as chairman of the Southampton College Council, saying that he was embarrassed to look students in the eye after this.

After many delays, the gym was finally completed two years later. A dedication ceremony on October 22, 1970, marked the official opening. Arthur Hull, who had remained as a member of the college council, spoke in praise of the students and members of the local Southampton community who had played a role in the fundraising campaign. Glanz noted that the campus had grown from two buildings to thirty, but none, he said, "had so unusual a history" (*Windmill* Nov. 2, 1970). As was the case with the dorms, the building was constructed on the cheap. It was a prefabricated steel structure with locker rooms and showers in the basement. The original plans had to be scaled back in size and in quality. There was no multipurpose room, no handball and squash courts, and no classrooms. Nevertheless, for the students it was a victory. For LIU and for Southampton College, however, it was a serious public relations setback. Arthur Hull's disappointment and embarrassment after he had given his assurance that the gym would be completed in 1968 gave potential local donors yet another reason not to support the college. LIU's reputation for uncertain leadership and suspect finances was again reinforced.

The gym campaign provides other insights into the history of the college. It illustrates the changes in student culture that emerged in the 1960s. The students were organized, outspoken, and no longer hesitant to challenge adult authority. Secondly, it documents one of the problems that continued to plague the college throughout its history. The dorms and the gym were in constant need of repair because of the poor quality of the materials used in the original construction. Repairs were often deferred until they reached a crisis point, and worn-out parts were generally replaced with more of the same poor quality. These repairs and the costs of heating the poorly insulated buildings were a drain on the budget. The condition of dorms was also a factor in another important area. Alice Flynn, who worked in several offices related to admissions and student services for thirty years, believed that the design and general condition of the physical plant hurt student recruitment and retention (It. 19). In an exit survey of students who were transferring to other colleges, Flynn found that the poor quality of the physical plant was frequently mentioned.

Chapter Five

Drift and Uncertainty, 1968–1972

> The administrative history of LIU-Southampton reminds one of Laurel and Hardy moving that piano up the long flight of stairs to a house on the top of a high ridge, only to lose control and see it roll back down into the street.
>
> —Robert Pattison

Committees, Policy Councils, and Models, 1968–69

When the Board of Trustees dismissed Hoxie at the beginning of the 1968 fall semester, they had given little thought to the consequences that would follow. There were no plans for the transition to new university leadership. George Stoddard, the vice chancellor for academic affairs, who was in East Africa at the time, hastily returned to serve as an interim chancellor. It was a chaotic state of affairs at a time when the university needed stable leadership to respond to the recommendations in the Heald Hobson Report (see ch. 4). The trustees were urged to become more "intimately involved with the life of the university," to revise the university statutes so that there would be a more rational relationship between the university center and the major campuses, and to establish a more professional fundraising program (SCC, Archive A, I-k, Heald Hobson, 76). The fact that these statutes had only been in place since 1965, yet were already deemed to be outdated and inadequate, underscores the continuing pattern of ineffectual leadership at LIU. The Heald Hobson report recommended that some functions of the university needed to be more centralized. The positions of provost at the centers, said Heald Hobson, should be discontinued and be replaced by executive deans who would report to the university vice president for academic affairs. This would ensure a closer uniformity in the university policies and programs. In the absence of firm leadership over the next two years, however, events moved the university in the opposite direction.

The Board of Trustees, stung by the criticisms that they had never included the faculty, students, and campus administrators in the decision-making process, established a committee on reorganization consisting of five board members and a faculty-student-alumni committee to draft a revision of the university statutes. The committees began their work by reviewing the Heald Hobson Report but the prevailing mood of the faculty, students, and administrations in the university centers was at odds with many of its recommendations. There was little support, in particular, for a more centralized university administration. Disillusioned by the past experiences with the central administration under Hoxie and his predecessors, a majority of the students and faculty at the centers wanted more local autonomy. Van Camberis, the president of the SGA, spoke to the Southampton Faculty Assembly in the fall of 1968 urging them to establish a new university structure that would ensure a large measure of independence from the university center (*Windmill* Oct. 18, 1968). Camberis articulated feelings that were widely shared at Post and Brooklyn.

Provost Glanz established a local campus-wide college policy council to draft its own proposal for the restructuring of the university. The council submitted their proposal, which they published in a special edition of the *Windmill* (Dec. 6, 1968). The council agreed with the university committee on reorganization and called for a federal model with virtually autonomous centers linked together by support services, such as financial accounting, computer databases, and legal counsel. The university would be governed by the chancellor and a university council that included the chairmen of the campus faculty senates, the presidents of the campus student governments, the university officers, and the center provosts, whose title would be changed to "president." The primary difference between the Heald Hobson recommendations and the Southampton college council's proposal is most sharply marked by the designations for the chief executive officer at each center. Where the Heald Hobson report called for the provosts to become executive deans with limited autonomy, the Southampton council wanted the provosts to become presidents with increased powers.

The university trustees' committee on reorganization chaired by Dr. Emilio Collado and the faculty-student-alumni committee reviewed the proposals from Southampton and the other centers and presented a unanimous report to the Board of Trustees on April 1, 1969 (*Long Island University Magazine* Summer 1969, 22–23). Collado's report closely followed the organizational model suggested by the Southampton College policy council. The report called for a classic federal structure wherein the local centers were to have greater autonomy. The provosts now became presidents, and the powers not specifically granted to the central administration were reserved to the centers. Each center was to have a college council made up of local community supporters, campus officials, and alumni. This new structure, said Collado, more accurately reflected what had been taking place over the previous years anyway. "In revising its structure, statutes, and perspectives," said the report, "the University has simply been shaping them to fit the facts" (*Windmill* April 18, 1969). The official names of the centers, which deemphasized the university identity, were to be The Brooklyn Center of Long Island University, The C. W. Post Center of LIU, and The Southampton Center of LIU. Acting chancellor Stoddard supported the new statutes and at the annual May meeting, the Board of Trustees voted for them to take effect on July 1, 1969.

Glenn Ferguson Chancellor for a Semester, Fall 1969

Running concurrently with the work on the statutes was the search for a new chancellor. Stoddard opened up the search process to representatives from the faculty, students, and administrators for the first time in the history of the university. When it came time to make the appointment, however, Stoddard ignored the campus committees and named Glenn W. Ferguson to the position. Ferguson had excellent credentials. He served as an administrator at the University of Pittsburgh from 1956 until 1960 when he was tapped by John F. Kennedy to become the first director of the Peace Corps in Thailand. He was next appointed to be the first director of VISTA, the domestic Peace Corps. Following that assignment, Lyndon Johnson made him ambassador to Kenya, where he served for three years prior to his selection by George Stoddard to head LIU.

Ferguson brought to LIU a level of credibility unmatched in the history of the university. Unfortunately, the announcement of this appointment at the LIU trustees' meeting on June 26, 1969, was overshadowed in the press by a lawsuit the Brooklyn student center brought against the trustees charging that the university had broken its agreement to consult with them on the selection of a university chancellor. At the meeting, a show cause order issued by a New York State Supreme Court judge, was presented to John McGrath, the chairman of the Board of Trustees (*Long Island University Magazine* Summer 1969, 2). The faculty senates at Brooklyn and Southampton also protested the arbitrary appointment. The faculty and student critics made it clear that they did not object to Ferguson, who they agreed had excellent qualifications, but with the process of selection by the university. Four days later, Ferguson met with the Brooklyn students to repair the damage. He negotiated a settlement with the students and faculty with a promise that the appointment of university officers would be made in consultation with the students and faculty. It was a most awkward beginning for the new chancellor, but it heralded even more serious troubles ahead.

Less than two and one-half months after Ferguson took office he came to Southampton and delivered a candid and provocative address outlining his assessment of the university and his suggestions for future policy. After a brief mention of the well-known financial problems; the 97 percent dependence on tuition, the lack of a sufficient endowment, the $40 million debt, and the $70 million debt service, which he concluded was due in part to "inept leadership, [and] disinterest of individual members of the Board of Trustees,"

Ferguson launched into a more far-reaching critique. In the first place, he noted that the university appeared to be more of a "holding corporation" than a university in the traditional sense. "I have searched in vain," he said, "for the existence of programs which point to a willingness on the part of faculty, students, alumni, community or administration of [the centers] to work together, to nurture common interests, to develop a meaningful rationale for the existence of a university" (SCC Archive B, II, d, Address to Southampton Faculty Sept. 18, 1969). He delineated several areas where he hoped to develop university-wide programs, but noted that these areas of cooperation did not require "a legal entity called Long Island University."

Ferguson noted that attempts to create a university-wide community of scholars had failed. There was little interest shown by the centers in the university as a whole, nor was there much interaction among the centers. The attempt to sustain a university faculty senate was frustrated by the quorum failures. Few Southampton faculty were willing to drive for more than an hour on the Long Island Expressway to attend a meeting at C. W. Post and then return at a snail's pace in the congested highway. This notoriously crowded roadway, often referred to as the world's longest parking lot, discouraged much interaction and guaranteed a measure of independence for Southampton. The author, who taught in the History department at Southampton College for more than three decades, cannot recall a single occasion when he met with colleagues at either Brooklyn or C. W. Post to discuss common academic interests. Ferguson believed that in addition to geography the lack of a common university identity was related to differences in demographics and educational philosophy. These differences were most dramatically expressed in the attempt to sell the Brooklyn campus, described in a previous chapter. The Southampton campus, continued the new chancellor, had two major assets which were wisely being developed by the administration and faculty; the marine environment and the presence of a well-established community of artists and writers. He concluded his address by inviting Southampton and the other centers to explore several models of university organization for the future. "I have no vested interest in whether Long Island University proceeds as a single entity, as three separate legal entities, or as two."

The address was most remarkable for its candor and for its timing. Here was a newly hired chief executive beginning his administration by calling his Board of Trustees incompetent and questioning the institution's rationale for existence. This, of course, made Ferguson very popular with the faculty and administration at the three centers, but it alarmed and infuriated many of the University Center officials and some members of the Board of Trustees. Mary Lai, in particular, was greatly distressed. She had become concerned during the months after Hoxie's departure with the absence of leadership at the University Center. She watched in dismay as the committees reviewing the statutes dismissed the Heald Hobson recommendations for strengthening the central administration. She was unhappy with the new chancellor because she felt that he had been hired to support the move toward decentralization. Lai feared with good reason that Ferguson's approach might lead toward the eventual dismantling of her beloved university.

Shortly after his address to the Southampton faculty, Mary Lai's fears were nearly realized when Ferguson submitted a proposal to the Board of Trustees suggesting that Southampton, C. W. Post, and Brooklyn become independent colleges. Even the trustees who favored the federal structure recommended by the Collado committee felt that this was going too far. The majority rejected Ferguson's proposal curtly. "It is regrettable that the Chancellor has found it necessary to pursue a search for an hypothetical rationale instead of seizing the helm and providing leadership necessary to assure a viable future for the university as a whole" (Quoted in Lai 1970:1, SCC Archives A I, K, 8). Ferguson's administration was over almost before it began. He could do little more than serve as a ceremonial officer until he left the university after the June 1970 graduation. An ongoing debate over the future of the university took up the time and energy of the administrators, faculty, and students until the appointment of Ferguson's successor, Albert Bush-Brown, in the spring of 1971.

Prompted by Chancellor Ferguson's invitation to consider alternative models for the future of Southampton, President Glanz had initiated campus-wide discussions beginning with a candid assessment of the current status of the college. He began by stating the obvious and then went on to propose four models for the future direction of the college. The absence of an endowment, he noted, left the college entirely dependent on tuition, forcing the admissions office to admit weaker, high-risk students. Attracting additional students was hampered by the limited scholarship funds available and a marginally adequate physical plant. Without a sufficient endowment there were few resources to improve the facilities or to enrich the curriculum. Peter Schilling, in an uncharacteristic break with his antiestablishment posture, praised Glanz's candid analysis in a *Christmas Camel* editorial, remarking on his emergence as "a dedicated, innovative, and sensible leader."

The first model presented by Glanz was the existing one under the new university statutes, which gave the centers considerable autonomy but offered no solutions to the problems he outlined. This model closely resembled the call for a federal structure in his 1968 proposal (see above). The second model called for Southampton College to be absorbed into the C. W. Post administrative structure. A variation of this model was implemented unsuccessfully in 1983 and abandoned a few years later. Another more drastic variation was finally imposed in 2004. At the time, however, there was no interest expressed by the Post administration for a merger of any sort. The third model was very popular in the Southampton College community because it envisioned an independent status as a private college.

The major barrier here, of course, was the debt the college owed to the university for the purchase of the property and for the construction of the campus dorms. The fourth model, with no small measure of historical irony, was to become a part of the State University of New York. There were two major problems with this model: LIU would likely oppose any attempt to join SUNY, and secondly the state appeared to have no interest in absorbing Southampton. The last model would be a partnership with the state system similar to joint ventures linking private and public institutions in Connecticut and Pennsylvania.

Mary Lai was also at work during the fall of 1969. She rallied support from among the university officers and trustees to turn back what she believed was a disastrous move toward decentralization. She outlined her arguments for a return to a centralized university in a twenty-seven-page position paper, which went out to the university community on December 30, 1970 (SCC Archive A I, k, 8, Lai 1970). She began by citing the 1964 Middle States report, which endorsed a corporate model. The home office in a corporation made general policy with input from the local branches. "The local manager moves along with little interference as long as he stays within the guidelines of the home office, but the home office has a tight rein if he begins to veer off in directions other than those agreed upon" (quoted in Lai 1970, vi). She reminded her readers that Hoxie's mandate had been to strengthen the central administration and that this policy direction had been supported in the Heald Hobson Report. During George Stoddard's laissez-faire administration, lamented Mary Lai, Post, Brooklyn, and Southampton asserted their independence, moving the university back to the policies advocated by William Birenbaum. The revised university statutes, continued Lai, reflected the parochial interests of the three campuses, further undermining the power of the university center. The campuses were establishing separate identities that confused the public perception of LIU. Lai had been concerned about the ambiguity over the identity of LIU since the opening of the Post campus.

Lai argued that the most important consideration was financial survival. The university financial structure was not only more economical than three separate budgetary systems, which duplicated many services, but it also provided important financial leverage for long-term low-interest loans. She also rejected arguments from the local centers that they would have more success in raising funds if they were not burdened by LIU's negative image. Post and Southampton administrators were convinced that the wealthy residents around Brookville and the summer community in Southampton would be more likely to give money to a local independent college. Lai dismissed this argument, noting correctly that the wealthy elites in these communities gave to their Ivy League alma maters. Although she was well aware of the university's public relations problems, she saw some areas of strength. There was strong appeal, Lai believed, in the larger corporate image of LIU. Money, she said, could more easily be solicited from industrial and governmental donors. Her position here was not very convincing because LIU had never had much success raising funds from any sources.

Lai's strongest argument was a firm warning that the centers were all in debt to the university and that "for all practical purposes, the debts of the university bind the three centers together" (Lai 1970, 18). Separation was not possible as long as the university, as a corporate entity, held title to all assets. The university might be, as Ferguson said, "merely a holding company," but it was, nevertheless, a legal entity with debt obligations to federal and state authorities and to individual bondholders who were not likely to approve a division of assets. Mary Lai chastised the Board of Trustees as well as the administrators in the centers for their naiveté. "One wonders," she said caustically, "why so much time and effort is spent discussing an almost impossible dissolution" (ibid., 18). Mary Lai was a force to be reckoned with. It was abundantly clear who was running the show.

Glenn Ferguson saw no future for himself at LIU and resigned after the fall semester. A few months later he was appointed president of Clark University in Massachusetts in and 1973 went on to serve as president of the University of Connecticut. Mary Lai and her allies quieted much of the talk about alternative administrative models. The tensions between the campuses and University Center at Brookville, however, remained. When Ferguson left in the spring of 1970, John McGrath became acting chancellor. It was Mary Lai, however, who handled much of the day-to-day operation of the university in her role as the chief financial officer. "I pretty much held the university together during the last days of Ferguson's administration and until a new chancellor was hired. McGrath was seldom around. He would ask me about most everything" (It. 31). During this period the three campuses enjoyed a great deal of local autonomy, but that was soon to end.

Enter Albert Bush-Brown

> I am confident that faculty and students will embrace Dr. Albert Bush-Brown as their leader with the spirit of the old Long Island University. Together, we can look forward to a great future.
>
> —John P. McGrath, Chairman of the Long Island University Board of Trustees

Albert Bush-Brown became chancellor on March 29, 1971. He was the fourth chancellor in a three-year period marked by acrimony, discord, and financial stress. When board chairman John P. McGrath announced his appointment he spoke of the dedicated university leaders of the past: "[W]e are thankful to divine providence for those leaders, in times of past crisis. And we dare to hope that we are again blessed with a capable leader, in this new critical phase in our history" (*Windmill* April 5, 1971). McGrath's hopes were not realized. After thirteen years, Bush-Brown had lost the confidence of the faculty at all three centers. There was a widely held perception that his drinking may have interfered with his capacity to administer the university. The chancellor usually ended his meetings with drinks all around. When he came to Southampton, Bush-Brown reputedly expected the college president to have a bottle of Jack Daniels ready in the bottom drawer of his desk (It. 38). Stories about his drinking were undoubtedly exaggerated in the telling, particularly by those he had humiliated in one way or another.

Not surprisingly the Southampton College faculty overwhelmingly endorsed a resolution passed earlier by the other campuses calling for his immediate dismissal and charging the chancellor with depleting the university's limited resources, injuring its reputation, and fostering a division between faculty and administrators (*Southampton Press* Dec. 20, 1984). In a recent analysis of the role of university presidents, Birnbaum and Eckel note that "regardless of what may appear in the charter and bylaws, the authority of the president, his real leadership, depends on the willingness of the campus to accept him as a leader. If it will not, well there are other ways of making a living" (Birnbaum and Eckel 2005, 343).

Ironically, Bush-Brown came to the university with the much better credentials than all of his predecessors, except, of course, Ferguson. He held a PhD from Princeton, had teaching experience at Harvard and M.I.T. and had served as the president of the Rhode Island School of Design. He had written three books and numerous articles on architecture and urban development. The Board of Trustees believed that these credentials would give LIU the credibility it needed to attract major contributions from donors and large government contracts. The impressive resume, however, could not compensate for aspects of the new chancellor's personality that undermined his effectiveness at LIU. In fairness, he was a very bad fit for LIU. His experience in high-powered, well-endowed, prestigious universities did not prepare him for the problems he would face. Accustomed to dealing with Ivy League administrators and faculty who had impressive resumes of their own, he came to LIU with an air of condescension that alienated many. His failure to raise funds was due, in part, to his discomfort at having to plead for money from a position of weakness and even desperation, whereas in the past he had represented well-established institutions.

Edward Glanz: Successes of an Orphan Child

> In many ways we were an orphan child, third in line behind Post and Brooklyn.
>
> —Timothy Bishop

> We are a pimple on the butt of LIU.
>
> —Thomas Haresign

One of the first to feel the brunt of the new chancellor's arrogance was President Glanz. Bush-Brown saw Glanz as something of a country bumpkin who was barely adequate to handle his job. The chancellor complained openly that Southampton College had failed to raise money from the wealthy summer residents on the East End, ignoring the assessment made by Mary Lai that wealthy elites tended to give their support to their exclusive alma maters. He also asked why Southampton had failed to maintain and increase the enrollments of 1967 and 1968. These were the years when the Vietnam draft had inflated the enrollments to nearly 1,700, about four hundred more students than had enrolled in 1966 In the fall of 1971, the enrollment held at about 1,300, a number that was a bit above the average for most of the remaining history of the college. The chancellor followed these complaints with orders to make cuts in all areas. The brief period of local autonomy ended abruptly, much to the dismay of President Glanz and the other center presidents.

Glanz, anticipating these developments, decided that he would remain as president for one more year. His resignation marked an important transition in the history of the college. As he looked back on nearly a decade of service to the college he could take satisfaction from his role as founder and as chief administrator during difficult times. There were also many disappointments. He came to Southampton with a vision of a small elite college that would nurture students and prepare them for the world. In the ten-year plan (1966–1976), Hoxie had promised that LIU was embarking on the development of "a university of the highest order in terms of quality of education and physical plant." Glanz, in his progress report to the New York State Department of Education in April 1967, added that his model for Southampton College was an elite college such as Bates, Bowdoin, or Colby.

This admirable but somewhat naive vision was immediately challenged by the New York State Department of Education. In its 1967 report, the state evaluators advised the Southampton administration that it was unrealistic and misleading to claim that admission standards could be significantly raised as long as the college was entirely dependent on tuition. When Southampton submitted its report to the state in 1969 the same goals were set forth. In response, Charles Meinhart, from the state department of education rather impatiently retorted, "We still sense a serious discrepancy between theory and fact. . . . It is understandable that goals must be in advance of practice; but when its goals are at odds with experience and with the financial, student, and faculty resources that can be expected within the foreseeable future, they must be considered unrealistic" (SCC Archive I, K-6, Memo: Meinhart to Glanz Oct 18, 1969, 1). The illusion that the college could one day become highly selective remained in the mission statements for the next two decades.[1] It was a dream that died hard, even in the minds of people who in their sober moments knew that it was highly unlikely without a substantial endowment. For Glanz, it was a particularly painful acknowledgment because of his initial, albeit naive, vision of the college.

Perhaps the more unsettling experiences for Glanz were personal. He saw himself as a sympathetic mentor to students with their best interests at the center of his concern. When some students wrote mean-spirited caricatures of him in the *Christmas Camel* or called for his resignation in the *Windmill* it must have hurt. His relationship with Chancellor Bush-Brown was also troubled. Glanz worked very hard to lobby for funds from the university that would benefit the Southampton faculty and students, only to find his efforts rebuffed by the chancellor in condescending tones. Donald Baker told of a time when he was in Ed's office while some administrator from Brookville was on the phone, "demanding this or that, and I realized the shit and duress he was under as he tried to fashion an institution" (pers. comm. Aug. 12, 2006). Glanz would sigh and give a polite answer, swallowing his frustration. He knew, said Baker, that any direct confrontation would have gotten him fired.

Another frustration was with the younger faculty, fresh from graduate campuses where the discourse with administrators was often confrontational and contentious. Glanz made a sincere effort to form collegial relations with the faculty. He often invited individuals or small groups to his office in the late afternoons to have some sherry and engage in informal discussion on any topic that might arise. This worked well with many, but some of the younger, more radical instructors had little patience with what they viewed as a relic of the 1950s. Rather than finding himself in a collegial setting surrounded by appreciative students engaged in the quiet pursuit of knowledge, he had faced the more challenging and contentious world of the sixties for an exhausting decade.

Donald Baker recalled sitting with Glanz one late afternoon in 1971 sipping sherry as they discussed their experiences at Southampton. Glanz told Baker that he was tired of all the hassles from Brookville and wanted to get back to teaching and writing. The orders, often in the form of demands, from Bush-Brown, said Glanz, "undercut nearly everything I wanted to do." It was evident, said Baker that Glanz's original idea of what he wanted for Southampton was somewhat in shambles, and as a consequence he was looking for a way out.

The Search for Cultural Diversity

When the college opened in 1963, there were only a few black students enrolled, and most of them were on the basketball team. During the 1965–66 season two of the African American players, Marvin Lewis and Roland Stansbury, came to the author and Joseph d'Oronzio, a colleague in the History department, with their concerns about racism on the campus and in the village. They said that they wanted to raise awareness of the prejudices and discriminatory practices that black people faced every day. Some were blatant and many were more subtle, but the message was clear. Some local landlords would not rent to black students and the churches in town were only beginning to integrate their parishes. Many merchants would not hire blacks or Indians from the Shinnecock reservation to work "up front" in the stores where they interacted with white customers. Minorities worked in the back at lower-paying jobs where they unloaded and shelved goods. Some restaurants, said Lewis and Stansbury, delayed service to black patrons until they left in frustration. The four of us co-signed a letter outlining these concerns, which we published in the December 16 edition of the *Windmill*.

Shortly after the article appeared a Sociology class made a survey of the local merchants asking them about their racial policies. Many were quite candid admitting that they did discriminate. Much to the discomfort of Provost Glanz and the civic leaders in Southampton, *The Suffolk Sun*, a short-lived newspaper with circulation that covered eastern Long Island, picked up the student survey and published it on the front page. Glanz was left with the task of smoothing over relations with the Southampton town and villages leaders. It was a task that frequently occurred during the 1960s. For the remainder of the 1960s, the numbers of minority students was miniscule. The few black students were either basketball players or Africans who came to Southampton on a special U.S. State Department program for southern Africa. One exception was Russell Beavers Jr., an African American student from Virginia, who majored in the Natural Sciences and later earned a medical degree from Rutgers.

Members of the Shinnecock Nation, in contrast, were involved with the college in many roles from the beginning. Shinnecock elder Harry Williams recalled being on the work crew that moved furniture and equipment into Claflin Hall to prepare for the opening in 1963 (pers. comm. 2005). Peter Silva, class of 1969, was the first of many Shinnecocks to attend the college. He was an active participant in the campus community. Silva was the vice president of his freshman class and became an important liaison between the college and the reservation. After graduation he became a guidance counselor in the Southampton elementary school and later moved on to a career in business. The college hosted many events celebrating Shinnecock traditional culture. Harriett Crippen Gumbs, a tribal historian and owner of the Shinnecock Outpost, graduated with honors in 1975. Gordell Wright, an alumnus, who has served as an elected Shinnecock Nation trustee for several terms, led a Shinnecock dance group in the annual celebration of ethnic diversity on campus. Melissa Arch-Walton, who graduated in 2000, was a dean's list student, ran for the office of town trustee in 1995, and in the following year was a candidate for the New York State Assembly.

Figure 5.1. Gordell Wright, Southampton College alumnus from the Shinnecock Nation, leading a dance group from the reservation in an event on campus celebrating ethnic diversity. *Courtesy of Southampton Town Historian.*

Shinnecocks also joined the campus community as administrators, secretaries, and custodians.

Ronald Richard and Lisa Bowen served as administrators in the Higher Education Opportunity Program (HEOP). Many Shinnecocks worked in the offices and in the physical plant. Victoria Williams, Cheryl Franklin, Kathleen Bess, and June Marshall held appointments in several administrative offices during their lengthy careers at the college. Marshall and Franklin both worked for twenty-five years in campus administrative offices. Nelson Cause, Kenneth Thompson, William Lee, Walter Wise Sr., and Anthony Smith were among the Shinnecocks who worked in the physical plant department. Walter Wise organized the first maintenance workers association and played an important role in union movement at the college. He also sang in "A Visit With Gilbert and Sullivan," a college theater production. Wise took advantage of the Sherry Institute of Career Opportunity (SICO), an educational program initiated by Sherry Morris, a Southampton student, to earn his high school equivalency diploma. Some of the Shinnecock staff members also took advantage of the tuition remission policy for employees and their families to attend Southampton College. For example, Nelson Cause, a custodian from the Shinnecock Reservation, completed a BA degree with honors in business.

The college also initiated interactive programs that strengthened ties with the Shinnecock community over the years. The Social Science department offered courses in community studies which required students to work directly with the Shinnecocks and with African Americans in Southampton. The primary focus was on tutorial programs for the school children. College students went to the community center on the reservation and to family homes to tutor Shinnecock children on a one-to-one basis. Peter Silva helped to establish the program and served as the student supervisor. The program bridged a cultural gap, enriching the lives of the participants from both communities.

Other academic departments also became involved with the Shinnecocks. Under the direction of Ral Welker, the first director of the Marine Science program, the college assisted the Shinnecock with the tribal oyster hatchery facility. The Natural Science faculty provided access to the college labs and frequently visited the hatchery on the reservation to consult with the Shinnecock staff. The Humanities and Fine Arts departments made the campus auditorium available for tribal events on occasion. In the spring of 1974, for example, the Shinnecock Nation Cultural Coalition staged a presentation of traditional music and dance introduced by ceremonial chief Henry Bess and trustee Charles Smith.

The interactions with the Shinnecocks were reciprocal. Tribal members made important contributions that enriched the college. David Martine, Shinnecock artist and current director of the Shinnecock Nation Museum and Cultural Center, frequently participated in anthropology classes as a lecturer and discussion leader on Native American art and culture. Lamont Smith, a Shinnecock who experimented with traditional cultivation of native plants, worked with the author on a native garden project at the college. Students in my Native American History class planted a garden using Native American planting practices witnessed by John Winthrop in Massachusetts Bay Colony in the seventeenth century. The garden project produced enough corn, beans, and squash for a class dinner prepared by Josephine Smith, a member of the Shinnecock Nation Museum staff.

Elizabeth Haile (aka Chee Chee), a Shinnecock elder and tribal storyteller also enhanced the college curriculum. She took part in several Sociology programs with Sociology professor Barbara Peters. In 2000, Chee Chee, at the age of seventy, was given an honorary degree, and she attended all the subsequent graduation ceremonies as an honored guest. In 2003–05, Courtney Leonard, a Shinnecock ceramicist, participated in an interdisciplinary seminar on prehistoric pottery from the Southwest. The seminar combined materials, experiences, and insights from anthropology and fine arts. The students made replicas of prehistoric vessels and studied the cultural context (see chs. 9 and 10). Ms Leonard served as a studio assistant to Professor Phyllis Kudder-Sullivan and was a discussant in the author's anthropology segment of the seminar.

The number of Shinnecock students increased after 1973, when the college established a scholarship program named after Mandush, a Shinnecock leader who greeted the first white settlers in 1640. The Shinnecock signed a treaty allowing the English to settle in Southampton. The scholarship covered the difference in tuition and fees between the funds available from other sources such as the New York State grants in aid to Indians living in state. It was the least the college could do for people who had lost the land where the campus was now located. The scholarship was also consistent with the college's commitment to the local community and its social problems (SCC Archives B II-F, Box 6, Mandush File, Memo June 16, 1972; Admissions office to Shinnecock and Poospatuck Trustees Jan. 5, 1973).[2]

Leon Parks, a starting member of the basketball team, took advantage of his high profile to keep the issues of race and prejudice before the campus community. He wrote a series of articles called "Leon's Views" in the *Windmill* which appeared regularly during 1968 and 1969. One of his first articles followed the assassination of Martin Luther King in the spring of 1968. Martin Luther King had been assassinated in a Memphis motel where he had been staying while he worked in support of a strike by the city sanitation employees. Parks took the opportunity to criticize the college for ignoring the lack of diversity and called for the establishment of a Martin Luther King scholarship. The scholarship was established and funds were also raised to purchase library books on African American culture and racial issues.[3] Parks and the other African American students acknowledged the importance of these gestures, but felt that this only began to address the larger problem of racial diversity at Southampton.

Parks continued to press for increasing the numbers of black students on campus. He was particularly concerned with providing educational opportunities for young people in the black communities on eastern Long island (*Windmill* Nov. 15, 1968). He also reminded the campus community that the nation faced serious racial problems that must be addressed by his generation. Parks commented on the summer race riots of 1967 and '68 in Newark and Watts and the lynching of Emmett Till (*Windmill* Nov. 22, 1968). There is a need, he said, for more educated black people to take the lead in resolving these problems and we can play a role in dealing with the national crisis by graduating more black students from local communities (*Windmill* Dec. 13, 1968). Parks recognized that the major impediment to bringing in more blacks from the East End was economic. Working-class families could not afford to pay the tuition, which had been increasing nearly every year since 1963. He urged the college to provide aid to poor students, but the lack of an endowment precluded any allocation of significant funds for scholarships.

The small percentages of students from working-class families was a national concern, which was partially addressed in the spring of 1969 by the New York State Legislature when it began the Higher Education Opportunity Program (HEOP). This educational program assisted students from economically disadvantaged backgrounds, providing funds for tuition, room, board, and support services such as tutorial assistance and summer workshops designed to enhance study skills. The guidelines further specified that the students must come from educationally disadvantaged backgrounds and be provided with tutorial assistance. C. W. Post and Brooklyn quickly applied for the program, but there was no university-wide policy established, in part, because of the confusion caused by the transition from the Hoxie administration.

The university administration lurched from Hoxie's centralized structure to a decentralized system and back again in a two-year period. When Dowling College, Southampton's East End rival, began a program in the summer of 1970, the Southampton administration began to take a closer look at HEOP, but feared that the program might cost too much. Financial difficulties continued to plague the university. Operational costs were increasing and enrollments at Southampton were dropping. There was talk, once again, about closing the campus. Chancellor Bush-Brown pressed the Southampton administration to cut costs, thereby limiting any options for innovation. The strategies used to reduce costs almost always cause problems for an administration. Eliminating faculty lines get them into trouble with the faculty and raising tuition angers the students.

In the spring of 1971, Glanz was in the midst of angry confrontations with both of the college's primary constituents. Some faculty members angrily protested the loss of eight academic positions. Glanz defended the cuts by pointing out that there was a sharp drop in enrollment from 1968, when the draft had pushed the full-time enrollments to an all-time high of nearly 1,700. The chancellor pressured Glanz to cut faculty positions because LIU was facing a projected drop in enrollment at the Brooklyn center.[4] The accompanying strategy, calling for an increase in tuition and fees, made it much more difficult for minority students to come to Southampton.

Glanz weathered the storms and imposed the tuition increase. Not surprisingly, in the fall of 1971 there were still only twenty-seven black students in an enrollment of 1,200 on campus. Although small in number, they decided to organize and express their concerns about racial issues on campus. Led by Al Gee, Edith Horne, Linda Smith, Richard Winfield, and Josephine Dalmeda, the Black Students Alliance (BSA), which had been formed the previous year, began to speak out on racial issues (*Windmill* Oct.

1, 1971). They also organized social events open to the whole campus and called for the college to apply for a HEOP program. A lead editorial in *Windmill* (Nov. 3, 1971) supported the BSA demands for increasing the number of black students. The real problem, said the editorial, is a familiar one at Southampton, the lack of finances necessary for any progressive educational reform. The college scholarship committee acknowledged that the problem was indeed financial, and noted that "if the college ever expects to bring more than token members of minority students, particularly Black students, it will have to make a real commitment in this area" (SCC Archive A, I-C, Scholarship Committee Report Dec. 1, 1971).

Edward Glanz's Legacy

Although Glanz may have been discouraged about his failure to accomplish many of his goals, he took pride in his contributions to the emergence of the Marine Science program into national prominence. In spite of severe financial limitations he managed to squeeze out funds for faculty positions in the natural sciences, bringing in young scholars who strengthened the division and formed a core of committed faculty. In 1971, he established and gave support to an innovative calendar reform which provided for a four-week "winter session" in January between the fall and spring semesters. The unique session allowed for experimental courses on campus and off campus. Many faculty developed research experiences abroad in such places as London, the West Indies, Israel, and Central America. Three of the new faculty members, Gil Bane, Howard Reisman, and Ed Hehre, took a class to study the coral reefs near Puerto Rico.

The Marine Science major eventually drew students from all over the United States. Glanz negotiated the purchase of a small parcel of land on Fort Pond Bay, an easy five-minute walk from the campus, for a marine research center. This location also provided access to Shinnecock Bay, Peconic Bay, and the Atlantic Ocean. The property had two small buildings; an apartment and a wood working shop. In 1965, on the recommendation of James Baumann, the Natural Science division director, Glanz had hired John R. (Ral) Welker, an experienced marine scientist from the Seattle Estuarine Research Center, to develop a marine science program. Welker began with a small number of enthusiastic students and set about converting the buildings on Fort Pond Bay into a laboratory and a small classroom. They put in pumps and hoses to bring salt water into the labs and scrounged around for donations of lab equipment from local high schools. Welker recalled, "Whenever someone closed a lab, we drove up there and took whatever we could." They didn't stop there. They solicited the donation of boats, many of them in various stages of disrepair, reconditioned them, and used them or sold them. Donald Getz, who graduated in 1968, recalled those early days:

> There was a great feeling of camaraderie felt by the students, the faculty, and the staff at the station. Ral Welker was the right man at the right time. We all loved and respected him. We worked hard at often unpleasant jobs that kept us long hours at the station after classes. We didn't care. We did it because Ral was there working alongside us. (pers. comm. October 10, 2007)

Alvin Siegel, a marine oceanographer from the Woods Hole Oceanographic Research Institute, on Cape Cod, joined the faculty and worked with Welker to develop an interdisciplinary Marine Science program with concentrations in Biology, Chemistry, and Geology. Many of the professors hired by Glanz were still on the faculty when the college closed in 2004. They represented a common pattern at Southampton. Faculty and staff tended to stay on at Southampton because they liked the area and they enjoyed teaching at a small college where there was a sense of community. Robert Danziger, a chemistry professor hired in 1968, personified this sense of community. He regarded the students as a part of his extended family, working closely with them as he developed many innovative student-centered programs.

Glanz also added a new laboratory building to the marine station and negotiated the donation of a thirty-eight foot, oceangoing, twin engine diesel trawler. He shifted budget priorities to support the growing program. In 1968–69 the Natural Science budget increased by $38,000 over the previous year while the Social Science share of the budget declined by $8,000. Another important component in the growing program was the development of opportunities for international research. By the fall of 1971, Southampton College was attracting students from throughout the eastern coastal states because it was one of the few Marine Science programs available. The admissions office was pleased with what they called "the Jacques Cousteau" effect. More than half of the applicants to the college now came from students interested in the natural sciences, and the great majority of them selected Marine Science as a major. These students came in with SAT scores about one hundred points above the scores of rest of the student body. The development of the Marine Science program is one of several examples of innovations that came up from the faculty, students, and administrators at Southampton without any significant input from the central administration at LIU. Another important development was the focus on environmental concerns initiated by Natural Science director Bill Burke, faculty members Gil Bane, John Andrews, Joe Sullivan, and students Sandra Shumway, John Poley, Michael and Janet Pawlukiewicz, and Jacob Akindle. In 1969, the group edited *East End Environment*, a small ten-to-thirteen-page typewritten newsletter with brief articles on the local environment, and organized a *Festival of Life* celebration with a teach-in, lectures, and films on the first national Earth Day in 1970 (Gregory 2003, 9–11; SCC Archive B, II, f

Box 6). This early initiative would soon give rise to student organizations and academic programs dedicated to environmental issues. In 1973, John Andrews hired Tom Twomey, a local lawyer and political activist, to develop one of the first courses to focus on environmental law in the country. Like an orphan child, the campus community had to depend on its own energy, commitment, and creative imagination, not only to implement innovative programs but also just to survive from one year to the next.

The frustrations that characterized the relations between the University Center and the Southampton campus are illustrated by two episodes involving the purchase of property with great potential. The first, purchased in 1967 at Hoxie's insistence, was a thirty acre parcel of land owned by Henry and Helen Simonson. The property, which included a summer cottage and a small pool, lay to the west of the college across Tuckahoe Road. The faculty, with Glanz's encouragement, developed an innovative proposal for the parcel which included a site for a gymnasium, a volleyball court, a large area for two softball fields and bleachers, a separate soccer field, a track, an outdoor pool, a small conference center, and an area to be preserved for ecological research. A draft of the ambitious project was prepared by architect Alfonso Alvarez and landscape architect Richard C. Ward. The excitement about the potential for the college soon turned to frustration when LIU informed Glanz that not only were there were no funds for developing the parcel, but also that the $175,000 purchase price and the routine maintenance costs of the buildings for repairs, water, and electricity had to come out of the Southampton budget. The only part of the plan that ever reached fruition was the gym, which was built on Tuckahoe Road. Instead of an exciting prospect that would enrich the academic and student life of the campus and make it more attractive to potential students, the Simonson purchase became one more strain on a sparse budget.

In spite of his frustrations over the Simonson property, a few years later Glanz negotiated the donation of a three-acre parcel on Little Neck Road at the mouth of Fort Pond Bay where it opens into Shinnecock Bay. The anonymous donor stipulated that the land be preserved as a college facility and never be developed. The Natural Science division was excited about the potential for the future development of the program. Division director Bill Burke told the press, "Nature made it and we'll preserve it" (*Windmill* Feb. 22, 1971; *Southampton Press* March 25, 1971). There were no costs for the preservation of the site, so it did turn out to be quite useful for the college over the next decade.[5] Unfortunately, in 1983, Bush-Brown sold the parcel to a developer. It would be yet one more example of a decision driven by desperation to save the present by selling off the future.

In spite of these frustrations, Glanz could take some satisfaction in the development of the Theater and Fine Arts programs. In the spring of 1964, John Willoughby, the Humanities division director, organized an annual arts festival, which brought prominent artists, classical musicians, writers, actors, and dancers to perform on campus. The following year, the college joined with local art museums, cultural centers, and public schools in a coordinated program that included forty events at venues throughout eastern Suffolk County. In the summer of 1967, an ambitious program brought nineteen artists, six sculptors, two filmmakers, two photographers, an architect, and four art instructors from the Museum of Modern Art to campus, where they formed a faculty for workshops. Guest appearances by Lee Krassner Pollock, Hans Namuth, and Alfonso Ossario enriched the program. Two years later, the arts festival invited fifty local artists, including Ilya Bolotowsky, Fairfield Porter, Willem de Kooning, Larry Rivers, and Louis Trakis, to show their work in a campus exhibit. Robert Shaughnessey, a member of the humanities faculty, and Harold Kohon performed Paganini sonatas for violin and guitar. Margaret Mead, Sydney Hook, and Shirley Chisholm also participated in the festival. It appeared that the college was on its way to becoming a center for the thriving art community in the Hamptons.

For the students, one of Glanz's major accomplishments was, no doubt, the opening of the college gym in the fall of 1970, after a long and frustrating struggle with the university officials (see above, ch. 4). The basketball team, coached by James Colclough, took full advantage of the new facility. Led by captain Ronald Cargill, Richard Blue, and Glenn Barry, they won twenty games that season and went on to win an NCAA college division title in the spring of 1972.[6] President Glanz rarely missed a game at his new gym.

President Glanz's major contribution, of course, was nurturing the college through its early years, no small accomplishment given the shaky financial base and the uncertain leadership at the university center. President Glanz must have taken some measure of satisfaction from a unanimous resolution passed by the FSG Assembly when he finally announced his decision in December of that year. The assembly praised Glanz for his contributions to the college. "In a very real sense, whatever good qualities Southampton College has today owe more to Dr. Glanz than to any other individual. The Faculty-Student Assembly thanks Dr. Glanz for his services to Southampton College as its first Provost and President. The Faculty-Student Assembly salutes Dr. Edward C. Glanz as an outstanding educator and administrator" (SCC Archive B, IV, b Dec. 1, 1971). Glanz also took comfort and satisfaction from his professional publications. Prior to his arrival at Southampton, he had published six books on psychology and guidance which were well received in academia. Several were adopted as standard texts, and he was invited to give workshops on guidance at universities.

Chapter Six

Great Potential amid Continuing Deficits

The Marmion Administration 1972–1978

The 1970s saw many important developments in the college's history. The newly appointed president, Harry Marmion, struggled to fend off efforts by an unsympathetic chancellor to eviscerate his yearly budget requests while he was, at the same time, addressing the concerns of African American students, faculty union organizers, and students eager to expand their role in administrative decisions that had a direct impact on them. His every move was carefully watched by reporters from the *Windmill* and *The Christmas Camel*, a popular and irreverent underground newspaper that gave no ground to people in positions of authority (see below, p. 123 ff). Marmion got off to a good start after Southampton students, who went to interview him at Xavier College, where he was serving in his third year as president, reported back to the *Windmill* that Marmion was a very popular and successful administrator, who had turned around a financial decline at Xavier. They felt confident that he was just what Southampton needed.

"Super Marm" Comes to Southampton

> Southampton College's future has become immeasurably brightened with the appointment of Dr. Harry A. Marmion as its second president.
>
> —Don McIntosh, *Windmill* editor

Marmion shared Glanz's enthusiasm and lifetime commitment to Southampton College. The new president spoke with great enthusiasm and optimism at the opening convocation on September 27, 1972. "In its tenth year, Southampton College, in my judgment is the campus of the future within

Figure 6.1. President (1972–1978) Harry Marmion (center) with students (left to right) Kevin Burns, Diane Ormsby, and Cathy Childs. *Courtesy of Southampton Town Historian.*

Long Island University. There are so many reasons why I am so happy to be here," he continued. "We are small enough to be personal, we can instill pride in Southampton College . . . we can turn this beautiful physical location into a showplace of academic quality." Noting that the college had balanced the budget in the previous year (1971–72) he said, "We are already operating on a balanced budget concept. We can begin immediately to plan for the future." Actually, there was still a shortfall of $50,000 but it was a significant improvement over the previous year when the deficit was more than $500,000 (*Newsday* May 11, 1973). Marmion's speech was met with a prolonged standing ovation (*Windmill* Oct. 5, 1972). The next time he met with the campus community, only a year later, the mood would be quite different.

In the spirit of Marmion's inauguration day, the president and his appreciative audience can be forgiven for putting aside some less pleasant concerns. While it was true that the budget had been nearly balanced in 1971–72, it was one of the very few years in the history of the college when there had been such a small deficit. The reduced deficit, however, made little impact on the growing cumulative debt. The "balanced budget concept" was, therefore, more of a fleeting thought than a newly entrenched concept. The deficit in the following year was $220,021 and the cumulative debt had reached $3.2 million. The selection committee emphasized the shaky financial resources of the college and laid down four primary challenges that would face the new president. They wanted him to: increase the enrollment to an average of 1,200 to 1,400 full time students, reduce the cumulative debt, raise funds, and improve the academic programs. The college could avoid annual deficits and make some small progress on the other goals as long as the enrollments held at about 1,300, but it could not significantly reduce the debt and make major improvements in the academic programs and the physical plant without an infusion of funds from private donors. The illusion that the wealthy summer community would contribute significant funds to the college remained in spite of the previous failures.

In order to increase and maintain enrollment, the college had to aggressively recruit students and then keep them from leaving before they graduated. Although the fall enrollments occasionally reached above 1,200, an average of about two hundred students left before the spring semester began. The overall attrition rate generally ran above 50 percent throughout the history of the college. Marmion increased the enrollments slightly during the last three years of his administration by reforms in the admissions office, but the attrition problem remained unresolved. Several studies conducted over the years indicated that students left for a number of reasons. Some left because they lacked the necessary skills and motivation, some because they were unsatisfied with the conditions in the dorms and in the physical plant, some because they wanted a more prestigious college, some because they wanted programs that were either limited or not available here, some because of financial need, and some for a variety of personal reasons.

It was impossible, of course, to address all of these factors, so Marmion focused on improving the academic programs and the physical plant. This had to be done with very limited funds. Chancellor Bush-Brown and Treasurer Mary Lai issued a report on the fragile financial state of the university in the fall of 1973. "We were in a downward trend," she recalled, "so I urged that unallocated expenditures should be frozen at Southampton and that new promotions, appointments, and tenured appointments should be restricted" (It. 31).

One of Marmion's first initiatives was to commission a master plan for the college which included input from students faculty and the administrative staff.[1] This was welcomed by the campus community, but the chancellor was not pleased with Marmion's show of independence. The architectural firm of Warner, Burns, Toan, and Lunde published their plan in July 1973, which called for three stages of growth; consolidation (1973–76), expansion (1976–1980), and reassessment (1980–82). The first stage called for renovations of existing buildings rather than new construction. The plan anticipated that population growth in Suffolk County would lead to as many as 1,600 full time enrolled students (FTE) and, as a consequence, a stronger financial base which would make stages two and three possible. Unfortunately, the crucial assumption that Southampton would benefit significantly from the population growth in Suffolk County did not take into consideration competition from Dowling College, St Joseph's College in Patchogue, and the state university at Stony Brook.

The failure to bring in the necessary tuition money meant that the last two stages of the master plan had to be abandoned. Marmion went ahead with renovations that he hoped would have a positive impact on recruitment and retention. The college completed significant renovations in the library, the dining hall, the natural science building, and the business center. Marmion's modest campus improvement program also included the conversion of space for classrooms and offices in two sections of the Montauk dormitory complex and on the third floor of Southampton Hall. These changes were welcomed by the campus community, but the students still wanted improvements in the dorms.[2] Marmion, under constant pressure to reduce costs, argued that a major renovation of the dorms would cost about one-quarter of a million dollars. The university finally did allocate $56,000 to make some much-needed repairs in the spring of 1978, but most of the serious maintenance problems continued to be deferred. This small amount was allocated because the university expected to bring in a rental fee from a diet camp for overweight youth, which was scheduled for the summer. It didn't happen.

Marmion's first year, however, was marked by some small successes: Robert Orndoff introduced a Psychobiology major which attracted students; the Southampton Drama Society, directed by William Patten, played to large audiences; student travel courses went off to the Yucatan, Big Bend National Park, the Virgin Islands, Guatemala, the prehistoric archaeological site at Cahokia in Illinois, Greece, Italy, and Ireland; the first annual environmental conference coordinated by John Andrews was a success; the university gave the faculty a 5 percent pay raise; William Burke, the popular chairman of the Natural Science department, was named the new dean of the college; and Marmion added to his early popularity by playing Jethro Tull and the Rolling Stones on his campus radio program. The only sour notes were the annual spring drop in enrollment and an early morning drug bust by the Suffolk County Seventh Squad, which netted ten students who had been trafficking in a variety of controlled substances.

FIGURE 6.2 The author (far left) with students on field trip to Tikal, Guatemala (1974). Front row (L. to R.): Linda Melton, Mike DelliGatti, Peter Hirsch, Bonnie Gallentine, Second row: Sharon Keyes, Gary Chorst, Susan Kunzeman, Third row: Charles Juidice, Bill Stafford, and Lisa Gordon, Top row: Bob Brill and Bob Cosgrove. Not shown Todd Tolkoff. *Photo by Todd Tolkoff, Courtesy of Southampton Town Historian.*

The *Long Island Press* published a glowing report on the state of the college (July 19, 1973) praising its new president for improving administrative procedures, continuing the development of the Marine Science program, and for his efforts to support the visual and performing arts. Marmion told the reporter about his enthusiasm for the future, projecting a growth in enrollment to about 1,600 in a few years. Faculty and students echoed Marmion's positive mood. Richard Bergman praised Marmion as "the man of the hour, providing leadership we badly needed." The college, he said, had tried at first to be all things to all people, offering too many courses and majors. At the beginning of the fall 1973 semester Marmion repeated his upbeat message about his vision of the college to another reporter for the

FIGURE 6.3. William Burke, Academic Dean, 1973–1980, also served as director of the Natural Science Division for several terms. *Courtesy of Southampton Town Historian.*

Long Island Press (Sept. 28, 1973). Southampton, said Marmion, was "the campus of the future . . . we are very young and very much on the make as an institution. We can influence our destiny." The college was getting good press, but his comment about Southampton being the campus of the future did not sit well with LIU chancellor Albert Bush-Brown.

The president's brief honeymoon ended sharply shortly after the articles appeared in the press. The fall enrollment dropped by about 15 percent. The excited enthusiasm expressed in Marmion's opening convocation and in the press reports was gone, replaced almost overnight by rumors that the college would close. Bush-Brown warned Marmion sternly that Southampton needed at least three hundred more students to survive. He added, gratuitously, that Post was bringing in students; "What's the matter with you people out there?" he asked. The chancellor's brusque, unsympathetic manner characterized his relationship with the beleaguered Southampton administrators throughout his tenure. Bill Burke recalled the phone calls from the chancellor, which so often began with a curt "What's going on out there?" Burke and Marmion dreaded their trips to the chancellor's cabinet meeting in Brookville (It. 56).

In an effort to address the growing concern among students and faculty, Marmion called for a campus-wide "day of discussion" on November 2, 1973. He opened the first session with an assurance that the college would not close.[3] The fact that this was deemed necessary only a year after the college had finished a year without a deficit demonstrates the roller coaster pattern of the college's finances. The slightest drop in enrollment often brought predictions of doom. Marmion gave a candid assessment of the hard times ahead and called for a commitment from the whole campus community to improve enrollment. The faculty and students responded with an agreement to help with recruiting by accompanying the staff when they visited high schools. Marmion added a young man named Tim Bishop to the admissions staff and increased the admissions budget. Enrollment rose slightly every year beginning in the fall of 1974 until the end of Marmion's tenure in the fall of 1978, but unfortunately these increases were undermined by the high attrition rates and increased annual operating costs. Although Marmion had managed to reduce the annual deficits slightly, the accumulated debt was about $4.5 million in the fall of 1978.

Which Side Are You On? The Faculty Union

The university's long history of financial instability and acrimonious labor relations played a major role in the success of the union movement. At Southampton the custodians were the first to form a union. Edward Dawson, the crew chief, took the lead in organizing the custodians and mechanics to form a chapter of the International Building and Service Employees Union in the fall of 1967. Their success encouraged the secretaries to form a union shortly after that. In the summer of 1972, Dan Duberman, a member of the Natural Science faculty began organizing a union movement. It was a timely move because public school teachers and college faculty across New York State were beginning to unionize. In September 1972 the AFL-CIO consolidated all the New York state public school and college teachers' unions into the New York State United Teachers (NYSUT). The Brooklyn and C. W. Post faculties also began union movements.

The union movement on the three campuses alarmed Chancellor Bush-Brown and the Board of Trustees. It was undoubtedly this concern that prompted the university to grant a 5 percent pay increase for the LIU faculty in the spring of 1973. The chancellor pressed President Marmion to use his influence to block the union movement. The university argued that negotiations between the faculty and the administration should be resolved on the basis of "collegiality" in the university faculty senate rather than in an adversarial context. This position was supported by some of the more conservative faculty members such as Alan Berkebile and Larry McCormick from Natural Science and Robert Cristal from Social Science. Duberman and a majority of the faculty rejected this option believing that "collegiality" was a concept from the 1950s that no longer had any credibility. This was particularly true for LIU faculty at all the centers because of the university's history of contentious labor relations.

If there was to be a faculty agency, the university preferred to work with American Association of University Professors (AAUP) because they were a less formidable adversary. There was a chapter on the campus already, but the association did not endorse strikes, nor could it provide labor lawyers or other financial support. A group of faculty members argued that the softer approach of the AAUP would be better in light of the fragile financial condition of the university. The same issues had been debated at Brooklyn and Post, resulting in a defeat for the AAUP. John Turner, the chair of the C. W. Post union, said that their faculty had concluded that they needed an agency with teeth to protect their interests.[4] The National Labor Relations Board (NLRB) scheduled an election on October 11, 1973, which gave the faculty three choices: the AFL-CIO-affiliated NYSUT, the AAUP, or neither of the two. The third option would leave the faculty with no outside support. A week before the NLRB election, President Marmion, under pressure from the chancellor, sent out a letter urging the faculty to reject both the AAUP and NYSUT. He repeated the university administration's argument that outside bargaining agencies would limit flexibility in dealing with economic hard times. The faculty saw "flexibility" as a code word for cutting jobs and limiting pay raises, and they also knew that Marmion's heart was not in his letter. "We knew that Harry was an old union man, so we read between the lines," said Duberman. Marmion later acknowledged as much: "I went through the motions, but most of the faculty knew that I had been a union member in the past" (It. 34). The chancellor undoubtedly suspected that Marmion had not tried very hard to block the union, and it added to the growing tension between the two men.

When the votes were counted, the union had won a clear majority over the other two options and opened negotiations with the university. This proved to be a lengthy process because neither side wanted to set a precedent that would work to its disadvantage in the future. A year later, the union negotiating team led by Radh Achuthan, a professor in the Natural Science division, finally reached an agreement on a three-year contract. The formal signing of the agreement took place on April 2, 1975. The meetings, attended by student observers, were not acrimonious, as was frequently the case at the other two campuses where tempers often flared and insults were exchanged during negotiations. At Post, for example, as the Southampton union was reaching a settlement, the negotiations nearly broke down and the union passed a resolution supporting a strike if necessary (*C. W. Post Pioneer* Nov. 19, 1974).

Two years later, the Southampton union negotiators, led again by Radh Achuthan, signed a three-year extension which included an 8 percent pay increase each year (*Windmill* April 20, 1977). At Post, however, the situ-

FIGURE 6.4. First LIU Southampton College Federation of Teacher's agreement, April 2, 1975. First row (left to right), Southampton president Harry Marmion (standing), union president Radh Achuthan (seated), and LIU chancellor Albert Bush-Brown (seated). *Courtesy of Southampton Town Historian.*

FIGURE 6.5. Faculty Union representatives in first labor action, c. 1977. (Left to right) Arnold Sklare, Rene Easton, Robert Danziger, Larry Liddle, Keith Serafy, Howard Reisman, Tom Haresign (rear), Robert Meltor, and Alvin Siegel. The dog, Canis, always accompanied Professor Serafy on botany field trips. *Photo courtesy of Howard Reisman.*

ation was quite different. The negotiations dragged on over the summer until the university team, led by vice chancellor David Newton, called off the meetings on the weekend before classes were to open, apparently hoping to force a settlement. Instead, the union president, John Turner, called a strike that lasted nearly three weeks, seriously disrupting the fall class schedule and causing a drop in the enrollment. The Southampton union had offered its concern and support, which, albeit limited, was acknowledged by John Turner in a letter to the newly elected Southampton union president, Dan Duberman. The Southampton union never became any more deeply involved with labor relations at the other campuses. Negotiations over the years with the administration were generally conducted in a civil manner, a point often commented on by university teams who remarked that it was such a relief to move from the rather stressful meetings at Post or Brooklyn to the more peaceful and relaxed climate in Southampton. The pattern of labor relations at Southampton set during these early years continued throughout the history of the college.

Marine Science Wags the Dog

In spite of annual deficits and the chancellor's mantra calling for "cuts, cuts, and more cuts," Marmion was able to make some improvements in the campus facilities and strengthen the Marine Science, Humanities, and Fine Arts programs. The Marine Science major had grown dramatically in the late sixties and by 1972 was attracting more than one-half of the college applications. The success of this program posed some problems for a liberal arts college. By 1975, nearly half of the full-time students were in the Natural Science division. The imbalance inevitably impacted faculty hiring and related budgetary considerations. Donald Baker had expressed concerns about the increasing amount of funds allocated to the Natural Science department back in the fall of 1968. Betty Ruffino, the Social Science representative to the student assembly noted that between 1966 and 1976 the number of Social Science faculty had dropped by nearly 50 percent while the Natural Science faculty had remained stable or increased slightly. The Natural Science program attracted a number of well-established scholars because of its reputation, its access to the ocean, and its emphasis on close relations with students. Larry Liddle, for example, who joined the faculty in 1976, came to Southampton from the University of Puerto Rico where he had developed a course in tropical marine biology. Liddle chose Southampton because he wanted a place where he could continue his research and still work closely with undergraduate students.

The growing reputation of the sciences was small comfort to Social Science majors. In an article in the *Christmas Camel*, the campus underground newspaper (see below), Betty Ruffino wrote, "The way it looks now Social

Science is on its deathbed." (*Christmas Camel* Nov. 3, 1975). Ruffino's fears, albeit overstated, were shared by some faculty members. There was, in fact, a proposal put forward by Alan Berkebile, a Natural Science professor, suggesting that the Humanities and Social Science majors be reduced to programs that would be service options for the Natural Science majors. Berkebile presented these ideas in the campus self-study report to the Middle States evaluators for their campus visit the following year. He stated bluntly that while Southampton purported to be a liberal arts college, it was not! (*Windmill* Sept. 30, 1972). Rather than keep up the pretense, which requires us to provide financial support to "weak departments," Berkebile proposed that the college should develop a "state of the art" marine science program. The Middle States reviewers discussed this issue briefly, noting that Berkebile's proposal could lead to severe problems once the market for marine science was saturated (SCC Archive A I, K, Middle States Dec. 3–6, 1972, 8). They concluded that the more likely option was that the college would remain "nominally" a liberal arts college with the social sciences and humanities playing a "de facto" service role to the sciences. The only way to address this "identity drift," suggested the evaluators, would be for the university to make a significant financial investment in Southampton College.

The university administration rejected any suggestion calling for a large shift of funds to Southampton. They had little choice anyway because there were no financial sources available. What did happen, in fact, was that the Natural Science division continued to receive a larger share of the budget and the faculty positions throughout the history of the college. The admissions staff, under extreme pressure to increase enrollment, gave the Marine Science program top priority in all their publicity. As one staff member put it bluntly, "We have a hot item, we would be crazy not to give it top billing!" Although Marmion and his successor, Donald Wilson, had some minor success in strengthening other academic programs, particularly in the Fine Arts, the success of the Marine Science program discouraged any significant shift in budgetary emphasis. It was not until the "final days" of the college, when the Marine Science program could no longer compete with newly established and far better financed Marine Science departments along the Atlantic coast that a radical shift in curricular emphasis would be considered.

In desperation, Marmion raised the possibility of selling the Simonson property (see previous chapter). In 1973, he inquired about the value of land and approached several developers, but no further action was taken at that time. Two years later, Bush-Brown asked him if he had any suggestions about real estate agents who might be consulted. Marmion told the chancellor that some developers had advised him not to sell the whole parcel to a single buyer. They told him to subdivide the property and sell off individual parcels because the profit would be much higher. Although no further action was taken for several years, the decision to sell the property, which had so much potential, clearly suggested that the university had abandoned any hope of developing and upgrading the Southampton campus.

Although the university provided him with only meager support, Harry Marmion, in the spring of 1978, could look back on his six years at Southampton with some satisfaction. When the Middle States Association visited the campus in the spring of 1977 to review the Master of Science in Education program they issued a positive report. The evaluating team found that "[a]lthough the institution is not without problems, it seems fair and accurate to state that these issues have been recognized by the President and his staff and are being faced openly"(quoted in *Tilting at the Mill* Winter 1977, SCC Archive B, V, b). The team also praised the "friendliness, openness and spirit of cooperation manifested by students, faculty and administrative staff."

Marmion took particular satisfaction from the success of the Southampton students. Many of those who graduated in the 1970s went on to very successful careers in diverse areas (*Alumni Profiles*, SCC Archive A, I., K-47). In 1975, Jeffery Coderre, the first Southampton College Fulbright recipient, spent nine months at the University of Reykjavik studying plate tectonics.

FIGURE 6.6. Jeff Coderre, the first Fulbright recipient (1975). (Left to right) Coderre, Ral Welker, Harriet Fulbright, Provost Tim Bishop. *Courtesy of Southampton Town Historian*.

He later earned a PhD from Yale University and worked on research related to the treatment of brain tumors at the Brookhaven National Laboratory. The informal program of encouragement and support initiated by Professor Danziger resulted in an unprecedented string of Fulbright awards. The following year, Lisa Morehouse went on a Fulbright to New Zealand where she studied geochemistry. In 1977, Robert Bernatzky, a Biology major, took his Fulbright to study marine pollution and plant biochemistry at the University of Melbourne in Australia, and in President Marmion's last year Steve Post also went to Australia to study marine biochemistry at the Roche Research Institute of Marine Pharmacology.

Douglas Love (1977), an English major who edited the *Windmill*, went on to work as the senior correspondent on the *Southampton Press* and serve on the board of directors of the Press Club of Long Island. Sandra Shumway (1974) received the highly coveted Marshall Fellowship and earned her PhD in Marine Science/Biology from the University College of North Wales in 1976. Charles Pelligrino (1975) majored in Marine Science/Biology, but pursued a career as a writer. He has authored twelve nonfiction books and five novels. One of his articles was acknowledged as a basis for a Michael Crichton novel and for Steven Spielberg' screenplay for *Jurassic Park*. Andrew Novick (1976), a Fine Arts major, earned an MA from Brooklyn College and worked in multimedia communications for the New York District Attorney's office. Most of these graduates commented on the close relationship they had with faculty members and on the nurturing cultural climate at Southampton.

The best-known local graduate from Southampton College is Fred Thiele (1976). He graduated from the top of his class in Sag Harbor in 1971 and entered Cornell University. He had to leave after his first year to help his parents who lost their jobs in the economic downturn that hit Long Island in the early 1970s. He was working as the manager of a shoe store when he began taking courses at Southampton College. He went there at first, he said, simply because it was closer than Hofstra and Stony Brook, but he soon came to appreciate the unique aspects of the campus community. "The professors, would spend time talking with me after class and made me feel that they really cared about me, something that seldom happens at a large university. I had no interest in going back to Cornell after that" (It. 48).

Donald Baker arranged for him to have an internship with the New York State Assembly that Thiele said was the turning point if his life. It happened, in part, because the college allowed for a great deal of flexibility in its programs and in part, because Baker took a personal interest in him. Thiele went on to graduate from Albany Law School in 1979 and was admitted to the bar the following year. He has represented the Second Assembly District in the state legislature since 1995, defeating his opponents by an average margin of 60 percent. When the college closed in 2004, Assemblyman Thiele immediately came forward as an advocate for the continuation of a four-year college on the Southampton campus, a struggle that continues as this book goes to press.

Marmion had also made progress toward two of the mandates set for him when he was hired. He had increased the enrollment every year since 1974 and he had strengthened some of the academic programs. He promoted a Presidential Scholarship program, which paid one-half of the tuition for students with a combined SAT score of 1,200.[5] During his tenure the Natural Science department initiated several innovations which enriched the curriculum. In the spring of 1974, Robert Danziger introduced an internship program, which provided students with the opportunity to spend a full semester in an off-campus research facility. The following year, twenty Natural Science students worked with scientists at such prestigious places as Brookhaven National Lab, Woods Hole, and National Oceanic and Atmospheric Administration laboratories. Danziger went on to develop a highly successful "hands-on" approach to mentor potential Fulbright scholars at Southampton.

Another innovation was the Seamester, which launched its maiden voyage in September 1976, beginning what was to become a signature program for the college. C. Douglas Hardy, a marine scientist, supervised the program and taught the Marine Science courses. A gifted teacher, he became the face of the Seamester for the next two decades. Some twenty to twenty-four students, three or four faculty members, and a couple of seasoned professional sailors stuffed themselves aboard the *Harvey Gamage*, a two-masted sailing ship, for a nine-week trip to the Caribbean. The students took a full semester of courses, including Navigation and Seamanship, Literature of the Sea, Maritime History, Physical Oceanography, and Fieldwork in Coastal Ecology. They also served as the crew under the direction of the fully licensed captain, who taught the navigation course. The fall Seamester went south to the Caribbean ports and ended in Saint Thomas, U.S. Virgin Islands. The students then flew home. In the spring, the students flew down to board ship in Saint Thomas and sailed around the Caribbean and then back up north. The Seamester soon attracted national recognition and became an important part of the admissions office recruitment package.

The environmental programs continued to develop on Marmion's watch. In 1974, after John Andrews left the faculty, Chemistry professor Art Goldberg established an Environmental Science major in the Natural Science division. Sanjeeva Nayak developed an Environmental Science major in the Social Science division. Students took an active role in protests against the proposed nuclear plant at Shoreham only a short distance from the campus and campaigned for legislation to protect the whales.

Although the Humanities and Fine Arts did not flourish along with the sciences, there were some modest accomplishments during this period.

FIGURE 6.7. Seamester ship *Harvey Gamage Courtesy of Southampton Town Historian.*

Humanities professor Elly Welt, for example, taught a Creative Writing course in the Canary Islands, where she and her husband had a house. The students were placed with local families and assigned to write about their experiences and observations. One of her students, Jenifer Auger (1982), recalled that it was a life-changing experience. She had entered the college as a Science major, lured by the "Cousteau Factor" and the proximity to the ocean. As was the case with many others, her first Chemistry class cured her romantic notions about this area of study. Influenced by Welt, who encouraged her to begin writing for the college *Windmill*, she changed her major to Fine Arts and Creative Writing. Auger later earned a master's degree in creative writing.

In the area of Fine Arts, the students took the initiative and developed a creative program that had great potential. The Southampton Dramatic Society, organized by students including Merrill Plaskow, Tim Burke, and James Dugan, staged plays that drew favorable reviews in the local press. In the 1973 winter session, William Patton, a professional actor and director who lived in Westhampton, served as the director, taking the small company on the road where they performed in several high schools in Massachusetts, New York, and Pennsylvania (*Windmill* Feb. 22, 1973). Unfortunately the

FIGURE 6.8. Doug Hardy (far right), Humanities Professor Richard Weber (far left), with Seamester students. Weber taught "Literature of the Sea." *Courtesy of Southampton Town Historian.*

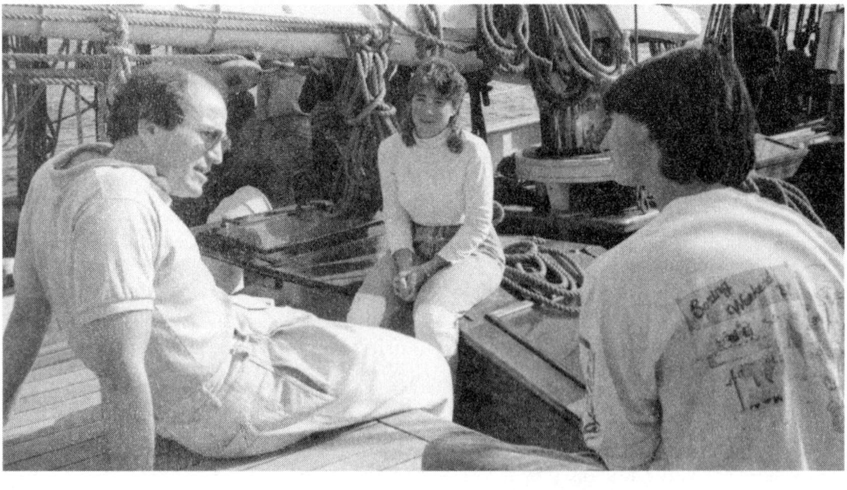

FIGURE 6.9. President Steinberg visiting with Seamester students. *Courtesy of Southampton Town Historian.*

lack of funds prevented this program from ever developing its potential. At the time, the Fine Arts department had only two faculty members, William Storrer and Robert McEntire. The position of technical director had been cut because of the lack of funds, a familiar story at Southampton where potential was frequently lost in a cycle of impending crises.

President Marmion did his best to encourage these programs in Fine Arts and Humanities by supporting faculty and student initiatives where possible. In the fall of 1975 he announced the formation of a new theater company, the Southampton Repertory Theater, directed by Tom Ewing, the new Fine Arts faculty member, who came with professional theater experience. The company, which drew upon local people in the Hamptons who had some theater experience to work with the students, opened with a successful music and dance adaptation of *The Spoon River Anthology*. The company was able to engage Bran Ferren, a technical consultant to the Kennedy Center, and Leila Katalyn, a professional dance instructor. The history of the college theater, albeit uneven, continued this rich interaction with the pool of professional talent in the Hamptons.

That same, fall Humanities professor William Peterson returned from his sabbatical in England to initiate another involvement with local talent. He invited Edward Albee, a two-time Pulitzer Prize winner who resided at the time in Montauk, to join in a "Conversation with Two Professors and Two Students" on the stage in the college theater. Peterson, his colleague Eric Kruh, and students Linda Gronlund and Christina Skoniezny engaged the author in an informal discussion of his work. Many prominent artists and writers were willing to make such appearances on campus with no remuneration. Lanford Wilson, for example, once attended a rehearsal for one of his plays, and Thomas Berger made a memorable appearance in my Native American History seminar when we discussed his novel *Little Big Man* and the film adaptation. John Mac Whinnie, who graduated Magna Cum Laude in 1972, and went on to have a successful career in art, remarked about the extraordinary opportunity that Southampton afforded him to study with several of the prominent artists who lived near the college. "I have been studying under Fairfield Porter since 1966. He has been a great teacher for me. I have been extremely fortunate to have him guide me in my painting" (*Windmill* March 1, 1973). Mac Whinnie also mentioned his interaction with Ilya Bolotowsky, Larry Rivers, and Willem de Kooning.

Marmion also encouraged local authors to become more engaged in the college. In the spring of 1978 he announced the opening of the John Steinbeck Room in the college library. The idea, which Humanities professor William Peterson initiated, was to provide local authors with a quiet place to work in the college library. John Steinbeck's widow, Elaine, who lived in Sag Harbor, enthusiastically supported the idea. Robert Gerbereux, the library director, arranged for a room with four cubicles and a computer terminal, which would be available for any writer who had a book contract. Several prominent authors, including Truman Capote, Willie Morris, Wilfrid Sheed, Alden Whitman, Betty Friedan, and George Plimpton, endorsed the initiative and agreed to help raise funds at an annual book fair hosted by Elaine Benson in her Bridgehampton gallery. Authors sat at tables behind piles of their own books, which had been donated by their publishers. They talked informally with the public and signed books for them. The money from the book sales went to support the Steinbeck Room. The affair soon became a fixture in the Hamptons, marking the "official" beginning of the summer season.

Marmion was particularly pleased with his efforts to recruit outstanding faculty who would strengthen the fine arts and humanities. In 1978, he hired Robert Pattison, a promising young scholar with a PhD from Columbia University, who went on to a distinguished career in the humanities. The following year he was the first Southampton recipient of the TASA award given by the university to recognize scholarly accomplishments by faculty members. He continued his scholarly productivity and was later to be awarded a Rockefeller Foundation Fellowship and a Guggenheim Fellowship. His five books all received high praise from the critics in his field. In addition to his scholarly contributions, he took an active role in the campus community as Humanities division director, chairman of the faculty council, and as president of the faculty union.

The Black Students Alliance continued to press for more black students and called for more courses related to black culture, taught by black professors. They placed members on all of the important campus committees to make sure their voices were heard. In the spring of 1972, the long-range plan for 1972–1980 proposed that an HEOP program be established, but still no action was taken. The BSA members on the scholarship and financial aid committee raised the issue every semester and gradually built support. In a memo to Dean of Admissions Tracy Scudder, his assistant Vam Maggipinto acknowledged the responsibility to attract more black students to the campus and noted the continuing efforts of the BSA to increase scholarship funds. He applauded their work and proposed an increase in financial aid to black students (SCC Archive A I, c, Maggipinto to Scudder Feb. 9, 1972).

BSA leaders also met with other campus administrators, reminding them of the need to diversify the student body and the faculty. They played a role in convincing the college committee on long-range goals to include a commitment "to increase the ability of the college to attract and to serve minority groups" in the self-study prepared for the Middle States Association in 1972 (SCC Archive A I, k, Report to Middle States 1973). The following fall, however, the BSA was disappointed to learn that all of the seven new faculty members were white. They were not sympathetic to the reasons given for the failure to recruit black faculty. Division directors said that they were unable to find black candidates with doctorates even when they contacted black colleges in the South. Ironically, one of the problems was a history of institutional racism throughout the country, which had discouraged blacks from continuing their education beyond the master's level. The BSA leaders felt that the best way to change this historical pattern was to keep the issue in front of the college community.

In the spring of 1973, the BSA was not making much progress on some of their goals, but they continued to organize social and cultural events. They invited black actors, artists, journalists, musicians, dancers, and educators to participate in a Black Artists Festival (*Windmill* March 29 and April 5, 1973). President Marmion gave them encouragement, but he was faced with a projected decline in the enrollment for fall of 1973 and could not commit the funds necessary for a HEOP program. Marmion faced the same pressures for cutting costs that had so frustrated his predecessor. The projected decline in enrollment proved accurate as the number of full-time students dropped from 1,236 in the fall of 1972 to 1,070 in the fall of 1973. The loss in tuition, of course, seriously limited the potential for improving existing programs or facilities. Allan Finger, the director of athletics, wrote a letter in the *Windmill* announcing that his department was nearly out of money and would have to drop several minor sports.

In the fall of 1973, the BSA, in spite of the frustrations caused by the university's financial weakness, continued to place its members on strategic campus organizations. Juanita Jay Hayden, Frank Rover, and Thomas Gant won seats on the Student-Faculty Assembly (*Windmill* Oct. 4, 1973). They wrote an open letter to President Marmion in the *Windmill* pointing out their successful efforts to enhance multicultural awareness and criticizing his administration for not taking more aggressive action to increase the number of black students and faculty. Gregory Stansbury, the new president, began a renewed campaign to establish a HEOP program on campus, but the timing was not good. The college was now in the midst of yet another financial crisis which sparked rumors about closing the campus (see above). The BSA and other student representatives found themselves in workshop discussions about dropping majors, reducing student services, and eliminating minor sports. There was to be no further discussion about any new programs or additional faculty that fall.

The BSA decided that they could not sit by quietly during the financial crisis lest their cause fade from the campus consciousness. They took a symbolic action by calling for a boycott of the few classes dealing with minority issues. Stansbury met with Chancellor Bush-Brown, who professed to know nothing about the strike but promised to discuss the matter with President Marmion. The chancellor's response came as no surprise to those familiar with the pattern of intrauniversity communications. The BSA did receive support from President Marmion, Hoyt Suppes, the president of the political science club, Frank Trotta, president of International House, the international student association, and from the seven instructors who taught the boycotted courses. These faculty, including the author, Donald Baker, Sanjeeva Nayak, Richard Weber, John Snyder, Robert Cooke, and Charles Hitchcock, published a joint statement in the *Windmill* (Feb. 22, 1974). The faculty statement noted that students of all races were ill-served by the absence of a significant minority presence in the campus community. "How can we, in good conscience, prepare students for life in a pluralistic society with a lily-white faculty in a lily-white campus?"

President Marmion responded in the next issue of the *Windmill*, acknowledging the legitimacy of the BSA's concerns and promised that a HEOP program would be in place when the college opened the next fall (*Windmill* March 7, 1974). He kept his word. In the summer of 1974, thirty HEOP students attended a workshop designed to help them make the transition to college and to strengthen their study skills. *Windmill* reporter Shari Freeman interviewed several of these students. Linda Hopson, Larry Moreland, Lorna Brackett, and Ro-Ann Smith praised the program and told Freeman that without HEOP they would never have had the opportunity to attend college. Brackett graduated and went on to work on the staff of the Head Start program in Riverhead, New York.

The impact on the college campus was significant. The black student population doubled overnight. Sociology professor Charles Hitchcock, who was serving as the HEOP administrative director, recruited Clarence Johnson, an African American who lived in Southampton, to serve as the assistant director. Johnson later took over as director. Although HEOP was open to all races, a majority of the students who came to Southampton under the program during the early years were from black and Hispanic families.

Some students were unable to overcome the deficiencies in their previous educational experience, but many graduated and went on to satisfying careers. HEOP staff members developed successful strategies for improving study skills. Jane Strong, who served as a tutor and academic counselor for more than twenty years, worked closely with individual students and served as an effective liaison with the faculty. She developed lifelong relationships with many of her students. Over the years, the HEOP center played a major role in the campus community. In addition to its primary goal of providing tutoring and academic counseling, the center sponsored social, educational, and cultural events which focused on multicultural themes. Under the dedicated and innovative leadership of such directors as Helen Smith and Ronald Richard, HEOP enriched the experiences of all the students at the college.

FIGURE 6.10. Helen Smith (center), director of the HEOP program, Walter Jones (left), Academic Vice President, and Eric Posmentier (right), Natural Science Division. *Courtesy of Southampton Town Historian.*

STUDENT POWER: THE STUDENT-FACULTY GOVERNMENT, 1970–1973

Two student initiatives that began during the Glanz administration help to define the campus "cultural climate." The first was a unique experiment in college governance and the second was the emergence of an independent underground newspaper. In the late sixties, students across the country were challenging university administrations, calling for a larger student role in decision making. Students at many of the largest universities, such as Columbia, Cornell, and Berkeley, seized buildings and presented campus administrators with "non-negotiable" demands for representation on primary decision-making bodies. In the fall of 1968, SGA president Van Camberis called for more student involvement in campus governance (*Windmill* Oct. 18, 1968). He believed that this was possible, he said in a memo to the faculty assembly, because President Glanz and some faculty leaders had acknowledged the legitimate concern of students and the necessity of their involvement in the campus governance. Our students, he continued, have not engaged in the sort of demonstrations that disrupted Columbia and polarized the campus. There is potential, he suggested, for instituting procedures and structures that would empower students. The SGA sent a petition to the faculty assembly asking for a voice in such areas as curriculum, financial aid, and academic standards. In the spring of 1969, the faculty senate agreed in principle to form a student-faculty government with fifty-fifty representation.

The following fall, the students again petitioned the faculty assembly, requesting "the creation of a new faculty-student governing body with 50% voting representation of the students. This assembly will supersede the existing faculty senate and will be the final decision-making body for all college matters, academic and administrative" (SCC Archive B IV-e, Faculty Assembly minutes Oct. 9, 1969). President Glanz supported the proposal and suggested that a constitutional convention be organized. The faculty assembly established a constitutional committee, consisting of fifteen faculty and fifteen students. The committee held a series of hearings that continued into the following spring. Co-chaired by Donna Grogan (class of 1972), representing the students, and Richard Weber from the Humanities division, the committee completed a draft in August 1970 which they presented to an open campus meeting after classes began in September. This was followed by a campus convocation held in the new gym on October 5. Grogan and Weber urged the campus community to support the constitution because it would "open the doors for Southampton College to become one of the most innovative colleges in the country" (SCC Archive B IV-e, Faculty–Student Government Files Sept. 18, 1970, hereafter cited as FSGF).

Although a number of faculty members had serious reservations, a concurrent majority of faculty and students ratified the constitution. At the time, no one on the faculty or in the administration raised a question about obtaining the approval of the chancellor or the LIU Board of Trustees. The campus community simply proceeded as usual with little thought about Brookville. The new government consisted of an assembly with one hundred members, fifty students and fifty faculty, an executive council elected by the assembly from among their members, and a college court consisting of three student members and three from the faculty. The assembly election procedures ensured that all of the academic areas, the library, student personnel, and general services would be represented. The votes by student and faculty representatives would be counted separately and all legislation required a concurrent majority.

At the first meeting of the faculty-student government (FSG) assembly on November 10, 1970, some of the political interplay inherent in a democracy surfaced. Joseph Ratti, a skillful and aggressive political player, organized a group of fellow students to vote for a bloc of candidates in the elections for the ten student seats on the FSG Executive Council. His success prompted immediate criticism from Emerson Hasbrouck, who had won a seat on the council. Hasbrouck and Peter Schilling, the editor of the *Christmas Camel*, accused Ratti of manipulating the democratic process. Schilling, however, praised the new government as "one of the most progressive college governments in the nation" (*Christmas Camel* Feb. 22, 1971). Ratti's tactics, continued Schilling, were legal, but "morally questionable." The students were getting some insights into the real world of politics in a democracy. Hasbrouck went on after graduation to become director of the Marine Program for the Cornell Cooperative Extension of Suffolk County and a well-respected fisheries biologist.

The executive council was convened the following week by Dean Vincent Aloia and elected William Gormley, a Philosophy professor, chairman, and Donna Grogan secretary. President Glanz urged the council to reconstitute the campus committees so they could begin operating as soon as possible and warned them to give careful consideration to the role of students on the faculty tenure and promotion committee. The faculty and administration were wary of giving student members access to the personnel files of faculty members. Professor Sidney Sherter recommended that all the campus committees except this one be restructured to have an equal number of faculty and students (FSGF Nov. 30, 1970). Joe Ratti countered with a motion to have a fifty-fifty representation on the committee. After some debate, Ratti's motion was tabled, avoiding a potential point of conflict. The new government, it appeared, was off to a good start with support from faculty, students, and even from the administration. Gormley was enthusiastic about the new government. "I feel strongly that the Assembly is a definite step in the right direction for us, it will bring faculty, administrators, and students to a position where they must cooperate. Furthermore, I am really very impressed with the membership of the Executive Council" (*Windmill* Nov. 20, 1970).

The new government immediately faced serious challenges that would have daunted any governing body. In the fall of 1970, City University of New York (CUNY) announced that they were putting in place a policy of open admissions, and that alarmed the LIU Board of Trustees. CUNY's new policy had a serious impact on LIU enrollment because the Brooklyn Center drew heavily from the pool of students who could not meet city university's admission standards. The anticipated drop in tuition income was certainly a factor in the decision to raise the tuition and cut faculty positions at Southampton. This was most unpopular because the tuition and fees had more than doubled since the college opened in 1963. When Glanz announced that there had to be another tuition increase and the elimination of faculty positions, the students angrily rejected the decision and called for Glanz's resignation.

Kevin O'Doherty, the student representative on the SGA budget committee came to the campus budget meeting in November, shortly after the elections of the new government, and announced that the students had voted to accept a tuition hike only if it was accompanied by President Glanz's resignation (*Windmill* Nov. 20, 1970). O'Doherty argued that Glanz was responsible for the financial crisis because he had failed to raise funds for the college. Others criticized the Southampton administration for incompetence and a poor leadership. O'Doherty noted that the tuition and fee increase, which he calculated to be about $74 a credit, was way out of line when compared to other colleges in the area: Dowling $59, St. Johns $55, Hofstra,$65, and Adelphi $60. He added that the increase would mean that Southampton students were going to pay as much as those at Columbia University ($73). The student proposal prompted a sharp response from Dean Aloia in the *Windmill* (Dec. 11, 1970), who argued that President Glanz was not responsible for the rising costs of higher education. This problem, said Aloia, faces private universities across the nation. These increasing costs, Aloia rightly noted, are mostly fixed budget items, such as faculty salaries, which must be met, but he avoided any discussion about the failure of the college and the university to raise funds for an endowment or the charges of incompetence.

When the FSG executive council met with Glanz and Aloia in a special session to discuss the budget for 1971–72, it became clear that the administration was most uncomfortable with the new government. The students, in particular, had very high expectations about their new role in the decision-making process. The council members pressed for cuts in nonacademic areas and more aggressive pursuit of government grants instead of a tuition increase and cuts in faculty. Joseph Ratti made a motion that there be no tuition increase, but this was defeated and the contentious issue was tabled. The semester ended with no resolution in sight. The executive council agreed to meet over the winter break because of the budget deadline.

Unfortunately, Gormely was unable to deal effectively with the challenges posed by conflicting interests. His naive optimism and his patience had disappeared completely. He announced his resignation at the January 4, 1971, council meeting, citing medical problems and his frustrations with what he termed "poor communications between members, between the Council and Assembly and between the Council and the administration" (FSGF Assembly minutes Jan. 11, 1971). Not surprisingly, Ratti was elected to replace Gormley until a formal election could be held at the beginning of the spring semester. Ratti, it should be noted, was not viewed by the students as a radical. Peter Shilling and Emerson Hasbrouck, who identified themselves as radicals, referred to Ratti as a "moderate liberal." As it turned out, Ratti proved to be a pragmatic leader who could negotiate a compromise without great fanfare. In a show of confidence from both faculty and students, Ratti was elected chairman in March.

The impasse over the tuition increase and the faculty cuts continued into the spring semester. In addition to these tensions, several actions taken and suggestions proposed by the executive council early in February infuriated the administration. The council went over the head of Dean Aloia and called the state education department in Albany to clarify a question about the newly established winter session. Aloia promptly denounced this as an unconstitutional infringement on the powers of the administration. At the same meeting, Professor Sidney Sherter proposed that the dean's office should be eliminated to save money. His duties, said Sherter, could easily be taken over by the president. There was another proposal to abolish the president's office and have his duties absorbed by the dean. Neither one was approved by the assembly, but the message was clear.

When the dean issued letters of termination to seven first-year faculty members, Ratti demanded that the notices be rescinded and a letter of apology be sent to each recipient because the dean did not consult with the executive council first, in accordance with a resolution passed the previous semester. The motion did not pass, but things were heating up. In March, the executive council established a six-person subcommittee to meet regularly with Glanz and Aloia in an effort to end the polarization.

President Glanz, caught between pressure from Brookville and local opposition on his own campus, had no solutions to offer. The college could not continue to operate without increased tuition revenues or extensive cuts in the current operating budget. At the next executive council meeting, Glanz himself came under attack. Bill Burke put forward a motion calling for President Glanz to resign effective at the end of August 1971. Claudia Koonz, a member of the History faculty, seconded the motion, but it was tabled. Negotiations continued over the next few weeks and both sides cooled down a bit. Burke withdrew his motion calling for the president's resignation at the next meeting and assured Glanz that he would do all he could to work with him for the good of the campus community. Burke's call for an end to the hostilities marked the beginning of a more cooperative relationship with the administration. The meeting between the subcommittee and the administration was successful in working out some compromises, but the tuition did go up by about 16 percent and the seven faculty positions were cut. The tuition increase was followed by another the following year, making Southampton more expensive than any of its competitors.

In the fall of 1971, the FSG began to have problems with student attendance. Assembly meetings often had to be rescheduled because there was no quorum. In fairness it should be noted that often members, usually faculty, would move for a quorum call when they feared that a motion they opposed might pass. This did not mean that there were frequent disagreements between students and faculty; quite the contrary, the concurrent vote tabulations reveal a pattern of agreement on most issues. Student representative Mitch Granat voiced a concern about student attendance, warning that "the continuation of the FSG is in jeopardy unless something is done." He proposed an amendment to the FSG constitution that called for the replacement of any member who missed two consecutive meetings. "It would be a great loss to this college community and the rest of the academic world if we let our new and innovative form of government pass away" (FSGF Nov. 3, 1971). Unfortunately, his remedy did not solve the problem.

Although the failed quorum calls continued to disrupt the work of the assembly, a surprising amount of important tasks were completed. This was due, in part, to the successful functioning of the campus committees. These smaller bodies carried on much of the weekly routine of campus administration. One of the important issues concerned the implications of the open enrollment policy. Many of the students were very poorly prepared for college-level studies and often flunked out or lingered on as part-time students until they became discouraged and dropped out. There was a feeling that the college had a moral responsibility to help these students rather than to simply take their money and then flunk them out. The FSG, therefore, recommended that the college provide tutorial support for these students, but no action was taken at the time. A faculty committee on admissions addressed the issue three years later, concluding that the open admissions policy "carries with it the obligation of offering remedial non-college-credit courses" (SCC Archive A, I-b Admissions File Oct. 3, 1974). Charles Hitchcock, who directed the college counseling staff that year, agreed and recommended that support services be provided on a regular basis. It would be another year, however, before the Special Academic Services (SAS) was established to "re-enforce students' verbal and quantitative skills" (SCC, Archives B, V, b-3, Southampton Catalogue 1975–76).[6]

The FSG also addressed the drug problem on campus, which had led to several highly publicized raids by the Suffolk County police. The executive council prepared a policy guideline that called for the student services to inform students about their rights and obligations and to provide confidential counseling. The college would not knowingly cooperate with the use of undercover agents and "sting" operations on campus, but would not interfere with the normal process of law enforcement. This evenhanded approach endorsed by students and faculty would have been much more difficult to negotiate if the two constituencies had confronted each other from separate organizations.

The FSG also implemented important curricular and administrative changes. The foreign language and the physical education requirements were dropped in response to several disparate pressures. One, of course, was financial. Getting rid of a whole department saved money that could be shifted to other areas of the operating budget. The decision to abolish the language requirement was related to the fierce competition for new students. As the admissions department pointed out, most of the colleges that competed with Southampton for the same pool of students were dropping their language requirements. The weaker students who had not taken a language in high school avoided colleges with such requirements. Another concern was student retention. For many of the Southampton students, the language courses were a difficult hurdle on the way to graduation. These pressures reveal, once again, the tendency in a private college without an endowment to sacrifice quality to ensure economic survival.

The fall 1971 semester ended on a tragic note. Dean Vincent Aloia collapsed in the campus cafeteria and died of a heart attack in December. His death came at a time when the college faced the challenges of a transition to a new president and a Middle States review. In the spring of 1972, the FSG had to organize committees to prepare a comprehensive self study for the 1973 Middle States evaluation. This was the first time that the college faced a comprehensive evaluation by the Middle States Association. The stakes were high, involving all of the college operations and personnel. The study was successfully completed on schedule in June 1972. The Middle States team visited the campus the following fall to conduct a series of interviews and issued its report on February 12, 1973. The report congratulated the college for being so well prepared and for providing the team with "a very thorough, concise, thoughtful document. The report gives a clear picture of the college's educational programs and mode of operation, as well as the major issues confronting the college" (SCC Archive A I, k, Middle States Report Feb. 12, 1973, 1).

Ironically, the report, after praising the self-study that had been organized and implemented by the FSG, concluded that the FSG was unworkable, agreeing with a number of the more outspoken critics on the faculty (Middle States Report, 16). The report cited the problem with quorum calls and stated that faculty dissatisfaction with the FSG had been a factor in the movement to form a faculty union. According to Daniel Duberman, no such charge was ever made by the leading advocates of a faculty union. The assertion, he believed, more than likely came from faculty members who opposed both the union and the FSG. The faculty who supported the union movement were motivated, said Duberman, by the concerns that always give rise to unions: low wages, lack of such benefits as pensions and health care, and working conditions in general (pers. comm. Sept. 7, 2006). The Middle States Association ended its report commending the college for its achievements and renewing the college's accreditation. The report, however, doomed the FSG, one of the more innovative initiatives implemented by the college.

President Marmion shared a negative view of the FSG with several influential faculty members. Tom Haresign and Alan Berkebile from Natural Sciences and Eric Kruh from Humanities were outspoken critics of the FSG.

They felt frustrated with the frequent failures to meet the FSG assembly quorum calls, which necessitated a rescheduled meeting. Kruh, in a letter to LIU chancellor Bush-Brown, spoke for a majority of the faculty when he described the FSG as cumbersome and inefficient. Supporters among the faculty and students argued that because the assembly was only scheduled to meet two or three times a semester to ratify actions of the executive council and the campus committees, the daily business of governance continued without serious interruption. Vam Maggipinto, a Southampton College graduate who returned to serve as an admissions counselor, believed that the innovative governance system was a positive factor in student recruitment. These supporters, including Radh Achuthan from Natural Sciences, John Willoughby from Humanities, and Peter Green from Social Science, recognized the attendance problems, but called for amendments to the constitution that might remedy the situation.

President Marmion asked Dean Gormely for his advice on a procedure for abolishing the FSG. In a memo to Marmion, Gormely advised him to issue a proposal to abolish the FSG just before the students left campus for the Christmas break. This will give the campus community, said Gormely, "time to assimilate your suggestions, and time to let sweet reason prevail over emotion or frustrated ideals" (FSGF, Memo to Marmion Dec. 7, 1972). The tone of the memo reflected the very thing that students had been rebelling against for the past decade. Marmion, to his credit, ignored the dean's advice and decided to leave the issue to the faculty. Gormely's memo undoubtedly reenforced Marmion's conviction that he needed to replace Gormely, who was a carryover from the Glanz administration.

At the end of March, the faculty voted by a margin of two to one to abolish the FSG. The meeting, recalled Marmion, was not as rancorous as he had expected. There was, however some outspoken opposition. John Willoughby, the chairman of the FSG assembly, challenged the faculty vote, charging that it was unconstitutional for one constituency in a government to unilaterally abolish the elected body. Haresign countered, saying that "the college faced a long period of economic crisis . . . [and] that we should not worry about the sophistry of who has the right to dissolve the existing government" (*Windmill* April 5, 1973.

The student response was surprisingly subdued. The *Windmill* and the *Christmas Camel* made little outcry. Don McIntosh's editorial in the *Windmill* (April 5, 1973) rejected the faculty decision and called for a campus-wide referendum, but ended on a conciliatory note: "In conclusion, while the faculty's actions were of questionable wisdom, they made a good start of re-establishing the sense of community that this college has recently been needing." It appears that 1973 may have marked another sea change in the student mood at Southampton and across the country as well. The Vietnam War was ending and the civil rights movement had achieved a relative degree of success. The moral clarity of the sixties had faded. Students became more focused on personal career concerns as the times continued changing.

The Underground Press

Student protest went underground and turned from vocal public demonstrations to caustic satire directed at those in authority. Mario Savio's Free Speech Movement played a role in the spread of underground newspapers on campuses across the country in the 1960s. The movement found expression a bit later on the Southampton campus. Ronald Smith told a reporter for the *Windmill* about the origin of Southampton's first and longest surviving underground paper, *The Christmas Camel*. In the fall of 1970 he and his friend Peter Schilling decided that there should be an alternative to the *Windmill*. Peter got the name, *Christmas Camel*, from an old Procol Harum song (their first album, 1967). "He never really came up with a reason one can put on paper," said Smith. "It's a song about insanity reaching limits" (*Windmill* March 7, 1974). Schilling and Smith had a small staff, but they did a great deal of the work on the paper themselves. They knew that as long as they did the editing, typing, stapling, and distributing of the paper themselves, they could remain relatively independent from the administration.

The *Camel* ran from 1970 until the spring of 1978 (SCC Archives B, V, b-7). The issues in the first year printed poems by students, serious comments on campus issues, and enough four-letter words to upset Frank Gambacorta, the coordinator of student services. Gambacorta told Randal Alfred, a sociologist from the Social Science department who advised the *Camel* staff that first year, that he wanted "normal and decent standards observed." Alfred responded to Gambacorta's criticisms with a defense of student free speech and noted that standards of what was "normal and descent" were in flux today. Obscenity, like beauty, said Alfred, is in the eye of the beholder. The times, he added, quoting Bob Dylan, "are a-changin." Alfred went on to say that he rejected any attempt at prior restraint by the administration and threatened to resign if Gambacorta pressed the issue (*Camel* March 29, 1971). The administration backed off, probably because they knew that any attempt at censorship was unenforceable.

The next year, Jack Kenneally from the English department, replaced Randy Alfred, who returned to graduate school. Kenneally also gave the students full freedom to run the paper. The *Camel* now turned to satirizing the faculty and the administration, particularly the food service, with irreverent, often unfair, sometimes insightful, but always interesting, commentary. Smith and Schilling and their staff went after both liberals and conservatives with their pointed barbs. They even wrote letters attacking themselves.

Ronald Smith complained that the administration was purposely trying to undermine the paper by withholding mimeo paper and access to the copying machines (*Camel*, Oct. 20, 1970). The administration denied the charges and pointed out that the paper did receive funds from student services. It was certainly true, however, that the administration would have liked very much for the *Camel* to go away. Dean Burke once banned the *Camel* from being distributed in Southampton Hall during Parents Weekend where visitors to the admissions office might see a copy. Burke argued that the parents might think that the *Camel* was the official college paper. It was, of course, a losing cause, and the administration made no serious attempt to censor the paper.

After Schilling and Smith graduated, the paper struggled to survive. In the fall of 1975, a new group of students led by Jack Schwartz, Richard Coffey, Susan Erickson, Lisa Morehouse, Catherine Matz, Christopher Reed, Richard Czerniak, Harold Berger, Susan Banahan, and Barbara Severns took over. The group eschewed any hierarchy or staff listing and had no official contact with the administration. There was no editor in charge and no faculty advisor. The students responsible for each issue were listed on one line with no spacing between them. The paper now printed cartoons featuring genitalia along with scatological poems and letters and the standard *Camel* fare. The food service and the physical plant remained prime targets of satirical barbs. Tuition increases, which had in the past sparked an angry outcry, were met with only token resistance in the *Camel*. This was due, in large part, to the open administrative policy, which encouraged student participation on the campus budget committee.

The *Camel* was clearly on the decline in the spring of 1976. The March 18 issue appealed to the student body for support with a message in capital letters warning that the paper "will cease to come out unless we get more support from our fellow students." There was little response, but the paper did manage to come out sporadically for two more years. The last issue that has survived in the campus archives is dated February 27, 1978. The *Camel* ended without apology, in characteristic fashion. The last page of the last issue featured a caustic satire on selected faculty and administrators replete with four letter words under a cartoon showing a nude female on a pool table.

"Bush-Brown just wore me down" (Harry Marmion)

Marmion's accomplishments were overshadowed in the eyes of the chancellor by the steadily increasing debt. The chancellor viewed Marmion and the Southampton administration condescendingly as "country cousins" who just could not resolve their financial problems. In fact, the other centers were also having serious fiscal problems. The 1977 strike at C. W. Post, mentioned above, hurt enrollment. The times were difficult for many private universities as well (Wormley 1978, 210–14). Several scholars had predicted a "New Depression in Higher Education" in grim articles published between 1968 and 1973. The LIU central administration had imposed draconian cuts in response to the projected decline in enrollments and available grants, with minimal results.

In the annual financial reports, beginning in 1973, Mary Lai frequently warned about the fragile economic conditions and the uncertain future of the university. In 1976, the university auditors issued a warning that the university's liabilities exceeded its assets by about $5 million and advised that it might be necessary to liquidate plant assets or borrow funds. Mary Lai responded to the auditor's report with concerns about the ability of the university "to sustain fiscal strength and academic quality" (LIUBCL, RG 2, Financial Report 1976/77, 8–9). The accumulated debt had risen from $3.6 million in 1974 to $4.5 million in 1978. She was also concerned about deferral of capital expenditures for plant replacement and renovation. Without the cushion of an endowment all the savings went right into the operating budget. The chancellor, unfortunately, was markedly unsuccessful in raising funds for the endowment; instead, he now chose to take out his frustrations on Harry Marmion.

In October 1978 the officials from the New York State Tuition Assistance Program (TAP) notified Southampton College that seven majors listed in the catalogue had never been registered with the state Department of Education. The TAP program, instituted in 1974, provided funds to students from low- and middle-income families. The students had to be enrolled in accredited majors at their institutions. The majors in question at Southampton were innovative interdisciplinary programs that had been introduced in 1973 and '74 in an effort to attract students. Unfortunately, there was no university oversight on curriculum development. As Ferguson had noted in 1969, there was no real academic center to LIU. Each campus maintained its own relationship with the state agencies. Although the Southampton administrators took full responsibility for the failure to inform the state, it is fair to say that the university administration bore some responsibility as well.

The situation was not difficult to remedy. Dean Burke assured the students that the necessary paperwork would soon be completed and sent to Albany. Charles Hitchcock, the Social Science division director at the time, noted that most of the courses in these majors were selected from existing clusters of courses in traditional majors which had been accredited when the college began in 1963. The problem for the university was nowhere near as serious as the scandal a year earlier in the C. W. Post Graduate Education Department. Five faculty members were charged with padding their enrollments and giving unearned grades to receive additional overload stipends. Two of them were fired for professional misconduct after an investigation by the university. Local media including *Newsday* reported the developing scandal in glaring headlines over a two-year period (*New York Times* Aug.

1966; *Newsday* Sept. 10, 1977; *University Bulletin* August and Mid-September 1977). There was no action taken against the senior administrators over this lack of oversight. The chancellor, however, reacted very differently to the administrative lapse at Southampton.

President Marmion and Dean Burke went up to meet with the chancellor at the university center and inform him about their plans to work out a solution with the department of education in Albany. To their dismay, Bush-Brown would not listen. Without ceremony, he abruptly asked Marmion for his immediate resignation. "I shouldn't have been surprised," said Harry years later. "It had been building up for two or three years. I fought him on all his budget cuts and he was not a man to take criticism or resistance from people under him. I even think he was a bit jealous of the success we had with our academic programs, the Fulbrights, and all that" (It. 34). The chancellor would not even allow Harry to finish the semester as a graceful face-saving exit. There was to be no decent interval. A week after Harry sent out a memo to the Southampton faculty, students, and staff informing them that that he had resigned, David McGregor, who had joined the university center administration in 1977 as university officer for academic resources, arrived on campus to take his place.

Marmion went on to have a successful career in administration at Fairleigh-Dickenson University where he served as vice president for academic affairs for more than a decade before he retired. He later was elected president of the United States Tennis Association, in 1997, and was instrumental in having the stadium in Forest Hills named after Arthur Ashe instead of a corporate sponsor. He kept his home in Southampton and continued his personal relationship with many of his friends in the college community. Marmion gave generously of his time and his expertise whenever it was requested, and he was to play an important role in the turbulent days following the closing of the college. "I loved the college and the local community and in a way I never really left the college. It was always an important part of my life" (It. 34).

McGregor's Brief Interlude

McGregor's arrival on campus came as a complete surprise to everyone at Southampton. Many saw this as yet another arbitrary action by the central administration. The students held a rally to protest the lack of communication about a matter as important as the appointment of a new president. The anger and unrest continued for several weeks. Ninety-six students presented acting president McGregor with signed withdrawal petitions, threatening to leave the college unless he and the chancellor engaged in an open-ended discussion with the student representatives (*Windmill* Nov. 29, 1978). The chancellor held a meeting just before the end of the semester and assured the students that the search for a new president would begin immediately and would include faculty and students.

McGregor moved quickly to resolve the problems with the unregistered majors. His open and friendly style soon won the confidence and respect of the students and faculty. Erich Kruh, a member of the presidential search committee, recalled that there was considerable support for McGregor to stay on as president. McGregor, however, declined to be considered, telling the *Windmill* reporter (Dec. 6, 1978) that he did not want to move his family out to Southampton only a year after they had settled in at Brookville. "The faculty and students are a pleasure to work with," said McGregor, and, "contrary to some rumors which persist in the face of reality, we are stable financially." It was a very diplomatic public statement, but as he confided to Kruh, he was not at all optimistic about the future of the college. "He told me," said Kruh, "that he declined to be a candidate for the presidency in large part because he thought it was an impossible job." Although he did not elaborate, he was undoubtedly pessimistic about the financial capacity of the university to support the growth and development of the Southampton campus. He may also have been concerned about the predictions in the educational journals that there would be sharp decline in the college-age population beginning in the 1980s. McGregor had his own candidate, a man that he had worked with when he was an administrator for the department of education in Vermont. He had been impressed with Donald Wilson, who had served for three successful years as the president of Castleton State College.

Chapter Seven

High Hopes and Hard Realities

Donald Wilson and the Merger, 1979–1985

President Donald Wilson: The Man with No Home Town

Over the winter session the search committee completed most of its interviews, and in February the chancellor announced the appointment of Donald Wilson to take over the leadership of the college beginning in June. Wilson had an unusual background. His parents were Seventh Day Adventist missionaries serving in Poona, India, when he was born. The family later moved to Indonesia, where Wilson completed his secondary school education. He then came to the United States for his graduate studies. He traveled widely and had a speaking or reading knowledge, he said, of French, Indonesian, Malayan, Greek, Swedish, and Dutch. These experiences, he said, had given him a unique global perspective. "I don't really have a home town," he said. "When I come here this will be my home town" (*University Bulletin* April 1979).

Wilson's education was also a bit unusual. He attended a Seventh Day Adventist mission school for his elementary and secondary school education. When he came to the United States he attended Southern Missionary University, a Seventh Day Adventist Bible college in Tennessee where he earned a BA degree in religion and speech. For his graduate studies he attended Andrews University, another Adventist school located in Berrien Springs, Michigan, a short distance from Battle Creek, where the Seventh Day Adventist church was formed in 1863.[1] At Andrews, Wilson earned an MA in "systematic theology" in 1961. His first experience outside the rather narrow intellectual horizons of the Adventist institutions came when he entered a doctorate program in speech communications at Michigan State. He completed his PhD from there in 1966. When he came to Southampton he attended the Methodist Church, perhaps because of the negative perceptions about the Adventists held by many in academia.

Wilson had taught communication and speech at Olivet College in Michigan for three years and then served as president of Castleton State College in Vermont from 1976 to 1979. The presidential search committee highly recommended Wilson after visiting Castleton and interviewing faculty, administrators, and students. Tom Haresign, chair of the Natural Science division, who led the campus visitation, recalled that "they all seemed very concerned about the survival of the college without him. We came back with high hopes for the future" (It. 26). Chancellor Bush-Brown was also enthusiastic. The university purchased a large house on Hill Street in an exclusive area of Southampton for the new president. This would give Wilson an entry into the heart of Southampton Village and, it was hoped, make it easier to contact potential donors. The historical experience of the previous Southampton presidents who failed in their appeals to the wealthy summer community was ignored, perhaps out of desperation.[2]

Bush-Brown described Wilson as a "witty, insightful man who can engage students." Commenting on the appointment in the *University Bulletin* (March 1979) he said, "We studied more than 175 candidates. We looked for those essential qualities of experience, commitment, vigor, and leadership. Dr. Wilson's candidacy was endorsed unanimously by representatives of the student body, faculty, administration, community and trustees. It was a happy process, and we welcome Dr. Wilson to Southampton and to the University." Some wondered, however, how men with such markedly different backgrounds, values, and lifestyles would be able to work together for very long. Wilson was a staunch social and political conservative who firmly believed in a vigorous lifestyle and a healthy diet free from alcohol and tobacco. He exercised daily, enjoyed white water canoeing, sailing, swimming, tennis, and held a high ranking in the martial arts. Robert Pattison remarked about the contrasting lifestyles, "Wilson was honest, intelligent, and upright with a strong sense of personal dignity, qualities that were sure to bring him into conflict with Bush-Brown sooner or later" (It. 38). What they did share in common, unfortunately, was a touch of arrogance.

Although Wilson could be charming, witty, and gracious in social settings, he often seemed aloof and somewhat enigmatic. Carol Gilbert, who worked in the admissions office, recalled that he always gave her a pleasant "How are you?" each morning, but never seemed interested in getting a reply. "When he talked with me, he usually listened with a stoic face that never revealed what he was thinking" (It. 23). He seldom opened up to others in the campus community. Mary Lai described Wilson as "a very nice man, quite pleasant. I liked him but I noticed that whenever anyone disagreed with him, he generally fell silent rather than engaging in a dialogue" (Lai, pers. comm. Sept. 12, 2007). Faculty and administrators who worked with him could seldom recall very much about him except that he seemed to ignore unpleasant realities that called into question some of his policies. John Agria, the academic dean, called him a "stubborn optimist," but Tim Bishop and others in the administration were less generous. "He seemed to create his own separate reality and to ignore or dismiss contradictory facts" (Bishop, pers. comm. Sept. 8, 2007).

There was no question, however, about his enthusiasm for his new job. He wasted no time in making his presence felt on campus. In the spring of 1979, while he was still a full-time president of Castleton, he sent Kevin Coveny, his own admissions director, to Southampton to review the operation of the admissions office, which he rightly viewed as crucial to the success of the college. In April, he came himself to address the campus community and stayed for three days, meeting with faculty, administrators and students. In his address to the campus community, he stressed the potential that the college had and remarked about its ideal location and its excellent programs, although he was concerned about dominant role of the Natural Sciences. He said that he wanted to strengthen the other programs, but he gave assurance that he would not do that at the expense of the sciences, a promise he did not keep. Ironically, his efforts to build up the Fine Arts programs proved to be his undoing. He ended his talk with a pledge to "pursue and achieve excellence" (*University Bulletin* April 1979).

Tim Bishop and Bob Danziger: "The Everywhere Men"

Wilson said that he was impressed with the faculty and the dedicated administrative staff. The staff's responses to the challenges of running their departments on a shoestring were indeed remarkable. Several worked at two, sometimes three positions that were full-time jobs at other colleges. They often took on these responsibilities with little or no extra pay and frequently stayed on job long after five and came in on weekends. Tim Bishop, for example, seemed to be everywhere in the administration building. In 1975, two years after he was hired at an entry-level position as an admissions counselor, the admissions director, George Hiltner, resigned abruptly. Tim agreed to take on the job until a replacement could be found. The next year, he served as assistant to Fran Mullin, the new director of admissions, and then took over the office of financial aid in 1978. Wilson, recognizing Bishop's experience with so many of the administrative operations of the college, appointed him director of institutional research and planning in the fall of 1979. The following fall, when the registrar, Richard Lotito, resigned in the middle of the semester, Bishop took over that job in addition to his other two positions.

Wilson was off to a fairly good start. The enrollment at 1,420 was the highest since the Vietnam era. Dean Burke sent him a list of twenty-nine rather ambitious goals that he had set for himself, which included increasing the rigor and quality of the academic programs, peer and student evaluations of faculty, developing a computer program, applying for grants, renovating campus buildings, and expanding adult education. Wilson used the list as a base to develop his own set of planning steps for the college. He noted, as had his predecessors, the advantages of the college location for Marine Science and the arts, but he cautioned that general inflation, the rising costs of such basics as fuel oil, electricity, and fringe benefits for the faculty and staff were a constant drain on a sparse budget. Additionally, the constant and ever-increasing deficit burden now averaged about $300,000 per year and only a little more than a quarter of the freshman students remained until their class graduated. Overall, however, he struck an optimistic tone, perhaps too much so, listing his "assumptions" for the future that included a program of annual deficit reduction of $100,000, a selective and stable student enrollment, and a continued striving for excellence in programs and personnel. He seemed oblivious to the clear impediments to his plans posed by the hard realities.

If Bishop was everywhere in the administration building, Robert Danziger was everywhere else on campus. He spent a great deal of his personal time nurturing potential Fulbright applicants as soon as he spotted them, often in his Introductory Chemistry classes. In the fall of 1979 his internship program sent twenty-five Southampton students to gain a full semester of valuable hands-on research experience in such diverse areas as a marine biology lab in Israel, Scripps Institute of Oceanography and the National Marine Fisheries Service, and the state legislature in Albany. Danziger was also developing a cooperative education program (Co-op) that would place students in paid positions for a semester or over the summer break.[3] The Co-op program was not as restrictive as the internship program, which was designed for junior and senior students with high grade point averages. Co-op opened up the opportunity for off-campus experience to most of the full-time students. Rather than emphasize primary research, this program was designed to provide paid work experience in an area related to the student's career objective. The following spring, Danziger wrote a proposal for a five-year grant to establish a cooperative education program at Southampton. The program, said Danziger, "will not only increase the likelihood of obtaining a good job upon graduation, but will also allow the student to earn money, as well as to apply principles learned at college to the workplace" (*Windmill* Oct. 8, 1980). In the summer of 1980, the federal government informed Danziger that the Co-op grant was approved. It was one of the largest grants that the college had received up to that time.

Mary Topping: Marking a Milestone in College Athletics

In another area, Southampton College made history that same summer. It was a moment that was not fully appreciated at the time. Mary Topping was hired to serve as the director of athletics. The appointment was actually quite accidental. Mary Peterson, the dean of students, met Topping on a social occasion shortly after the athletic director resigned in protest over budget cuts in the athletic program. Topping had recently returned to her family home in Southampton after serving as director of women's athletics for several years at the University of Northern New Mexico. Peterson encouraged her to apply for the new opening at Southampton. She was hired along with Cindy Corwith, a young woman just out of college, to run the athletic department.

This marked a sea change in college athletics. Mary Topping was one of the first women in the country to become the director of a college athletic department at a coed four-year college or university. She was one of the

Figure 7.1. Mary Topping (center), director of Physical Education, Pat Dzintarnieks (right), director of Off-Campus and Contract Programs, and Dorothy Clarke (left), former director of the National Center for Women and Retirement Research. *Photo by author.*

pioneers in advocating for equal opportunities in college sports programs. In the 1972, she went to Washington, D. C., to lobby for the passage of Title IX, which called for women to have equal access to sports programs at all institutions receiving federal funds. The bill was passed, but it had no teeth until a number of lawsuits forced compliance. Although female athletes did gain access in the 1980s most of the women's teams in coed colleges had male coaches and few women held top level administrative positions. Mary recalled:

> When I went to national athletic conferences I was the only woman among the white males at many of the meetings. They didn't know what to make of my presence. That didn't change until the 1990s. Gradually over the years, I would look around and see women in the meetings. At Southampton, however, I never felt any awkwardness in my interaction with the male coaches, the faculty, or the administration. (It. 48)

Mary went on to have a most successful career at Southampton. She and her assistant Cindy Corwith developed strong programs for both male and female athletes. These teams won numerous championships over the years.

The sea change in college athletics was closely related to demographic changes in the general college population. The percentage of female students increased to a point where they often exceeded 50 percent of the total enrollment. At Southampton, the ratio in the fall of 1979 was only slightly below 50 percent. Faculty appointments also reflected these changes, but to a much lesser extent. In 1969, there were six women out of sixty-five full-time faculty members, and by 1979 the number of women faculty had doubled. The number, however, didn't change much after that. Although the percentage of female students increased to nearly 70 percent by the time the college closed, there were only seventeen female members out of about sixty-five full-time faculty. Many of the women interviewed for this book said that they did not feel that there was discrimination in the hiring, but that women did not advance through the ranks and get tenure as quickly as did the male faculty. There were, it should also be noted, at least two acrimonious lawsuits brought against the college by female faculty members who charged that they were the victims of gender discrimination. These women left the college and the settlements they received were never made public.

Messages from Byzantium

The co-ops, internships, and the hiring of the first female athletic director certainly pleased and encouraged the new president, but there were, of course, problems as well. The attrition rate remained high and there was a costly strike that fall by the Brooklyn Center faculty. Wilson revived WPBX, the college radio station, and made good on his pledge to improve the college plant. He added an auxiliary section to the gym, had a new entrance built on the library, and closed two dorms in the spring of 1980 for much needed renovations. The dorms could be closed because of the persistent pattern of attrition between the fall and spring semesters.

In the fall of 1980 the enrollment dropped sharply from 1,420 to 1,305, reflecting national trends for college populations. A drop of one hundred students meant a loss of a half-million in tuition revenue. Wilson responded at the beginning of the Spring 1981 semester by hiring a consultant to write a new "Master Plan" for the college and by announcing plans for the construction of a new library learning center, which would cost an estimated $1.4 to $2 million. Wilson said that he expected to break ground in 1982. There seemed to be a sharp disconnect between the reality of the declining enrollment and Wilson's rather ambitious plans for the library. There was no disputing the need for the library nor that the library might attract more students to Southampton. The problem was that without a sharp increase in enrollment there were only two possible sources of funds available, donor gifts and the LIU coffers.

The LIU coffers, unfortunately, were always near empty. The strike by the Brooklyn faculty in the fall of 1979 cost LIU an estimated $700,000 to $900,000 according to Brooklyn center president Edward Clark. The faculty at Brooklyn charged that Bush-Brown had purposely provoked the strike. When a group of Southampton students met with the LIU trustees to request more funds for the campus they were reminded of the college accumulated debt, which had risen to nearly $5 million, and were told that LIU was already doing as much as it could to keep Southampton alive. The trustees, however assured them that they viewed Southampton as the "jewel in the LIU crown," a mantra that was oft repeated by LIU officials right up to the closing in 2004. It was clear, however, that for Bush-Brown and some of the trustees, a more apt metaphor in their minds was that of an albatross around the neck.[4] Wilson had either been purposely misled by Bush-Brown about the amount of capital investments that LIU could provide for Southampton or he had misunderstood statements made by Bush-Brown when he was being courted in the spring of 1979. Whatever the reason, the lack of financial support from LIU led to a growing tension between Wilson and Bush-Brown.[5]

Wilson seldom spoke about his relationship with Bush-Brown. He kept things inside, but the tensions occasionally surfaced. One instance came when the chancellor insisted that Wilson replace Bill Burke with a new academic dean. Burke was popular with the students and faculty, but Bush-Brown was adamant, perhaps because of Burke's close relationship with Harry Marmion. Wilson apparently did not agree with Bush-Brown's assessment of Burke. Burke later told Tim Bishop that his meeting with Wilson was extremely awkward. The president sat across his desk and could not seem to make eye contact. He paused looked down at papers on his desk and kept saying that he was sorry, but he had no choice. Wilson never opened up with any explanation for his action. Charles Hitchcock, chair of the Social Science division at the time, remarked that relations with the Bush-Brown administration were "Byzantine" and that he felt sorry for Don Wilson. Wilson replaced Burke with John Agria, who had been the academic dean at Alma College, a small Presbyterian school in Michigan. Argia's church-affiliated background undoubtedly struck a positive note with Wilson.

Wilson's most serious problems with Bush-Brown centered around the larger issue of fiscal survival. Disappointed with the lack of financial support from LIU, he now turned to the local community. Wilson was certainly aware of the past failures by his predecessors, but he was confident that he could succeed where others had failed. He believed that one of his goals for curriculum development was closely related to his goals for fundraising. The most effective means of access to the wealthy, he reasoned, was through the fine arts. He was convinced that if he could develop a fine arts program with a reputation for excellence, it would attract financial support. He wanted to shift emphasis, at least in the short run, from the Marine Science program to the fine arts. He was quick to assure the Natural Science division that he would only put the growth of the sciences "on hold," until he could develop a more balanced liberal arts program for the college.

Capping the Golden Goose

The Marine Science program had, by 1980, become a dominant force on campus. The 650 Natural Science majors comprised nearly half of the 1,305 student body. There were twenty-six full-time science faculty and only seven in the Fine Arts department. Wilson proposed to "cap" the number of Marine Science majors at six hundred while he expanded the Fine Arts programs and promoted more involvement with the cultural arts institutions in the Hamptons. Meanwhile, the Marine Science program continued to flourish, pretty much on its own. The faculty successfully applied for a $10,000 grant from the National Science Foundation for equipment. The Marine Station under the direction of Ral Welker expanded to include a facility to store and repair the boats and an annex with two large classrooms and a research lab. The boat repair facility enabled the Marine Station staff under the direction of Don Aldrich to repair and sell damaged boats, which were donated to the college in exchange for tax deductions. The sale of these boats continued to provide a small source of income for the college. The department also continued to develop reciprocal relationships with the local community. Ral Welker, along with other faculty members, served as voluntary consultants to the Shinnecock Indian Oyster Project. The Shinnecock Tribal Trustees invited Welker and local elected officials to attend the opening of the Shinnecock Oyster Hatchery in the spring of 1981.

The Marine Science travel courses to increasingly more exotic locales added an important dimension that attracted students and drew very positive press reports. In the 1982 winter session, for example, Larry Liddle and Howard Reisman took twenty-four students to the Great Barrier Reef in Australia. On the way they visited Tahiti, the Cook Islands, Rarotonga, and New Zealand. They did their research, which involved scuba diving and collecting specimens at the Heron Island Research Center in Australia. They also participated in seminars and lectures by prominent local scientists. "It was a rich experience," said Liddle, "not only the scientific research, but also the travel and exposure to different cultures. Just getting there was an experience in itself" (It. 33). Following the return of the students from the far reaches of the South Pacific, the spring seamester made a port of call in Havana, Cuba. Doug Hardy had managed to navigate the diplomatic channels and received permission from the United States and Cuba to spend a few days in Cuba. A Cuban gunboat met their sailing ship and escorted them into Havana harbor, where they were treated as guests of the Cuban government. William Peterson, who had taken a leave for the semester to teach the literature course on that voyage, recalled,

> Representatives from the Cuban ministry of foreign affairs met us and arranged tours of the Hemingway House, a school, and a training workshop for maritime machinery. We saw a country remarkable for its achievements in education, health care, workers' housing, and economic equality. But we also knew that the Castro regime had little tolerance for dissent. After an evening of debate some students decided to take part in the annual 1982 May Day Parade, others declined. The visit was a most extraordinary experience for everyone. (It. 40)

Another important accomplishment of the Natural Science division, mentioned above, was the number of Fulbright awards received by Southampton College students. Robert Danziger had developed a successful strategy for monitoring potential Fulbright students. Beginning in their sophomore year he encouraged them to formulate research proposals that required work at international research centers. Then he monitored them regularly as they went through the necessary paperwork, and made sure they met the application deadlines. He also remained in contact with individual scholars at many of the international centers that had accepted Fulbright Scholars. The combination of student potential and Danziger's tireless monitoring led to steady stream of successful Fulbright applicants. During Wilson's five years as president, the Marine Science students received six more Fulbrights.[6] Wilson believed that he could develop a Fine Arts program that would eventually earn a similar reputation.

Wilson's Big Gamble: The Performing Arts Festival, 1981–1983

The development of a Fine Arts program that was closely integrated with the cultural arts community in the Hamptons had been one of Edward Glanz's major goals, but neither he nor his successor Harry Marmion had been able to make it happen. Wilson also believed that classical music was the key to opening the coffers of the summer elites. Tim Bishop, the director of institutional research and planning, was not so sure. The assumption that most classical music enthusiasts were wealthy and that they would show their appreciation to the college for providing them outstanding classical artists, thought Bishop, was questionable and unsupported by market research. President Wilson dismissed such concerns, as he did most everything that did not support his own thinking. He was convinced that he could succeed where his two predecessors had failed. Wilson decided that the best way to establish Southampton College on an equal footing with Guild Hall in East Hampton and the Parrish Art Museum in Southampton was to invest in a program that would bring performers with an international reputation to the college. The annual fine arts festivals which had been initiated under President Glanz relied on local artists and operated on a very modest budget. In the summer of 1981, President Wilson hired L. Kenneth Simsarian, an experienced event organizer, who was familiar with world of classical music. He asked Simsarian to organize and direct a high-profile arts festival and charged him with the task of raising funds to pay for the advertising, the catering, and costs of the performers.

Simsarian launched an ambitious program he called "The International Prize winning Young Artists Series of the Southampton Performing Arts Festival 81." The series featured several well-known international musicians including Nadja Salerno-Sonnenberg, a Julliard student and winner of the Naumberg International Violin competition, pianist Peter Orth, a soloist with the Chicago Symphony; flutist Linda Chesis; harpist Sara Cutler; and Yugoslavian cellist Walter Despalji, a soloist with the Zagreb Philharmonic, who had performed at the Kennedy Center.[7] These performances were sold out to enthusiastic audiences who gave some of the performances standing ovations. Simsarian announced that his fundraising was also going well. He said that he had raised a total of $15,000 from the Mobil Foundation, the North Fork Bank, and individual donors. Convinced that these successes heralded an even brighter future, he began spending large sums on advertising and on recruiting more high-profile musicians for the second season.

Wilson allowed him to increase his budget from the $34,000 he had spent in the first year to $139,000 for the 1981–82 festival.

In a related effort to woo the wealthy donors, Wilson had decided, in the spring of 1981, to take the college radio station out of the students' hands and replace the student managers with a salaried professional who would shift the emphasis from popular to classical music. He also increased the station wattage from ten to one hundred watts to reach a wider audience. This required more expensive equipment, which Wilson proposed to pay for with anticipated donations from appreciative classical music enthusiasts. The students were outraged. Kevin McEvoy, the student program director, wrote a front page article in the *Windmill* protesting Wilson's action. This decision was made, said McEvoy, "without the consent of the student staff who operate the station" He added, "Our staff cares too much and works too hard to allow the joy of WPBX to be taken away from them" (*Windmill* Feb. 19, 1981).

Wilson defended his decision in his own front page article. He argued that a professional director would help the students improve their skills in radio communications as well as establish rapport with the local community. McEvoy was quick to note that this reference to the local community really meant the wealthy summer community. McEvoy suggested that if Wilson's primary concern was to raise money it would be better to hire a professional fundraiser and a new faculty member to teach courses in radio broadcasting. Paul Martin and Roger Snyder, who had been student volunteers for several years, expressed their concerns. Martin also criticized Wilson for his attempt to engage the wealthy elites as "open and arrogant snobbery," and protested that WPBX should not become "an economic and political machine." Snyder joined the voices of protest, charging that "it appears to many that the president's drive for quality is actually a drive for money, it also amounts to censorship" (*Windmill* March 6, 1981).

Disregarding the students' concerns, as well as those voiced by Bishop and Joseph Carbone, the director of administrative services, about the mounting expenses, Wilson hired Joseph Valerio, a professional station manager to run WPBX. Valerio, much to the dismay of many faculty members, had worked for the Voice of America, a major outlet for United States propaganda during the cold war. Valerio and Simsarian shared Wilson's conviction about the potential of classical music to bring in large donations. Wilson did not ignore the potential of other connections to the cultural resources of the East End. He initiated a lecture series associated with the Steinbeck book fair and the Steinbeck Room in the library. Kurt Vonnegut, E. L Doctorow, Wilfrid Sheed, and Gloria Emerson were among the nationally recognized local residents who participated in the series. Although the stipends and publicity costs were modest they did add to the growing burden of Wilson's investment in the arts. In anticipation of a windfall from the pockets of the appreciative elites, Wilson announced a fundraising campaign for a new library and a tennis complex with four indoor courts, a large center court for major tennis tournaments, and seating capacity for more than six thousand spectators. The courts would be completed, he said, by July 1982, and a dome and clubhouse would be ready by the following October. Wilson could not be faulted for thinking small. He envisioned the college hosting televised international tennis matches, which would greatly enhance the college image, bringing in donations and additional students (*Windmill* Dec. 10, 1981).

There were clear signs in the spring of 1982 that the donations were not going to meet Wilson's expectations, nor was there any more talk about the tennis complex or a new library. The disconnect between what Tim Bishop called "Wilson's reality," and the real world was becoming increasingly evident. Bishop recalled that whenever he, along with Dean Agria and Joseph Carbone, asked about the money, Wilson brushed their concerns aside saying that promises had been made and that the money would soon be coming in. "After awhile," said Bishop, "we realized that nothing could shake what we saw as his extreme overconfidence, even wishful thinking; we often looked at each other with raised eyebrows and just shook our heads" (Bishop, pers. comm. Sept. 13, 2007). In June 1982, Simsarian organized what he called "a gala benefit to commemorate and to raise funds for the arts festival." He invited Anne Jackson, Lanford Wilson, Rod Steiger, and New York City Ballet dancer Edward Villella to participate in the event. Simsarian told Wilson that he expected to raise about $40,000. To Simsarian's great dismay the event brought in only $8,000. "Not even worth talking about," he lamented (*East Hampton Star* Aug. 25, 1983).

Undaunted, Simsarian launched the 1982–83 festival, which would open with pianist Walid Howrani on June 11. He scheduled eighty musicians from six countries in a series of performances, including the Joffrey II Dancers and the Eglevsky Ballet, to run through the summer and fall. The central theme would again be "the young prize winning artists." On September 16, a sold-out performance by Santiago Rodriquez, silver medal winner at the Van Cliburn Festival ended with a standing ovation. "We have built a loyal and diverse audience," said Simsarian, "we have had Nobel Prize and Pulitzer Prize winners, Hollywood stars, and corporate executives (*Windmill* Sept. 16, 1982). By the end of 1982, however, the festival was nearly $90,000 in debt and there was little hope that there would be any significant donations. The festival was cancelled in May 1983 and Simsarian's contract was terminated abruptly.[8]

In a desperate effort to cover the debt, Wilson, probably with considerable pressure from Bush-Brown, removed $200,000 from a restricted account in the fall of 1981. The account, which came from the sale of boats donated to the college, had been set aside for the construction of a small lab and classroom building at the Marine Station. The Marine Science students and faculty had been working for some time on architectural plans for the building. Al Siegel, who was serving as the Natural Science division director at the time, discovered the empty account in the spring of 1982 and angrily confronted Wilson.

> I was very angry. It was bad enough he acted in bad faith by taking the money last fall, but he never even consulted with us about it. He said, "What difference would it have made if I told you?" I was surprised about his attitude, here he was missionary's son and all. I told him that if we had been informed we would not have spent the last five months planning for the building. It made us look foolish. We had unknowingly been misleading our students. It made us look like liars. (It. 45)

Sometime later, when Siegel complained to Abraham Krasnoff, a university trustee, the funds were quickly returned to the account. Krasnoff and a growing number of the trustees viewed such incidents as examples of serious lapses in Bush-Brown's attention to the challenges of university administration.

The Fine Arts Festival was later revived in its previous form featuring modest programs run by volunteers from the local art community. Wilson's gamble had failed, but in fairness to him, it is quite possible that if the university had been able to sustain the losses for a few more years Southampton might well have joined Guild Hall and the Parrish Art Museum as fixtures in the Hamptons' cultural scene. One could argue that the failure was another example of opportunities lost because of LIU's inadequate resources. The Fine Arts program in the college curriculum was never able to achieve its potential for the same reason. As William Peterson, who served as the director of the Fine Arts department for several years, noted, "The LIU administration had no idea what funds were really needed for a fine arts facility, we lacked the necessary studio space and the equipment to establish and maintain a quality program" (It. 40).

Saving the Present by Selling the Future: The Simonson Estate

There were many examples of opportunities lost for want of capital investment. The college accepted collections of papers from local congressmen which it could not store or curate properly. They were piled in remote corners of the campus and forgotten. Donated works of art suffered a similar fate because there were no climate-controlled facilities. When Beth Giles, the director of the college Avram Gallery, inventoried the eighty works in the collection in preparation for removal in 2004, she found that a mural painted by Ilya Bolotowsky and valued between $50,000 and $75,000 was so badly damaged that it required nearly $20,000 to restore it (*New York Times* March 27, 2004). There was never enough money available, said Giles, to develop the collection and establish a focus.

In the 1980s, a similar fate befell an internationally acclaimed horticultural collection. In 1982, the Thompson family, who were nationally known begonia collectors, approached the college with an offer to build a state of the art greenhouse on the campus if the college would provide the land and maintain the facility. The offer appealed to Wilson because he saw in it another way to raise the status of the college and attract financial support. The Thompsons' highly reputed collection of 1,900 varieties of begonias would fit in well with the art collection and the classical musical performances. Although Bishop warned Wilson about the maintenance costs, he accepted the Thompsons' offer. The Thompsons financed the construction of a $40,000 greenhouse thirty feet wide by seventy-two feet long. The college was responsible for heating the facility, a cost estimated to be between $2,000 to $3,000 a year. Unfortunately, the building was located behind several rather rundown storage sheds and the college was unable to complete the promised landscaping. Larry Liddle, professor of Botany, took his classes there regularly, but there were few other visitors. Much to President Wilson's dismay the university was unable to provide the funds for maintenance. The Thompsons, angry and discouraged, finally had to remove their collection, and the greenhouse became a storage place for assorted groundskeeping machines. Rather than enhance the college image, the greenhouse became an embarrassment. The lost opportunities with the art and begonia collection, however, pale when compared with the fate of Simonson property.

After the plans for developing the Simonson property had to be abandoned in 1967, the Conference Center building near the eastern end, which had six bedrooms, a kitchen, and a large living room, was used for many purposes over the years. In the 1970s, students used it for club meetings, social affairs and, on two occasions, wild parties that caused significant damage.[9] The regular use by various groups put a strain on the center, causing it to deteriorate. As a result, it later became a residence for academic deans and occasional overnight guests. No attempt had been made to renovate or significantly improve the property after the decision in 1973 to put it on sale. One of Wilson's first tasks when he arrived in Southampton in the summer of 1979 was to begin actively marketing the thirty-acre parcel. Wilson, undoubtedly to his great frustration, was to spend a disproportionate amount of time during his three-year administration dealing with real estate lawyers, town zoning regulations, potential buyers, and, most frustrating of all, with Albert Bush-Brown, who seldom responded promptly with the necessary official signature at each stage of negotiations. It must have been a bit depressing for Wilson, who saw himself as an educational leader in the process of developing an institution of high quality, to take on the rather pedestrian role of a real estate salesman.

The first step was to sell three small plots on the eastern edge of the property, which bordered on St. Andrews Road. When the lots, which were valued at $64,500, did not sell quickly, Wilson told a local developer that he would be willing to accept $55,000 if a buyer could be found by the end of 1979. There were no takers. The following March, the college applied for permission to develop fourteen lots for sale. The town planning board asked for more specific information about demands for public water, storm water drainage, and sewage disposal. This, of course, took more of Wilson's time and energy. At the end of 1980, the college received an offer of $30,000 for two plots near the Conference Center, but it fell through. A few months later, the Greek Orthodox Church of the Hamptons purchased those lots for an undisclosed amount.

In October 1981 Fruitbine, Weiner, Harwin, and Herman, a company owned by a C. W. Post alumnus, donated a parcel of land on the northern boundary of the Marine Station to Southampton College. Richard Pellicane, the real estate lawyer who represented the college, offered to exchange property he owned north of the donated parcel for two lots in the Simonson subdivision.[10] Wilson recognized the importance of this acquisition for the college and readily agreed, but he needed approval from LIU to consummate the exchange. In September, Wilson wrote to Bush-Brown strongly urging that LIU give approval. Six weeks later, Pellicane wrote to Wilson complaining that he had no word from LIU. In February 1982, Judith Tytel, the university counsel, wrote a sharply worded letter to Wilson telling him not to proceed with the exchange until they had the Simonson property appraised by a qualified real estate appraiser and asked him to collect "all letters, notes, contracts, etc., having anything to do with Mr. Pellicane and his swap" (SCC Archive B, II, F Box 6, Simonson File Feb. 2, 1982). The clear implication of the letter was that the university administration did not trust Wilson and Pellicane to handle the exchange on their own. This must have infuriated Wilson, not only because of the insulting tone, but also because it meant further delay in obtaining an important acquisition for the college.

On January 6, 1983, Wilson wrote to Pellicane apologizing for the many delays and thanking him for his patience. Pellicane's patience was running thin. The university tried to reduce the original agreement to one of the Simonson lots for Pellicane's Marine Station lot. Pellicane angrily reminded Wilson of the wording in the original negotiation and threatened to put his parcel on the market. Wilson quickly responded, telling Pellicane that the original agreement was again in place and implying that there had been an error in the records and not an attempt to alter the agreement. Wilson wrote to Bush-Brown two weeks later urging him to complete the exchange. Pellicane, said Wilson, "is doing us a favor if we intend to continue the Marine Science Program. . . . I would appreciate your expediting a decision on this matter and having someone who is authorized to finalize the trade speak with him so that Mr. Pellicane is not disadvantaged any more that he already has been by the delay" (SCC Archive B, II-F, Box 2, Wilson File).

A month later, Pellicane had not heard anything from the chancellor's office. After another month, Wilson wrote to Pellicane in exasperation, "I will honestly never understand how the University functions. You have bent over backwards to help us and in return for your help with the property you have been treated shabbily" (Simonson File March 24, 1983). In May, Pellicane, wrote directly to Bush-Brown asking curtly "for the courtesy of a reply." Please, implored Pellicane, "have someone talk to me." The delays continued. The final subdivision of the Simonson property did not come until November 1983 and the sale was completed in January 1984.

One opportunity, however, was not lost, but that was because of the dedication and "hands-on" work of a faculty member. John Bridge, a psychobiologist who came to Southampton in 1979, took advantage of an offer from the Museum of Natural History to give the college a colony of a rare spiny mice bred for experimental research. At the time there were no facilities and very limited funds available for research. Bridge, with the help of some students, renovated a small storage shed to serve as a laboratory. He revived a moribund psychobiology major and established a highly regarded research program focusing on the relationship between stress and alcohol abuse. The program produced some professional papers authored jointly by Bridge and his students. The success of the major was due in large part to Bridge's infectious personality. He soon had an enthusiastic student following in and out of the classroom. Bridge organized a Frisbee Club that set a Guinness record for the longest game ever played in 1988. The students played a marathon game lasting thirty-seven hours.

President Wilson's Perfect Storm

At the beginning of the Fall 1982 semester, Wilson addressed the campus community in the *Windmill*. "In spite of gloomy predictions for private universities . . . I believe that Southampton College will continue to advance towards the vision of excellence that we have articulated in our planning." He cited accomplishments of the past year, which included an addition to Marine Station to begin in the fall, the extension of Danziger's Co-op grant, and a Title III grant for a three-year period to establish and develop a learning resource center and programs in computer science and graphic design. The latter was the second large grant that the college had received in a two-year period. Dean John Agria received high praise from the grant reviewers for his work on the proposal. The president added that he anticipated a second year in a row with a balanced budget. The tennis project and the fundraising for the arts festival, "is progressing well. I know that you share my belief in the future of the college. Together we can work for the shared vision of excellence" (SCC Archive B, II, f, Box 2, Wilson Papers).

There were other positive accomplishments that Wilson could have mentioned. Sanjeeva Nayak and Sociology professor Ralph Herbert developed an Environmental Studies major in the Social Science division that was approved by Albany in 1981 (Gregory, 17–19).[11] The 1981–82 basketball team had a winning record for the first time in ten years. Led by Coach Vinnie DeCerbo, a Southampton College alumnus, and team captain Herb Beach, who scored more than one thousand points in his college career, won first place in the Big Apple Conference. The other starting members of the team were Roy Jordan, Elroy Carr, Juan Rodriguez, and Keith Jackson (SCC Archive A, II, b, Sports).

Early in the spring of 1982, the *New York Times* published its annual *Selective Guide to Colleges* and placed Southampton College among the top 265 in a survey that included two thousand college and universities. The guide praised the Marine Science and Co-op programs and the "young and enthusiastic faculty," but noted that the campus buildings were rather shabby and that the library was inadequate (*Southampton Press* Feb. 18, 1982). Undoubtedly, the guide's comment that "Southampton is the best and most interesting of the four centers of Long Island University," did not sit well with Bush-Brown and the administrators at the other centers. Karl Grossman, a local journalist, wrote an article celebrating the listing in the survey and quoted Wilson: "We do not want to be known as just a good, small liberal arts school. We want to be known as an excellent liberal arts college." The admissions office reprinted Grossman's article and included copies in the packets sent out to prospective students. The faculty were also pleased that spring because the union, under Robert Pattison's leadership, negotiated a three-year contract with a significant pay raise. Students were not so pleased, however, when the drinking age in New York State was raised to nineteen in January.

There was little to suggest in Wilson's address that within five months he would be out of a job and a house, and that Southampton College would be administered from C. W. Post. The clouds of a perfect storm that hit LIU and Southampton in the late fall of 1982 had begun to gather the previous fall when President Ronald Reagan implemented sharp reductions in federal aid to education. The Reagan policy posed a real threat to LIU and to other private, tuition-driven, universities that drew a majority of their students from the middle and lower middle classes. These students now tended to seek out state-sponsored universities and community colleges. This came at a most unfortunate time because the total population of

FIGURE 7.2. Donald Wilson (left), president of Southampton College, 1979–1983, Robert Pattison (center), union president, and LIU Chancellor Bush-Brown signing labor agreement, 1982. *Photo by Davis Gaffga.*

college age students was in decline. Most private universities faced a "perfect storm" of difficulties. The following February, Wilson went to Washington to protest the Reagan cuts and Sue Taylor, director of financial aid, asked students to write their congressmen to protest the Reagan cuts in student aid. On March 1, 1982, the Southampton students sent ten representatives in join with five thousand students from across the country on a protest march to Washington. "Higher education," said Dean Agria in an address at the college academic awards convocation, "is in deep trouble. It is beset by financial problems fed by declining enrollments and increasing costs." The Reagan administration, he continued, has given education, especially private education, a low priority. Unfortunately, the policies went into effect in spite of the protests and appeals, and had the feared outcome. In the fall of 1982, the National Institute of Independent Colleges and Universities estimated that "the Reagan cuts had forced about 200,000 lower middle and working class students to either drop out of college or attend state community colleges. . . . The migration out of private colleges began as a trickle in January, but has grown to a steadily flow now." Southampton enrollment fell from 1,305 in 1980 to 1,130 in the fall of 1982; by 1984 it had dropped to one thousand.

There were, of course, other factors contributing to the storm. The debt incurred by Wilson's art festival certainly played, as Tim Bishop indicated, an important role, but there were several other events that came together at that time. The operational costs had increased, in part caused by faculty and staff raises, but heating and facility maintenance also contributed. In the spring of 1981, Southampton announced a tuition increase of 12–16 percent which priced the college about $700 more than its closest rival, Dowling College. Dowling, drawing its students from the same pool as Southampton, increased its enrollment to more than two thousand students during the early eighties. St. Joseph's, in Patchogue, another close rival, was $2,000 cheaper than Southampton (*Chronicle of Higher Education* Aug. 4, 1982, 14). Many prospective Southampton students were undoubtedly lost to those less-expensive colleges. Stony Brook, of course, was much cheaper and offered state of the art educational facilities, but few of the students who applied to Southampton, Dowling, and Saint Joseph's could meet Stony Brook's admission standards.

FIGURE 7.3. President Donald Wilson handing diploma to Jenifer Auger at 1982 Commencement. *Photo by Davis Gaffga.*

The last and most critical devastating event in the final storm were the evaluations from the New York Department of Education and the Middle States team. Chancellor Bush-Brown, recalled Mary Lai, set a very negative tone for the review process by treating Robert Kirkwood, the director of the Middle States team, with arrogant condescension. Kirkwood complained to Mary Lai that the chancellor, "played me like a cat with a ball of yarn and seemed to be saying, Who are you to evaluate me?" (Lai, pers. comm. Oct. 4, 2007). There is no evidence that Kirkwood let this interfere with his objectivity, but it speaks volumes about Bush-Brown. He was unable to restrain his arrogance even in a situation calling for sensitive diplomacy.

The Middle States team came to the Southampton campus for a four-day visit at the end of October 1982 and gave a brief oral report before they left. They began with a grim warning that, contrary to Wilson's upbeat address a month earlier, the financial situation for Southampton was so dire that "time was running out . . . and that many members of the college community did not appear to recognize the harsh realities." There were words of praise for the Marine Science program, the Fine Arts division, the Co-op, the HEOP program, the Internship programs, and for a dedicated faculty which was the "the most attractive feature of the college," but Wilson's administration did not fare so well. The most damaging critique was the lack of any progress in dealing with the problems cited in the 1973 Middle States report. In that report, the evaluating team warned that the "fiscal well being of the college was in doubt," and ten years later the evaluating team made a similar assessment, stating that "the financial viability of Southampton is seriously in doubt" (SCC Archive A, I, k Middle States 1973 and 1982). Student services remained inadequate: "There is a lack of clear goals, clear leadership, professional staff, and direction in the student affairs program at the college. One major outcome from this situation is the high attrition rate (60%)." The visiting Middle States team also reported that: the facilities were still in disrepair; the library was still inadequate; and there was still no major full-time fundraising program. The team was also concerned about the lack of any provision for an outcomes assessment which could measure the progress of the college toward its stated goals. In fairness to Wilson and the administrative staff, it should be noted that most of these problems were directly related to the university's continuing budget crisis.

After the holidays, the chancellor came to Southampton and described several models for Southampton's future. He said, almost in passing, that he could not exclude the possibility that the Board of Trustees might sell the campus and convert it into a retirement home or some such enterprise. He got everyone's attention with that, and then told them that he did not think that the college could survive without making substantial structural changes. By this time the relations between Bush-Brown and Wilson had become very strained. The chancellor, recalled Tim Bishop, was often heard making demeaning comments about Southampton College; "a blight on Shinnecock Hills," he once said. (Bishop, pers. comm. Sept. 13, 2007). Carol Gilbert, another long-time staff member who had served in many departments, said that she believed that Bush-Brown, "considered us out here as a bunch of country bumpkins and I don't think he cared much about what happened to us" (Gilbert, pers. comm. Oct. 2007). Al Siegel remembered one of Bush-Brown's addresses to the faculty on a foggy spring day: "His first words were about the miserable weather. He said no wonder you can't get students to come out here! It seemed to us that we were even getting blamed for fog" (It. 45).

The chancellor never appreciated the aspects of the college that meant the most to the students, nor did he seem at all aware of the success achieved by many Southampton College graduates during this period. In addition to the Fulbright recipients, there were many other success stories. David Krasnow (1982), who majored in Chemistry and went on to earn a law degree from George Mason and serve as a clerk for the U.S. Supreme Court, cited the "close working relationships between students and teachers that turned into multiple lifelong friendships" (*Profiles of Alumni* SCC Archive A I, K-47). Katherine McLane Francis (1983) a Business major, won several awards after graduation. She received the Suffolk County Human Rights Commission Award in 1983 and was named East End Women's Network Woman of the year in 1989. In 1992, she was the recipient of the Southampton College Distinguished Alumni Award. She also commented on her continuing relationship with her professors and fellow students. Mary Rojas (1982) a psychology major who earned her PhD from New York University, praised her former professors for their help "well beyond the call of duty." Another Psychology major, Lester Owens (1980), who went on to a successful career in banking, remarked about how much the small classes and interaction with the faculty had meant to him. Arthur Levitt III (1980) majored in Biology but changed his career interests after graduation and went to Harvard Business School. He later served as the president/CEO of the Hard Rock Café. Levitt told the alumni office that "Southampton College holds a special place in my heart because of its caring people dedicated to education and to the students." The chancellor, to be fair, was only one of many faculty and administrators in the LIU system who failed to appreciate the unique nature of the academic culture at Southampton.

Brookville must have been a very busy place in January 1983. The administration had to deal with the fiscal problems at Southampton while it prepared for its own Middle States visit. The University Center at Brookville had followed the same Middle States process as had the three campuses the previous fall. The evaluation team visited Brookville from January 23 to 25, 1983. Their oral summary at the end of the visit was just as negative as the one they had issued at Southampton. The team faulted the university for not doing sufficient institutional research and academic planning and development (LIUABCL RG 3:2, Middle States Report to the University Jan. 23 to 25, 1983, 4–5). There were, for example, no enrollment scenarios for the next three to five years, "even though such expectations are key to determining actions to be taken this year and in coming years, particularly in a tuition sensitive institution" (ibid., 9). The Board of Trustees, noted the team, was too distant from the important operations of the university. The trustees did not even receive the reports of the internal auditor, which went directly to the treasurer. There was a lack of leadership and coordination in the development of the budgetary process.

Another criticism concerned the failure to establish a coordinated and effective means of fundraising from private sources. The existing fundraising structure, noted the team, is viewed within the university "with a sense of confusion and misunderstanding" (LIUABCL RG 3:2, Middle States Report to the University Jan.23 to 25, 1983, 11). This structure needed to be reevaluated and given a higher priority if the university was to meet the challenges of the eighties. Unless the Board of Trustees themselves became more actively engaged in the process, "any fund-raising structure or organization will not be effective" (ibid., 13). The team also noted that a factor related to university fundraising was an identity crisis, a confusion of image and identity, which the university projected to the public. Each campus, as has been noted several times in earlier chapters, had its own identity and its own constituency (ibid., 14–15). The report was certainly unsettling, and it very likely caused some members of the Board of Trustees to lose their confidence in Chancellor Bush-Brown. They all knew that something had to be done quickly to save their accreditation. In a dramatic gesture, designed, in part, to impress their Middle States' critics, they took away Wilson's job and sold his house. Wilson went to Kansas, where he served as the president of Pittsburg State University from 1983 until 1995 when he was forced to resign because he improperly provided in-state tuition waivers to foreign students. Wilson left the country and lived in self-imposed exile for nearly a decade. He suffered a heart attack in Thailand and died in 2003 at the age of sixty-five. Donald Wilson remained a man with no hometown until his untimely death.

The Great Decapitation: Southampton Merges With C. W. Post, Feb. 2, 1983

The decision to remove the office of president at Southampton and absorb the administrative structure into C. W. Post came right after Bush-Brown received the Middle States oral briefing. Abraham Krasnoff, a board member since 1979, was the primary architect of the merger. He had become increasingly disillusioned with Bush-Brown's leadership and now came forward with his own solution to the criticisms outlined in the Middle States evaluation. His action made it clear that Bush-Brown's days were numbered. The idea of a merger with Post was, of course, not new. It was, as noted in an earlier chapter, among the proposed models discussed in the late sixties when the first fiscal crisis loomed. Wilson informed Dean John Agria, Tim Bishop, and Kevin Coveney about the merger shortly before the Board of Trustees voted their approval in February 1983. Agria, Coveney, and Bishop all recalled that they were completely surprised because there had been no consultation with any of the administrative staff at Southampton and no advance planning about anticipated consequences. Carol Gilbert said that she first heard about the merger from an article in *Newsday*. Although Wilson claimed that he had been involved in planning the merger, Tim Bishop was convinced that Wilson was given no choice and had made the claim as a way of saving face. Many at Southampton agreed with Bishop and suggested further that Krasnoff had moved quickly to deflect the negative Middle States review.

The decision to merge was officially approved by the Board of Trustees less than a week after they heard the Middle States oral briefing, but their action did little to offset the negative final reports from Middle States. The evaluation team would not renew LIU's accreditation, but it did allow the university to continue under the previous accreditation for two more years with the understanding that the university would take significant action to restore fiscal stability. They made it quite clear that while the merger was a quick response to the fiscal problems, "the commission is less interested in immediate actions than in a careful and deliberately developed plan identifying priorities among the recommendations of the evaluation reports and a reasonable timetable for dealing with the issues on which the evaluation teams reached a remarkable and virtually unanimous consensus" (LIUABCL RG 3:2, Middle States to Bush-Brown). The stern warning indicated that Middle States wanted serious change and would not be placated with superficial administrative shuffling. It was also quite clear that the LIU administration had no idea what to do after they announced the merger.

The chancellor decided that Wilson would continue in his office until the end of the spring semester while the university developed a new administrative structure. In place of a campus president, Tim Bishop and John Agria were to run the daily affairs of the college beginning in the fall of 1983. Agria was responsible for academic programs, and Bishop served as the senior campus administrator. They would report directly to Edward Cook, the president at Post, but there was no decision about the place of the academic division directors in the new structure. The cost savings were expected to come from a significant reduction in administrative personnel at Southampton. The tasks formerly assigned to these staff members would now be done by the Post staff. According to the merger plan, a skeleton staff at Southampton would now report to their counterparts at Post.

A week after the merger was announced, Tim Bishop sent a list of forty-two questions to the chancellor, which included basic concerns about campus governance, admissions, financial aid, and lines of authority for administrative offices. There was no immediate answer. Not surprisingly, the spring semester was a time of great chaos and uncertainty. The reorganization process moved with glacial speed. There was some reshuffling of administrators, but no movement toward academic integration, which might have resulted in more significant savings.

Where changes were implemented, they often created unanticipated problems. It was a nightmare for the admissions office. Kevin Coveney was angry and frustrated. Carol Gilbert, who served as his assistant at the time, lamented that "overnight we lost twenty years of effort to build our identity. The windmill logo was gone from the stationery and the venerable campus newspaper changed its name from the *Windmill* to the *Overlook*. "*The Directory of American Colleges*," said Gilbert, "now listed Southampton College under LIU, not separately under Southampton, and that confused prospective students. Another problem was that the admissions people we reported to at Post didn't know anything about us and didn't seem to care. They seldom came out to our campus and they often put out misleading and sometimes outright false information. They didn't note, for example, that certain majors were only available at Post" (Gilbert, pers. comm. Oct. 2007).

At the end of March, the faculty were becoming more outspoken in their demands for some progress on the merger. Many charged that the university was not serious about making any significant changes. Most of the changes thus far were superficial. Southampton Center now became Southampton Campus, the only center was the University Center, at Brookville. The former center presidents would become provosts and Bush-Brown's title was be changed from chancellor back to president, as it had been under Hoxie.

Robert Pattison sent a blistering memo to the Southampton union members describing a meeting called by Bush-Brown in June 1983 to discuss the plans for the future with twenty-five representatives from the three centers. The invited guests included board members, faculty, and administrators. "We were mollified," said Pattison, "with crab legs and cocktails. Dinner was four courses with wine and salmon for the main event" (SCC Archive B II. f, Merger file, Memo to SCFT members June 2, 1983). The plan presented to them, said the memo, began with platitudes and continued with a list of very general issues which previous Middle States reports had urged the university to address. There were no specifics about how to address these problems. In the midst of the current crisis, said Pattison, the "hideous reality" is that "the university is without any plan of action and is playing games." He characterized the merger as an attempt to deflect attention from the real issues and to get university faculty and administrators "wrapped up in nebulous and "dead-ended" committees. How depressing it was, he continued, to see that Bush-Brown hoped to seduce the guests to endorse the plan with eight ounces of salmon and warned the Southampton faculty to steel themselves "to resist blandishments of salmon." Although Pattison's memo may have been somewhat overstated, it reflected the general concerns voiced by Bishop earlier in the spring.

Implementing the Merger during Another "Messy Exit," 1983–1985

> The decision was made to merge, and then people got to the task of deciding how it would work.
>
> —Tim Bishop

Robert Pattison's analogy of Laurel and Hardy's piano (see ch. 5) certainly applies to the merger. The administrations in the three centers of Long Island University, in the absence of any preplanning, struggled to deal with the day-to-day problems with hasty crisis management solutions. The faculties simply ignored the new structures and continued to teach their classes as they had in the past. After five years of efforts to bring the piano to the top of the hill, it had come tumbling back down to where it was at the beginning.

In the fall of 1983, the problems with the hastily defined lines of administrative authority began to surface. John Agria recalled that some decisions were often delayed because they had to be discussed with President Cook at Post. Cook had promised that he would regularly visit the campus and become directly involve with campus affairs, but that did not happen. "We were left pretty much on our own," said Agria. "Tim and I had to drive up to Post weekly to meet with Cook or to attend 'cabinet meetings' which seldom addressed our concerns." The drive on the Long Island Expressway, often described as the world's longest parking lot, took an hour and a half each way in good traffic conditions. It amounted to a full day away from campus. "This took our time away from Southampton campus affairs and increased our frustrations," said Agria (It. 3). Many faculty members were also frustrated with the rather amorphous administrative structure. One commented that while Dean Agria was "a good, a very descent, sincere guy," the general impression was that nobody was running the place.

Krasnoff's election to the chairmanship of the LIU Board of Trustees in September 1983 was more bad news for Bush-Brown. Krasnoff was convinced that new leadership was needed to see the university through the crisis. Bush-Brown, however, had enough support on the board to prevent Krasnoff from ousting him that fall. Concerns about the president's leadership increased in the spring of 1984 when the board learned that the

Southampton deficit remained at $500,000 on a $10 million yearly budget (*East Hampton Star* April 5, 1984).

In December 1983, Dean Agria outlined the new university-wide structure, which was intended to address the concerns about academic leadership. Agria, whose four-year contract with the university ended in the spring of 1984, would be replaced by seven "University Deans." Beginning in the fall of 1984, these administrators would be responsible for all academic programs at the university. "Streamlining for Strength" was the term used in the university public relations releases (SCC Archive B, *Tilting at the Mill* Fall 1984). Maithili Schmidt, the dean of fine arts at C. W. Post, with a doctorate in Philosophy and Logic, was appointed interim university dean for the arts and sciences. She was now responsible for all of the arts and sciences departments in the university. The Social Science and Natural Science and Humanities division directors at Southampton would report to her. For her, the commutes to the other two centers posed an additional problem. She could not drive. Dean Schmidt had to rely on a volunteer from among her junior faculty or a staff member from the university center to drive her to Southampton (Siegel It. 45).

In March 1984, the university appointed Dennis Murphy, the former director of the Brentwood extension campus, to serve as the Southampton provost beginning in the fall of 1984. Murphy described his job as "pretty much what Wilson did" (*Windmill* April 5, 1984). He did not add the obvious, "but much cheaper." A number of Southampton faculty and administrators expressed uncertainty about where the authority of the university dean left off and the provost's began. The faculties at C. W. Post and Brooklyn made it clear that they would oppose any attempt by the deans to change their curricula and their teaching assignments.

Throughout this unsettled period in university administration, the Southampton campus faculty continued with their innovative academic programs. In April, Bob Danziger initiated an honors program, which enriched the educational and cultural life of the campus. He raised funds to bring in nationally known speakers who addressed current issues in their fields. Larry Liddle and Howard Reisman took a class of twelve students to do research on tropical marine biology in Micronesia and Chemistry professor Nancy Peters organized a conference on "Women in Science," which focused on the contributions of women in the sciences and their struggles with gender discrimination. Dr. Sandra Shumway, a distinguished alumna now employed at the Marine Resources Laboratory in Maine, came to participate in the program. The campus radio station flourished under the direction of "Buffalo T."—Terry Jones, a popular and charismatic figure with a colorful background that included songwriting and performing in rock and blues bands. Jones had a way with students, particularly those who had never spoken before a mike before.

FIGURE 7.4. Jon Frazier (left), Fine Arts, Buffalo T (Terry) Jones (center), director of campus radio station WPBX, Southampton Chancellor Angier Biddle Duke (right), December 1986, at the WPBX Christmas party. *Courtesy of Southampton Town Historian.*

In the summer of 1984 the conflict between Chairman Krasnoff and President Bush-Brown was finally resolved in a most unusual manner. The impasse between Krasnoff's supporters and those who remained loyal to Bush-Brown was broken when Krasnoff offered to resign as board chairman if Bush-Brown would also fall on his sword. Both sides were placated, in what soon became known throughout the university as the "double suicide pact." President Bush-Brown announced that he would resign during the 1984–85 academic year, but did not give a specific date. Both men stated publicly that this had nothing to do with personal disagreements, nor was it related in any way to questions about Bush-Brown's leadership. Krasnoff gave a polite, carefully worded, obligatory statement to the press praising Bush-Brown's leadership and his many accomplishments, which, he said, greatly enhanced the university. Two months later, Abraham Krasnoff resigned and was replaced by William Zeckendorf Jr., who organized a search committee to find a new university president.

Bush-Brown's final exit, however, was nearly as messy and unpleasant as was his predecessor's. As the fall semester proceeded, Bush-Brown remained involved in university affairs and gave no hint of his departure. The faculties at the three centers viewed him as a very "lame duck" who no longer had any credibility. They resented his continued presence, which they felt hampered the development of university programs. In response, Bush-Brown announced in December that he would not leave until June 1985. The Brooklyn faculty drafted a resolution, which was later endorsed by Post and Southampton, demanding that he step down immediately and added that he should not be given a "golden parachute," which would divert much-needed funds from the university coffers. A Southampton faculty member reported that Bush-Brown had asked for a half-million in severance pay and insisted that a theater on the Post campus be named after him. The resolution described the president's leadership over the years as marked by "disruption, confusion, and waste, and accused him of provoking three strikes, causing divisiveness between faculty and administration, injuring the University's academic reputation, and depleting University resources" (*Southampton Press* Dec. 20, 1984). The Board of Trustees would not respond to questions from the press about the petition nor about severance pay, but an administrative building at the Brookville administrative center was later named Bush-Brown Hall. The issue was quieted in the spring semester when David Steinberg, who would become president of the university the following fall, visited the three centers, engaging the faculty, students, and administrators in discussions about the future of LIU and thereby making it clear that Bush-Brown no longer had any significant influence. Although he was memorialized by a building at the university administrative center, the accusations in the faculty resolution followed Bush-Brown to his grave. When he died after a brief illness at the age of sixty-eight in 1994, the *New York Times* obituary quoted directly from the faculty resolution (*New York Times* July 25, 1994).

Chapter Eight

A Decade to Build

The Bishop-Steinberg Era Begins

> It is my sense that both a great task and a great opportunity lie before us. Together we can achieve the founder's vision of a University that stretches across four counties of this Island and beyond, providing quality, effective, affordable education.
>
> —President David Steinberg, introducing the Long Island University Plan, January 13, 1988

In July 1985, David Steinberg, the former vice president of Brandeis University, was chosen for the presidency of Long Island University. Steinberg was a Harvard-educated scholar with an international reputation as an expert in Southeast Asian affairs and had been a very successful fundraiser at Brandeis. His preliminary visits to the university centers in the spring of 1985 had already raised questions in his mind about the merger. Although he hesitated to make any significant change in the new structure, he did make one very important intervention soon after his inauguration in July. During the Fall 1985 semester, Dean Bishop and Provost Murphy traveled to the University Center regularly to discuss matters related to the Southampton campus. Mary Lai recalled that at these meetings Murphy frequently deferred to Bishop when more detailed questions about finance or administration were being discussed. After one of these meetings late in the fall, she pointed this out to Steinberg and suggested that Murphy's role was peripheral at best.

Murphy, however, had the conventional academic credentials for the position as provost, and Bishop had neither a PhD nor experience as an educational administrator. Both Mary Lai and President Steinberg realized that the absence of these standard items in his resume was more than offset by other strengths. Bishop had more than a decade of hands-on experience in every one of the most important campus administrative offices, he was respected and well liked by the administrative staff, and he had a very good relationship with the Suffolk County elected officials and with the local press. In January 1986, Steinberg announced that he had appointed

Murphy to serve as the university dean of continuing education and had named Bishop the new provost at Southampton.

Steinberg's second important appointment was Walter S. Jones, the former senior vice president and provost at Wayne State University, in Detroit. Jones, an expert in international law and diplomacy with a doctorate from the Fletcher School of Law and Diplomacy at Tufts University, was appointed the university vice president for academic affairs. The two senior university administrators found themselves in an untried and hastily conceived university structure with no clear direction forward.

The Collapse of the Merger, 1986–1988

The university deans reported directly to Walter Jones. Michael Soupios, a Political Science professor at C. W. Post, had replaced interim dean Maithili Schmidt in the fall of 1985 (see ch. 7 above). He recalled that it was an exhausting, frustrating, and thankless job. The long hours on the Long Island Expressway, the constant infighting between the academic departments, who all resented any attempt to "streamline" the campus administration, and the competition between the university centers for funds combined to wear him down. "On some occasions I would drive an hour out to Southampton for a lunch meeting then drive back to Post for a late afternoon meeting and then to Brooklyn for an evening meeting" (pers. comm. 2006). He figured that he often spent nearly ten hours a week in his car, more if the traffic was bad.

Some of the other deans faced similar problems. The faculty at C. W. Post was particularly antagonistic to most of the deans. In a survey conducted by the Post faculty union, only Soupios and Schmidt were given satisfactory ratings along with complimentary comments by individual respondents. The others were rated below average and received comments that were often quite personal and rather nasty (SCC Archives B, Merger Files, SCFT Newsletter May 27, 1986). There were, however, some bright spots. Liz Granitz, the Business Division director, recalled having a positive relationship with Carl Figlioa, the university dean for business: "Carl and I were pretty much on the same page, and we developed a successful university wide master's degree program" (pers. comm. July 2010). Sidney Sherter, who was serving as the director of the Education department, also remarked that he had established a good working relationship with Helen Greene, the university dean for education (pers. comm. Nov. 12, 2010). Granitz and Sherter felt that the merger worked fairly well for the professional programs such as Business and Education.

In the fall of 1986, as a part of the sixty-year anniversary of LIU, President Steinberg announced a university-wide campaign called "a Decade to Build" to raise $100 million by 1995. Among the projects that would be funded was a library-learning center for Southampton. Steinberg called for support from "our more financially secure" alumni.[1] The campaign was, in part, a response to frequent criticisms that LIU had never made any serious and well-planned attempts to raise funds. It was hoped that the appointment of Angier Biddle Duke in 1986 as honorary chancellor of Southampton College would bring in donations from the wealthy summer residents in the Hamptons. Duke, who had served as ambassador to Spain, El Salvador, Denmark, and Morocco and had served as the chief of protocol to presidents Kennedy and Johnson, used his influence and his international connections to organize and develop the World Affairs Council, which brought distinguished speakers from around the world to the campus. These dignitaries regularly drew appreciative audiences. Carol Gilbert, the director of admissions, quipped, "This place can only improve now that we have a Bishop and a Duke running it." Duke saw his role as a bridge between the college and the summer elites in the Hamptons. "I want my hometown to use and to respect the college," he said (*Windmill* Feb. 7, 1986). Unfortunately, this population remained, as they had in the past, aloof from any significant involvement with the college.

At about that same time, Steinberg convinced the board to establish a university-wide planning committee. The total Southampton enrollment in 1986–87 dropped from 1,090 in 1985–86 to fewer than one thousand students, causing concerns about the future. The accumulated debt had increased from $6 million in 1986 to $7 million in 1987. The population of people in the Northeast between the ages of seventeen and nineteen had dropped by about 6 percent. The newly established planning committee of the Board of Trustees conducted student surveys, marketing assessments, and held dialogues with faculty and staff. This was one of the first times that a LIU administration had ever engaged in such thorough planning that involved the faculty, students, and staff.[2] Provost Bishop drafted a candid assessment of the state of Southampton Campus and sent it to the trustees' planning committee for their meeting on April 30, 1987. It was a remarkably frank document for a newly appointed administrator (SCC Archives B II, F Box 2, Bishop to Planning Committee April 24, 1987).

Bishop began by noting that Southampton charged a higher tuition than any other college on Long Island: "By several available measures, we are an average institution charging an above average price." These measures included SAT scores, admission standards, number of honors received by graduates, and retention rates. Southampton, said Bishop, rated below its primary competitors in all these areas. The sobering report recommended that recruitment focus on average to good students rather than recruiting and giving scholarship aid to "exceptional students," who would be in a position to demand more financial aid. The report urged that more funds be devoted to remedial programs that would aid the marginal students and thereby reduce the number of students who would drop out. He recommended a related shift for financial aid, calling for funds to be given primarily for need. Rather than give full scholarships to exceptional "honors" students, he argued, the aid would be spread around to the much larger group in the campus population. Ironically the Marine Science program at Southampton continued to attract talented students with above-average SAT scores, who remained on campus until they graduated.

The planning committee, somewhat sobered by Bishop's assessment, requested a report from Jan Kurkowski Associates, a consulting firm commissioned by the planning committee for a university-wide study evaluating the current student body and the marketing position of the university (SCC Archive A, K-25 Nov. 2, 1987). Based on interviews conducted on all three campuses, they developed a very negative profile of the "average" LIU student. The Kurkowski study concluded that the students tend to fall in the lower ranges of the SAT scores for colleges across the nation, are the first in their families to attend college, have not been admitted to their first choice of a college, and begin their college experience with little focus and generally end it the same way. The students are unsure about how to relate to the faculty and administration and seldom seek out any contact outside of the classroom. When they get discouraged about their grades or about any other aspect of campus life they simply drop out without ever speaking with any of the available counselors. This population, continued the report, "presents a difficult pedagogical problem that few colleges have dealt with successfully," adding, "What LIU has done so far has not won any accolades, either from most of its own students, or college counselors and others who can directly influence recruitment" (Kurkowski 1987, 5).

Although there were Southampton students who fit the negative profile, there were many outstanding exceptions, particularly in the Natural Science division. Lisa Frederickson (1990), for example, majored in Marine Science/Biology and worked as an educator at the New England Aquarium. Catherine St. Hill (1992), another Science major, went on to study Veterinary Medicine at the University of Minnesota. Southampton graduates during this period from Social Science, Business, Humanities, and Fine Arts, as well as from the sciences, provide many exceptions to the characterizations in the Kurkowski report. Alexandra McCarty (1990), a communications major, played a significant role in the development of the college radio station, WPBX-FM, into a major force in Long Island radio. After graduation, she took over as the director of the station. Deborah Shurberg (1988) earned her PhD in Psychology at Hofstra University in 1995 and later served as a scientific associate at Brookhaven National Laboratory in Upton, New York. She traveled to Russia and Ukraine to assist in the development of training programs for nuclear power plant personnel. Jean Abiuso (1992) completed her BA in Elementary Education and went to earn her Master of Science Education in 1994. Jonathan Ji (1991), a Marketing Management major, received the Provost Citizenship award and was named Co-op Student of the Year. After graduation, he worked for Bell Atlantic Corporation where he became director of marketing and sales. Carol Taylor (1987), an English major, worked as an editor for Random House in New York and was profiled in *Essence* magazine. Lorna Libert (1989) studied art with Yoshi Higa and Robert Mumford and then taught for two years before entering an MFA program at Central Washington University. As noted in chapter 3, many of the "average to good" students turned out to be "late bloomers," who graduated and went on to successful careers.

The Long Island University Plan

The Kurkowski report recommended that the university emphasize programs that lead directly to career opportunities and establish a program that enables the students to earn money and gain firsthand experience in a profession while they are in college. The report urged that a program of cooperative work placements in career-related work experience that generated income for tuition would clearly distinguish LIU from its competitors and give it a much better market position. Noting that the first-generation students are insecure and often become isolated, the report recommended that programs of more intensive academic, career and personal counseling be established.

Based on these reports and the results of the year-long study, Steinberg outlined a new direction for the university which he called "The Long Island University Plan" (SCC Archive A I, k, 27, Memo to LIU Community Jan. 13, 1988). President Steinberg's remarks introducing the plan in 1988 made reference to his sense of the "great task" to achieve the "founders vision of a University that stretches across four counties of this Island and beyond, providing quality, effective, affordable education," ignored both the history of the university and the current conditions highlighted in the Kurkowski Report. When Ralph Jonas founded the university in 1926, his vision was to establish a multicultural university in the heart of Brooklyn. There is no evidence whatsoever that Jonas and those related to the founding ever envisioned expanding beyond Brooklyn. Jonas' s vision was severely compromised in 1953 when President Metcalf decided not to use the funds generated from the influx of World War II veterans to improve the Brooklyn facility nor to establish an endowment as recommended in the Middle State critique. Instead he invested in an expansion to Brookville, Long Island. Partly as a result of that decision, the vision of providing quality and affordable education remained beyond the reach of Long Island University.

The LIU plan had four key elements: an intensive program of advising, orientation, and guidance throughout a student's academic career at LIU; more opportunities for co-ops and internships; an expanded core curriculum focusing on writing skills; and expanded financial counseling related to the anticipated income earned by students on their internships. The plan also marked the end of the ill-conceived merger. The new structure, he said, eliminated the university dean system and returned most academic decision making to the campus faculties. No one mourned the end of the dean system and, in fact, most faculty had never paid much attention to it anyway. Steinberg and Jones were also happy to be rid of a group who might challenge their authority and limit their administrative powers. Bishop and the other campus provosts had found that the structure was unwieldy and delayed administrative action. For Carol Gilbert and the Southampton admissions office, it meant that they got their campus identity back.

The Southampton faculty executive committee voted unanimously to support Steinberg and his administration during the period of reorganization (SCC Archive B, IV, e, Faculty Council Minutes May 11, 1988). The Southampton campus had already established programs that addressed many of these concerns. Bishop had introduced a "Freshman Program" three years earlier that was designed to help the new students with their adjustment to college life. The centerpiece of the program was College 101, a one-credit, required course, with small classes. The seven-week course was taught by volunteer faculty who were sympathetic to the goals of the program. This course introduced the students to the campus support facilities available to help them with career direction, counseling, recreation, financial guidance, and academic problems. The faculty were encouraged to establish informal relationships with the students by inviting them to their homes and organizing short field trips. In 1988 the three-year-old program was credited with a slight reduction in the attrition rate and with strengthening a feeling of community on campus. Bishop was invited to an international conference on the first-year experience sponsored by the University of South Carolina. The conference was held at Cambridge University in England (*Windmill* April 25, 1988). The following year, the program won a national award for excellence from the Noel/Levitz National Center for Student Retention (*Southampton Press* Sept. 14, 1989).

Bishop pointed out that the college programs developed by Robert Danziger also addressed these issues. Danziger, as noted above, had developed an internship program in 1974 and a program of cooperative education in 1978. The internships were designed as a culminating experience in the junior year. Some were paid and some were volunteer positions. By 1991 the program was nationwide and had expanded to Europe, the Caribbean, Latin America, and the South Pacific. The co-ops were for shorter time periods with nearby employers. These positions enabled a student to continue attending other classes on campus. Ellen Avenoso, the current director of cooperative education, began work immediately on an expansion of her contacts with employers. There was already a data bank of more than two thousand employers in the Co-op office files. Steinberg was aware of these programs and heartily endorsed them. The problem was at the other campuses, where the faculty tended to resist any interference in their curricula and their workloads.

The five-year interim report prepared for Middle States in 1989 noted that the enrollment had recovered significantly from 949 in 1987 to 1,190, and that the freshman program had improved the retention rate between the freshman and sophomore years. Nevertheless, the overall retention rate, running at about 35 percent, was "alarmingly low" given the heavy dependence on tuition revenue for the operation of the college (SCC Archive A, I, K, Middle States June, 1989, 110). The retention rate in the sciences, however, was higher than the college average. An internal report on retention in the sciences written by Math professor Russell Meyers pointed once again to the higher mean SAT scores in the sciences in general and to the even higher test scores for Marine Science majors. The SAT scores for the Science majors were about one hundred points higher than the college mean. The sciences were more likely to remain in the college through graduation. The low retention rates for the non-Science majors was, of course, directly linked to an open admissions policy driven by a need for a constant flow of tuition money each September.

The visiting Middle States team toured the campus and reported, not surprisingly, that in spite of improvements to the Marine Science and Fine Arts facilities, the campus plant remained a problem (Middle States, 112). The team also noted that the library and computer facilities were substandard. Another unaddressed problem from previous reports was the heavy reliance on adjuncts in the humanities and the social sciences. These issues were unaddressed, of course, because of financial limitations. The following fall a review by the New York State education department reported similar findings (SCC Archive A II, K-32, NYSED Sept. 24, 1990). The university responded to these criticisms with a statement of confidence in the newly established LIU plan. The small improvements were cited as a basis for new growth leading to a more stable financial situation. Like Sisyphus, we kept rolling the stone up the hill. Unfortunately, as Mary Lai noted, "the Long Island Plan just never took off." The "Decade to Build" fundraising effort also fell far short of expectations.

Alvin Siegel: The Reluctant Dean

The new university structure did not replace the university deans with an administrator for academic affairs at Southampton. The Southampton faculty asked the university to appoint an academic dean, but Jones and Steinberg were reluctant to provide funds for a national search and a salary that would attract a highly qualified experienced academic administrator. The faculty continued to press for a dean until Steinberg finally agreed to a search that was limited to the Southampton campus. The search committee interviewed several faculty members and sent their recommendations to Vice President Walter Jones. In 1989, Jones appointed Al Siegel, who had served as Natural Science division director for several years. Siegel, who described himself as a "life long learner," joined the faculty in 1968 after seven years at the Woods Hole research center in Massachusetts. He had turned down a higher-paying job in industry because he wanted to be a part of a campus community where he could interact with faculty and students. Siegel's first love was classroom teaching. Siegel accepted the deanship, but insisted that he continue teaching two of his chemistry courses. Some faculty were unhappy with this arrangement. They wanted to have an academic officer who would devote his full time to the job without the distractions of classroom teaching. Three years after the failed merger with C.W. Post, one of Dean Siegel's first challenges was to oversee a merger of a very different sort.

The Bride Comes Without a Dowry: Friends World College Merges with LIU, 1991

Friends World College (FWC), a nontraditional Quaker school, was founded in 1965 with a mission to educate students who would play an active role as world citizens dedicated to the betterment of humankind. The college expanded from its campus in Lloyd Harbor, New York, on the north shore of Long Island, to include seven overseas centers in England, Kenya, China, India, Japan, Israel, and Costa Rica. FWC had a nontraditional curriculum with an emphasis on experiential education. The students had to spend a full year of immersion on two of the overseas campuses. Working with faculty advisors, they developed research projects and documented their progress in a portfolio that would be the only evaluation tool used by the college.

Friends World College, unfortunately, had a history of financial mismanagement that prevented it from obtaining Middle States accreditation. Without accreditation it was difficult to recruit a sufficient number of students to pay off the college debts. In the 1980s the college, which was located on prime real estate, began to sell off small tracts to lower their accumulated debt. By 1989, there was no longer an option unless they relocated the college and freed up the last parcel. With the college facing bankruptcy in 1989, President Nancy Lester and the college council reached out to private colleges on Long Island seeking an agreement of affiliation that would provide them with accreditation and alleviate their financial problems. Once they relocated the college, the real estate could be sold to pay off the debts and, it was hoped, have enough left over to fund an endowment for the college (It. 35a). The FWC, therefore, could offer a package that included a student body of about two hundred and the possibility of an endowment. With this attractive bait FWC approached several Long island institutions.

Adelphi, Dowling, and Hofstra were not interested, but David Steinberg and Walter Jones, who visited the Lloyd Harbor campus on several occasions, were intrigued by the emphasis on experiential education and by the international campuses. They saw a connection between these aspects of the FWC and the Co-op and Internship programs at Southampton. The Southampton campus seemed a good fit for the FWC. Undoubtedly, Steinberg and Jones were also attracted by the prospect of two hundred new students for Southampton and the possibility of an endowment. They opened negotiations with President Lester and signed an affiliation agreement on April 4, 1991. The LIU officials were disappointed to learn, several years later, that after the FWC council settled all the debts there was no money left for the anticipated endowment. As Kathleen Mudrowski, the director of the FWC North America Center, quipped, "The bride came without a dowry" (It. 35a).

The following fall, the Friends World Program (FWP) opened on the Southampton campus. Two administrators from the former FWC came with the program: Jeff Halper, the former director of the FWC Middle East Center, and Kathleen Modrowski. They arrived on campus to greet the Friends World freshman class. Shortly after the program was established in the new setting, Lewis Greenstein replaced Halper as the program director. Halper's unconventional approach to education had made Walter Jones most uncomfortable. Greenstein had a PhD in African History from the University of Indiana and had served as a Peace Corps volunteer in Kenya.

The program varied little from the previous years at Huntington. The new students lived on campus for two semesters, taking a foundation program that included an introduction to cross-cultural studies, the goals and philosophy of the FWP, global history, languages, and basic research skills. They worked with a faculty advisor to develop an independent research project. The next two years were spent at selected overseas centers where the students immersed themselves in the local culture. In their last year they returned to the Southampton campus for a capstone seminar. In 2002, the foundation year was shifted to the London center to introduce the students to an overseas experience at the beginning of their educational program.

The students in the FWP were bright, with firmly held views on political and social issues. During the first years, there were some clashes with the Southampton students, who were more interested in their personal career concerns. It was as if a time machine had transported a group of student radicals from the sixties into the more conformist culture of the nineties. The "strange dress," the focus on contemporary issues, and the understandable tendency to remain aloof from the Southampton students fostered some animosity that, on one occasion, led to a serious act of vandalism. The FWP offices and classrooms in the Amagansett Dorm basement were, in the words of Modrowski, "trashed so severely that even the window frames were torn out" (It. 35a). Over the years, however, the two divergent student cultures

FIGURE 8.1. Friends World students at the 1997 World Conference on the Southampton campus. *Photo © Gary Mamy 2012.*

managed to get along. By the end of the nineties, many of the Southampton students had studied at the overseas centers and some had transferred into the FWP as full-time students.

The innovative aspects of the FWP are best illustrated in the experience of two students who graduated during the first two years on the Southampton campus. Hallie Stone (1991) spent semesters in Costa Rica and Kenya. During her time at the Southampton center she studied at the Alvin Ailey American Dance Center in Manhattan, where she met Pearl Primus who encouraged her to combine anthropology and dance. She later entered the master's program in Anthropology at Indiana University. Daniel Osei-Owusuh (1992), a Ghanaian student, who came to the program after receiving a diploma in French, studied sustainable agricultural development at the Middle East Center. In 1993, he took an internship in sustainable agriculture with the Rodale Institute.

BISHOP'S "KITCHEN CABINET"

The close social relationships among the secretaries and staff in the college administration had been noted by many of the people interviewed by the author (It. 11; It. 19; It. 23; It. 28; It. 52; Ulrich, pers. comm. July 2005;

Zimmer, It. 65; Peterson, M., pers. comm). Joan Zimmer, who was a part of the college community for more than four decades, believed that the sense of family was related to the small size of the workforce and the relative isolation in the Hamptons. Mary Peterson agreed. She began assisting with the tutoring program in the study center, then came to work with Alice Flynn on the freshman program until David McGregor appointed her associate dean of student advising in 1978. Mary recalled that another bond uniting these people was that many, including Tim Bishop, had experience in several administrative offices. Vicky Mulvey, who replaced Mary in 1995, had been administrative assistant to the provost. She had graduated from Southampton College and earned her master's degree at C. W. Post, where she had worked for several years. Mulvey told Peter Wells, a student reporter, that what she liked best about her job was that she loved "the students, the small campus, and the fact that we seem like one big family here at Southampton Campus" (SCC Archive A, I, k-52, *Faculty Profiles* Vol. 1(2) 1997, 10). John McCrudden began his career at Southampton as a counselor in the HEOP program, then served as the director of the continuing education program for a year before Bishop appointed him director of career development and cooperative education. They all understood each other's problems and frustrations with the perennial lack of funds and the constant need to improvise.

There were some critics of Bishop's "folk style" of administrative management. To them, it appeared to be an inclusive cadre of personal friends who moved from one position to another. When questioned about this criticism, Alice Flynn defended the "kitchen cabinet," arguing that "we knew each other's strengths and weaknesses and we got along well as a team. We knew how things worked and we were all deeply committed to Southampton College. A new person coming in needed time to adjust and, on occasion, in spite of their glowing resumes they turned out to be a disaster" (It. 19). Although these arguments did not silence many of their critics, the "folk style" worked as well as any management style in a small college and most of the staff agreed that it was a comfortable place to work.

Here We Go Again: Middle States, 1993–1994

In the spring of 1992, preparations began on the self-study required by Middle States as the first step in their scheduled evaluation. The visiting team of evaluators planned to use this document as a basis for their campus visitation in 1993. Their primary focus was on a program they called "outcomes assessment." The purpose of this program was to establish a set of college-wide goals that would then be measured against the outcomes recorded yearly in a database. This database included records from the administrative offices, faculty departments, and student service areas, and from surveys of alumni.

The writing of a mission statement was a fairly simple task. All this required was to go back through the many drafts that had been prepared from time to time since the college opened. It was a fairly simple matter of piling one cliché on top of another. The draft prepared for the university, for example, set as its mission: preserving world culture, providing the highest ideals of scholarship and community service that would serve as a basis for fulfilling lives and careers, fostering intensive self-discovery through enhanced holistic counseling, ensuring access to the American Dream, providing library collections, computer networks, and laboratories, and meeting the academic and social needs of a diverse student body (SCC Archive A I, K-35 Mission Statement for LIU Oct. 12, 1992).

The real challenge for LIU was the establishment of the database that would be used to measure the progress toward meeting all those stated goals. Middle States had distributed a guide, *Characteristics of Excellence in Higher Education*, for colleges and universities to follow that called for the establishment of a program for "continuous self-study" based on data collected yearly from academic and administrative offices. The outcomes assessment should include a "multi-dimensional evaluation of scholastic achievement using qualitative and quantitative measures." Curriculum and program review and teacher evaluations should be made on a regular basis. The success of the alumni should include surveys focusing on job satisfaction and performance evaluations by their employers. This assessment model required a university-wide institutional research office with a staff and computer facilities. The university did have a university office of institutional research, but it did not collect the types of data required for an adequate outcomes assessment program. Institutional research was described as a "decentralized and somewhat informal" responsibility left to enrollment services and the alumni office.

The response of the LIU administration to the clearly stated emphasis on outcomes assessment by Middle States can best be described as a mixture of confusion and denial. In April, when the Southampton campus steering committee, which had received no direction from the university administration, submitted their self-study design to the Middle States Association, they placed "outcomes assessment" at the very bottom of the list of nine committees (SCC Archive A I, K-34, Self Study April 1992). The outcomes committee set as its goal a review of the current instruments in place and a set of recommendations for improvements that would bring the university into compliance with the Middle States model.

In August, Robert Pattison, chairman of the outcomes committee, sent a memo to Provost Bishop asking for nine specific databases required for the completion of an outcomes assessment. The most important among them were comparisons of Southampton graduates with college graduates nationwide in writing and math and assessments of alumni job satisfaction five years after graduation and/or success in graduate school. Pattison also asked what procedures were in place for gathering and analyzing such data. There was, of course, no response. As Bishop later lamented, we had no institutional memory at all. In fact it was not until the following October that a copy of the 1983 Middle States report was found by Lee Stanley, the Social Science division secretary, buried in her office files. That same month, Pattison, having received no response from the administration, outlined a proposal for an office for institutional research. There should be, said Pattison, a senior academic officer in charge of an assessment program supported by an office staff and computers, assistants who would collect educational data, and outside consultants.

The university administration was eager to avoid making such an expensive commitment. Dennis Payette attended a Middle States outcomes assessment workshop held at Hunter College shortly after Dean Siegel received Pattison's memo. Rather than finding the workshop instructive, Payette reported to Lee Kelly, Steinberg's executive assistant, who had been given the responsibility to oversee the preparations for the Middle States reports on the university centers, that the director of the workshop had been "maddeningly vague" in her explanations about the intent of the Middle States Association in the matter of outcomes assessment (SCC Archive A, I. K-35, Middle States File, Payette to Kelly Oct. 23, 1992). Payette concluded that each center should go ahead with whatever plan was most suited to their needs. This was the message that the university wanted to hear. Pattison and Dean Siegel, however, did not find the intentions of Middle States difficult to understand.

On November 10, Dean Siegel sent a memo to Lee Kelly urging that the university establish an outcomes assessment office on each campus. Without the information from such offices, wrote Siegel, we cannot make major progress toward the goal of outcomes assessment (SCC Archive A, I. K-35, Siegel to Kelly Nov. 10, 1992). He also asked Kelly to help establish better communications between the centers during the Middle States process. Two days later, Pattison sent an angry memo to his committee attaching Payette's memo, and commented with a characteristic note of sarcasm that "certain members of the administration seem to be of the opinion that Outcomes Assessment means whatever they would like it to mean. . . . I don't think Middle States will take this opinion very seriously, nor should we" (SCC Archive A, II. K-35, Pattison to Outcomes Assessment Committee Nov. 12, 1992).

Kelly responded to these concerns with a brief memo telling Siegel that Southampton was on their own. There would be no new offices established at the centers for outcomes assessment. She informed Siegel that there already existed a university office of institutional research and a data center that would provide the centers with the data they needed (SCC Archive A, I, K, Kelly to Siegel Nov. 13, 1992). The existence of these offices came as somewhat of a surprise to Siegel and Pattison. They soon learned that these offices were not at all what was needed for an outcomes assessment program. On December 28, for example, Provost Bishop finally responded to Pattison's August memo with a brief note and an attachment from a report submitted to him by the career development office on Dec 16 that gave excerpts from the results of an alumni survey and a list of mean SAT scores. This fragmented and sparse data demonstrated the need for a more comprehensive data collecting process that could serve as an adequate basis for a professional analysis.

In the fall of 1993, the Middle States visiting team arrived on campus to begin their evaluation. The team reviewed the campus self-study and interviewed faculty, administration, students, and staff. In October, the college received an assessment, which noted strengths and areas of concern. The first two on a list of eight concerns came as no surprise to Pattison and Siegel. The committee was very concerned about the lack of significant planning for academics and finances and the related absence of any significant progress on a plan for outcomes assessment. The primary recommendation was for the campus and the university to develop a strategic campus plan and an outcomes assessment program. The committee noted that "there is little outcomes assessment and no campus-wide plan to develop such assessment." They also noted that there was no university process for assessing educational objectives. The collection and analysis of data was hindered by the absence of a uniform computer format for the university. The Middle States evaluators recommended that the university centralize its database. The concern about inadequate planning and assessment was repeated several times throughout the evaluation reports.

The campus outcomes committee questioned the level of commitment for an outcomes assessment program on the part of the university administration. The problem, of course, was, once again, a matter of available funds. The university was unable to implement a program that would lead to an improvement in academic quality and institutional effectiveness. There was, however, praise for the Freshman 101 program, the Marine Science program, the experiential learning programs, and the increase in the freshman enrollment. The areas of criticism reflected the historical problems related to undercapitalization. The financial condition of the campus, said the report, was serious; the physical plant was deteriorating; the classroom space was inadequate, and the library was substandard. The annual deficits had increased dramatically from an average of $200,000 to $500,000 for the years from 1971 to 1981 to range from about $3 million to $5 million beginning in 1991. What was most unsettling, however, was that many of these same problems had been noted by previous Middle States reports in 1973 and in 1983. The campus remained undercapitalized and unable to address any of these concerns.

It was these areas of criticism, of course, that received most attention from the press. The headline in *Newsday* (Jan. 12, 1994) read "Review Rips Southampton Campus." The article continued with a brief discussion of the positive findings, but the damage was done by the headline. This was President Steinberg's first Middle States review and he was very upset. In an angry letter to *Newsday* reporter Robert Fresco, he denied that LIU was in trouble, but noted that the article would most certainly have a negative impact on the university. The *Southampton Press* (Jan. 20, 1994) was much more positive, focusing on Steinberg's response to *Newsday* and comments by Dean Siegel, Provost Bishop, and Lewis Greenstein, the Friends World Program director. In February 1994, the Middle States Association reaffirmed the accreditation of LIU, but requested a followup report by September 1996 that would focus on the outcomes assessment program and on university finances (LIUABCL, RG 3:2, Middle States Association to President Steinberg March 8, 1994).

Bishop and Siegel acknowledged that the Middle States criticisms were well founded, but noted that these problems tended to overshadow some very positive accomplishments. The success of the Fulbright program and the co-ops and internships, it could be argued, were, in effect, a much more significant measure of outcomes than some of the statistical measures required by Middle States. During the four-year period from 1990 to 1994, four Southampton Marine Science students were awarded Fulbright grants. Kristin Loop (1991) spent a year in Australia studying the endangered hawk-bill sea turtle. Katherine Barneau (1992) traveled to Belgium to examine the relations between trace elements and phytoplankton. That same year, Carol Kosman was in Antarctica studying a rare species of sea-ice plankton. In 1993–94, Patrick Perl studied zooplankton ecology at the Taupo Institute for Scientific Research in New Zealand. The great irony was that the Natural Science department, which produced most of the Fulbright Scholars, was the primary source of the annual deficits.

Chapter Nine

A Decade of Treading Water, 1993–2002

It is undeniable that the financial condition of the Southampton Campus is serious. It has to be a concern for the whole university.

—Report of the Middle States Evaluation Team to the Faculty, Administration, Trustees, Students, of Long Island University, Oct. 24–27, 1993

[T]he seeming intractability of these enrollment and financial problems,[at Southampton College] . . . require immediate and dramatic action.

—Report of the Middle States Commission Site Team, April 17, 2003

The Dollar a Year Chancellor

Every spring, the Southampton administrators traveled to the University Center to meet with the LIU trustees and juggle the budget projections for the following year. Every spring, some trustees proposed closing Southampton, and every spring, optimistic budget projections gave enough promise to keep the college open. Often these projections assumed that fundraising campaigns would produce more than they had in the previous year. Every fall, the optimism faded as budgets had to be revised. In the spring of 1993, however, there was new hope. The college appointed Robert F. X. Sillerman to replace Ambassador Duke, who had retired from his position as Southampton's "dollar a year" chancellor. Sillerman, a graduate of Brandeis University, had amassed a huge fortune in the radio business by buying poorly performing stations, improving their management, and then selling them at a considerable profit (*Newsday* March 17, 1996; *Boston Globe* Nov. 15, 1998). His association with the college, however, began in the mid-seventies and was not related to a fundraising campaign. He and his wife Laura had an informal social relationship that had developed over the years with several members of the college staff. Carol Gilbert, who had been friends with Laura from their college days, introduced the Sillermans to the rest of Bishop's "kitchen cabinet." During the summer months, recalled Alice Flynn, the group met on weekends to play volleyball on Road D off Dune Road, where you could park without a sticker. In 1979, Sillerman built a house nearby that he called the "Road D annex" (Flynn, It. 19).

Shortly after Bishop became provost, he came under pressure from David Steinberg to engage Sillerman more directly with Southampton in the hope that he would be a primary benefactor. Bishop hesitated because he knew that Sillerman was often pressed by people around him with their hands out, and he did not want his relationship with Sillerman to be compromised. As it turned out, Sillerman was more than willing to help the college. His close friendship with Bishop and the others was undoubtedly a factor, but Sillerman was also very impressed with the record number of Fulbrights and the national reputation of the Marine Science program. In 1992, Sillerman launched a concert series called *All For The Sea* which continued until 2004, bringing in more than six million dollars for the Marine Science scholarship program. Sillerman used his media contacts to get such performers as Tina Turner, Bob Dylan, Jimmy Buffett, Rod Stewart, and Tony Bennett to play at no charge for the college.[1]

FIGURE 9.1. Provost Tim Bishop, Mary Welker, Honorary Chancellor of Southampton College Robert Sillerman, and Long Island University president David Steinberg. *Courtesy of Southampton Town Historian.*

There were some skeptics, however, who put a very negative spin on Sillerman's interest in the college. Corey Dolgon, a member of the Friends World faculty, asserted that Sillerman was seeking to bolster his personal reputation and offset allegations that he was a "junk bond hustler." Dolgon, in his book *The End of the Hamptons* (2005), characterized Sillerman as one of the new "hyper bourgeoisie," who arrived in the Hamptons in the 1970s. Sillerman, argued Dolgon, was among those who sought to "claim a legacy of wealth and status, legitimizing their ascendency and demonstrating their fitness to rule" (Dolgon 2005, 9). Sillerman, said Dolgon, merely sought "to dress in the garb of an academic elite."[2] Dolgon's subjective opinion of Sillerman resonated with some of Sillerman's critics. Among them were a few LIU trustees who were receptive to anything negative about Sillerman. These individuals tended to disparage what they saw as a rather shabby road to wealth in contrast to their own "high road" of conventional business activity. Roger Tilles, who later became chairman of the board, frequently clashed with Sillerman. Another trustee allegedly commented that there were many negative feelings about him in the Hamptons that would prevent him from finding donors. Carol Gilbert dismissed this criticism, noting that Sillerman successfully brought in donations from his business contacts in Manhattan and not from Dune Road or the Hamptons in general. She also noted, as had many, including Mary Lai, that the wealthy summer residents in the Hamptons had never given significant donations to the college. Justified or not, these personality conflicts among the trustees remained close to the surface and would later erupt in heated exchanges during the days of crisis in 2004.

Sillerman's appointment as chancellor, of course, did not immediately alter the college's financial distress. Shortly after the negative report in *Newsday*, Robert Pattison, who was now the chairman of the faculty budget and finance committee, issued a report which was sent to Bishop, Lai, Jones, and Steinberg (SCC Archive A, I, k Feb. 10, 1994). The report warned that the college deficit, in spite of an increase in enrollment, was "chronic, growing and unless quickly addressed, terminal." Part of the problem was that the increase in enrollment was offset by the scholarship aid that the college had to give to attract new students and to keep those already enrolled from leaving. The more students we enroll, continued the report, the larger our deficits will grow. The percentage of a student's tuition paid by parents and family had dropped from 56 percent in 1989 to 37 percent in 1993. The percentage of tuition that came from college scholarships had risen from 19 percent to 26.8 percent during that same period. The remainder of the tuition came from government grants.

The committee concluded that the reason for the drop in family support was that there was a perception that the college's educational programs, with the exception of the Marine Science program, were not worth the price the institution was charging. The committee urged the faculty to "offer an educational program of higher quality, manage its academic life more professionally, and market its educational product more effectively. . . . The college must move quickly to establish programs that have the potential for real quality." The specific recommendations included appointment of a single powerful academic officer, increased standards for all faculty reappointments, elimination of faculty lines in poorly enrolled programs, and recruitment of experienced, highly paid scholars who would give direction to new programs.

The recommendations were discussed in a number of meetings over the next three semesters. The task of "improving the product," involved a long-range commitment that made some administrators who wanted a "quicker fix" somewhat uneasy. Steinberg, for example, appeared to be more interested in improving the customer. In the fall of 1994, when he answered questions about the state of the university at a Southampton faculty meeting, he said, "We need to attract more students who can contribute more towards tuition" (SCC Archive B IV, b, Faculty Council minutes Oct. 12, 1994). The assumption that richer families who had a greater choice of colleges would be willing to pay more for a less than adequate product was questionable to say the least.

Some faculty and staff argued that more attention should be given to the programs such as HEOP, which played an important role in retaining students and increasing the graduation rate. In 1994, the Southampton College HEOP program celebrated its twenty-fifth anniversary at the annual conference in Albany, where staff member Jane Strong and HEOP student Mary Thornhill received statewide awards. Strong, a founding member of the college HEOP program in 1974, received the Trailblazers Award for her work as academic coordinator. The award is given to those individuals "whose contributions exemplify the diversity of the challenges that HEOP has met and the leadership that has made it possible." Mary Thornhill, who started her college career at the age of twenty-nine, received the Distinguished HEOP Alumni Award. Thornhill graduated Summa Cum Laude with a degree in Business Administration. "If it weren't for HEOP," said Ms. Thornhill, "I would still be waitressing. I couldn't have afforded the tuition . . . but it was not only the financial assistance. It was the support and guidance I received" (*Around and About the Windmill* Feb./March 1994).

All agreed, however, that there was a need to improve and expand the fundraising programs. At the same meeting Jerry Kleinman, the vice president for public relations and development, announced that LIU was going to hire Tom Lloyd, a professional fundraiser "with a distinguished track record and use [his] expertise and resources to develop fund-raising activities." A new fundraising endeavor called "The Capital Campaign" was launched in the hope that it would be more successful than the "Decade to Build" project. Even with the help of professionals, fundraising was an uphill struggle for LIU. Muriel Siebert, one of the LIU trustees who had become increasingly critical of the LIU financial model that was based on separate budgets for the three main campuses (Bishop, pers. comm. Aug. 5, 2010), resigned from the board, allegedly at the same lunch meeting where Steinberg was pitching her for a large donation and offering to have a building named after her.

In February 1995, Pattison's budget and finance committee issued a report highly critical of both LIU and the campus administrations. The fall enrollments had dropped slightly and the deficit, projected to be $2.9 million, was, in fact, more than $3.5 million. The cumulated deficit had increased by $10 million, from $7.1 million in 1987 to $17 million in 1995. In the committee's view, the university administration "had been remiss to the point of negligence" (SCC Archives B IV. b, Finance Committee to Executive Committee Feb. 27, 1995). Clearly, the LIU administration had ignored the admonition in the 1992 Middle States report (cited in epigraph at the beginning of this chapter). The committee called for a "top to bottom review of academic policies and programs, conducted by qualified and objective outside observers." This did not happen.

In the spring of 1995, the faculty agreed to defer a 3 percent wage increase as a gesture of their concern and their commitment to the survival of the college. The decision came after a number of heated debates in the union meetings. Elizabeth Granitz argued against the wage freeze, which, she noted, would hit the younger faculty the hardest because it would amount to a significant loss over a number of years. Robert Pattison and the union leaders, however, held that it was necessary in order to avert the closing of the campus. They also held out the hope that this action would gain the faculty leverage in any future negotiations with the university.

In July 1995, Bishop announced that Robert Sillerman had pledged a gift of one million dollars to the college if the trustees would pledge two million. It was the largest pledge ever made to the college up to that time (SCC Archive A I., b, Bishop File, Memorandum to the faculty and staff July 25, 1995). These funds would help to support a campus master plan that called for a new library and a 35,000 square foot building for classrooms and laboratories. Sillerman's challenge was welcomed by the university administrators, but it did not sit well with some of the other trustees who resented the implication that they were not giving the university their full support until prodded by Sillerman. Tensions related to the system of pledged donations was nothing new. The system of pledged donations had frequently resulted in some delicate negotiations when the donors were delinquent in making their promised payments. Roger Tilles, for example, pledged a gift of $50,000 in 1995, but three years later he was still $10,000 short of fulfilling that promise. This pattern for most donors must have been very frustrating to the university officials and fundraisers who had to be careful not to alienate the donors by pressing them too hard. They were well aware that these donors might close up their wallets and resign from the board if they became annoyed.[3]

The following fall, the faculty was able to use some of the leverage gained from the wage freeze they had accepted. The faculty and administration agreed to designate four "lead programs"—Marine Science, Visual Arts, Professional Writing, and Environmental Studies and Psychobiology—for development at the expense of programs with low enrollment and limited potential (SCC Archive B II. e, Report of the Committee on Academic Planning and Deficit Reduction Sept. 8, 1995). That same fall the Social Science department hired Paul Forestell, who had a PhD in Comparative Psychology from the University of Hawaii, to replace John Bridge who was suffering from a terminal illness. Forestell's background in the study of whale and dolphin behavior was a perfect fit for a college with a strong Marine Science program. Within a short time, under Forestell's leadership the Psychobiology program became one of the fastest-growing majors in the college.

In the 1990s, a resurgent emphasis on environmental issues was led by Scott Carlin, a geographer who joined the faculty in 1993, and Robert DeLuca, an adjunct professor in the Social Science division. Students formed a new environmental organization they named PEACE (Protecting Every Aspect Concerning the Environment). In 1994, DeLuca and Carlin worked with Michele Koestner, Vince Pascarella, and other members of PEACE to form a movement called "Greenprint Campus," designed to encourage campus-wide interest in a plan to turn Southampton College into a "green" institution. They advocated recycling, energy conservation, an environmentally friendly sewage system, and integration of environmental content into all of the college's courses across the curriculum. The movement drew enthusiastic support from New York State Assemblyman Fred Thiele (class of 1976) and from State Senator Kenneth LaValle. Although the call for curricular reform met resistance from the academic divisions, a program was developed in environmental studies by Ralph Herbert, a Sociology professor who had extensive contacts in Australia. In the spring of 1996, Herbert began taking students to Australia for a full semester to study sustainable systems and alternative agriculture. These were exactly what Pattison's committee had in mind when they wrote the 1994 report.

The reference in the 1994 report to the need for a "single powerful academic officer" was directed at Dean Siegel, who was regarded by many faculty as a part-time dean with limited authority. In the late fall of 1994, the faculty prepared an evaluation form for the faculty to use in evaluating administrators. Although Dean Siegel had strong support from some faculty, he did not fare well on the evaluation. The university agreed to give Dean Siegel a sabbatical for 1995–96 and use the "deanless" year to do a nationwide search for an experienced academic dean. It appeared to many that the

Figure 9.2. Robert DeLuca, president of the Group for the East End, Provost Tim Bishop, New York State Assemblyman Fred Thiele (class of 1976), New York State Senator Kenneth LaValle, and Southampton student Michele Koestner at the founding of Greenprint, 1994. *Courtesy of Southampton Town Historian.*

university had reversed their previous opposition to a national search for a high-priced academic dean as a quid pro quo for the wage freeze. Provost Bishop, however, denied that this was the case.

The new agreement also called for the hiring of an outside director of enrollment services who had national or regional experience in marketing and recruitment and a professional director for computer services. In the summer of 1996, President Steinberg, in an effort to deal with the budgetary and planning challenges, announced the appointment of Red Owl, a Native American of Cherokee descent, to serve as executive assistant to the president, and as planning officer. Dr. Red Owl who insisted that he be addressed by his Cherokee name, came with an impressive resume. He had earned his PhD in Public Administration from the University of Georgia and had taught in the graduate school of public affairs at the State University of New York at Albany. He was versed in the use of computer systems and had conducted workshops on the Middle States accreditation process. These changes in policy reflected a feeling among many in the faculty that the college had too long relied on administrators without extensive professional experience in outside institutions. The days of Bishop's "kitchen cabinet" were drawing to a close.

The Dean Parade Begins

The turn to professionals with extensive experience on the job did not, as Alice Flynn had noted, always work as well as expected. Over an eight-year period beginning in 1996 and ending with the closing of the college eight years later, the college had six deans. The parade of deans provides some insights into the administrative problems and uncertainty the college faced during its last years. The resurrection of a full-time academic dean at Southampton appeared to be getting off to a good start in the fall of 1996. A yearlong national search brought more than one hundred candidates before the search committee. The finalists came to campus where they were met with faculty, students, and staff. The search committee recommended Wayne Miller, who had served as an academic dean at the University of Houston before taking a position at the Kodiak Island Center of the University of Alaska. He had experience in the classroom and had published two books on literary criticism that had gone through several printings. In 1980–81, he was a senior Fulbright lecturer in Rome and served as director of the American Studies Graduate Center there. His resume and his smooth handling of the interview process led most of the LIU community to believe that Miller would provide the strong academic leadership that it needed. Michael Arons, who had replaced Walter Jones as vice president for academic affairs, announced Miller's appointment with great enthusiasm. "I anticipate that his appointment will bring vitality and continued excellence to Southampton's academic programs" (SCC Archives B I-d, Arons to Southampton faculty and staff May 13, 1996). What could go wrong?

The Community Disrupted: Outsourcing the Custodians, 1997–1998

The sense of a close campus community was manifest throughout the history of the college. The staff and administrators in Southampton Hall, however, were less aware of the informal social network that had developed over the years outside of their building. The students, faculty, department secretaries, and the custodians also felt a sense of community which had developed "below the radar." The academic division secretaries often became "surrogate mothers" to the students. Lee Stanley, the Social Science Division secretary nurtured many students who were having difficulty adjusting to collegiate life. Alumni who visited the campus often came by the office to thank her for her support during their student years. The custodians, in particular, were in a different world, seldom noticed by the administration until they raised grievances or threatened to strike for better wages and working conditions.

Mae Anderson, who cleaned the rooms in the Montauk Complex for thirty-seven years, recalled her warm memories of the students over the years. She said with a smile, "I remember more than one time after a very messy party in the dorm that the students told me, Mae don't worry, we will clean up the mess ourselves, just leave the mop and stuff" (It. 5). Pete Dosch, who cleaned the Social Science offices and classrooms, was on friendly terms with Lee Stanley, the division secretary, the faculty, the students, as well as the author who served as the Social Science division director for nearly a decade. If we needed any help or had any problem related to the building, we went directly to Pete and he promptly took care of things. George Harney, the foremen of the custodial staff, who had come up from Virginia in the 1950s to find work in the Long Island potato fields as a migrant laborer, was also popular among the students (Dolgon 2005, 167). He would often talk with them during his coffee break or when he finished work. When alumni returned long after graduation, they would look up Harney just to talk about their memories of their student years (Harney, pers. comm. 2005).

Wayne Hudson, who came to the college in 1987 after working as a bayman, a truck driver, and a mason's helper, had a similar relationship with the students. "After work sometimes I would sit with them and just talk about all sorts of things. When they complained about a teacher or a problem with the bursar, I would tell them to go and talk to them and I would remind them that they should appreciate what they had here, small classes and all that" (It. 29). Many of the students who came from working-class families may have felt more comfortable talking to the custodians than they did with the professional counselors. Hudson also told about how the students, on occasion, thanked him for keeping their dorm clean with a "Wayne Appreciation Day." They would clean the dorm for him (It. 29). The greatest honor, however, was when the students voted to have Wayne serve as a marshal at graduation. This position was traditionally filled by faculty or staff, who were selected by the graduating class after lengthy discussion.

On December 20, 1996, Provost Bishop sent a memo to Mary Lai, asking her permission to begin negotiations with Laro Service Systems regarding the outsourcing of the custodians' contract with the college. Laro, founded in 1981 by Robert Bertuglia, an enterprising high school graduate, had grown into the largest building service company in the country, employing 1,800 workers and bringing in $50 million in annual revenues (Winerip 1998). Laro was able to underbid their competition by paying minimum wages and by other "efficiencies of scale." Building operators were particularly interested in ridding themselves of the union employees, who pressed them for better wages and demanded decent working conditions. The aggressive anti-union tactics used by Laro had been cited by the National Labor Relations Board (*Laro Maintenance Corporation v. National Labor Relations Board* June 9, 1995). In an interview several years later, Dan Gearon, the director of the physical plant, acknowledged that they knew Laro was a "bottom feeder," but that it had come in with the lowest bid (It. 21).

Bishop denied that he planned this move as a transition to a nonunion contract when the current agreement with the custodial union expired in September 1998. Bishop noted that the contract with custodians' union Local 424 permitted outsourcing as long as the new contractor (Laro) assumed the existing conditions of employment (SCC Archive B II. G, Laro file, Collective Bargaining Agreement by and between Southampton College and Local 424 Oct 1995). He argued that the Laro contract was a "budget neutral" move to improve the efficiency of the custodial staff. George Harney and many of his custodial staff disputed the claim that they were inefficient, arguing that the problem was understaffing and outdated equipment, not inefficiency. Peter Dosch and Wayne Hudson pointed out that they were frequently asked to meet deadlines at the beginning of a new semester or between sessions of summer school, which often forced them to rush jobs with insufficient help (It. 29; Dosch, pers. comm. May 31, 2005). The custodians' real concern, however, was about what would happen after their contract ran out. Knowing Laro's reputation, they feared that Laro would not bargain in good faith.

When the contract was signed in January 1997, the workers felt a strong sense of betrayal by the college administration. What particularly hurt, said Wayne Hudson, was the feeling that they were disposable and had never really been a part of the college community: "Most of us had always felt that we were fully accepted as members of a small community because of the way we got on with students, secretaries, and some faculty, but we were suddenly cast adrift" (It. 29). "We came in on a Monday," said Hudson, "and were told that we didn't work for the college anymore; our jobs were gone and we would find out on Friday which of us would have jobs with Laro" (It. 29). Many in the meeting thought Dan Gearon, the director of buildings and grounds, appeared to take great pleasure in making the announcement and seemed to be relieved to be "washing his hands" of the custodians. They could take their complaints, their demands, and their grievances to Laro now, he said. Gearon later acknowledged to the author that the meeting became heated and that he lost his temper.

There was an immediate response from the faculty union. Robert Pattison sent out a memo to the members, noting that Gearon's heated threat about the loss of jobs was idle and asked any of the members who wished to help the custodians to meet with him and the author of this book (SCC Archive B II. g Laro file, Pattison to SCFT members Feb. 12, 1997). We felt that Gearon's outburst expressed an unfortunate negative attitude toward the workers, who now felt alienated from what they had viewed as a caring college community. George Harney said bitterly that they want to "sell us off like we were on the auction block" (quoted in Dolgon 2005, 177, fn.

FIGURE 9.3. Dan Gearon (right), director of physical plant, and George Harney, foreman of the custodial staff, adversaries in 1998, at the campus farewell party in 2005. *Photo by author.*

39). Pattison and the author met with George Harney to discuss the situation. We assured Harney that we would help him with any legal problems and offered our support and counsel. In particular, we would make sure that Laro honored the terms of the contract.

The custodians took action in their own behalf. They circulated a petition asking the students, faculty, and staff for their support and for their affirmation that the workers were still a part of the campus family. The petition asked, "If you feel this is unfair treatment to the dedicated custodial staff—some of who have been with LIU for over thirty years and you feel you deserve the security and familiarity of knowing who is cleaning your living and working areas on a day to day basis WE URGE YOU TO HELP US AND SIGN! We are family people with children, spouses and mortgages. Thank you for your support." The petition circulated quickly through the dorms and the faculty and staff offices, garnering an impressive number of signatures.

The most dramatic show of support, however, was organized by the faculty and students in the Friends World Program. Corey Dolgon and Bob Zellner, a civil rights activist who had organized protests for voting rights in the South during the 1960s, organized weekly meetings in the FWP offices and classrooms, bringing together custodians and students to form an organization called the Coalition for Justice (Dolgon 2005, 178). Dolgon and Zellner were convinced that racism had played a major role in the decision to outsource the custodial staff because a majority of them were black or Native American. Bishop denied this charge, and there was disagreement about this assertion among the custodians and the students. Dolgon, to his credit, noted that Brian Quist, one of the FWP students who interviewed Bishop at some length, concluded that "I no longer felt appropriate accusing the university of acting with racial bias. I feel that Tim [Bishop] is a good person who is not a racist and who simply made a stupid and unfair decision about switching to Laro" (quoted in Dolgon 2005, 188). Bishop himself later told the author that, in effect, he agreed with Brian's assessment. "It was," he said, "one of the worst mistakes I have ever made as an administrator."

The coalition wrote letters, distributed leaflets, and put up posters to draw the attention of the campus community to the issue (for a detailed account of the role of the coalition, see Dolgon 2005). Although, as Dolgon noted, most of the support came from FWP, there were some students involved, such as Melissa Arch-Walton, a pre-law major from the Shinnecock Reservation. In the late spring when the FWP students returned to campus from their study in the overseas centers, they took an active role in the Coalition for Justice. They held a rally in front of Southampton Hall on April 16 and invited the custodians to speak out about their concerns. Some faculty, including the author, also addressed the rally, calling for Provost Bishop to void the Laro contract. A group representing the coalition also staged a sit-in in Bishop's office.

In the fall of 1997, Bob Zellner taught a course for Friends World students that focused on the Laro issue. His students were invited to take active roles in the Coalition for Justice and in any other community organization that pressed for human rights. The students kept the pressure on Provost Bishop with several large demonstrations outside of Southampton Hall and in front of the main entrance to the campus. Although Wayne Hudson and several other custodians disagreed with Dolgon's emphasis on the role of race and class in the controversy, they all appreciated his support. "He put his job on the line for us," said Wayne, "and I think the student protesters just wore Bishop down" (It. 29).

Finally, in the late summer of 1998, Bishop terminated the Laro contract, which was not due to expire until the end of the year. He then began negotiations with the custodians on a new contract. Bishop acknowledged that he had not fully appreciated the feelings of the custodians about being a part of the campus community, but he denied that the protests had anything to do with his decision and he was particularly incensed about the accusation of racism (*The Southampton Independent* Sept. 23, 1998). In spite of his denial, the student demonstrations and sit-ins undoubtedly had created a distraction that Bishop was eager to end.

Wayne Miller's Seven Hundred Days, 1996–1998

In July 1996, President Steinberg sent out a "State of the University" memorandum in which he said with great pleasure, "the University is in a stronger financial position than it has enjoyed for many, many years. He also noted with pride that the university had made several key academic and administrative appointments and that in all cases "our first choice accepted our invitation" (SCC Archive B, II. d, Memorandum July 1, 1996). Roger Rosenblatt, author, critic, and frequent essayist on the PBS news hour, had agreed to accept an endowed chair in professional writing. Dean Miller was the next appointment mentioned by Steinberg. He was off to a good start.

At the beginning of the Fall 1996 semester, Steinberg repeated his enthusiastic assessment of the university's finances and went on to affirm his "unequivocal support" for Southampton College (SCC Archive B IV, e. Faculty Council Minutes Sept. 25, 1996). The enrollment was up slightly from 1,090 in 1995 to 1,106, and construction had begun on a $6.5 million 30,000- square foot building that would house classrooms, a larger lecture hall, and WPBX-FM, the campus radio station. The building, later called "Chancellor's Hall," was to be paid for with a municipal bond issue through the New York State Dormitory Authority and with the funds raised from the LIU trustees in response to Sillerman's "challenge pledge." This was to be the first new facility on campus since the construction of the art studio and the Marine Science Station laboratory in 1985.

What Steinberg did not mention, however, was that the annual deficits were continuing to increase. In the spring of 1996, the college had projected a $2.5 million budget deficit for 1996–97 (*Southampton Press* May 2, 1996). The projection was off by over $2 million. In the fall of 1997, Mary Lai announced that the deficit was actually $4.2 million, in part because the financial aid to students had increased by nearly $1 million. There was, therefore, some understandable skepticism among faculty and administrators about Steinberg's rosy description of the university's financial situation. The accumulated debt continued to increase like a cancer on the fiscal health of the college.

Miller, however, appeared not to notice the implications of the deficits. After his first semester on the job, he distributed his "talking points" for a campus-wide discussion about the future of the college. The perceived strengths, said Miller, included the obvious: the Marine Science program, the appointment of Roger Rosenblatt, and the opportunities for interaction with the artists and writers on the East End. No surprise here, but his list of "perceived weaknesses" did have one surprise. He mentioned the understaffed programs, the aging physical plant, and the inadequate library facilities, but made no mention of the lack of university resources for development. Miller, whose previous administrative experience had been at two large universities with extensive funds for development, appeared to be in denial about the fact that LIU was a tuition-driven institution with no significant endowment (SCC Archive B II. d, Miller Memorandum Jan. 24, 1997).

Dean Miller began ambitious plans to develop master's degree programs. "We have always had a good marine science/biology department," he said, "what we want to do now is to have four or five other excellent programs" (*Southampton Press* July 17, 1997). These words could have been lifted verbatim from comments made earlier by Glanz, Marmion, and Wilson. Miller worked with Robert Pattison, the Humanities division director, to develop what became a successful master's program in Fine Arts and Writing and he encouraged the expansion of a master's degree in Gerontology, which had been put in place earlier by Chris Hayes, a professor in the Psychology department. Miller also worked with professor Donald Baker on the plans for a Women's Studies program. The attempt to develop such programs was, of course, not new; it had been a policy goal from the opening of the college. The problem, as Miller was soon to discover, was that the university simply did not have the capital necessary to establish competitive programs in such areas.

Miller also paid no attention to institutional history. His plan for the development of the MFA in Fine Arts, for example, was based on the assumption that the program would be supported by an "inner circle" of artists and by linkages to East End organizations devoted to painting and sculpture, particularly museums and galleries. When one faculty member told him that this approach had first been proposed by Edward Glanz in 1962 and pursued actively by Harry Marmion and Donald Wilson in the 1980s with similar unsuccessful results, Miller dismissed these warnings with an offhand comment about senior faculty members burdened with defeatist perspectives. Miller's plans envisioned seven more master's programs over the next five years. By the spring of 2002, he hoped to have sixteen graduate majors in place. When that time came, however, there were five master's programs, only one of which had been launched by Miller. The Gerontology master's that had received disproportionate funds and attention from Miller had been phased out because of persistent low enrollments. The successful master's in professional writing, however, did turn out to be Miller's lasting legacy.

In the fall of his second year as dean, there were indications that Miller was having trouble dealing with the demands of his office. He had difficulty with very simple things. The author recalls bringing Miller the Social Science department's recommendations for promotion and tenure in a large packet, which included resumes and copies of faculty publications, well in advance of the deadline. After a brief conversation in his office, the author placed the packet on the dean's couch and left as a small delegation from the Bay Street Theater group came in for a meeting. To the author's surprise, the day before the deadline Miller sent out a frantic request to the Social Science department for the materials. After a time of confusion, Miller's secretary discovered the packet under the couch in his office. Miller or someone in the visiting delegation had cleared them off the couch and put them underneath, where they had remained for at least two weeks. There were other much more serious lapses. As a result of Miller's inaction, the new master's in Fine Arts and Professional Writing had been placed in jeopardy, requiring last-minute revision, in part because Miller had given the grant's authors inaccurate information about the budget.

Faculty and staff mentioned similar incidents and noted that his decisions often seemed a bit erratic and sometimes contradictory (It. 25; It. 28). Rumors about a drinking problem were fueled by the report on a local radio station that Miller had been arrested for driving under the influence of alcohol (Charles Hitchcock, pers. comm.) One campus administrator told the author that Miller "seemed to be unraveling before our eyes." The following spring, Professor Charles Hitchcock, the chair of the faculty executive committee, sent a memo to Michael Arons, the academic vice president, expressing the faculty's "great concerns about the academic leadership on campus. . . . Faculties have been demoralized, divided and politicized by inappropriate or questionable actions by the Dean. Members of the Academic Standards Committee, which reviews appeals submitted by students who have been dismissed for academic reasons, reported that Dean Miller all too frequently arbitrarily reversed their decisions." Another serious complaint noted by Hitchcock was Miller's attitude toward women. "Although a proponent of the women's Studies Program," continued the Hitchcock memo, "the Dean refers to the 'lovely' Miss X or the 'beauteous' Miss Y, demeaning these women in the eyes of the full faculty. Equally as important are concerns voiced by several women who feel that his off-handed comments are inappropriate and disturbing . . . there is also a sense of unequal treatment" (SCC Archives B, II. F, box 3, Memo, Hitchcock to Arons May 13, 1998).

That was the final nail in Miller's coffin. During the summer, the university negotiated a settlement terminating his contract, which included an agreement not to mention his problems with alcohol. Miller was later hired by the University of Tampa in Florida. Although the university kept its word, a faculty member, acting independently contacted the university in Florida and informed them about Miller's drinking. Miller then sued LIU for violating the agreement. The outcome of his suit was never disclosed. Miller left administration soon after he arrived in Tampa, and ended his academic career teaching freshman English. The student evaluations for 2004 through 2008 were most complimentary. Miller died in his sleep at the age of sixty-seven, in February 2008.

The Southampton Five Year Success Initiative, 1998–2003

The disconnect between the LIU Board of Trustees and the Southampton campus was underscored on April 1, 1998, a month prior to Miller's dismissal, when the LIU Board of Trustees passed a resolution affirming their "historic commitment to the University's campus in the Hamptons," citing as evidence of its commitment to Southampton College the appointment of Wayne Miller in 1996 (SCC Archives B II. d., Board Resolution April 1, 1998). Clearly, the board had not been informed about the growing dissatisfaction with Miller over the past two years, which finally led to his dismissal before the ink was dry on their resolution.

In August 1998, the board acknowledged that the yearly deficits at the campus continued to increase the campus debt, but anticipated that the enrollment would increase significantly and lead to "fiscal sufficiency." The board pointed out that they had explored every available option, even a proposal to close the college. They "unanimously rejoiced in the conclusion that we have a very good chance of turning the Southampton Campus into a profitable division of LIU." The deficit reduction in the five-year initiative that would begin immediately would, by 2003, bring Southampton a break-even point. This would be accomplished by an increase in enrollment, improved retention rates, reduced tuition discount rates, and increased fundraising (SCC Archive A, I, k, Steinberg to Jean Moore, Middle States Association Aug. 28, 1998). The trustees, said Steinberg, went on to resolve that "this board reaffirms its unequivocal belief in the promise of Southampton College and commits the University to make those investments deemed necessary to enable the College to achieve fiscal sufficiency, national prominence, and continued academic excellence."

Although the trustees stated that the university would make investments, it soon became clear that Southampton College would be expected to share the burden of fundraising. This was always a considerable challenge. The Southampton College board of overseers, formed in 1996 to replace the moribund president's advisory council, which had been established during the early years of the college to engage potential donors, had never been able to raise significant funds. The group was a loosely structured advisory body of about twenty members including alumni, local businessmen, faculty members, members of the Long Island University Board of Trustees, and former president Harry Marmion, who had continued his interest and his support for the college over the years (SCC Archives B, II, g). Marmion, who had kept his primary residence in Southampton, had become involved in campus affairs after his retirement from Fairleigh Dickenson University. The overseers met three or four times a year to discuss the state of the college, but it had no decision-making power. Although the overseers, with the exception of the faculty members, had been appointed expressly to help raise money, either from their own resources or from their personal contacts, they were frequently evasive when asked for firm pledges or hard cash. Two years after the initiative was launched, Tom Lloyd wrote a memo to Bishop and Sillerman lamenting the anemic response from the overseers who had been asked to support the library addition (SCC Archive B, II, g Nov. 15, 2000). Fifteen of the twenty-three members had made no commitment and three said "maybe." Referring to one member, Lloyd wrote with some sarcasm that an appeal by letter was "not worth an additional stamp." In another case, Lloyd suggested to Provost Bishop that he sit down over a beer with one of the reluctant overseers and "shame him" into a pledge.

There were, however, some good omens in 1997 and 1998, which supported the board's optimism. In the fall of 1997, Michael Brophy, the newly appointed assistant provost for enrollment services, announced with pride that the enrollment had increased by about thirty-five students and spoke enthusiastically about the new building. The following year, the enrollment reached 1,477, the highest since the 1960s. LIU received a $12 million gift from Edmund Pratt Jr. in June as Miller was making his exit. Pratt, whose son had graduated from C. W. Post, was a friend of Eugene Luntey, the chairman of the LIU Board of Trustees. His gift was the largest ever received by the university. One-third of the funds were designated for the Southampton campus. A week later, Robert Sillerman pledged a donation of $4 million, quieting some of the LIU trustees who had expressed skepticism about Sillerman the year before. The *Sag Harbor Express* ran a story with the headline "Southampton College's Future Looks Bright" (Oct. 29, 1998). Another grant came through the efforts of Congressman Michael Forbes, who secured $1 million in federal funds for the Marine Science Center (*Southampton Press* Nov. 19, 1998). The summer workshops for writers and artists, which featured participation by Peter Matthiessen, Leon Uris, Larry Rivers, and Roger Rosenblatt, also drew positive attention from the press. In 1999 the Greenprint committee successfully lobbied for the administration to prepare a plan to develop a solar aquatic waste treatment plant that would replace the antiquated septic system. The outdated system had to be pumped out regularly and could not prevent some seepage into Shinnecock Bay. A new, modular, waste management system would be moderately expensive to install, but in the long run it would be much cheaper and more efficient.

The number of Fulbrights continued to grow. An unprecedented number of seventeen students received Fulbright awards in a three-year period from 1995 to 1999. No other small liberal arts college in the country had earned that many Fulbrights in any three-year period.[4] These awards brought the number of student Fulbrights to thirty-one over a twenty-three-year period. In 1998, the author received a Fulbright to teach Native American Studies in Hungary. These Fulbright awards were quite an accomplishment for a small college. The Fulbrights and other honors earned by Southampton graduates were cited by the Cousteau Society in France as reasons for choosing Southampton College to be its sole North American affiliate at a ceremony in La Rochelle, France (*Southampton Press* June 11, 1998).

There were other honors for Southampton faculty and administrators. Professor Sandra Shumway and two scientists from the University of North Carolina were awarded a $512,000 grant to study a microbe that destroys fish. Shumway (class of 1974), one of Southampton College's distinguished alumnae, had been hired by Dean Siegel in 1995. In 1998 Shumway and the author received the Trustees Award for Scholarly Achievement (TASA).

FIGURE 9.4. Professor Sandra Shumway and the author receiving Trustees Award for Scholarly Achievement (TASA), Spring 1998. *Courtesy of Southampton Town Historian.*

FIGURE 9.5. Professor John Neill and Psychobiology student Hillary Downes-Vogel. *Courtesy of Southampton Town Historian.*

In addition, the Co-op career development program under the direction of John McCrudden received an award for its outstanding work in preparing students for careers on Long Island. In 1998, John Neil, an instructor in Neurology from the Harvard Medical School in Boston, with a research emphasis on autism and epilepsy, joined the psychobiology faculty, adding another important dimension to the major. Neill supervised the Long island "Brain Bee," for advanced and highly motivated high school students. This contest, which brought many talented students to the campus, gave the college some very positive publicity. One of these students, Saroj Kunnakkat, from Lynbrook, Long Island, placed first in the International Brain Bee held in Baltimore (*Newsday* April 20, 2003). Others coached by Neill took top places each year in the Brain Bee.

In addition to the Fulbright recipients, other graduates from the Natural Science programs helped to improve the college image. Three of them joined the Peace Corps and served in very demanding circumstances in rural

African villages. Kate Honeywell (1992) put her Environmental Science and Geology background to good use as a volunteer in the Ivory Coast where she worked as the manger of an environmental management project. Kelly Ernst (1995) majored in Biology and went to Malawi in East Africa to serve as a child survival officer, vaccinating children and monitoring prenatal care and infant nutrition programs. Kerith Lewis (1994) a Marine Science/Biology major went to Cameroon to work in an aquaculture program. The students wrote back to professors Tom Haresign and Howard Reisman, describing their experiences and thanking them for their help and support during their undergraduate years (SCC Archive B, IV, c).

The 1998 graduation marked the first time that the children of alumni were among the graduates. Caprice Crippen, a Communications major and a Shinnecock Indian, whose mother, Annette Crippen, earned her degree in 1982 and then went on to work at the college, serving at that time as the assistant director of the higher educational opportunities program, graduated Summa Cum Laude. Melinda Meyer, a Marine Science major, whose father Charles graduated in 1969, was vice president of the sophomore class, and David Jaycox whose father Larry graduated in 1967, was a Chemistry major, who worked, as his father had, as a lab assistant on campus.

In the fall of 1998, the new academic center was opened in a ceremony hosted by Provost Bishop and Chancellor Robert Sillerman. The new building was named Chancellors Hall by Sillerman, whose generous donations helped pay for the $10 million facility. The building in its final form housed four laboratories, six classrooms, a lecture hall, three seminar rooms, and a studio for WPBX-FM. The campus had also undergone new landscaping and several of the dorms had been renovated. The administration hoped that these improvements in the facilities would help with recruiting and retention and would build on the romantic draw of off-campus experiences such as the Seamester, which continued to attract students from across the country. An article in the Allentown, Pennsylvania, *Morning Call* (Feb. 4, 1999), for example, celebrated the Seamester experiences of Jamie Druckenmiller, a student from Zionsville. Jamie, who participated in the fall 1999 Seamester, spoke enthusiastically about life on the ship where the students served as the crew and about her visits to exotic ports of call in the Caribbean.

Mary Topping's emphasis on the development of women's sports continued with great success. In the spring of 1999, the women's basketball team won its second straight ECAC basketball championship, and Rita Breivaite, a foreign student from Lithuania, was selected tournament MVP for the second consecutive year (*Windmill* March 31, 1999). That same spring, the *Windmill*, under the editorship of Richard Rosentreter, won journalism awards from *Newsday* in the categories of layout design (John LaFountain) and local history (Jaime M. Saberito). The paper won four more *Newsday* awards the following year and a second place in a statewide prestigious New York Press Association competition.

Although these accomplishments were cause for optimism, endemic problems remained. In addition to the problems with the local fundraising, there were other some sobering notes during this same period. The graduation rate was still around 40 percent. In the fall of 1998, Dr. Shumway sent a memo to Brophy and Bishop with unsettling news. She had received promotional literature from the University of Maine announcing a new program in undergraduate Marine Science and a new state of the art Marine Station in Walpole. Southampton no longer enjoyed the "luxury of being one of the few schools in the country to offer an undergraduate degree in marine science," and Dr. Shumway warned that "at our current rate of growth we are going to fall behind the pack very quickly." If we do not diversify very quickly, she added, we will not remain competitive (SCC Archives B, II, f, box 3 Shumway to Brophy/Bishop Sept. 28, 1998). Another related warning was that these competitive Marine Science programs were much more generously funded by the host institutions. The concern for a more diversified academic offering was, of course, a mantra that had been recited for decades by Southampton administrators and faculty, but Shumway's warning put it in a much starker context.

Lewis Greenstein, who served as interim dean for 1998–99 while continuing as director of the Friends World Program, was in no position to initiate a response to the challenge articulated by Shumway. There was nothing much to do except mark time while the search for a new, full-time academic leader was completed. Fortunately the crisis was still a few years away. The new Marine Science programs gradually taking shape in several universities along the Atlantic coast would not be a serious threat until the end of the millennium, but clearly time was running out. The golden goose was in danger.

A search committee for a new dean began its work in the fall. The committee, chaired by Southampton's Charles Hitchcock and Bonnie Bernstein from the University Center, reviewed the resumes and had narrowed the field of more than seventy candidates to four by November 1998. The process continued into the following spring as each of the four finalists came to the campus and was interviewed by faculty, staff, and students. In April, academic vice president Michael Arons announced the appointment of Dr. Margaret Madden as the new dean of academic affairs at Southampton. Dr. Madden had an impressive resume, which included a PhD in Social Psychology from the University of Massachusetts, experience as an academic dean at Lawrence University, in Wisconsin, more than fifteen years in the college classroom, awards for teaching excellence, active participation in academic organizations, thirty publications in professional journals,

FIGURE 9.6. Dean (1999–2000) Maggie Madden and Lawrence McCann, director of Education. *Courtesy of Southampton Town Historian.*

thirty-five presentations at professional conferences, extensive work in community organizations, and a leadership role in campus programs focusing on women's issues.

DEAN MARGARET MADDEN'S 700 DAYS, 1999–2001

In the fall of 1999, there was again cause for some optimism. Enrollment had increased by about 4 percent. Sillerman and his wife Laura pledged another $5 million gift to support the construction of a new library. The popular undergraduate program in Psychobiology, under the direction of Paul Forestell, continued to grow, as did the graduate programs in Education and Writing. Allison Wright, one of Forestell's students, won an award of $1,000 to support her study of dolphins in Costa Rica. Professors Chris Gobler and Robert Turner won a $18,562 grant to study coastal morphology. Jill Mandel, a senior majoring in Marine Science, spent the fall semester on an internship, arranged by Professor Shumway, studying penguins and sea birds on the Dassen Island Nature Reserve in South Africa. The students in PEACE expanded the Greenprint initiative to include the Institute for Sustainable Development, revived the campus recycling program and advocated the development of a composting program and a solar aquatic sewage treatment plant (Gregory 2003, 33–36).

The success of women's sports was matched by the men's soccer team, which went undefeated that fall. At their annual convention in Baltimore, the National Soccer Coaches Association honored coach Edward Goodhines and the players, led by Johan Kron, a foreign student from Sweden. Coach Goodhines, named Coach of the Year, was on his way to becoming the winningest coach in the college's history. The college faculty, in stark contrast to the faculties on the other LIU campuses, was willing to work with the local administration in search of solutions to the problems facing the college. Yoshi Higa, the popular Fine Arts professor, biked his way across the country to raise funds for a fine arts scholarship. The "Pedaling Professor," as he was dubbed in the media, raised funds and drew attention to the college.

That was the good news; the bad news, not surprisingly, involved the college finances. Provost Bishop told a *Windmill* reporter that the college had accumulated a $40 million debt and would run a deficit of about $2.9 million in an annual operating budget of about $30 miliion for the 1999–2000 college year (Dec. 14, 2000). These were ominous figures. In the seven years

FIGURE 9.7. Yoshi Higa, Fine Arts Division, Professor Higa rode his bicycle across the continent to raise money for scholarships. *Courtesy of Southampton Town Historian.*

from 1986 to 1993 the cumulated debt had risen by $10 million and in the following six years from 1993 to 2000 the debt had risen by twice that amount. Little progress had been made on the outcomes assessment program in spite of the strongly worded recommendations from Middle States. Madden moved quickly to revive the campus efforts on the outcomes assessment. Dr. Donna Ferrara, the outcomes assessment coordinator, had begun work in 1996 in a delayed response to the recommendations made in the 1992–94 Middle States report. The progress of the outcomes assessment had also been interrupted by the lack of consistent leadership from the dean's office prior to the arrival of Dean Madden and had been hampered by the inadequate investment of funds in the program. The outcomes staff had managed to establish a system for collecting the necessary data to evaluate academic programs and administrative policy, but little else had been accomplished. There was growing concern that the 2002 Middle States team would be extremely critical if their 1992–94 recommendations had not been acted upon.

Madden established a faculty long-term planning committee to deal with these concerns. Her approach was marked by transparency and inclusivity. She wanted the faculty to be directly involved in the process. Faculty committees focused on the familiar problems of recruitment and retention, which had historically plagued the college, as well as on the costs of academic programs. The latter involved such contentious issues as class size, the use of adjunct faculty, and scholarship aid.

At the commencement ceremony in May 2000, preceding a commencement address by Billy Joel, Chancellor Sillerman announced that he had pledged a new donation of $15 million to Southampton College. Ten million was designated for scholarships and $5 million went to the college library. President Steinberg sent a memorandum to the Southampton College community noting that "[t]his is the largest single gift ever for Southampton College and is a stunning reaffirmation of the University's mission" (SCC Archive A, b, Steinberg Memo May 22, 2000). Another, smaller gift of a half-million from Michael Avram actually posed a bit of a problem for Provost Bishop. Avram wanted to have the Fincke Fine Arts Theater renamed after him. Bishop had to approach the Fincke family and persuade them to relinquish this well-deserved honor. Surprisingly, they agreed. Ironically, their willingness to accept this loss of official recognition gracefully should have earned them a place of honor as well.

Shortly after these successful fundraising endeavors, Chancellor Sillerman and President Steinberg made a decision that resulted in a sharp drop in tuition revenues and significantly increased the accumulated debt. During the fall of 2000, the faculty planning committees met regularly to address a series of goals set at the beginning of the semester. There were complaints that the central university administration was too often attempting to micromanage affairs at Southampton without taking the time to consult with the local administration, a familiar theme in LIU history. The case in point made by many in the faculty was a decision the previous spring by Michael Brophy at the urging of Steinberg and Sillerman to change the recruitment strategy. Instead of placing emphasis on the same demographic areas where we had been successful in the past, the recruiting advertisements and visitations would shift to wealthier areas where students had higher board scores. This decision was made at a time when the faculty was making a great effort, begun in 1994, to improve the academic quality of their programs. The new strategy simply ignored that long-range goal in favor of a quick fix based on an attempt to "improve the customer rather than the product." It was an idea that Steinberg had mentioned informally at a faculty meeting in 1994 (see above).

The disastrous result of this strategy did not surprise Pattison and the other faculty members who had served on the faculty budget and finance committee in 1994. Their report had warned that the problem with enrollment was the perception that, with the exception of Marine Science, the academic programs were not worth the money charged for tuition (see above). The freshman enrollment for September 2000 fell by nearly one hundred students, at a time when the accumulated college debt was over $40 million. The Board of Trustees, acknowledging that their "quick fix" had failed, now put more pressure on Dean Madden to speed up her progress on program improvement. At the same time, administrators at the University Center bypassed Madden and began micromanaging class schedules and teaching assignments. These interventions undermined Dean Madden's authority and caused confusion and resentment. Madden felt that these efforts were, in part, motivated by a subtle bias against women (pers. comm. July 28, 2005). There were coded statements referring to "weak leadership," incapable of "pushing things along faster." These were contradictory signals from the understanding she had when she was hired. She had been told that she had three to five years to develop an improved academic offering. Now it appeared the board and the university administrators had panicked a bit following the consequences of their own poorly advised interference with recruitment.

Madden, nevertheless, went ahead with a comprehensive proposal for the evaluation of academic programs. In January 2001, she asked for a review of the progress made in the previous fall and the development of an "action plan" for the spring. The planning group also began work on the accreditation self-study for the 2002 Middle States review. Specific tasks were assigned to individual faculty members and administrators. No one from the university administration advised her that the timetable had changed and that she needed to speed up the progress of her reform program. It is unlikely that such an endeavor would have been possible anyway without arbitrarily imposing solutions on the faculty that would surely have caused long-lasting resentment.

On April 12, when a reporter for the *Windmill* interviewed her, Dean Madden was unaware that the university administrators had already decided to fire her. She was popular with the students and spoke with enthusiasm to the reporter about the work she was doing with the faculty on academic program reform and on the outcomes assessment. She also said that she looked forward to the many good changes on the college horizon such as the new library and the renovations on the dorms, the Marine Science Station, and the science laboratories. Shortly after the interview, academic vice president Michael Arons asked her to come up to the University Center for a meeting, but said nothing about the agenda.

"I was totally blindsided," she said. Arons told her that she was being given a face-saving appointment as university dean for learning technology. Arons said that her replacement, James Larocca, a friend of President Steinberg, would take over the deanship beginning in September. Larocca was a lawyer who had served as New York State commissioner of energy and transportation and was currently the president of the Long Island Association, a business group. "What does he bring to the job that I don't have," she asked. Arons replied that he would bring a more decisive, "business approach" to the position. The reference to "decisiveness" could certainly be read as a code word covering a gender bias. It inadvertently highlighted the panicked "decisive" decisions made by the male administrators and the board of trustees. Steinberg also felt that although Larocca had no experience in academic administration, his business and political contacts would bring in donations. Dean Madden suspected that there was another factor involved. She believed that Steinberg and Arons wanted to make a dramatic gesture that would deflect criticism from the board about the drop in enrollment and what appeared to them to be the slow pace of program reform. The LIU trustees, she noted, had little understanding about the challenges involved in curricular and academic program reform. They were looking for the sort of "quick fix" that was possible in their own business operations.

When the author asked Larocca about Madden's administration, he responded quite candidly: "I was stunned when she was fired; I thought that she was doing a good job." He added that "she had prepared the groundwork for the Middle States evaluation and had resolved other problems related to academics" (It. 32). It was a humiliating and insulting affair for Dean Madden. She was given a small office in the back of the Montauk dorm next to the boiler room, where few people ever ventured. The negative assessment of Margaret Madden by LIU administrators was in sharp contrast to the view held by the state university at Potsdam. Dean Madden was hired the following semester to serve as Potsdam's provost in charge of academic affairs. She continues to perform successfully in that position as this book goes to press.

Dean James Larocca's 240 Days, Sept. 2001–May 2002

There was no academic leadership at Southampton from April through the following September. Michael Brophy scrambled to regain the "market share" of potential student recruits that he had lost in 2000 (SCC Archive B IV b, Memo: Brophy to Southampton Faculty Dec. 6, 2001). He returned to the areas where the college had traditionally recruited and did manage to increase the number of freshmen by about fifty in the fall of 2001. It was not possible, however, to do much better after a year of lost contacts. Rivals quickly stepped into the opening. Other four-year colleges on Long Island were offering more attractive financial packages. Tuition and fees for Dowling College were $12,849; St. Joseph's charged $10,424, and Stony Brook charged $4,268. Southampton, in sharp contrast, charged $18,077. The freshman enrollment, projected by Brophy's office in the spring of 2001 to be 430 students, was only 405, and if the current pattern for graduation rates continued, 67 percent of them would leave the college prior to graduation. The national graduation rate for average for schools similar to Southampton College was about 50 percent (SCC Archive A, II, k, Student Development and Enrollment Services Report Fall 2001). Brophy estimated that it would take another three years (2004) to bring the enrollment back up to what it had been in 1999. In the absence of academic leadership, the momentum on the academic reform programs was slowed and would later be abandoned entirely when Sillerman, Steinberg, and Jeffrey Kane, who had replaced Michael Arons as university vice president for academic affairs in May 2002, pressed the faculty to develop a radical new interdisciplinary curriculum and a new organizational structure that eliminated the existing academic divisions.

The new dean came with a heavy burden. There had been no campus search committee, no vetting process, no letters of recommendation, and no advance warning. For the campus community Larocca's appointment was a classic reenforcement of the longstanding complaint concerning the arrogant and arbitrary actions by the University Center administrators. Larocca was an unknown outsider, with very limited academic credentials, who had been suddenly parachuted onto the campus. It was insulting for many at Southampton to hear that Larocca, in his own words, had been hired to "turn the college around," suggesting that a "man on a white horse" was the answer to their problems. These clichés had surfaced every time a new administrator was hired in the wake of a fired predecessor.

There were also cynical comments about the nature of Larocca's contract. Larocca had hired a legal consultant to negotiate a ten-year contract with a stipulation that he would retain his title as dean and the opportunity to teach an adjunct course at another university center in the event that the college closed. It was a somewhat counterintuitive arrangement. He was being hired to "turn the college around," at the same time he was guaranteed a job in the event that he failed.

The new dean understood that his task was to move as quickly as possible to deal with the financial problems rather than to devote his time and energy to the challenging tasks involved with academic program reform, which had been the focus of the previous dean. Larocca soon found that his attempts to employ the organizational approaches he had successfully used in government and in nonprofit systems did not work in academia. He discovered that the dean's limited authority over personnel and budgetary matters prevented him from making rapid and significant changes. When he tried to make changes in the recruitment procedures, he was rebuffed by Michael Brophy. When he tried to make changes in faculty office assignments, he was ignored. His discretionary funds, he said, were open to raiding by other administrators (It. 32). He also felt that Provost Bishop and Jeff Kane, from the University Center, too often interfered in matters that should be handled by the dean.

By the middle of his first semester as dean, Larocca was convinced that the campus was dysfunctional and had been so for the past twenty years. His relationship with President Steinberg now became quite contentious. It was clear that Larocca's frustration stemmed from his inexperience with educational administration, and in part, from his own personal attributes. Although he had support from some faculty, he often came across to others as arrogant and inflexible, qualities that may not have been a problem in another organizational setting. He had experienced considerable success in the business world, but he was clearly not a good fit for Southampton College. When Larocca resigned in May 2002, he said, "I came into this business to teach and to write and found myself consumed with paperwork and administrative duties" (*New York Times* May 2, 2002). This was a somewhat surprising comment for an academic administrator to make. One had to wonder why he expected that the role of an academic dean would not involve paperwork and be burdened with administrative duties.

In spite of the financial clouds and the administrative problems, there were many positive things happening on campus. John Neill continued his research on brain function and worked with local fifth and sixth grade students on a community grant related to music and cognition. Paul Forestell took students on field trips along the Atlantic coast to study whale behavior and collaborated with Dr. Maria Kretzmann, a colleague in the Natural Science department, on a survey of harbor seals around Long Island. In 2001, Dr. Arthur Goldberg took his Tropical Field Studies class on a research trip to the upper reaches of the Amazon in Brazil.

The one consistent positive note in the Middle States evaluations over the years was praise for the quality of the college faculty, for the creative ways

FIGURE 9.8 Students in Dr. Goldberg's Tropical Field Studies class in the Amazon rainforest 2001. *Courtesy of Arthur Goldberg.*

that they integrated their teaching and their research. Southampton students were regularly involved in primary research. The students in PEACE successfully lobbied for a voluntary "green fee" of $20 on all students to pay the salary of a full-time administrator who would coordinate all of the campus environmental activities. In Fall 2002, Peter Maniscalco, who was hired to fill this position, began an energy audit of the campus buildings with the cooperation of LIPA that resulted in recommendations that would save the college about $459,697 in energy costs over a ten-year period. In the spring of 2002, the Greenprint Committee and the PEACE members led by Kasey Jacobs, Valerie Sudak, and Aatisha Singh negotiated an $80,000 grant from the U.S. Department of Energy and LIPA (Long Island Power Authority) to erect a one hundred foot high ten kilowatt windmill on campus that was linked into the campus power grid.

Charles Hitchcock, a Sociology professor who had served the college for thirty-five years, was appointed as interim dean. Hitchcock, the recipient of the Newton Prize for teaching excellence, had served as the director of the Social Science division for several terms and had held a number of other administrative positions. He had been the founding director of the HEOP program and had served as director of counseling. He was another "everywhere man." Hitchcock said that he would accept the position on a permanent basis provided that he received strong support from the faculty.

The End of an Era: Provost Bishop Goes to Washington

On March 12, 2002, Provost Bishop, with the encouragement and considerable financial support from Robert Sillerman, took a leave of absence from the college to run as a Democratic candidate for the First Congressional District in New York State. He left with a feeling of some satisfaction for his accomplishments at Southampton.[5] The freshman program that he initiated served the college well. It reenforced the student-centered campus culture that was one of the more significant legacies of Southampton College. Bishop was an important stabilizing factor during the times of chaos and crises that had so often plagued the college throughout its sixty-year history.

Tim Bishop had literally grown up with the college. He had a very special connection with the campus community. Even his critics respected his honesty and his total commitment to the college. Tim attended most of the college events from athletics to theater programs and guest lectures. His "people skills," developed over the years at the college, served him well in his new career. Bishop is beginning his sixth term in office as this book goes to press.

There are many who felt that his departure was a foreshadowing of 2004. Mary Lai, who retired in December 2003, and Bishop were the two people in the university who had struggled so hard to keep the campus running. They were replaced by professional administrators, who were moved primarily by cold numbers rather than sentiment and loyalty to Southampton College. Lai and Bishop were most comfortable with a hands-on, somewhat "folksy" approach to administration. Tim attended most all of the college events, wore T-shirts and caps emblazoned with the college logo, developed personal relationships with students, staff, and faculty, and fought as hard as he could to protect the interests of Southampton College in the ongoing struggle against competing forces within the university. Those cold hard numbers, however, were telling a very sober story. The annual deficit for 2002 was nearly $5 million.

Chapter Ten

Inventing a New College, 2002–2003

Southampton has a very exciting future ahead in the 21st century.
—President Steinberg, Nov. 22, 2002

The Price Waterhouse Report: "No more business as usual"

In the spring of 2002, the LIU Board of Trustees, concerned about the Southampton College debt, which had reached $50 million, and the budget that was projected to run a $5 million deficit for 2001–02, established a special subcommittee to focus on Southampton. There were other concerns as well. The disproportionately high cost of the college tuition, noted in the previous chapter, was offset by the high discount rate. The rates were necessitated by the income level of the families who were sending students to Southampton College. These families, mostly from suburban Long Island, who were bringing in an average of about $50,000 per year, could not afford to spend half of their yearly income on tuition and fees. As a result, the college had to offer discounted rates in order to bring in an adequate critical mass of new students. The result, of course, noted in many previous reports, was that the loss of this revenue made it difficult for Southampton to develop new programs or to improve those currently being offered. The Marine Science program, for example, had lost its competitive edge to better financed programs in Roger Williams College, Coastal Carolina, University of Tampa, and Eckerd College.

Although the problems facing the college had been identified ad nauseum over the years by the faculty and administration at Southampton, the trustees, at the urging of Roger Tilles, hired a consultant firm, Price Waterhouse Cooper (PwC), to study the college and make recommendations to them. This company, the second-largest professional services firm in the world, is best known for supervising Academy Awards ballots and establishing tax shelters for the wealthy. The cost of their services was not revealed, but it must have been a very expensive undertaking for a board concerned about financial problems facing the university. On August 4, Interim Provost Lee Kelly and Charles Hitchcock sent a memo to the faculty introducing PwC consultants Dr. Greg Lozier and Joanne Michael, who would be speaking with a broad range of people on campus during the month.

There was, however, some good news that summer. In July the college received a check from Sillerman for $3.4 million in partial payment of his earlier pledge. This contribution was earmarked for the college scholarship fund. In August, while Price Waterhouse was preparing its report, Bob Dylan performed to a sold-out audience at the annual *All For The Sea* concert. More than nine thousand people attended, bringing in an estimated $1.6 million in related donations and ticket sales.

When the Southampton College faculty council met on September 18, Dean Hitchcock announced that the LIU Trustees had received the PwC report and would discuss their recommendations at their September meeting. The report, said Hitchcock, would soon be made available to the Southampton College faculty and administration. At this meeting Dean Hitchcock introduced Rory Shaffer-Walsh, the new director of admissions, and announced that the search for a new provost would be delayed pending the recommendations from the PwC team. Shaffer-Walsh had served as director of university admissions at Adelphi University where she had established an effective recruitment program. There was also a brief discussion about Dean Hitchcock's status. Three options were under consideration: make Hitchcock's appointment permanent immediately, begin a search immediately, or continue his interim status until the following year. No action was taken at the time. The college now faced very difficult challenges with an interim dean, an interim provost, a new admissions director, and a new university vice president for academic affairs.

The Board of Trustees was shaken by the blunt assessments and the recommendations in the PwC report. The full report was never made public because, according to President Steinberg, it reflected so poorly on the university and would undermine morale at a time when the college was in "crisis mode." The most striking conclusion made by the PwC team was that the campus needed a $100 million endowment in order to survive. This figure was apparently based on a conventional formula holding that a college needed to have an endowment that was twenty times the annual deficit. This was a significant challenge for a college with no endowment, but it was actually a very modest figure in comparison with other small private colleges. Sewanee College in Tennessee, with an enrollment of 1,500, for example, had a $350 million endowment.

For many in the faculty and administration the report merely stated the obvious once again. It was simply ridiculous, remarked Mary Lai, that the board spent all that money to hire an expensive firm to tell us what we already knew. Red Owl and Robert Sillerman came to the same conclusion. Sillerman dismissed the "$1 million dollar solution" as something out of "fairy tale land." Financial assessments made throughout the history of the university had issued the same warning about the inherent risks of operating without an endowment. The best that could be said was that the PwC report was yet another very sobering reminder of an old problem. The university itself had an endowment of only $40 million at that time. According to trustee John Kanas, the board had discussed closing the school, but were convinced by Sillerman that Southampton could be saved by "repackaging the curriculum" (Rothfeld and Winslow 2004). This approach, said Sillerman, would involve developing a new curriculum with an emphasis on innovative interdisciplinary courses. This was an opportunity, said Sillerman, to redefine higher education in the twenty-first century. Kanas himself was very skeptical of any proposal put forth by either Sillerman or Steinberg.

The executive summary of the PwC report was made into a PowerPoint presentation and presented at a campus faculty meeting in October. Dean Hitchcock recalled Jeffrey Kane meeting with him and Lee Kelly and advising them that they should begin thinking of appropriate strategies for closing the college. Sillerman and Steinberg, however, were adamantly opposed to this solution. They urged the board to consider a radical agenda designed to address the factors that contributed to the spiraling deficits. Sillerman, in particular, saw closing the college as a personal failure for himself. Tim Bishop had observed on more than one occasion that "Bob prides himself with being associated with successful enterprises." Sillerman firmly believed that his business acumen, his problem-solving ability, and his gift for making astute decisions under stress would not fail him here. One of the trustees, who declined to give his name, told *Newsday* reporters that Sillerman's "ego was driving the process" (Rothfeld and Winslow 2004). In fairness to Sillerman, it should be said that he did have a genuine commitment to the college and that he had a legitimate concern with the inadequate support from many of the other trustees. Sillerman and Steinberg made a persuasive appeal to the board in the face of the open skepticism from members such as John Kanas.

Dean Hitchcock recalled driving to the University Center and waiting outside the room where the trustees were meeting to make their decision about their response to the PwC recommendations. Steinberg and Kane emerged all smiles and gave him the "thumbs up." They had convinced a majority of the trustees to keep the college open on the condition that the college faculty and administration embark immediately on a plan to "transform the college" (SCC Archive A, I, k, Decennial Self Study Feb. 2003, S-95–96). The specific goals set forth by the trustees were: (1) Establish a revised core curriculum that is innovative and focused on a theme that is related to the academic majors; (2) Restructure the academic majors by consolidating some into stronger programs and eliminating those with low enrollments; (3) Develop new graduate degree programs, strengthen existing graduate offerings, and undertake new entrepreneurial programs that will take advantage "of the rich cultural institutional and environment of the Hamptons"; (4) Increase enrollment by improving the academic image of Southampton College; (5) Reduce administrative and academic management costs through administrative reorganization and more effective management controls; and (6) Identify and seek funding for critical investments required to meet the above goals. The trustees made it quite clear that if they were not satisfied with the progress made by the Southampton College faculty and administration to meet these goals they would close the college. The restructuring of the academic majors was to be completed by the end of the Spring 2003 semester and the new curriculum was to be in place for the Fall 2004 semester. The most difficult goal by far was number 6. Anyone familiar with the history of fundraising campaigns at LIU was well aware that these efforts always fell far short of their expectations. Sillerman's presence did give some hope that with his help the historic pattern might be changed. Steinberg grasped desperately at that one last straw.

There was an immediate response to the report on the Southampton campus. The faculty executive committee established a core curriculum committee with at least one member from each of the academic divisions. This structure ensured that each division would be involved in the development of a program that directly impacted them all. At the October meeting of the executive committee, the faculty core curriculum committee was asked to gather information on core curricula in private small colleges and make recommendations for a revised core at Southampton.

Almost forgotten in the near-panic over the PwC report was the work of the campus Middle States committees, which had begun preparing in the fall of 2000 for the 2003 Middle States evaluation. A coordinating committee and seven subcommittees made up of students, faculty, and administrators representing all of the academic and administrative areas had begun meeting that fall and continued into the early spring of 2002 when they began a review of the report. Not surprisingly, the self-study pointed to many of the issues outlined in the PwC report. The report called for the development of new academic programs that would improve recruitment and retention, for upgrading the physical plant, and for better marketing strategies (SCC Archive B, II, a, Middle States Decennial Self Study Oct./Nov. 2002). There was one noteworthy exception. The Middle States report called for better communication between faculty, administration, the University Center, and the Board of Trustees. Before the ink was dry on the report, President Steinberg, Jeffry Kane, and Robert Sillerman established a presidential task force to monitor the development of a "New Southampton," thereby setting in motion a "top-down" process that ignored the concerns raised by the campus self-study committee.

Parallel Universes: The Academic Steering Subcommittee and the Faculty Core Curriculum Committee

Creating a "New Southampton" was an ambitious undertaking that would be closely monitored by Jeffrey Kane, Robert Sillerman, and President Steinberg. Although some latitude was granted for the college faculty and administration, the final decision about everything was in the hands of Kane and Sillerman. On November 22, 2002, the presidential task force formed an academic steering subcommittee (ASC) that included interim Provost Kelly, interim Dean Hitchcock, and four members of the Southampton faculty: Paul Forestell, the chair of the faculty council, Liz Granitz, a member of the faculty council executive committee, and Marc Fasanella and Robert Pattison, representing the faculty union. It was clear, however, that Kane, Sillerman, and Steinberg were running the show. The new committee was charged with overseeing the faculty core curriculum committee, but the relationship between the two committees was never clearly articulated. Robert Turner, a professor in the Natural Science division, who served on the faculty committee, said later that their recommendations were either sent back for revision or were simply ignored: "We thought that we were

Figure 10.1 Faculty representing Southampton College in the whaleboat race at the annual SagHarborfest (2001) L. to R. Chris Gobler, Keith Serafy, Liz Granitz, Robert Turner, Dean James Larocca, and Tac Hostetter. *Courtesy of Southampton Town Historian.*

a significant part of the process, but we soon discovered that this was not the case" (It. 50).

When the faculty committee was pushed into the background, there was no longer any significant involvement of the Natural Science division in the development of the "new Southampton." Paul Forestell asked Steinberg why no faculty members from the Natural Science division were included on the steering committee. Steinberg dismissed his question, stating that it was sufficient to have the elected faculty council and faculty union officials on the committee. Forestell accepted the rationale, but questioned the political wisdom of Steinberg's response. The decision to go ahead without a representative from the Natural Science division was one of two poorly considered decisions made in this first meeting, particularly in the face of the appeal for better communication voiced in the Middle States self-study. The ASC members also agreed that they should keep the discussions in the meeting in "strict confidence," to encourage the freest possible discussion of alternative strategies. Whatever justification there may have been for these decisions, they served to reinforce the suspicions of many on a faculty that was already under considerable stress. Not surprisingly, resentment grew, particularly among many members of the Natural Science division.

The first meeting of the ASC, held on the Southampton campus, was attended by Kane, Sillerman, Mary Lai, Red Owl, and two trustees, Edward Travaglianti, and Tess Mullarkey. Their presence made it clear that the University Center was giving full support to the process. Dean Hitchcock reported that there would be a five-day faculty retreat at the end of January to "jump start" the reformation. The tone of the meeting was positive and upbeat. There were, however, some references to the Natural Science division as a "separate entity from the rest of the college." It was clear some believed that the Marine Science major was the primary cause of the yearly deficits. There was a consensus in the meeting that the dominant role of the Marine Science program had to be carefully reexamined. Forestell, concerned about what might well be perceived as a shroud of secrecy thrown over the proceedings on the steering committee, asked Steinberg to write a letter to the faculty stressing the importance of the committee's task and assuring them that there would be open discussions of proposals made by the committee. This message was not well received by Arvind Borde and Donald Baker. Borde, who taught Mathematics and was serving as the director of the Natural Science division, objected to what he charged were clandestine meetings with an agenda imposed by the University Center. Baker, who spoke for many in the Social Science division, also objected to what he described as a unilateral imposition by Jeffrey Kane.

On Dec. 9, 2002, Forestell and Hitchcock received a six-page memo from Jeff Kane that fueled the long-held faculty suspicions of University Center. Kane outlined the general parameters for the development of a new core curriculum and for the reorganization of the academic majors. These were deemed to be the primary areas where deficits could be reduced. Kane proposed a new core curriculum be developed that would reduce instructional costs, be more attractive to potential students, increase student retention, and improve academic quality. A primary goal was to increase class size to an average of thirty students for the freshman and sophomore years. This arbitrary increase in class size, however, raised questions about the reference in the Middle States self-study (SCC Archive B, IV, a, Kane to Hitchcock Feb. 2003, S-1) stating that the "essential character" of Southampton college was its small class size.

Kane had acknowledged the previous fall that although there was no specific database in the literature on higher education that could document the impact of any given core curriculum on student recruitment, retention, or the overall enrollment of a university or college, "many of us have considerable practical experience in implementing and in marketing Cores and can identify a number of relevant considerations" (SCC Archive B, IV, Kane to Hitchcock and Forestell Nov. 22, 2002). Kane did not mention who besides himself constituted the "us" that had this experience in marketing core programs. It certainly was neither Sillerman nor Steinberg. The relevant considerations he cited as primary factors leading to an increased marketability were, small class size (twenty to twenty-five students), attractive majors, modern facilities, and university reputation. Core curriculums, at best, said Kane, play only a supplemental role.

If small class size was a primary factor in attracting students, it would seem that Kane's proposal for a core with an average class size of thirty students might work at cross-purposes with the goal of increasing the college enrollment. Kane never addressed this obvious contradiction. Another "relevant consideration" was that the core should be "tightly constructed" around a universal set of academic experiences that would define the college. Students who shared these experiences, argued Kane, would be more likely to remain at Southampton and graduate with their class. Whereas the assumption that the core would have a positive impact on retention and recruitment was open to serious question, there was no question that a tightly structured core curriculum with class sizes of thirty students would reduce the costs for instruction. A careful look at Kane's list of his "relevant considerations" was quite sobering, because Long Island University had outdated facilities and a poor reputation. The one criterion that Southampton College met was small class size, and that would end when Kane's plan to increase class sizes to thirty was implemented. That left only the possibility of developing more attractive courses, a slender reed, to say the least. Kane's initial acknowledgment that there were no data to indicate that a core curriculum, no matter how dynamic, would increase enrollment made it difficult to generate enthusiasm among the faculty for the "New Southampton."

Most of the faculty who did become enthusiastic supporters of the reformed interdisciplinary curriculum were not so much concerned about the impact on recruitment as they were excited about the opportunity to experiment with innovative educational approaches.

The second strategy addressed in Kane's memo was the consolidation and reorganization of the majors and the reduction of elective courses. Once again, the primary goal was to increase class size. Kane offered no specifics about implementation other than calling for the establishment of guidelines that would result in raising the average class size for the campus from eleven to twenty-two. He did make it clear, however, that the role of the Marine Science program in the college curriculum had to be reevaluated. "Under any circumstances," said Kane, "the program cannot serve as the mainstay of the campus and must be reduced." The Marine Science program offered students a choice of four majors that each required more than eighty credits. The Natural Science division had added three related Bachelor of Science majors in 2001, Marine Vertebrate Biology, Oceanography, and Marine Biology. Kane argued that these choices and the number of required courses resulted in far too many small classes. He wanted to reduce the number of majors and to cap all college majors at sixty-four credit hours. In his concluding paragraph he stressed that faculty had to be committed to these changes and that the new academic programs had to be in place for the Fall 2004 semester. The parameters had been set; now it was up to the faculty, monitored closely by Jeff Kane, to come up with the specifics.

On December 13, a week after Kane's memo, Steinberg wrote his own memorandum to the Southampton faculty and administration. He forcefully repeated the basic message that Kane had sent to the steering committee. The board, he said, "demands a new core curriculum." The faculty and administration, continued Steinberg, was now charged with "the collective task of repositioning Southampton College in the market place for students" (SCC Archive B, IV, a, Steinberg Memorandum Dec. 13, 2002). In an attempt to quiet the complaints that a small group was working behind a cloak of secrecy, Steinberg stated that "the Presidential Task Force for the New Southampton must manage the contradiction of working in strict confidence even while remaining open to ideas, suggestions and reaction from the larger community." Not surprisingly, given the faculty's historical suspicions of the LIU University Center, Steinberg's rather convoluted assurance was unconvincing to many, particularly those in the Natural Science division.

That same day, the Task Force steering committee met at Southampton. Once again the University Center came out in full force. Steinberg chaired the meeting and brought along with him Jeffrey Kane, Mary Lai, Richard Gorman, George Sutton, Red Owl, and four trustees, Sillerman, Mullarkey, Tillis, and Travaglianti. The Southampton administration was represented by Dean Hitchcock and Provost Kelly. The four faculty representatives, Granitz,

Forestell, Pattison, and Fasanella, were outnumbered by administrators, two to one. This did not go unnoticed by the rest of the faculty, some of whom saw it as a show of support and seriousness of purpose on the part of the university officials. Others, given the historic suspicion of the University Center so deeply embedded at Southampton, read it quite differently.

There was a clear sense of urgency shared by all of the people in the meeting. Sillerman wanted to submit the curricular and program changes to the New York State Board of Education by August 2003 in order to be ready for full implementation the following year. Kane agreed with the need to accelerate the move toward the "New Southampton." Fearing a prolonged resistance by the Natural Science faculty, Kane once again emphasized that "what is said around the table concerning the Marine Science program is confidential." The hope, apparently, was that the ASC would avoid a lengthy debate if it could confront the Natural Science faculty with a complete package already framed out.

The ASC met again on December 20 to review the majors, the core curriculum, and the structure of the academic divisions. The criteria for majors included enrollments, size of the market, costs, available facilities, quality, and relevance to the college mission. Using these criteria, the committee proposed that twenty-three majors with less than ten students be eliminated, among them seven majors in the Natural Science division. The new core curriculum was to have forty-two credits, an average class size of thirty students, and a coherent theme. The courses would all be interdisciplinary or experiential, with a focus on the "essential literacies" in the liberal arts. The ASC also proposed that the Business and Education majors be placed in the Social Science Division and that the Art majors be placed in the Humanities division. The committee also agreed to cap the credits required for any major at sixty-four. Although no representative from the Natural Science division had as yet been involved in these discussions, the committee was careful to note that all decisions would follow "collegial discussion and debate." When the steering committee met the next week, however, Steinberg made it clear that he viewed the Natural Science program to be a primary source of the yearly deficit. "[T]he more Natural Science students Southampton has," said Steinberg, "the more it loses financially" (SCC Archive B, IV, a, ASC Minutes Dec. 27, 2002).

When Jeff Kane met with the ASC on January 7, he decided that it was time to engage the Natural Science faculty and inform them about the proposed changes. Kane stressed that the subcommittee members "be of one voice" when they made their presentation at the January 13 meeting of the Natural Science division. Kane apparently hoped that the united front would discourage any significant resistance. He had seriously miscalculated. On January 14, Borde addressed an angry memo to Steinberg, Kane, Sillerman, and Hitchcock stating that his faculty received the information with surprise and with great dismay (SCC Archive B, IV, a, Memo: Borde to Kane et al. Jan. 14, 2003). We have a first-rate faculty, he said, and they have many options for employment. A reduced Marine Science program, he feared, would make it difficult to retain them. Borde argued that reducing the Natural Science majors to sixty-four credits would seriously weaken the program. Cutting what amounted to nearly a semester from the majors would put Southampton graduates well behind the graduates from the University of Rhode Island, the University of Maine, and Florida Institute of Technology, where the majors required eighty or more credits. This change would likely discourage prospective students, increase the rate of attrition, and seriously compromise Southampton's hard-won national reputation. These are factors, warned Borde, that I urge you to carefully consider. Borde also questioned the assumption that the new core would have any significant impact on the deficit or would attract more new students and keep them longer.

Borde did acknowledge that the new core was a "good, reputable, and successful program," but he objected to the way it was imposed on the Southampton faculty under the threat of closing the college (SCC Archive B, IV, a, Memo: Borde to Forestell Feb. 16, 2005). Kane was undoubtedly aware of these concerns, but he argued that the college could no longer afford such an expensive program. He was convinced that with faculty support he could develop an innovative program equally attractive to the top high school graduates. The bottom line, as Kane saw it, was that the yearly deficit hemorrhage had to be stanched no matter what the risk.

The Natural Science division was not alone in their concerns about Kane's rather heavy-handed role in the work of the academic steering committee. The faculty core curriculum committee included members representing Social Science (Stacy Horstman Gatti, History) Natural Science (Robert Turner, Geology, Steve Tettelbach, Biology, and Ed Himmelblau, Biology), Education (Kathleen Feeley), Humanities (Bill Roberson, English and Jon Haynes, English), Fine Arts (Michael Drexel, Theater, and Christa Bowden, Photography), administration (Vicky Mulvey, director of academic advising), library (Robert Gerbereux, library director), and students (Daniela Gregory). This committee had developed their own model for the new curriculum that varied in some details from the steering committee model (SCC Archive B, IV, a, Memo from Core Curriculum Committee to Steering Committee Jan. 14, 2003). Sillerman, speaking for the steering committee, rejected their model because he felt that it was "too specific and was created by a deeply entrenched faculty" that was motivated by self-interest. Kane concurred. The proposal, they said, "had no coherent theme," and the courses were not interdisciplinary (SCC Archive B, IV, a, Steering Committee Minutes Jan. 15, 2003). What Sillerman and Kane wanted were courses that were developed independently from the existing academic divisions.

The faculty committee responded with a sharply worded memo calling for better communication. Professor Turner charged that the ASC apparently "intends to continue as a top secret closed club from which menacing things leak now and again" (SCC Archive B IV, a, Memo, Turner to faculty committee Jan. 17, 2003). There were also concerns expressed by several faculty members that decisions were being made during the month of January when there were few faculty members on campus. Feelings were running high, especially in the Natural Science division. Arvind Borde sent a memo to the faculty steering committee voicing the feelings of his faculty. He argued that it was possible to reduce the over reliance on Marine Science by strengthening the other parts of the college, rather than by weakening Marine Science. By increasing the core and mandating a cap of sixty-four credits, Borde continued, you will destroy the Marine Science program. "Asking us to help design the core is like asking us to design our own noose" (SCC Archive B IV, a, Memo: Borde to faculty core committee Jan. 20, 2002).

In an effort to cool down the tensions, the faculty committee issued a statement to the campus community a week prior to the campus retreat. They reluctantly accepted the forty-two credits total for the core curriculum in spite of the opposition by Borde, but they argued that their model provided more emphasis on "essential literacies" in Math and English Writing. The committee did not get involved in the debate over the cap on the credits for the majors because that was not a part of their mandate. When they attempted to send their statement to the individual members of the ASC, they were informed by Elizabeth Ciabocchi, Jeffery Kane's executive assistant, that no one, not even Kane, was permitted to send material directly to an LIU trustee. All such communications had to go through President Steinberg's office. Stacy Horstmann-Gatti remarked caustically, "How's that for information control?"

Perish or Prosper: The Faculty Retreat, January 29, 2003–February 3, 2003

The university officials, anticipating resistance, came out to Southampton in full force. They wanted to make it clear to the Southampton faculty that the future of the college hung in the balance. The university officials were President Steinberg, Academic Vice President Jeff Kane, Southampton Chancellor Robert Sillerman, and Red Owl, vice president for information services. Former Southampton College president Harry Marmion also attended. There were thirty-eight of the sixty-three current faculty members in attendance and two student government representatives, Valerie Systak and Daniela Gregory. Nine of the twenty-one Natural Science members attended, but Borde was not among them.

Sillerman spoke first and set the tone for the retreat. He told about his battle with a cancer he discovered on his neck in 2001. "Over a thirty day period, I said to myself: perish or prosper." The treatment proved successful, he said, and now he was completely healthy. "Perish or prosper, that is my mantra," and it is "an absolute analogy of where we are today" (SCC Archive B-IV, f Retreat Notes Jan. 29, 2003, morning session). Steinberg added that he too had won a struggle with cancer of the prostrate. "The destiny of this place," said Steinberg, "is to be decided soon—choose life." Sillerman was careful to note that he was not suggesting that the college had a cancer, but only that the college was in a life and death struggle and that the institution could win the struggle with deficits and debt as he had done in his struggle against disease. There were those, however, who read it differently. Some on the faculty were convinced that Steinberg and Sillerman did believe the Natural Science division was a cancer that needed to be brought under control before it destroyed the college.

Although Kane and Red Owl could offer no such dramatic examples of personal triumphs, they underscored the seriousness of the situation at hand. It was quite clear that unless the faculty satisfied the LIU trustees that the changes advocated by Kane, Sillerman, and Steinberg were well under way by the end of the spring semester, the college would be closed. Sillerman also emphasized that his leverage with his fellow board members rested on the level of commitment and support he could get from the Southampton faculty. He noted candidly that the board was of three minds about him, "those that loathe, those that fear and those (very small percentage) that respect." Sillerman wanted to make it clear that he saw himself as an advocate of the "new Southampton College," not as an agent of the LIU trustees. He envisioned the curriculum changes as precedent-setting in higher education. "This is going to be a school that has a definable place in our educational process. . . . We are participating in an educational revolution long overdue in this country . . . we may be seen as one of the leaders in this revolution." He was excited about the prospect of continuing his success with failing institutions. Kane shared Sillerman's enthusiasm for the endeavor. He told a reporter from *Newsday* that "[w]e expect the result will be a new Southampton College that will be a polished gem rather than one so much in the rough" (Feb. 10, 2003).

Kane reported that he was working with the state department of education to make sure that the new core curriculum was registered and ready for the fall 2004 semester. In order to meet that deadline, he warned, the faculty would have to complete their work and give their approval by the summer. The faculty must resolve the differences between the proposed parameters in the next few days. "The decision you make in the next few days," said Kane, "will chart the future of this place for decades to come." The sense of urgency was palpable, and a bit unsettling, but the reference to "decades to come," was reassuring.

"I feel torn and exhausted by this process. Reason appears to be getting us nowhere" (Robert Turner)

Three days after the retreat ended, Rob Turner addressed a memorandum to both core committees, outlining his remaining concerns about the ASC model. His primary concern was what he believed to be an overemphasis on interdisciplinary courses at the expense of the basic courses in each discipline. He noted that several of his colleagues also feared that the students needed to have a solid grounding in at least one discipline in order to understand and apply an interdisciplinary analysis. He also feared that the proposed faculty of interdisciplinary studies might diminish the traditional role of the disciplines in the preparation of students for graduate schools and for employment in their chosen professions. "I urge that we take care not to let the pendulum swing carry us away into the demonization of the disciplinary approach to learning and growing" (SCC Archive B-IV, e, Turner Memorandum Feb. 3, 2003).

Members of the faculty core committee continued this discussion via e-mail over the next week. The messages were a mix of frustration, anger, and resignation. Jonathan Haynes, in a message to Stacy Horstmann-Gatti and Robert Turner, wrote: "In general I'm also prone to rage at affronts to the dignity of the faculty and to having my own time wasted and to being used as a flack for authoritarian edicts" (SCC Archive B-IV, e, Haynes to Horstmann-Gatti and Turner Feb. 7, 2003). He went on to add, however, that he realized that he had to "tamp down" his emotions and keep his eye on the larger picture. In fact, he acknowledged that sweeping change was necessary and that the academic subcommittee proposal did have some good points. Turner answered Haynes, noting that the Natural Science division overwhelmingly supported the faculty committee model, but that he was exhausted by the process and was now resigned to working with the subcommittee model. Stacy Horstmann echoed the tone expressed by Haynes and Turner. "We have a gun to our heads," she wrote, "the faculty has to buy into a plan that the Trustees approve or they will close down the school in eighteen months." The faculty executive committee (FEC) expressed the same state of mind at their meeting on February 5: "We need to have an integrated core curriculum ready for a vote on February 19th and it must be one that will satisfy the Trustees" (SCC Archive B-IV E, FEC Minutes Feb. 5, 2003). As it turned out, the faculty did give them the plan they wanted but the college closed sixteen months later anyway.

On February 12, the presidential task force addressed the fundraising goal set by the trustees in the previous fall. They issued a proposal for a five-year plan to improve the physical plant. This was the first step in a campaign to raise funds for extensive capital investments in Southampton College. The assumption was that potential donors needed to be assured that there was a plan in place that demonstrated a positive vision for the future. Donors wanted to know how their money was going to be used and to have confidence that they would be participating in a successful revitalization project. The language, therefore, was upbeat, almost breathless. There were to be renovations on the Natural Science building, the Marine Station, the Fine Arts building and the "old library" in the spring of 2003. Groundbreaking for a new library building was scheduled for the spring of 2003. During the 2004–05 academic year, the plan called for a renovation of the Natural Science building that included the construction of a dormer on the roof for the faculty offices. The Marine Station would be equipped with a solar-aquatic marine science facility, and the old boatyard would be replaced with a coastal plant research center. The old library building would be renovated for the use of the Fine Arts program, a reception area, and classrooms. The Fine Arts and Humanities building would house a digital photo and printmaking facility and several classrooms. In 2006–07 the dormitories would all be renovated. The old Federal-style dorms would now embody the "ambiance of a country inn, outfitted with Stickly Furniture and used in the summer for prestigious summer programs." There were also plans for a $13 million, 65,000 square foot athletic and recreation facility. The building exteriors and the grounds would be renovated to "create a bucolic sense of place consistent with . . . English rustic landscaping." The following year, most of the rooms in Southampton Hall, recently renamed the Pratt Center in honor of the benefactor, would be completely gutted and made compliant with building codes. There would be a pool house near the pool on the south lawn, and a continuous private garden would extend from the pool to the windmill residence. The funds for these projects would be generated by a capital improvement plan.

The Grand Experiment or the Big Gamble?

> The truth is that we are embarking on a "grand experiment." We are all in a new territory . . .
>
> —Faculty Minutes, Feb. 17, 2003

At a meeting of the whole faculty on February 17, the model for the new core was approved by a vote of forty-six to three with three abstentions. Those who voted in favor, however, were not of a single mind. About one-third of the faculty were genuinely excited and enthusiastic about the interdisciplinary approach and looked forward to developing experimental courses. Others who voted in favor saw the new program as a desperate gamble pressed upon the faculty by the University Center and the Board of Trustees. They were very skeptical about the assertion that the "New Southampton" with all its innovations would attract more students or reduce attrition in any significant way. The LIU trustees gave their approval at their meeting on June 17, 2003. The basic structural components of the new core were now in place and the work began on fleshing out the course descriptions. These needed to be in place by the next fall for the admissions office to develop their recruiting literature.

The freshman semester was to begin with a six-credit "global" lecture and seminar that would focus on an environmental theme. All of the class would attend a common lecture and then break off into discussion sections of twenty-five to thirty students. The other six required credits for the freshman year were either one set of linked interdisciplinary courses or two three-credit interdisciplinary courses. The linked courses were designed to bring together the methodologies from two distinct disciplines and focus them on a specific subject. One set of linked courses, for example, focused on prehistoric cultures of the American Southwest. Phyllis Kudder-Sullivan, a ceramicist in the Art and Media division, taught a class in prehistoric pottery techniques, and I came out of retirement to teach an Anthropology course on the prehistoric Southwestern cultures. We arranged to have space for my lecture-discussion class in the art studio building. When the students finished with my class, they moved directly into the ceramic studio where

FIGURE 10.2 Phyllis Kudder-Sullivan with student Jackie Sherman-Smith, in the interdisciplinary seminar on prehistoric pottery of the Southwest. *Photo by author.*

they made replica pottery, using the prehistoric coil method and firing the pots in an outdoor kiln, in conditions similar to those used by prehistoric potters. We were both very pleased with the results. It was, for me, one of the most exciting and satisfying teaching experiences I have ever had.

Each three-credit interdisciplinary course was taught by an instructor who drew upon perspectives from another discipline to study a topic. Robert Pattison, for example, designed a course on the relationship between science and literature wherein the students examined Mary Shelly's study of science and its consequences. In their sophomore and junior years the students took six more credits of integrated courses, three more interdisciplinary courses, two courses called "Foundations of Modern Thought" that introduced the students to the chronological development of the "foundations of knowledge in science, the arts, the social sciences and the humanities from diverse cultural perspectives," and two Experiential Education courses. The latter two courses would usually be taken off-campus in private or public agencies or overseas. There would be a final "capstone seminar" in the senior year "as a culmination of the core experience."

FIGURE 10.3 Students with their replica prehistoric pottery. *Photo by author.*

This innovative and demanding curriculum drew enthusiastic response from a number of the faculty, who began to develop course proposals during the remainder of the spring semester and submit them to the newly established core program office. Ann Algieri, who had been director of the learning and writing center at Southampton, was appointed director of the core program. Algieri was assisted by a core committee that included representatives from Natural Science, Social Science, and the Humanities. Although Kane was not on the committee, he played a major role in evaluating the course proposals. Each proposal had to specify how it addressed three or more of the following "essential literacies": aesthetic literacy, critical thinking, cultural analysis, environmental literacy, ethical action and citizenship, quantitative reasoning, scientific literacy, and verbal literacy. The committee was under pressure to have courses clearly defined for presentation to the New York State Department of Education in July. To encourage proposals, Algieri set up a "Course Development Workshop" for faculty who were interested in developing course proposals.

The New Provost

> I am excited by the challenges of Southampton College.
>
> —Dan Rodas

The provost search committee had interviewed several candidates during November and December and had narrowed the field down to two finalists, Robert DeLuca, the current director of The Group for the East End, a highly respected local environmental organization, and Daniel Rodas, an assistant vice president at Duke University. Rodas came with impressive credentials. He graduated from Williams College in 1985 and went on to earn a master's from Harvard and a PhD from Stanford. DeLuca had no experience in educational administration, but he was a very popular adjunct professor, who, as noted above, had been teaching environmental courses for several years and had strong support from those students. The students had encouraged DeLuca to apply for the position of provost. He agreed, he said, primarily because he felt that if the college was going to focus on environmental education, he would be a good fit.

Student representatives Daniela Gregory and Valerie Suzdak sat in on the interviews with the candidates, but, according to an article by Valerie Sudzak in the *Windmill* (Feb. 4, 2003), they were never asked for their opinions. Sudzak was angry. Student opinion, she said, "was not taken seriously." For the university officials, it was an easy choice: they wanted a provost with the sort of credentials that Rodas had presented. The way the appointment was handled, however, reinforced the historic suspicion and negative feelings about the LIU University Center that fueled the student unrest that erupted a year later. By the end of the Spring 2003 semester, there were significant undercurrents of resentment shared by many among the students and faculty. Steinberg told a local reporter that Rodas was "just the leader Southampton College needs at this moment in its history, bringing an understanding of the business of higher education as well as imagination, verve and leadership skills to his new role" (*Sag Harbor Express* Feb. 27, 2003). Rodas visited the campus several times that spring and was officially installed on May 1, 2003.

The new core was in place, but the discussions about the cap on the Marine Science major continued. On March 7 the academic subcommittee met with four members of the Natural Science division: Chris Gobler, Maria Kretzmann, Steve Tettelbach, and Robert Turner. They agreed, reluctantly to reduce the program to between seventy-two and seventy-six credit hours, but warned that any further reduction would put their graduates at great disadvantage when they applied for graduate schools. Gobler told the committee that 50 percent of the Southampton graduates in Natural Science go on to graduate school and that a majority of them complete their PhD programs. The Natural Science representatives convinced Sillerman that their proposal was an acceptable compromise, and the other members of the committee agreed.

Widening the Net: Aggressive Recruiting under Shaffer-Walsh and Rodas

The mistaken gamble taken by Brophy in the spring of 2000 had cost the college a place in its traditional market niche that had been difficult to reclaim. Although some progress had been made by the summer of 2002 when Rory Shaffer-Walsh arrived on campus, she implemented a more aggressive approach. Rory and Rodas realized that there needed to be a new approach based on the use of new recruiting tools as well as on a more aggressive use of the old methods. They increased the number of prospective student names purchased from the Educational Testing Center and the National Research Center from about forty thousand to more than sixty thousand. These national organizations sell lists of names of high school seniors who are intending to apply to colleges following their graduation.

Ms. Shaffer-Walsh also developed more attractive recruiting materials. She was appalled by the bland, unimaginative booklets and related materials in the packets sent out to prospective students. It was not the fault of my predecessors, she said, "They had little input into the decisions about the recruiting materials. I was told that the university public relations office kept tight control over the message and the budget for such materials." (pers. comm. April 29, 2011). As Carol Gilbert had often lamented, the public relations people at University Center seldom came out to visit the college and had little awareness about the unique nature of the campus and the "student-centered" focus of the faculty and administration. C. W. Post, in particular, was a different world entirely. Fortunately, she said, Robert Sillerman came into her office on one of his occasional unannounced visits to the campus administrative offices and asked her how he could help her improve the recruitment effort. Sillerman took what was for him, a characteristic "hands-on" approach to his relationship with the college. She showed him the materials that had been sent out the previous year and he agreed with her assessment of them. "I don't know what he did, but I was quickly given more control over decisions about a new recruitment package." Rory developed an attractive, colorful, forty-two-page "viewbook" that featured the interdisciplinary courses in the new curriculum and architectural drawings of the new library, the new recreation center with the eight-lane swimming pool and indoor track, and the $12.5 million renovation of the student center. She also included several smaller booklets that focused on financial aid, experiential learning, sports, residence life, and, of course, Marine Science. This revised recruitment program, unfortunately, was not fully in place until the following year.

Commencement 2003: The $60 Million Dollar Promise

> This is the best I have ever felt about the future of the college.
>
> —Dean Charles Hitchcock

On Commencement Day, Sillerman, Steinberg, Hitchcock, and several LIU trustees lined up, shovels in hand, to break ground for the 29,600 square foot new "green" library. When Sillerman addressed the graduates he told them that LIU had guaranteed $60 million to ensure that "the college they are leaving will bear little resemblance to the one they will find when they return for their five-year reunion." This investment," he continued, "will guarantee that your Southampton College degree will be worth even more to you tomorrow than it is today" (*Southampton Press* May 22, 2003). He described the new buildings in the capital campaign proposal and praised the "cutting edge" curriculum and new teaching methods that would "shake up the higher education world and increase enrollment." He added that $35 million of the $60 million had already been secured. He and his wife Laura gave $20 million, and $15 million came from private donations. The LIU Board of Trustees, said Sillerman, "have guaranteed that whether or not the college can raise the additional $25 million for the building fund, the university will make up the gap between what is secured and what is needed. . . . The Trustees are willing to cover a potentially multimillion dollar shortfall because they feel confident that the rest of the money will be donated." The chancellor went on to describe some of the courses in the new interdisciplinary curriculum and noted that "[t]his kind of teaching has never been done before." Although the interdisciplinary approach had been introduced in the early years by President Glanz and was later abandoned, this was no time to quibble with Sillerman's eloquent hyperbole. His words gave a welcome assurance about the future of the college. The renovations and the new buildings, he continued, were expected to be completed within five years. The upbeat tone of the ceremony was capped with a commencement address by Alan Alda, underscoring the college's connections with the community of creative artists in the Hamptons. Congressman Bishop, who had been awarded an honorary degree for his long service to the college, remarked enthusiastically about Sillerman's presentation: "This is more than I can comprehend." Indeed it was.

Sillerman's address demonstrated, once again, his ability to put the best face on a very risky prospect. This was one of the many entrepreneurial skills that had brought him so much well-deserved success in the business world. A closer look at the figures, however, removed some of the glitter. Generous pledges, as Mary Lai had often lamented, are not hard cash in hand. In fact not a single dollar of the pledged $60 million was actually in the university coffers that May. According to Mary Lai, Sillerman had once again made his pledge as a matching donation that would not be paid until the university raised an equal amount. The $40 million from the trustees and the private donors was scheduled to come in over the next four to five years. The promised makeover of the physical plant, however, depended upon having a sizeable chunk of that money in place. Provost Rodas was concerned about this slow trickle of cash. Although he fully supported the development of the new curriculum, he believed that what was needed much more than a new curriculum was an immediate transfusion of capital to begin the transformation of the physical plant as soon as possible (It. 42). University officials were later to claim that Sillerman's total personal cash contribution was only about $10 million. Sillerman disputed this, saying that he had given somewhere between $15 and $25 million, but declined to offer any additional information about his contributions.

In August, when Sillerman introduced Jimmy Buffett to another sold-out *All For The Sea* concert audience, he repeated his pledge to donate $20 million to Southampton College, part of a "bold $60 million strategic plan that will transform the college both physically and academically." Buffett, in that same spirit, donated his concert fee to the college. Provost Rodas added that "[i]t was a fantastic show, the most financially successful fundraiser ever for the college. The concert is a great example of the college community's ability to come together as a group, pooling our various talents to help the community grow" (SCC Archive B, V, c 2, *Alumni Newsletter* Fall 2003). Many shared the positive enthusiasm of the moment, but Rodas, in spite of the smile on his public face, remained very concerned.

Two other signs of hope emerged that summer. The Parrish Art Museum was looking for a place to build a new 80,000 square foot museum facility. Museum director Trudy Kramer and LIU officials had negotiated "a creative plan and reached a firm agreement that will expand the museum at a new location on the Southampton Campus." This project, said Sillerman, will "build upon the momentum we have established, further enriching our students' experience" (*Alumni Newsletter* Fall 2003). The relationship with the museum would certainly strengthen the college Fine Arts program and give students direct access to the rich cultural resources of the Hamptons.

The second promising development was the possibility that a fifty-four-acre parcel of land on the shore of Peconic Bay would be donated to the college. Michael Pascucci, a wealthy businessman, had purchased a three hundred-acre tract in 2001 for $45 million, intending to build an environmentally responsible "organic" golf course. Pascucci's offer was part of his strategy to obtain permission for a golf course that bordered on a wetland environment. Former dean James Larocca and Chancellor Sillerman represented the college in these negotiations. The plans included a joint relationship between the college and the Nature Conservancy to develop educational and research programs on the tract. In August, Larocca and a team of faculty from the Natural Science division, including Robert Turner, Keith Serafy, and Howard Reisman toured the site. Robert Turner submitted a brief report outlining the educational and research possibilities and affirming that the faculty were very enthusiastic about the project (SCC Archive B-IV, e, Memorandum Turner to Rodas Aug. 27, 2003). It was one more reason to feel good about the future of the college.

Honoring Dean Hitchcock

In August, Jeff Kane sent a memorandum to the Southampton College community thanking Dean Hitchcock for his more than three decades of service to the college and noting, "His integrity, his commitment, and his capacity to envision new possibilities for the college have been central to the academic renaissance of the campus" (SCC Archive B-II, d, Kane Memorandum Aug. 1, 2003). Hitchcock, continued Kane, "will continue to lead the college through the 2003–2004 academic year. His contributions are deserving of the title of Dean, the position he has in fact, assumed, and it is my great pleasure to inform you that during this coming academic year his title will now be Dean of Southampton." This was a long-overdue recognition for Hitchcock's years of service to the university. It was nevertheless, an

FIGURE 10.4. Dr. Charles Hitchcock. In addition to his teaching and administrative duties, Hitchcock coached the Southampton College Tennis Team. Front Row (L to R) Roger Svensson, James Grigo, Mats Selander, Freddie Rydell, Johan Kron. Back Row (L to R) Assistant Coaches Julia Denny and Vinnie DeCerbo, Andres Lindberg, Brett De Cerbo, Andress Lindquist, Coach Hitchcock (1999). *Courtesy of Charles Hitchcock.*

honorary title, because he was, in fact, still an interim dean. Kane wanted to bring in a career administrator with a significant track record of success as an academic dean, who would be in place when the new core curriculum was introduced in the fall of 2004. Kane announced that he would be working with the faculty council to establish a dean's search committee to select a "Dean for the future." The committee was to be formally convened and to begin its operations in early September. The dean parade was to continue.

Chapter Eleven

The Final Days, 2003–2004

Moving Too Fast with Too Few

The development of the core curriculum continued during the Fall 2003 semester. There was, however, still a great deal of faculty indifference. Kane reported to the academic steering committee (ASC) that only about one-third of the faculty was currently involved with the planning. Rodas also expressed concern about the possible negative impact on student recruitment and retention (SCC Archives B-IV, a, 4, ASC minutes Dec. 15, 2003). One of the reasons frequently noted was not directly related to pedagogy. Many in the faculty resented what they felt was Kane's "top-down" administrative approach. A second reason, expressed by some of these same faculty members, was that neither Sillerman nor Kane had sufficient academic credentials to make informed decisions about their disciplines. Sillerman, for example, was dismissed by Robert Pattison as someone who may have read an article on interdisciplinary education in a Brandeis alumni magazine or had perhaps seen a program on PBS (It. 38). Kane's graduate degree in Education led some to assume he was an intellectual lightweight who lacked wisdom and experience necessary to justify his interference in their "more rigorous" disciplines.

It was an uphill challenge for Kane, who was under considerable pressure from Steinberg and the trustees. He decided to go forward with a small group of faculty, who he hoped would serve as mentors for those faculty who were not openly hostile to the transformation. Kane offered to give them whatever support they needed, including funds for conferences, workshops, and consultants. Dean Hitchcock, for example, approved funds for Phyllis Kudder-Sullivan and the author to take part in a conference on prehistoric pottery in New Mexico in preparation for our linked interdisciplinary courses scheduled for the Spring 2004 semester. Kane also arranged for members of Anne Algieri's core curriculum committee to attend several conferences on interdisciplinary education. Julio Gonzalez, an instructor in the Education division, who had joined the faculty the previous fall, Liz Granitz, and Anne Algieri attended a workshop at the annual conference of the Association for Integrative Studies in Detroit. This organization had been established in 1979 by Professor William Newell, a nationally recognized leader in the field of interdisciplinary studies at Miami University of Ohio.

In December, Kane invited Newell to run a two-day workshop on interdisciplinary education at Southampton. The number of interested faculty remained small. Only twenty faculty members came for the first day and about half of them returned the next day. A severe snowstorm undoubtedly played a role in the poor turnout on the second day. According to Dean Hitchcock, however, Newell's question and answer session was "highly interactive and very effective" (SCC Archives B-IV, a, 4, ASC Dec. 15, 2003). Forestell was pleased with the workshop because it helped to underscore the academic legitimacy of the interdisciplinary focus. The critics on the faculty, he believed, would now be less likely to dismiss the approach as some sort of fad conjured up by Sillerman and Kane. He also felt that Newell had provided important direction to the faculty who were engaged in developing the new core.

Newell, however, in his post-workshop discussions, noted that the involvement of only one-third of the Southampton faculty might be a serious problem for such an ambitious project. Newell also believed the transformation project was moving too fast. He suggested the creation and assessment of pilot courses prior to full implementation of the new core. Kane rejected the suggestion. He was under considerable pressure to have the full core program in place for the Fall 2004 semester. This sense of urgency was increased somewhat by the deficit projections released in the fall of 2003. Kane warned the Southampton faculty council that the annual deficit had increased from $5 million at the end of 2001 to about $9 million in 2003 (SCC Archive B-IV, e, Faculty Council Minutes Nov. 19, 2003).

Whereas the faculty agreed, albeit reluctantly, to accept the new curriculum, considerable resistance to the restructuring of the academic divisions remained. The ASC presented a model that abolished the existing divisions and replaced them with twelve program areas all under the direct control of the dean of academic affairs. This more centralized structure, argued Kane, would be much less expensive to operate than what he saw as semi-independent "feudal fiefdoms" in the current academic divisions. Natural Science, for example would be divided into Marine Science and Biology and Environmental Science would be combined with Environmental Studies as a separate program. Each of the twelve programs would have a coordinator elected by the program faculty. It was not clear to many how this would be more efficient or save much money. Arvind Borde argued that this structure would create more paperwork and require stipends for all the coordinators. Herbert Sherman, who had served many years as the head of the Business division, agreed with Borde. Sherman wrote a memo to the faculty at large arguing that the plan would reduce efficiency and increase fragmentation. At the end of the semester, Dean Hitchcock reported to the ASC that a majority of the faculty had responded negatively to the proposed academic structure and that some faculty had alarmed the students about the arbitrary dismantling of the existing divisions.

As the fall semester came to a close, the university administration underwent a very significant "sea change." In December, Mary Lai, the grand lady of Long Island University administration, retired, ending more than a half-century of devoted, highly competent service to the university. After a nationwide search, the university hired Robert Altholz, a certified public accountant who had served as assistant comptroller at Yale University and went on to become the chief financial officer at St. Louis University, where he managed a yearly budget of $500 million. Unlike Mary Lai, whose maternal style had earned her so much loyalty and respect from everyone in the university, Altholz earned respect as a "numbers" man with a cold professional eye.

Forestell's Six Questions, February 11, 2004

The optimism from the previous summer dropped during the fall semester. A growing number of the faculty, although relieved that the trustees had approved the progress toward the new core, were raising serious questions about the state of the college. Some appeared to be just worn down by the constant feeling of angst fueled by what they saw as an atmosphere of desperation coming from the University Center. Some had worked very hard, putting in long hours on committees and developing courses and proposals only to have them rejected by Kane and Sillerman. Nancy Peters spoke for them in a letter that she wrote to Jeff Kane in January: "I currently feel worse about the transformation of Southampton College than I have ever felt. . . . The constant reminder of the enormous deficits that we hear from the University Center are delivered in such a way that we in the Natural Science Division feel somehow personally and professionally to blame" (SCC, Archive B-IV, e, Peters to Kane Jan. 21, 2004). Arvind Borde leveled more sharply worded critiques of the university officials, accusing them of incompetent bungling while the college ship was sinking. Don Baker echoed Borde's evaluation of the LIU administration, charging them with mismanagement, financial irresponsibility, and administrative ineptitude (SCC Archive B-IV, Baker Memo 2004).

Paul Forestell was in a very difficult position. He had been a strong supporter of interdisciplinary education throughout his academic career in Psychobiology. He had, as noted above, played a leading role in the development of the program at Southampton. Forestell also took his role as chairman of the faculty council very seriously. In an attempt to address the issues raised by several faculty members, he wrote a carefully worded list of six "discussion items" to Sillerman, Kane, and Steinberg, suggesting that they be the focus of a discussion at the next faculty meeting on February 18, 2004. Forestell introduced the list with a reminder about the enormous amount of time and effort put into the development of the core by members of the faculty. He also pointed out how much solid progress had been made in a very short period of time. The following questions, he said, represent the major concerns of the faculty "as we speed toward September of 2004" (SCC Archive B-IV, e, Memorandum Forestell to Sillerman, Steinberg, and Kane Feb. 11, 2004).

The first question noted the steadily rising yearly deficits and asked how the reduced number of courses, tutorials, and independent study programs offered in 2003–04 had resulted in actual deficit reduction. He also asked for a report on the current status of the capital campaign to raise a "healthy endowment." The next question concerned the recruitment problems from 2002 and the absence of any model that would predict the impact of the new curriculum on student applications and retention. The third question was much more provocative, expressing the long-standing concern about the role of the faculty in curricular matters. It began by noting that there was a majority view among the faculty that while they had accepted the chancellor's challenge to "choose life," critical decisions, such as the adoption and the character of the new core and the removal of divisions, "have been imposed on us by the administration with little regard for our preferred alternatives or our experience in delivering education." Where, they asked, was the faculty, staff, and student morale on the university radar? "How can we maintain excitement and investment in the programs we must administer when our collective will is routinely dismissed and efforts to enroll or support us in making programmatic changes are minimal?"

Next, he asked how much autonomy the new dean, currently being recruited, would have to administer the new curriculum. They also wanted to know about the funds and resources that the university would commit to support the transition to the new core and for the new administrative structure. The fifth question concerned academic matters. Would the emphasis on interdisciplinary programs interfere significantly with faculty members whose career paths depended on discipline-specific research and publication? Many remained convinced that valid interdisciplinary studies had to be based on a thorough command of at least one of the disciplines involved. The last question was closely related to the third concern about faculty involvement in decisions that directly affected their teaching. They acknowledged their gratitude for the investment in new and improved campus facilities, but noted, "We, however, will be the ones who must work and teach in whatever structures and facilities are added and modified. What plans are underway to seek faculty input on the nature and timing of the changes to the campus?"

The questions, of course, conveyed a mood of dissatisfaction and revisited issues that had been discussed frequently over the previous two semesters. Forestell welcomed Sillerman, Steinberg, and Kane to the faculty meeting on February 18, 2004. He then gave a PowerPoint presentation highlighting his six questions. Sillerman responded, but sidestepped most of the questions, shifting focus to an overview of the core curriculum. He repeated his conviction about the new core. It would, he believed, "revolutionize and redefine a liberal arts and sciences education in the 21st century" (SCC Archive B-IV, e, Faculty Council Minutes Feb. 18, 2004). This plan, he again warned, required significant faculty support and involvement. Sillerman reminded the faculty about the university's commitment to raising $60 million for the revitalization the college. This planned investment, he continued, was a strong vote of confidence for the college. His response did not satisfy many at the meeting. In the view of some, Sillerman had only offered a wildly hopeful vision of a prominent role in higher education for the core and an unfunded pledge of financial support. His implication, however, was clear. This was no time for the sort of questions that Forestell had posed. Kane, in contrast, simply dismissed the faculty concerns without comment. In so doing, he lost whatever shred of respect and legitimate authority he had left. Even those faculty who were committed to the new core became increasingly critical of Kane (R. Turner and J. Gonzalez pers. comm. 2011). Nevertheless, they put their feelings about Kane aside and turned to the task of developing the new curriculum.

Fine-Tuning the New Core

Once the parameters were in place, the faculty in the core program could turn to the details of specific course development. By the end of February, nineteen course proposals had been submitted to the core committee from twenty-three faculty members. Each course proposal included a brief abstract and a discussion of those aspects of the course that addressed the requirements for at least two of the "essential literacies." The larger challenge was the development of the global introduction to interdisciplinary studies for the incoming freshmen. Work on this "cornerstone in the drive to reinvent the college," had begun in 2002 but had become bogged down from time to time in disagreements between Kane and the faculty committee members. By the late spring of 2004, the faculty for the course had been identified: Liz Granitz, Scott Carlin, Susan Oatis, John Strong, Nancy

Peters, and Rob Turner, who served as the coordinator. The focus, suggested by Liz Granitz, was on an interdisciplinary approach to the study of water as a vital environmental and a cultural resource. Students were introduced to four disciplines: Hydrology, Ecology, Political Science, and Economics. Turner, who had received a grant from the Peconic Estuary Program, narrowed the course theme to the Peconic estuary watershed (SCC Archives B-IV, e, Turner Memo Feb. 2005).

The viewbook produced by the admissions office (see above) focused on the new core, with attractive photographs of faculty meeting with groups of four or five students along with descriptions of interdisciplinary courses, and off-campus experiential classes in exotic locales. Provost Rodas wrote an introduction that described Southampton as "one of the nation's most exciting colleges." The innovative curriculum, continued Rodas, was the only one of its kind in the nation. It was, he said, "revolutionizing higher education and reshaping the way you learn." Rodas went on to note that "an unprecedented $60 million commitment from the university's board of trustees will fund major campus projects." Sillerman could not have said it better.

The new innovations in recruiting under Rory Shaffer-Walsh were going very well. Alice Flynn and others involved in the recruiting campaign were convinced, however, that the students were responding more to news about the new buildings and the campus improvements than to the descriptions about the new core. As soon as the letters of acceptance went out, they were followed up with phone calls from Rory, from her staff, and from faculty members who taught in the academic areas identified by the students. The joint effort, she believed, brought the college community together in an unprecedented fashion. Rory recalled that, in the process, she developed fairly close personal relationships with many of the prospective students.

April-May: Mixed Messages Abound

The search committee for a permanent dean was called off in April. The new dean would have to be selected from among the campus faculty, none of whom had any experience as an academic administrator. The decision was made for financial reasons, raising questions about the enthusiastic public relations promotions describing all the new campus buildings and renovations and the new viewbook touting an innovative new curriculum to be implemented by an experienced, highly qualified academic leader. How was it the university could not afford to fill a position so vital to the functioning of the innovative programs and so crucial to the establishment of the controversial new academic administrative structures? In retrospect, it is clear that the university officials were becoming very concerned about the troubling reports from Robert Altholz, warning about the steadily growing deficits at Southampton. The efforts to raise matching funds from the trustees had failed. The issue was resolved with an informal decision to leave Hitchcock in place as the permanent dean.

During this time Dean Hitchcock was receiving occasional comments from Jeff Kane about the growing dissatisfaction among the trustees concerning the situation at Southampton. In 2002, the trustees noted the 29 percent discount rate at Southampton was more than twice that of Brooklyn and C. W. Post and asked for it to be lowered as soon as possible. It did not happen. Instead, by 2004 the rate had reached nearly 40 percent. This was the only way, said Hitchcock, we could attract students. The result, of course was a steep rise in the projected annual deficit. The only good news that spring was from the gym. The women's basketball team, coached by Pat McGunnigle, won the ECAC title. Senior Jill Jensen led the team to a 19–9 season record. (*Southampton Press* April 7, 2004).

Rob Altholz, who had been reviewing the financial situation at Southampton during the spring, advised the trustees' budget and finance committee that the projected budget losses for 2004 were unsustainable without an immediate infusion of cash. When this was reported to the trustees at their April meeting, a majority concluded that unless this cash became available the college should be closed. John Kanas, Southampton College's wealthiest alumnus, refused to help, stating bluntly that he would not pour any more good money down the drain. He recommended closing the college. There was a general agreement on the board, however, that they wanted more information before they made such a radical decision. The trustees remained unresponsive to Sillerman's demand for matching donations. Sillerman resented what he perceived to be an attempt by a majority of trustees to sit on their hands and shift the full financial responsibility to him. Some, including Tilles, would, no doubt, take great satisfaction in seeing Sillerman humbled by a very public failure.

The mood of the Board of Trustees was not mentioned at the April 21 meeting of the Southampton board of overseers (SCC Archive B-II, d, Board Minutes April 21, 2004). Relations between university administrators and the overseers required a delicate balancing act. The trustees were usually told that funds were needed, but any serious problems were always glossed over lest the potential donors be frightened away. This time, however, the news was all upbeat, with no hint of anything seriously awry. Sillerman opened by displaying a poster advertising the Marine Science program, "targeted to prospective students and their parents." It was sent to 2,500 yacht clubs and marinas in March. Sillerman, perhaps, had not entirely given up on his attempt to recruit students from wealthy families. Ironically he focused on the very department the "new Southampton" was in the process of diminishing. Sillerman invited the board members to attend the New York performance of Roger Rosenblatt's play "Ashley Montana Goes Ashore in the Caicos," starring Alan Alda and Mercedes Ruehl. There would be a buffet dinner for the board followed by a "Meet and Greet" the stars for the members and their guests.

Steinberg followed with a report about his initiative to bring world-class performances to the Avram Theater after they had played at the Tilles Center on the Post campus. Our plans, he said, are in the formative stages. His staff, he continued, were doing market research and developing a game plan. He promised to give a progress report at the July meeting. Rodas then discussed the new core curriculum, noting the hard work done by the faculty who had "embraced the program." He distributed course descriptions and a brief narrative about the "transdisciplinary" concept underlying the core curriculum. Rodas concluded his remarks with an account of plans to develop an "aggressive marketing strategy targeted to constituent audiences, a new website with video streaming of actual classes, and preview programs where prospective students can experience the new core curriculum."

After Rodas finished, Professor Chris Gobler from the Natural Science division described the accomplishments of the Marine Science program and outlined the plans for the renovation and expansion of the Marine Science Center. He recounted the successes of their graduates, many of whom had won Fulbrights and often gone on to earn advanced degrees. Gobler also noted that they often joined distinguished research centers and prominent university faculties. The college board of overseers, of course, were unaware of the irony in the decision by the university officials to give the spotlight at this meeting to the very program that they were in the process of diminishing.

Sillerman ended the meeting with a decidedly upbeat description of the capital campaign highlighting the commitments made by the university to build a new library, a new academic center, an ecologically engineered sewage system, a renovated Marine Science Center, a recreation center, and new dormitories. The Parrish Art Museum, he said, "may soon announce an architect and begin concrete discussions about a facility on campus." There followed a discussion among the members about priorities. Should the recreation center or the Marine Science Center be given priority? We should not make a choice, they concluded, we should do both through increased efforts in fundraising. One cannot help but wonder what was going through the minds of Rodas, Steinberg, and Sillerman during these discussions. They knew full well the capital campaign had failed to produce any significant funds, and consequently, the college was in danger of closing before the next scheduled meeting of this group.

The only real hope was a significant cash gift from Sillerman. Sillerman, however, wanted at least a token show of financial support from his fellow trustees, but, with the exception of Warren Schwerin, they continued to be unresponsive. Less than two weeks after the meeting with the board of overseers, Kim Woodhull, Provost Rodas's administrative assistant, sent out an open invitation to the campus community to attend a meeting in the Avram Theater, she described as "an important question and answer session." There was no stated agenda. The brief notice said only that, "Robert Sillerman will be here on Monday, May 3rd from 9–10:30 AM for a question and answer session in the Avram Theater. Please make every effort to attend this meeting. Questions welcomed" (SCC Archive B-IV, d, SH Provost List April 28, 2004). It was Sillerman's show: no other university official was there. Sillerman sat informally on the edge of stage as if he were addressing a small group in his living room.

He began by praising the faculty for the work they had done putting the new core program in place. This innovative curriculum, he said, would establish Southampton in the national spotlight as a leader in higher education. He spoke with great enthusiasm about the impact that the interdisciplinary core would have on universities and colleges across the country. Sillerman repeated the promise of a completely redone campus with new buildings and extensive renovations. There was no hint of the financial distress facing the college in his presentation, nor did the questions asked by the fifty or sixty students at the meeting reflect any serious concerns on their part. It was a somewhat peculiar performance given the existing financial conditions. Some thought he may have been attempting to gain support from the college community and put more pressure on his fellow trustees to come up with the matching funds.

During the next three weeks prior to Commencement, the impasse between Sillerman and the other trustees continued. Schwerin came forward with a small gift, but none of the other trustees offered their support. According to Steinberg and Mary Lai, a gift of $5 million in cash, not a pledge, would get the college through another year, at least. Sillerman, however, remained unwilling to give the money unless the trustees matched his donation. Steinberg, nevertheless, clung to the hope that Sillerman would come to the rescue.

There was some good news, however, from the admissions office. Shaffer-Walsh informed Rodas that she had received a very large number of inquiries from high school sophomores and juniors asking about Southampton College. It was most encouraging she said because it indicated that the enrollments for 2005 and 2006 would likely increase significantly (pers. comm. July 2011). Rodas, however, projected a drop in enrollment from 1,460 in 2003 to 1,280 in 2004, and another drop to 950 in 2005. He was apparently not at all optimistic about the prospects for converting the high school inquiries into cash deposits in spite of the enthusiastic publicity touting the marketing impact of the new curriculum and the new buildings.

The Final Blow, June 16, 2004

> Yesterday the University's Board of Trustees instructed the University Officers to relocate the undergraduate liberal arts and sciences currently offered at Southampton onto the C.W. Post Campus.
>
> —Steinberg Memorandum, June 16, 2004

According to Provost Rodas, the board met in his office on the morning of Commencement Day in an effort to convince Sillerman to put up the $5 million. The luncheon meeting, according to some, was acrimonious. Sillerman, in a dramatic gesture, once more challenged the other trustees. According to a widespread rumor, he defiantly waved his checkbook at his fellow trustees and said he was ready to write a check on the spot if any of the others would step up. Provost Rodas recalled the meeting, but said he did not remember the waving checkbook. Sillerman's refusal infuriated Steinberg, who had clung desperately to this one last hope. Sillerman later told reporters from *Newsday* he thought Steinberg and the LIU officers and trustees were acting erratically and that "this group of people, acting and operating the way they were, were not the people who we wanted to be the sole solution for" (Rothfeld and Winslow July 18, 2004). Sillerman's refusal to provide the necessary funds doomed the college. Steinberg, who had come to depend on Sillerman's generosity and on his frequently expressed commitment to the college, felt betrayed. The two men seldom spoke after that meeting.

Dean Hitchcock said he saw Steinberg looking "white as a sheet." Paul Forestell recalled seeing David "ashen-faced" following the trustees' luncheon. When Steinberg took the stage at commencement, he could not bring himself to make his traditional upbeat comments to the graduates. Instead of his familiar quote from *Star Wars*, "May the force be with you," he said only that he would spare the audience a speech in the hot sun. For those who believe in omens, there was another unexpected element. The highly publicized address by Vaclav Havel, the former president of the Czech Republic, was canceled at the last moment because of illness, disappointing many guests.

On the Monday after graduation, Jeff Kane told Forestell the closing of the Southampton campus was a very real possibility. A week earlier, the provosts of the Brooklyn and C. W. Post centers had pressed Steinberg not to take funds from their budgets to save Southampton. Enrollments at Post had suffered significantly as a result of a faculty strike in September 2003. When the opening of the semester was delayed, many students went elsewhere. During the next eight days the university officers, the budget and finance committee, and the executive committee of the Board of Trustees reviewed the financial reports prepared by Robert Altholz. A consensus was beginning to form around a "consolidation plan" transferring the academic programs from Southampton College to C. W. Post for the Fall 2004 semester.

The proposal was carefully worded to emphasize that it was "consolidation" and not a "closure" plan. The fundamental operating principle would be the preservation of the new core curriculum and the transdisciplinary learning program. The assumption was that only four hundred students would continue their studies at C. W. Post. The two hundred commuting graduate students would continue their studies on the Southampton campus. Fifty of the current sixty-four Southampton faculty would be moved to the other LIU campuses. If all went well the university would be free of Southampton's deficits by 2007. This approach would minimize the risks of litigation and a court-ordered temporary restraining order. Robert Altholz prepared a packet of documents supporting this proposal and sent it to all of the university trustees on Tuesday, June 8, for them to review prior to their meeting on June 15. There was little doubt that the consolidation plan would be approved by a majority of the trustees at that time.

On June 9, Dan Rodas invited the administrative staff, Dean Hitchcock, and Paul Forestell, the chairman of the faculty council, to a closed meeting in his office. Rodas told them that the Board of Trustees would vote to close the school at their next meeting. He made it clear that it was a "done deal." As Jennifer Browne recalled, "We were not completely surprised because we had all heard rumors about the mood of the trustees" (It. 11). Rory Shaffer-Walsh, however, was surprised and dismayed that the board had ignored the good news about the prospects for Fall 2005. There was a moment of stunned shock and disbelief as they reacted to the announcement. Paul recalled noting that everyone in the room except himself and Hitchcock were faced with the loss of their jobs. Tenured professors would have to be given jobs in one of the other centers, but the university had no obligation to help any of the administrators. "It was the end of the world as I knew it," lamented Alice Flynn, but no one in the room focused on their personal concerns. In spite of the unsettling implications for their jobs, recalled Forestell, their immediate thoughts were on the students. Their first concern was the decision to close the college at the end of August.

Rory's surprise and dismay quickly turned to anger. She had earned the trust of the incoming freshmen and their parents during her frequent communications with them over the past spring. She felt a moral obligation to make sure that the damage and the inconvenience was mitigated as much as possible under the circumstances. The decision to close abruptly in August would place the new students in an untenable position. Rodas was put on the defensive as he labored to explain why Steinberg and the trustees had decided to "transfer" the students to Post so quickly. The two arguments he presented sounded quite lame to the people in the room. Rodas explained that this plan would avoid any unpleasant student protests during the fall semester and would be the most "cost effective" for the university. When the author asked Steinberg about this strategy, he responded with a quote from *Macbeth* in his soliloquy contemplating the assassination of Duncan "If it were to be done when 'tis done, then t'were well it were done quickly." The university, as did Macbeth, wanted a quick ending that would "trammel up no consequences" (It. 46). Not only was the rationale focused entirely around the concerns of the university, completely ignoring the plight of the students, it was impractical in the extreme. "It's ridiculous," protested Alice Flynn, "it will never work, it's impossible" (It. 19).

Rodas brushed aside the objections raised by Flynn and the others, arguing that there would likely be few students left on campus in September anyway. They would either go to Post or enroll in another college in the fall or in the following spring. Rory Shaffer-Walsh argued that this was a callous failure to honor what she considered to be a professional and a moral obligation. The freshman class that she had worked so hard to recruit would have no time to go through the application process for a new college. All of the scholarship funds would have already been allocated at most colleges. It would also pose a hardship on students who had already signed agreements and made down payments on their rooms for the next academic year. More than half of the students lived in off-campus housing. More importantly, the move to Post ignored one of the primary reasons many students had chosen Southampton. They had responded with enthusiasm to the emphasis in the college recruitment literature on small classes in an intimate small community environment. Now they were told that they might end up at Post, a large campus with larger classes. There was also the possibility of class action breach of contract suits. The university had made an agreement with the incoming freshmen for a four-year program at Southampton. It was becoming clear now that any number of consequences would "trammel up."

Rodas told the group not to say anything about this in public until the board made it official at their meeting on the fifteenth. Paul recalled meeting with Alice Flynn, Jennifer Browne, Rory Shaffer-Walsh, Provost Rodas, and Dean Hitchcock to discuss their concerns about the decision to close at the end of August. It was an emotional time for all. Some lost their composure and momentarily burst into tears as they came to terms with the full implications of the decision. They all felt obliged to express their objections about the date proposed in the recommendation to the board. Steinberg remained adamant about the August closing. The group agreed that Paul, as the elected head of the faculty, should be the one to address the board if they would allow him to speak at their meeting. Paul had some doubts about his authority to speak before the board without consulting the faculty, but there was no way to assemble a quorum in time (pers. comm. 2010). The majority of faculty had left campus for the summer. He spoke with Sillerman, Harry Marmion, Roger Rosenblatt, Congressman Tim

Bishop, and Bob Pattison, who all agreed that the campus should remain open for at least the Fall 2004 semester. Steinberg, to his credit, called Paul and told him that his leadership role in the development of the new curriculum and his passionate concern for the students had earned him the right to address the board at their meeting on Tuesday afternoon. Bishop encouraged him, and told him to "speak from his heart."

Forestell spoke eloquently about the moral obligation that LIU owed to the students, the faculty, and staff of the college. He reminded the board that it was the Post faculty, not the Southampton faculty, who had engaged in the 2003 strike. An abrupt closure, he continued, would inevitably result in chaos, and, undoubtedly, in some very bad publicity for LIU. Here, he pulled out all the plugs in a dramatic flourish. "What if one of the students with a contract for off campus housing in Southampton were to have a fatal accident on the Long Island Expressway on the commute to their classes at Post." He then moved a pointed finger back and forth at the assembled trustees and asked, "Who among you is going to tell the parent you made this decision for financial reasons or to prevent student protest?" There was silence in the room. Paul went on to urge the board to grant at least one more semester to allow for a more humane and well-organized transition. The board listened and agreed to delay the closure until the fall of 2005, thereby avoiding yet another bad decision by the university.

Shock, Disbelief, and Anger

Steinberg addressed a letter to the Southampton College community on June 16 and sent a copy to the media. "It is with heavy heart," he wrote, "that I write to inform of a painful but necessary decision." He went on to cite the factors leading him to make the decision: the $9 million deficit for the year, the anticipated $12 million deficit for the 2004–05 year, the accumulated debt of $77 million by 2005, and the current low enrollment (SCC Archive B-II, d, Steinberg Memorandum June 16, 2004). University officials made the announcement to the campus community at a hastily convened meeting the next day in the Fine Arts Theater. Richard McIntyre, the director of the Marines Science research station, said the small number of faculty and students who attended the meeting were "stunned into silence" (*Newsday* June 17, 2004). Michele Pananan, a sophomore from Dix Hills, told a reporter from the *Southampton Press* that she was "just pissed." They didn't know anything, she said, about where students would live on the Post campus, how credits would transfer, and how financial aid would be handled (*Southampton Press* June 17, 2004). There had, of course, been no advance planning for the transition. The confusion and the inability to answer these basic questions simply fueled the perception of poor management and incompetence. Rumors about the reasons for the decision to close immediately began to spread. There was speculation about fraud, gross mismanagement, and a suspicion that LIU was doing this in order to sell off the campus to real estate speculators and use the money for undisclosed nefarious purposes.

Most of the faculty and students had left the campus and were, by then, busy with their summer activities. The public announcement to the press was lost in the local media hype about the 104th U.S. Open Golf Tournament, which had begun the day before on the Shinnecock Golf Course across the road from the campus. Not surprisingly, given the past history of the college's relations with University Center, many assumed that Steinberg had purposely released the announcement at this time to avoid media attention and to make it difficult for student and faculty protests to get organized. The manner in which most of the campus community received the word contributed to the feelings of conspiracy and betrayal.

Mary Topping received a call from a friend in Chancellor's Hall, followed by an e-mail. "I was in total disbelief," she said, "I was convinced that the college had potential and could have survived. I shouldn't have been surprised," she continued. "It was typical of LIU: chaotic, no vision and no plans for dealing with all the problems related to the closing. . . . We had no instructions for closing the athletic facility. What was I supposed to do, just throw the keys in the trash and walk away?" (It. 49). Many faculty and staff agreed with her assessment. For Professor Goldberg, who heard about the closing from Topping while he was shopping in the local hardware store, disbelief soon gave way to anger. "We have to do something," he said, and proceeded to call some colleagues, but he had trouble getting through to anyone. Professor Herbert Sherman reacted at first with disbelief. "I thought it was a joke," he said, "there was no consultation and then to get the news from an e-mail!" (It. 44). Bob Gerbereux was in his office looking over samples of carpeting that would be installed in the new library for its opening in September. The news was devastating for him. He had worked tirelessly for the past three decades to get a new library, which would be named the Bishop-Burke Learning Center in honor of Tim Bishop and William Burke. The *New York Times* had run a detailed article describing the "green" features of the library design. The 29,600 square foot building would be "energy efficient and harmonious in design with its setting" (April 18, 2004). The energy-saving components included a geothermal energy system and an overall design minimizing heat loss and large windows facing the north. Gerbereux was justifiably proud of the new building and the statement it made about the commitment of the college to its long-standing concerns about the environment. Now, just as he was so close to seeing his vision realized, his dream had collapsed and his job was gone. Many of those who received word by e-mail from the University Center were offended by this impersonal form of communication. The word, no matter how it was received, was met with resentment by most of the Southampton community. Robert Martin was particularly incensed that the board of college overseers was not consulted before the decision was made. Martin learned about the closing while he was attending the U.S. Open. His anger, however, stemmed from a rather naive belief that the board of overseers was something more than a means of stroking the egos of potential donors with the illusion that they were actually involved with the development of university policy.

The Situation Room

> We were traumatized. It was like being in a war room. Parents cursing us, berating us, accusing us of taking their money deceitfully and many more unpleasant things. Others broke out crying.
>
> —Alice Flynn

The University Center sent out letters by Federal Express to all of the freshmen, telling them the campus was closing but emphasizing that the academic programs would be continued on the C. W. Post campus. Most of these letters arrived over the weekend of June 19–20. Peter Saltanis recalled receiving his letter the weekend before his high school graduation:

> It was an Airborne Express from New Jersey and I thought to myself who do I know in New Jersey? Not only was it impersonal, but mailed from New Jersey? When I opened it I was devastated and my parents were furious. I had spent several months looking for a small school with a well-developed environmental studies major. I didn't know what to do. I was sort of depressed most of the summer, but I finally decided that I would go to Southampton for the year and then see how thing would work out. (It. 43)

Rory Shaffer-Walsh recalled that one student received the news as he was preparing for his senior prom. He was so upset that he decided not to go (pers. comm. 2011). Another heard the news at his graduation party. One of his presents was a Southampton College sweatshirt.

The university had made no plans for any other contact with the students. Rory and the other staff members involved with student affairs were appalled. They decided that this was inadequate, and proposed that all the freshmen be called and given some personal attention. Jennifer Browne, Rory Shaffer-Walsh, Alice Flynn, Jean Conroy, and Amy Urquart volunteered to take on the responsibility. Rodas, Hitchcock, and Forestell supported this approach. The women were told, however, that they were on their own, Steinberg would take no calls. All e-mails from parents and students that came to any of the university offices were redirected to them.

These dedicated administrators set to work, as one wryly noted, "cleaning up someone else's train wreck."

During a two- to three-day marathon the women phoned all the freshmen with the news. They set up a phone bank on the second floor of Pratt Hall to follow up the letters. They soon discovered that some had not yet received the letter of notification from the university. These calls were the most difficult. The people often thought that the call was to give them information about freshman orientation in the fall. The response to the news was a combination of shock, disbelief, and anger. Accusations were hurled at them charging deceit and fraud. High school guidance counselors turned on Shaffer-Walsh, accusing her of lying to them. This was devastating for her both professionally and personally. She had worked very hard to earn their confidence and their trust; now that was lost.

The women were subjected to shouting, rude comments, and abuse. Some of the recipients of the calls burst into tears. These latter calls, they said, were the most wrenching. "Our colleagues," said Alice, "gave us moral support and brought us coffee and food" during the ordeal. There was a strong feeling, shared among many of the staff, that the male officials responsible for the crisis, had taken a cowardly exit and left the women to deal with a disaster not of their making. Several mentioned with great annoyance Steinberg's refusal to take any calls.

Once the initial emotional response had subsided, the students were reassured that they would be able to take the courses in the new curriculum in the fall and that the process of transition to the Post campus would be as smooth a transition as possible. If they wished to transfer to another college immediately or at the end of the Fall 2004 semester, they would receive full support and assistance. Rory, however, felt that she had lost their trust. She had also, she feared, lost the confidence of the local guidance counselors that she had worked so hard to earn over the past two years. The five women remained in this stressful "situation" for two or three more days.

The faculty were stunned and angry. "I thought we chose life," quipped Professor Herb Sherman. Those faculty members who had supported the university in the development of the new curriculum and had worked long uncompensated hours on the new courses felt betrayed. All of the faculty were concerned about their terms of employment. On June 28, Bill Roberson and Bob Pattison represented the union in a meeting with university attorney George Sutton and Lee Kelly, the director of human resources, to discuss the implications of the campus closing for the union contract. In a memo to the membership, Pattison reported that the existing contract would be honored for the next academic year and that those with tenure would be guaranteed positions at C. W. Post, Brooklyn, and Brentwood. The unions at those campuses indicated that they would cooperate in the process of relocating Southampton faculty but wanted assurance that their own faculty would not lose tenure slots. Pattison and Roberson urged the university to do a better job about controlling rumor and speculation.

The Long Hot Summer

It was a public relations nightmare of historic proportions. It was the 1930s bankruptcy, the 1950s basketball scandal, the Hoxie and Brooklyn episode all rolled into one and there was no one at University Center with sufficient expertise or experience to handle it. Paola Curcio-Kleinman, the associate president for marketing and public relations, and her assistant Kimberly Volpe had little time to organize and prepare for the barrage of questions from reporters. They hoped to get out ahead of the story with a lead message emphasizing the word *transition* and avoiding any use of the words *shut* or *closure*. The college was not closing, they said, it was merely moving its programs to the C. W. Post campus. It was, however, immediately obvious to everyone that the most prestigious academic program could not be moved away from Shinnecock Bay. There was no Marine Science facility available at Post. There was one other serious concern. The initial message from the university also indicated that the campus might be sold to the highest bidder, leaving open the possibility that a developer might purchase the property and put up condos. This prompted former U.S. congressman Michael Forbes and Southampton town supervisor Patrick Heany, a Southampton College alumnus, to begin discussing a plan to change the zoning in order to prevent a sale to a developer.

The dimension of the public relations problem soon became clear. The attempt to convince the public that a "transition" was not a "closure" failed, and the alarm about condos was not even addressed at that time. Two days after Steinberg's letter went out, the *Southampton Press* carried the headline "College Will Be Shut Next Year" (June 17, 2004). The same article quoted state assemblyman and distinguished Southampton alumnus Fred Thiele's angry reaction to the news: "I vehemently disagree with the very short-sighted decision," he said, "Especially in light of the recent improvements at the college. This decision is like Pearl Harbor—with no forewarning whatsoever. To an outside observer, it looks like extreme incompetence on the part of the university to make millions of dollars of improvements and then shut the campus down." Thiele believed that a sale to a condo developer was a real possibility. It would only get worse for the public relations office. These words and sentiments were repeated in one form or another in the media throughout the summer. As noted several times in this book, LIU's history was a heavy burden for the public relations office. Observers on Eastern Long Island were most receptive to any negative news about LIU, accurate or not.

Stung by Thiele's charge of incompetence and panic, Steinberg told a *New York Times* reporter the following Sunday that "the decision was not taken lightly or precipitously, it was taken with great sadness and real pain." (*New York Times* June 20, 2004). The students had no sympathy for Steinberg's pain. Kathleen Graham, a Psychobiology major, told the same reporter, "I'm pretty angry about it," and went on to point out that she came to Southampton because she wanted a small school where you had a face. Post is huge, she said, there will be no intimacy there. Volpe responded to these concerns in a press release the next week, assuring the students that although there was no possibility of moving the Marine Science program to Post, the campus was accommodating and could offer "a rich array of things to take advantage of." The transition, said Volpe, will be as seamless as possible. The article in the *Independent*, however, was under a headline announcing, "LIU to Close Undergraduate Program" (June 23, 2004). A headline in the *East Hampton Star* read, "College Closing Blamed on Debt, Poor Enrollment" (June 24, 2004).

In the *Star* article, Provost Rodas again emphasized that the academic programs were simply relocating to a new campus, "It's just a new location." Dean Hitchcock assured the *Star* reporter that "the new core curriculum to be introduced at the Southampton campus in September will be a cornerstone of the relocated program." These comments were followed, however, by Professor Danziger's blunt assessment of the new curriculum. It went over, he said, "like a dead fish, it looked like a dead fish, it smelled like a dead fish, and it went belly up." Although many, the author included, disagreed with Danziger's assessment, his words added fuel to the growing public relations nightmare for LIU.

The few students who were on campus met to discuss their options. There was a naive hope that they could somehow raise the money themselves to save the college, but appeals to corporations such as MacDonald's and to celebrities such as Oprah were about all they could come up with. Their concerned response reflected the strong bond that students have historically made with the college.

In defense of the university, it should be noted that the administration had moved quickly to open negotiations with Shirley Strum Kenny, the president of State University of New York at Stony Brook, about the possibility of taking over the Marine Science Station and of admitting the Southampton College majors who might wish to transfer to Stony Brook. An article in the *Southampton Press* (June 24, 2004) reported that the move by Steinberg was endorsed by State Senator Kenneth LaValle, chair of the Senate Committee on Higher Education and by Assemblyman Fred Thiele. The same article, however, quoted Congressman Bishop, who noted that the college had been undercapitalized throughout its history and former

Southampton College president Harry Marmion, who cited what he believed to be the "routinely mismanaged" university resources. "They created their own mess," said Marmion.

It's a Land Grab!

Many events scheduled earlier now proved to be somewhat embarrassing. One of them was the annual Distinguished Citizen Award honoring local citizens who had made an outstanding contribution to their community. It was an opportunity to raise a modest sum and to develop a good rapport with the neighboring communities. The money was divided between the recipient's charity or nonprofit organization and Southampton College. This year, the recipient was John Halsey, a direct descendant of Thomas Halsey, one of the original settlers who founded the Town of Southampton in 1640. Halsey, a respected and much admired champion of land preservation, was the founder and president of the Peconic Land Trust. This organization is committed to protecting the remaining open spaces in the township from overdevelopment. Friends of Halsey, supporters of closely related environmental organizations, and members of the Southampton College community, including David Steinberg and Harry Marmion, attended the reception on June 25 in Chancellor's Hall.

The reception came the day after the *Southampton Press* ran an article quoting Marmion's disparaging remarks about the history of mismanagement by the LIU leadership. Steinberg was beginning to show signs of stress that must have been building since the confrontation at the trustees' Commencement luncheon. When Steinberg began his introduction of Halsey, he went sharply off message and launched into a defense of the decision to close the college. He repeated the mantra about the debt, the deficit, and the low enrollment to an audience who were becoming most uncomfortable. Marmion, in particular, felt that Steinberg's remarks were inappropriate, even insulting, to Halsey and those who came to show their support for his work in preserving farmland and open spaces from developers. Many other members of the college community were also dismayed. They felt that the people had come to honor Halsey, not to hear an unpopular LIU official defend an unpopular decision.

When Steinberg finished, Marmion stood up and blurted out an impromptu and most ironic remark, given the occasion: "That's a bunch of bull, and you know it, David. It's a land grab, pure and simple!" (Marmion, pers. comm. 2005) There was an awkward silence, but the program continued without any further mention of Marmion's accusation. His words, however, gave more fuel to the growing suspicion that LIU would not hesitate to negotiate with a developer. A few days later, an editorial in the *Southampton*

Press accused LIU of treating the campus like a "cash cow ready for the slaughter" (July 1, 2004). The editorial went on to raise questions that were on many minds. The editor found it baffling that the sudden decision to close the school was made only a year after the university announced, "with much pomp and circumstance, an ambitious plan to spend $60 million to improve the campus. . . . How did things fall apart so rapidly?" The plan to move the Marine Science program to Stony Brook was fine, continued the editorial, but "the college as we know it will still be dead."

Shortly after the reception for John Halsey, Marmion wrote a memo to Provost Rodas demanding that none of the funds raised at the reception go to LIU. Rodas responded with a politely worded letter thanking Marmion for his past support and informing him that "we find ourselves in an unusual circumstance but Southampton is open and operational and these funds are important to this coming year" (SCC Archive B-II, D, Memo: Rodas to Marmion July 22, 2004). Rodas's defense was not convincing to Marmion, nor to at least one other prominent donor.

At the beginning of July, Nancy Wendell, the executive director of the Evan Frankel Foundation, wrote to Provost Rodas requesting the return of any unallocated funds. The foundation, named after a wealthy East Hampton investor, had been a generous supporter of the Marine Science program. In 2001, the foundation gave $400,000 in matching funds to establish an endowment for Marine Science scholarships. Over a five-year period from 1998 to 2003 the foundation had awarded $184,000 in scholarship aid to Marine Science majors. Andrew Sabin, the president of the foundation had made it quite clear that while he was an admirer and enthusiastic supporter of the college Marine Science program, he was not at all impressed with Long Island University. He did not want any funds to find their way into the university's general budget. The sudden decision to close the campus may have raised the suspicions of Sabin and Wendell, because the week before closing Wendell had been assured the library was being completed and work would soon begin on the construction of a new Marine Science Station. In December 2003, library director Robert Gerbereux, wearing a hard hat, had signed the last steel beam as it was hoisted into place on the roof of the new library. Ironically, at about the time Wendell was writing her letter, the construction workers were ordered to complete the library roof, install the windows, and lock the doors for good.

Rodas wrote back to Wendell informing her he could not do anything until the university had a chance to evaluate "the impact of these actions on the designated gifts and grants to the University" (SCC Archive B-II, b, Rodas to Wendell July 9, 2004). He thanked the foundation for its gifts in the past and told Wendell the university must follow established legal procedures and receive clearance from the Internal Revenue Service before returning the gifts. The gift was later returned. In contrast to Rodas's insistence on protocol and delay, Barbara Grodd, the director of development for the college, immediately returned a check, by hand, to a donor.

The Last Deans

On July 21, 2004, Paul Forestell was appointed dean and mandated to lead the transition of students and programs to the C. W. Post campus. Dean Hitchcock was given the responsibility to oversee the graduate programs. Ironically, the dean parade finally ended with two campus deans. Forestell faced a daunting task with no existing precedents to work from. The students and parents were angry, the faculty and staff were still in shock, and reporters, frustrated with the secretive and confrontational attitude of the university public relations office, were constantly on the phone. Among the uncertainties were the number of students who would be on campus in September, the number of faculty and staff who would be needed, and the fate of the new curriculum. Did it make any sense, for example, to implement the new courses if they were not going to be continued at Post? Forestell and Kane believed that it would be possible to operate a "college within a college" on the Post campus. Many of the faculty who were committed to the interdisciplinary concept were skeptical about this possibility, but they wanted a chance to put all their hard work on the courses into practice even if the program did not survive the transfer to Post.

The followup telephone interviews of the freshman class made by Rory Shaffer-Walsh and the other staff members in the situation room indicated that about 130 to 150 would come for the fall semester. This was a surprise because early expectations suggested the number would be little more than forty. Many, however, came reluctantly because they had no other options. It was clear that the implementation of the vaunted new curriculum, a challenge under the best of circumstances, would test the patience, the skills, the commitment, and the character of faculty in the new program.

It was not until mid-August that the fall enrollment figures were becoming clear. The numbers surprised many. An estimated nine hundred students would attend in spite of the prevailing climate of anger and uncertainty. Pattison issued a memo to the union members assuring them that all of the full-time faculty would be needed on campus for the next academic year.

Fueling the Media Fires

> If you wanted a classic example of how not to run a public relations office, Paola at LIU would be it. She kept telling the press "No comment" or answered rudely, "don't ask me to do

> your job for you!" The media were really angry and, of course, the bad PR got worse.
>
> —Pekka Paavonpera, appointed director of public relations for Southampton College in the summer of 2004

In a desperate attempt to deal with the growing public relations disaster, Paola Curcio-Kleinman's office issued a press release on July 29 that actually confirmed the worst suspicions. The LIU trustees announced the formation of a special committee to explore the future use of the Southampton College campus. The title of the new committee made many wonder why this action had not been taken until more than a month after the college closed. Roger Tilles charged the new committee with formulating recommendations for the executive committee of the board and addressing ways the university could "fulfill its mission as an educational institution committed to learning, culture, scholarship and the advancement of knowledge." The subheading in the release read: "Trustees Focus on Preserving the Campus for Education and Culture." This was an attempt to answer the accusations such as the ones made by Harry Marmion and the editor of the *Southampton Press* that the trustees were looking for the highest bidder.

The third paragraph of the press statement, however, drew the attention of many in the Hamptons. Tillis stated that the board was committed to the preservation of the campus for educational purposes *if at all possible* (italics by author) and added that it was incumbent upon the board "to explore all options." It was these qualifying statements that fed the rumors and suspicions. The failure to reassure the public about the board's intent was evident a week later at a public hearing on the Southampton campus. The *Independent* (Aug. 4, 2004) ran a report about the hearing under the headline: "Growing Outrage Over College Closure." Professor Scott Carlin, who moderated a panel including Congressman Bishop and Assistant Deputy County Executive Ben Zwirn, expressed concern about the possibility that the campus would "fall prey to developers." The headline also made it clear that LIU's attempt to avoid reference to the word *closure* was not working.

Save the College at Southampton

> We will not go quietly into that last goodnight.
>
> —Save the College at Southampton (SCS)

Once the shock and disbelief wore off, a group of alumni, including Joan DiPaola Tutt (1968), Robert Martin (1968), V. Anthony (Vam) Maggipinto, Michael Director (1968), Alan Braveman (1968), Assemblyman Fred Thiele (1976), and recent graduate Nora Detweiler (2005), met with Donald Baker, Scott Carlin, and Harry Marmion and founded Save the College at Southampton (SCS), an organization dedicated, at the outset, to reversing the LIU decision to close the campus. When it became evident that this would not happen, the group began discussing alternative proposals to preserve the campus for educational purposes. Professor Scott Carlin was quoted in a press release stating that their mission was to save the college and to provide an intellectually vibrant and ecologically sound undergraduate program at Southampton (*Southampton Press* July 15, 2004).

One alternative was the establishment of an independent private college free from what they believed was the stigma of Long Island University. An independent Southampton College, they argued, would be in a much better position to raise funds from local sources that had been reluctant to give to LIU. The proposal called for the expensive Marine Science program to be turned over to Stony Brook. An interesting variation on this theme was drafted by Carlin, who suggested renaming the college, "Shinnecock College" and establishing a cooperative relationship with the Shinnecock Nation. The interdisciplinary curriculum would focus on environmental sustainability. These proposals were abandoned as the emphasis shifted to the hope that Stony Brook University under the leadership of President Shirley Kenny might take over the campus.

Three weeks after the 2004 Commencement, Edward Travaglianti, chairman of the LIU Board of Trustees, came out to Southampton and asked Sillerman to resign from the board. Sillerman agreed, on the condition that LIU sell the campus to Stony Brook University. "I agreed to step down," Sillerman told a reporter from the *Southampton Press*, "after receiving positive assurances from Board Chairman, Edward Travaglianti, that the Board was serious about SUNY's offer and that LIU will enter into a proactive dialogue about the offer" (June 23, 2004). The implication of Sillerman's remark undoubtedly infuriated many of the trustees. Sillerman, however, did not relinquish his position as chancellor of Southampton College.

> As on the *Titanic*, the Band Played on
>
> —*New York Times* headline, August 29, 2004

When the planning began on the 2004 *All For The Sea* concert, the intention was to put on a highly publicized and elaborately staged performance as a prelude to the implementation of the new curriculum for the "new Southampton College" (*Southampton Press* Aug. 26, 2004). Sillerman felt that Rod Stewart had the suitable star power for the event, described by Anne Rachel, the concert coordinator, as the celebration of an academic renaissance at Southampton. The concert, she said was the most expensive and extravagant that the college had ever produced. "We wanted this to be a huge success," she continued. It was certainly extravagant. The total cost of the event came to about $1.1 million. Stewart, who refused to waive his fee as he had done when he performed at the concert in 1998, wanted an elaborate sound stage and other unspecified amenities.

The V.I.P. guests, who had paid $400 a ticket for the privilege of viewing the concert up close in a lavishly catered tent facility, seemed satisfied with Rodas's assurance that the profits from the concert would be used for scholarships in the 2004–05 academic year. The ticket sales, of course, took a big hit. For the first time in twelve years, the concert was not sold out. Rachel said there were about two thousand tickets left unsold. The event raised $500,000, about one-half of the average profits from the previous concerts.

SCS volunteers attended the concert, passing out pamphlets and yellow stickers reading "Save Southampton's College." They also carried around a petition, signed by about five hundred people, urging the preservation of the campus for educational purposes. David Suskind, a Southampton town councilman, voiced his support saying: "If L.I.U. tries to do anything with this campus other than turn it over to another college, the town and the county and the people here will go to the wall, they will have to." Sillerman, wearing a large yellow button with the same message, told reporters the button expressed his support for continued existence of a four-year educational institution that was not associated in any way with Long Island University. "It is not an institution," he continued, "that, at the moment, has much courage" (*New York Times* Aug. 29, 2004). He was unwilling, he said to be the college's cash cow. When a reporter asked Paola Curcio-Kleinman for a response to Sillerman's remarks, she said that it was inappropriate for President Steinberg or any other university official to respond.

Two weeks later the new freshman students arrived to begin what was to be a most surreal academic year. As one student, thinking back on the year, quipped: "It was a year of living weirdly." Indeed it was.

Chapter Twelve

The Long Goodbye, 2004–2005

> Let's live it up and go out with a bang so that when we look back on our last year at Southampton College, the only thing anyone will be able to say is "that was one hell of a year."
>
> —Andrea Liebel, Student Government President

An Unpleasant Beginning

The freshman orientation program was understandably a challenge for Dean Forestell and the orientation committee. Peter Saltanis recalled the meeting with David Steinberg and Dean Forestell in the Fine Arts Theater on the first day. "Dean Forestell welcomed us and promised that the college was committed to making the transition to the C. W. Post campus as smooth as possible. He also said there would be full support if we wanted to transfer to another college at the end of the fall semester. The staff, he said, would give help in selecting another college" (It. 43). He was soon bombarded with questions, some delivered in hostile tone. "It got a bit rowdy," said Saltanis, "some people shouted angry comments at Steinberg." Dean Forestell did his best to address the questions as frankly as possible, but some in the audience would not be placated. They used the opportunity to vent their frustration. The negative tone of the meeting abated somewhat, but a palpable undercurrent of hostility toward the university remained well into the spring of 2005. For many in the college community, the wounds never healed.

Some believed there was still hope that the decision to close the campus could be reversed. In the summer, Scott Carlin, with the support of students and alumni, arranged with the owner of a house located across the road from the college to erect a sign six feet long and three feet wide, reading *Save Southampton's College*. "Everyone was enthusiastic about the sign," said Carlin, "because it is a nice reminder that a lot of work is going on behind the scenes to keep undergraduate studies here at the campus" (*Windmill* Oct. 2004). Sometime during the week of September 26 the sign mysteriously disappeared, and all realistic hope that LIU would reverse its decision disappeared about two months later.

The faculty arrived on campus in an angry mood. On October 14, the faculty council sent a letter to President Steinberg informing him that the council had passed two motions without a single dissenting vote.

> In the light of the mismanagement of Southampton College over the past several years, we the faculty vote no confidence in the President and administration of Long Island University.
>
> We the faculty at Southampton College strongly support the continuation of a 4-year undergraduate institution at the current site of Southampton College. (SCC Archive B-IV, e, Faculty Council Minutes Oct. 13. 2004)

The following day the letter was sent to the media and a press conference was held at the front gate of the college. Vam Maggipinto, a former president of the alumni association and a founding member of Save Southampton College, charged that the college closed because of poor leadership, not because of external factors over which the administration had no control. Maggipinto said his organization had sent a letter to the LIU Board of Trustees on September 22 requesting a meeting to form a coalition dedicated to maintaining undergraduate programs at Southampton. Another "good faith" letter was sent on October 5. There was no response, he said, to either overture. Steinberg and the trustees also declined to respond to the faculty resolutions.

Assemblyman Thiele had some good news. First, he promised that he would not allow the campus to be sold to developers, and then he reported that the State University of New York at Stony Brook was interested in going beyond the adoption of the Marine Science program. There had been some very preliminary discussions, said Thiele, about purchasing the campus and establishing a four-year undergraduate program. Don Baker followed with a brief discussion of the faculty resolution. There was more good news from another alumnus. Concerns about the sale to developers were allayed when Patrick (Skip) Heany, who was now serving as the town supervisor, announced his intention to impose a nine-month moratorium on development in the town. If successful, the legislation would block the consideration of any development plans by the town planning board until June 2005. Heaney's announcement to the press underscored the negative perception of LIU held by many on eastern Long Island. The moratorium was necessary, said Heany, because "I am concerned that we are dealing with at least some people who would not hesitate to involve themselves with the wholesale dissection of this property" (*Newsday* Oct. 15, 2004). Curcio-Kleinman responded in a manner that only encouraged suspicions. The university trustees, she said, are studying what to do with the property. Tilles could not be reached for a comment.

Soon after the new freshman class arrived on campus they began organizing a protest movement. They formed a loose coalition of students calling themselves the "Orphans of Long Island University." They dedicated themselves to reversing the decision to close the school. Their mission statement reflected the emotions stirred by their cause: "We believe that it was our destiny to come to this school, and now it has become out fight to save it." Peter Saltanis, one of the founders of the group, recalled that in the first week of the semester students seemed in shock, confused, angry, and uncertain about how to respond. In most classes, he said, teachers and students avoided talking about the situation. Two professors, Scott Carlin and Bob DeLuca, were the exception. DeLuca's class, Grassroots Environmental Advocacy, used the action by LIU as an opportunity for an exercise in experiential education. The instructors urged students to organize and to voice their opposition. By the middle of October, the "Orphans of LIU" was meeting every Wednesday evening in the student lounge. They chose the name to emphasize their conviction that the university had abandoned its obligation to provide them with a four-year education on the Southampton campus. At the beginning, their goal was to convince the trustees to keep the campus open, or at least to postpone the closing for another two or three years.

Waiting For Godot (or Anyone)

At the November faculty meeting there was some faint hope that Sillerman might support an attempt to found a four-year private college at Southampton. A few faculty members planned to raise this issue at a meeting the faculty council had requested with the chancellor. Sillerman had agreed to meet at a time convenient with his schedule. A week later, Arvind Borde, the faculty council president, reported, with some annoyance, that he had finally managed to get past Chancellor Sillerman's assistant's assistant to talk directly with the assistant. She told him the chancellor was out of the country and that she was trying to reach him. Borde asked her to try to arrange a meeting before the fall semester ended. A month later, the assistant told Borde that Sillerman would not be available until the next spring. There was now growing uncertainty about what Sillerman's role would be in college affairs. Although he kept his title until the following June, he was seldom seen on campus.

The student government representatives were experiencing similar frustrations in their attempts to arrange a meeting with the LIU Board of Trustees. No LIU officials, it seemed, wanted to venture anywhere near the campus. Student government president Andrea Liebel spoke with President Steinberg asking for a meeting with the trustees to discuss their decision to close the campus. Steinberg agreed and arranged for a meeting on October

26 at seven p.m. Shortly before the meeting, the trustees asked Liebel to reschedule the meeting because they did not want to drive home so late. In response and after what Liebel referred to as a "rescheduling nightmare" for her, she managed to find a twelve p.m. to two p.m. slot on November 17. Steinberg agreed on the date, but he did not inform Liebel that the trustees had once again found a reason to avoid the meeting.

It turned out to be very bad timing. On the day before the meeting, students from Southampton came to C. W. Post and staged a loud and colorful protest ending with an emotional confrontation at the University Center. In an effort to dramatize their concerns and put pressure on the university officials, the students, assisted by members of SCS and the Group for the East End (formerly the Group for the South Fork), organized the march. They were aware that Steinberg and the trustees were scheduled to come to the Southampton campus on the following day, but many, including Nora Detweiler, feared the university officials would find another excuse to avoid a confrontation with the students.

It was a colorful affair. On November 16, about fifty students came by bus dressed in a variety of costumes and carrying a set of bongo drums. There were grim reapers in hooded robes carrying scythes, and several homeless hobos wearing red and yellow bandanas carrying sticks with bedrolls tied to them. There were many protest signs urging the trustees to keep the college open. As is often the case in student demonstrations there was at least one unauthorized sign. The one at this march read, "Drop Acid not Southampton College." They marched across the Post campus to the student center chanting, "Truth and knowledge, save our college." TV cameras from News 12, and Channel 10 and reporters from *Newsday, The Southampton Press, The Independent,* and *Suffolk Life* were not allowed to follow the march across campus, but the students' dramatic arrival and the rally at the admissions office were well covered in what were, for the most part, favorable accounts of the protest. Paola Curcio-Kleinman, in a losing struggle to counter the negative publicity for the university, stated once again that the college was not closing, it was moving to C. W. Post, and added that the university "will maintain an open dialogue with the students." Her statement, tucked away in the middle of an article in *The Independent* (Nov. 17, 2004), received little attention.

After the rally at the admissions office, the demonstrators decided to pay an impromptu visit to President Steinberg's office in the Bush-Brown administration building in University Center. Caught completely by surprise when the busload of very loud and enthusiastic demonstrators pulled into the small parking lot, Steinberg and his staff scrambled to set up guidelines for the meeting. Four students—Elisha Gibson, Peter Saltanis, Kasey Jacobs, and Lindsy Sargent, each representing one class—were allowed into the conference room. They handed Steinberg 256 letters from students, all urging the college to remain open for two more years. Saltanis told Steinberg the students had lost trust in the administration and accused the university of mismanagement (It. 43; *Windmill* Dec. 2004). Outside the window in the parking lot, the students were chanting "Two Years More." Steinberg acknowledged the unfairness of the decision but argued in his defense that it would be even more unfair to the Post and Brooklyn students to take their tuition money to bail out Southampton. Not surprisingly, Steinberg who had no time to prepare for the meeting, appeared to the students to be aloof and somewhat cold. He held firm and made it abundantly clear that the college campus would be closed at the end of the Spring 2005 semester. There would be no extension beyond that time. As the meeting went on, Elisha Gibson, a sophomore, became distraught and began to cry. "She just sobbed," said Peter Saltanis. "He was so rude to us" (It. 43).

Steinberg, although somewhat shaken by the emotional session with the student protestors at the University Center, came to Southampton the next day. He was accompanied by some university officials, who the students assumed were LIU trustees. They were joined on stage by Dean Forestell and Provost Rodas. According to the three accounts of the meeting in the *Windmill* (December, 2004), the meeting got off to a fairly good start. Andrea Liebel wrote that Steinberg "was fairly reasonable and answered questions fairly well." *Windmill* campus life editor Carly Kenkel agreed, but noted that Steinberg seemed "agitated and far more abrasive than necessary." The first concern, said *Windmill* staff writer Lisa Steuer was the presence of signs and placards carried by several students and by alumni members of the Save Southampton College. Liebel asked this group not to stage an open protest at the meeting. This, she said, is our event and asked those with signs to place them in the back of the auditorium. She opened the meeting with a plea for a "calm question and answer session for students to get the answers that they deserve."

The mood in the room, nevertheless, was not a comfortable one for Steinberg and the university officials. Steinberg addressed the students and began answering their questions without informing them that there were no trustees among the officials on the stage. About halfway through the meeting a student asked Steinberg to introduce the LIU trustees. In an embarrassing moment, he acknowledged that the trustees were unable to come and defended their absence by claiming that Liebel and the students were at fault for changing the time of the meeting to the midday when it was inconvenient for the trustees. Liebel was furious, noting later that she had been told Steinberg and several trustees had played golf on the Shinnecock Golf Course at midday only two weeks before the meeting.

The response from the students was loud and angry. "That's when things started to get ugly," wrote Kenkel, "stupid and ugly." Kenkel, even though she was one of Steinberg's outspoken critics, expressed dismay at the personal attacks shouted at him. Steinberg promised to help Liebel arrange a meeting with the trustees in the future. Nora Detweiler, a member of the SCS executive committee, complained that the trustees had not even responded to their proposals for saving the college. Kenkel wrote, "Hopefully, the board will realize what they owe the students of this college and have the dignity to show up to the next meeting." Kenkel and Liebel both ended their articles with a pessimistic admonition to the students not to hold their breath.

The LIU Board of Trustees continued to be seen by many as a dark, mysterious, inaccessible force, but Steinberg was, to his dismay, a much easier target for those who wanted to vent their anger and frustration. All summer, beginning with Marmion's now famous outburst, Steinberg had been subjected to intense scrutiny and criticism by the Southampton College community and in the local press. Marmion, a popular former college president, who, many believed, had been thrown under the bus by a previous LIU administration, had over the summer emerged as an icon for the SCS movement and their supporters. Steinberg, patiently at first, repeated the same arguments about external forces beyond anyone's control only to have them summarily and more stridently rejected at every turn.

A week after the two confrontational meetings the students carried their signs to the Southampton Town Hall where Supervisor Skip Heaney was presenting his proposal for a twelve-month moratorium on development in Shinnecock Hills to his board. He spoke to a standing room only crowd who enthusiastically cheered when the proposal was approved. State Assemblyman Fred Thiele and State Senator Kenneth LaValle applauded Heaney's efforts. Paola Curcio-Kleinman, in an attempt to address the perception that the university had now been blocked from implementing a secret plan to sell off the campus, assured the press that LIU welcomed the moratorium and "looked forward to pursue educational and cultural uses for the campus"(*Southampton Press* Dec. 2, 2004). It would have been be difficult, however, to find many in the room at the time who believed her.

The difficulties in reaching the trustees and the dissatisfaction with Steinberg's responses prompted the faculty to become more aggressive. The executive committee prepared a letter to the New York State Board of Regents protesting the transfer of the undergraduate programs to C. W. Post (SCC Archive B-IV, e, Executive Committee Minutes Dec. 1, 2004). Most faculty realized it was a symbolic protest because they knew the regents were highly unlikely to interfere with an internal matter, even one as significant as this. The faculty was still struggling with a coherent response to the university when the Spring 2005 semester opened.

Options 05 Initiative

Amidst all the confusion and confrontation, the transition team led by Dean Forestell, Jennifer Browne, Alice Flynn, and Rory Shaffer-Walsh put in place an effective approach to the process of transition. On October 13,

Dean Forestell addressed a meeting of the student government association and announced the implementation of a support program designed to assist the students as they made their plans for the future. The following Monday, he announced, an "Options 05" counseling office would open in Chancellors Hall with a full-time staff headed by Flavio Bollag and Tracy Cleary from the admissions office. Students were invited to visit the C. W. Post campus on a shuttle bus. Options 05 staff would accompany them and introduce them to the student support services and the campus facilities. There were three available options. They could "transition" to Post and complete the new core curriculum and the majors they began at Southampton and graduate with a degree from Southampton College. If they wished to officially transfer to either Brooklyn or Post they could do so and receive full credit for all of the courses they had completed at Southampton. If they wished to transfer to another college or university, the admissions office would assist them in selecting a college and provide support to them as they went through the application process.

A majority of the faculty immediately raised questions about the first option. They argued that the students should have a choice to take either the new core or to complete the old Southampton core requirements. The faculty executive committee supported this position in a memorandum to Dean Forestell and Jeff Kane. The committee acknowledged the commitment and the long hours of work put in by the faculty participating in the new core program, but concluded that it would be both impractical and burdensome on the students to require them to complete the new core. Impractical because the Southampton faculty were being transferred to new positions in other branches of the university based on local needs, not on the concerns about the new core. The memorandum also noted the incomplete development of the new core. The final capstone course for seniors and the guidelines for the six-credit experiential requirement, for example, had not been developed. Without the coordinated efforts of a core faculty, it would impossible to complete this work. It would also be difficult to implement the interdisciplinary curriculum already in place. There was another impediment. Many faculty members who were not involved in any of the new courses characterized the courses as part of a boondoggle foisted upon them by a desperate and marginally competent university administration. At the first faculty meeting in the spring, the faculty council voted to allow the students to take the old core if they wished. Most took that option.

Introducing the New Core: Innovations on the *Titanic*

Dean Forestell, Jeff Kane, and many of us teaching the interdisciplinary courses disagreed with the negative assessment of the new core and were reluctant to see the innovative curriculum abandoned. Several of us were very pleased with our interdisciplinary courses (see ch. 8 above). We knew that our innovations would not likely survive the transition to Post, but we were enthusiastic about the opportunity to put theory into practice, if only for two semesters. Those classes proved to be satisfying to most of the professors involved. Unfortunately, the freshman global core course did not go so well. It was an uphill battle and a very hard sell from the beginning. The freshman students brought their resentments about the campus closing to bear on a course they saw as an imposition forced upon them. Had there been more time to prepare for the course in more settled circumstances, things might have worked out differently. The distractions of the summer, following the devastating news about the closing of the campus, stirred negative emotions and dampened the enthusiasm students normally felt about their first year of college.

Robert Turner worked tirelessly as the course coordinator, struggling with nonfunctioning audiovisual equipment and with an overstretched media staff. He carried the course on his shoulders, serving as a spirited and creative master of ceremonies for the weekly lecture series in an auditorium filled with "a disgruntled student body that was dragging its feet throughout the semester" (SCC Archive B-IV, a, Turner 2005, 4). The faculty teaching the six discussion sessions scrambled to develop new class plans. Out of desperation and commitment, we came together in a collegial spirit. Turner developed a close working relationship with local environmental groups such as the Peconic Estuary Program, The Suffolk County Department of Health Services, and the Cornell Cooperative Extension. Students had the opportunity to work with "hands-on" projects related to water conservation.

The student evaluations were mixed. Most liked the instructors, but many resented what they saw as an arbitrary requirement. The course soon became the primary target for all of their resentments. They also feared the course would not be accredited by any other college. As some put it most candidly, they were angry about being forced by an unfeeling university to take a "useless" course about a topic in which they had no interest. Some simply ignored the class and never participated. There was a disproportionate number of grades of C to D and F. As a result, given a choice, few students opted to continue the new curriculum.

The good works of Option 05 did not placate the Orphans or the SCS. The Orphans opened up a mock lemonade stand in front of the college front gate to raise funds "to save the college." On December 3, they staged an all-night slumber party in the Chancellor's Hall lobby. The brochure announcing the event stated that the slumber party symbolized "LIU's slumber during the last 40 years in managing the college's financial future. This was followed the next week by a rally in the Fine Arts Theater where student and faculty representatives again expressed their angry feelings

FIGURE 12.1. Jane Ellendorf and Peter Saltanis protesting the closing of the campus with a mock lemonade stand in front of the campus main gate. Their group called themselves, "The Orphans of LIU" (Dec. 2, 2004).

about the decision to close the campus. That same day, Peter Saltanis led a small group of supporters to stage a protest on Main Street in Southampton. Although they were well aware that the university was no longer listening to them, they continued to make the same demands for full financial disclosure, for a meeting with the trustees, and for a two-year postponement of the scheduled closing. On December 16, the *Southampton Press* printed letters from four students who asked for local community support in their efforts. Kathleen Graham (class of 2007) wrote, "We are not going to walk away from the college we love without a fight." We are waging a war, said Peter Saltanis, "against the beastly indifference of Long Island University." Seniors Lindsey Graham and Heather Black wrote about their affection for the college, noting the warm relationships with a caring, accessible faculty, the exciting field experiences such as Seamester and Australearn, and "the feeling of home," which could not be captured in the same way by any other school. At the beginning of the spring semester, the group announced they were collecting questions for a meeting with the LIU trustees.

FIGURE 12.2. Poster announcing the Orphans of LIU demonstration. *Photo by author.*

SPRING 2005 CONFUSION, SUSPICION, ANGER, AND DENIAL

The SCS joined the Orphans in their refusal to soften the condemnation of LIU. In February 2005 they wrote to the New York State Department of Education, asking them to investigate the legality of the decision to move the academic programs to the C. W. Post campus. Marmion told a *Newsday* reporter, "We want them to determine if the de facto closing of the college was legal and warranted" (Feb. 16, 2005). It was not, he stated emphatically, a "relocation." Clearly, the attempt by the LIU public relations office to define their action as a "transition" and not a closing had never gained much traction. Marmion repeated the charge that LIU wanted to use the property for commercial purposes.

In its defense LIU issued a statement from Rob Altholz repeating the now familiar statistics on the deficit and the enrollment, and said the university officials had kept the state education department informed about the decision at each stage of its implementation. The university added that it was acting responsibly in its relations with the faculty, staff, students, and donors. All of the tenured faculty and most of the probationary faculty had been reassigned, the staff had been provided with employment counseling and support, and the students who wished to transfer were compensated for their application fees to other institutions. Unfortunately for LIU, their defense was dismissed by most of the Southampton College community and by many of the editors writing in the local press on eastern Long Island. Little had changed in the public perception of Long Island University since President Hoxie had tried to sell the Brooklyn campus three decades earlier.

At the beginning of the spring semester, there were still some faculty members who believed it might be possible to save the college. The faculty council discussed three "action proposals" at their meeting on February 9. One was in fact a "non action" proposal to accept the situation as it was and to focus on concerns about the implementation of the move to Post. The second was to continue seeking a way to save the college, and the third was a variation of the first, adding only that there should be an appeal to the Board of Trustees to more forcefully address what the faculty determined to be the responsibility of Steinberg for the mismanagement of the college. The decision to take the third option was made at the next meeting.

The faculty would accept the decision to close the school but wanted to have the satisfaction of bringing down Steinberg. They sent a statement to the Board of Trustees asking them to call for President Steinberg to resign and to terminate his presidency if he did not comply (SCC Archive B-IV, E, FC Minutes March 9, 2005). The faculty presented a list of specific "management deficiencies," including a failure to raise endowment funds, inadequate use of the Internet's potential in the development of creative marketing strategies, a failure to consult with the faculty when important issues arose, a failure to assemble a competent administrative team at the university center, and a general intolerance of dissent at all levels. "With failures such as these on the track record of our present leaders," concluded the statement, "we fear for the health of the entire University." Two years earlier, the *Chronicle of Higher Education* (Nov. 22, 2002) published a list of salaries earned by presidents of institutions granting masters' degrees. President Steinberg's salary of $400,081 was ninth in the nation. Many faculty believed Steinberg to be an overpaid, underachieving university leader. The C. W. Post faculty council passed a resolution showing their support of the

Southampton faculty. The resolution expressed "a lack of confidence in the leadership and administration of Long Island University," but stopped short of calling for Steinberg's resignation" (*Newsday* April 4, 2005).

Newsday reporter Olivia Winslow (March 12, 2005) wrote about the faculty statement under the not so subtle headline "College's Faculty Rip LIU Chief." The article did, however, include a comment by board chairman Tilles, criticizing the faculty statement as inappropriate and unfair. The decision to relocate, he said, was made by the board for oft-repeated financial reasons. It was a decision, he continued, made by a fully engaged board after many years of "grappling with the myriad complex problems confronting Southampton." His defense was dismissed by most of the college community. The article noted that Tilles was stepping down from the board to take a seat on the New York State Board of Regents on April 1, 2005. His membership on the regents ended any possibility that the letter from the Save Southampton College group would result in an investigation of the LIU Board of Trustees.

The Stony Brook Solution

In March, Senator LaValle inserted an item in the state budget bill allocating $35 million for the purchase of the Southampton campus. Assemblyman Fred Thiele pledged his full support and Governor George Pataki voiced no objections to the purchase. President Shirley Strum Kenny supported the move with great enthusiasm. Steinberg, however, warned that the university was still in the process of evaluating the market value of the property and "was bound by state law to get fair market value for the property" (*Southampton Press* March 31, 2005). Steinberg said the university was in discussions with other nonprofit and educational institutions, but he refused to name them. He was undoubtedly aware of an assessment made by a real estate developer in Bridgehampton who arrived at a figure of $55 million based on subdividing the campus into 1.5 acre lots (*Southampton Press* May 26, 2005). Many suspected LIU was simply trying to get a better price and feared the university might end up alienating the state and lose out on what seemed to be a good solution for everyone. Chancellor Sillerman told a reporter for the *Southampton Press* that "when and if they begin negotiations with Stony Brook, I will make sure that they are successful" (May 26, 2005). The clear implications that he had this measure of influence over the board and that the board could not be trusted to make the right decision on their own undoubtedly infuriated many trustees.

The SCS and the Orphans endorsed the purchase and pledged to make every effort to pressure LIU into accepting the offer from the state. Harry Marmion, who had established a friendship over the years with Kenny, took the lead in this effort. The group urged its members to write letters of support to Governor Pataki. In April, after Governor Pataki approved the funds for the purchase, the LIU Board of Trustees again told the press it was awaiting evaluations of the property. For many in the SCS group their procrastination aroused suspicions about LIU's intent. There the matter rested when the last commencement was held in May.

During this time of confusion and confrontation, the majority of the 739 students who remained for the spring semester moved on to deal positively with their plans for the future. Most shared the feelings expressed by Campus Life Editor Carly Kenkel in a *Windmill* editorial: "After months of anger, confusion and bitterness, let me be the first to say, enough already!. . . . after nine months it's time to move on" (April 2005). The Options 05 Initiative played an important role in helping the students to do just that. One example of the students' character and determination in the face of their difficulties was told to the author, with great pride, by Mary Topping (It. 49). The Southampton "Lady Colonials" basketball team had been seeded fourth place in the Eastern Collegiate Athletic Conference (ECAC). Several top recruits had transferred after the fall semester, leaving behind a depleted team with only seven players. Five games into the season, their coach, Patrick McGunnigle, resigned. It should have been all downhill from there, but Cassie Arroyo, the college softball coach who had never coached a college-level basketball game, took over the team and led then to an 18–12 season. This record put them in the playoffs where they defeated the number one seed and went on to defeat Philadelphia University, 68–63, in the final. It was an inspiring and bittersweet comment on the resilience and spirit of the Southampton students. The parade of Fulbrights continued through the last years of the college as Matt Stutz studied Coastal Geography in Australia, Carol Kosman went to the University of Copenhagen to study Antarctic sea-ice plankton, John Richert studied oceanic fishes in the waters off the Baja Peninsula in Mexico, and Rebecca Langlois researched the role of iron in nitrogen-fixing organisms at the Ocean Studies Institute in Kiel, Germany. In the years following the closing of the Southampton campus, only one student from Long Island University has received a Fulbright.

Closing Time for a Very Special Place, May 22, 2005

You don't have to go home, but you can't stay here
So gather up your jackets
Move to the exits
I hope you have found a friend
Every new beginning comes from some other
Beginning's end.
(Lyrics by Dan White of the band, Semisonic. The song was nominated for a Grammy Award in 1999.)

The song "Closing Time" was taken by the 457 graduate and undergraduate students as their anthem. Carly Kenkel used the title and the song's first line as the headline for her article in the first edition of the Fall 2004 *Windmill.* Senior class president Joslyn Mills and Dennis Bonal wrote a parody of the song with several sharp and irreverent references to LIU. The student government leaders, however, did not want the commencement to become a forum for another protest against LIU. They made this clear to the Orphans and to the SCS. Nevertheless, many students made personal statements in one form or another. Some wrote brief messages in white on the tops of their mortarboards. Joanne Douglas, an English major, doffed her cap to reveal the letters "F.U. LIU" on the top. During the procession, students frequently tipped their caps revealing similar messages. Donelle Bright, a Dean's List Psych/Bio major, was one of several who refused to shake Steinberg's hand when he gave her the diploma.

FIGURE 12.3. Joanne Douglas, class of 2005, wearing her sentiments about LIU on her graduation cap. *Photo by author.*

FIGURE 12.4. Chancellor Robert Sillerman addressing the last graduation ceremony on the Southampton Campus, May 2005. *Photo by author.*

Congressman Tim Bishop spoke briefly. "Southampton College," he said, "was a very special place. It has made a significant difference in the lives of many people and it has made a great contribution to the community at large." Honorary degrees were awarded to Robert Gerbereux and Ral Welker for their long and distinguished service to the university. In what many in attendance considered an offense to Gerbereux and Welker, a third honorary degree was given to Roger Tilles. One has to wonder why the university chose Southampton rather than C. W. Post or Brooklyn to make this gesture to Tilles. The entry in the commencement program praised Tilles for providing "unwavering, visionary leadership that spurred the institution to reach new heights." One also wonders how the university could have missed the irony and, indeed the inappropriateness of the award and of this eulogy at the ceremony marking the closing of Southampton College.

Chancellor Sillerman spoke briefly, focusing on the plight of the 140 staff members who faced unemployment. He gave out his personal phone number and invited them to contact him if they had any financial trouble in the next year. It was not an empty gesture. Susan Ulrich, the associate director of the Co-op program told the author a few years later she had asked him for help with her graduate fees and said that he had responded generously. Both Sillerman and Bishop received enthusiastic applause, as did Dean Hitchcock when he received a university award for his distinguished service to the university. In sharp contrast, a cold silence greeted President Steinberg when he stepped forward to hand out the diplomas.

Although the history of the college was haunted by its troubled relations with University Center, that did not define the college. What defined the college was a sense of being part of a small, caring community in an idyllic environmental setting. The faculty expressed this feeling of community at this last commencement. They agreed among themselves to depart from the normal protocol and make a symbolic gesture demonstrating the unique nature of their relationship with the students. They declined to sit in the traditional place on the stage behind the university officials and special guests. Instead, they sat among the students alongside the stage. It was a fitting, final tribute to a very special place that survives in the memory of all who were fortunate enough to have been associated with the college.

Chapter Thirteen

Epilogue

Lost in Transition

In the fall of 2004, students in Professor Scott Carlin's Sustainable Development class and members of the campus environmental organization, PEACE, converted a 1980 Mercedes-Benz to run on vegetable oil. The idea was first suggested by Randy Spitzer, an employee of the Long Island Power Authority. The students solicited the local community for a used car, and Dr. Jonathan Korn of East Hampton responded with the gift of a maroon Mercedes. The students, with the help of Henry Adamczyk, the college mechanic, worked on the car for a year revamping the diesel fuel system. The project was financed with $1,300 from the "green tax" the Southampton College students had imposed on themselves to support environmental initiatives. The car had to be started on diesel, but once the vegetable oil was heated enough, a switch on the dashboard would be flipped to change over to the oil. The students set to work painting the exterior and decorating the inside with such environmentally friendly images as clouds on the roof and fish on the trunk.

After the car passed the New York State vehicle inspection, Professor Carlin and three students, Kasey Jacobs, Peter Saltanis, and Elisha Gibson, filled the tank with vegetable oil purchased from a local supermarket and used peanut oil donated by Janet Herbert, the mailroom supervisor, and drove the car on the Long Island Expressway from the Southampton campus to C. W. Post. "It was quite an experience," recalled Carlin. "We managed to get it up to fifty miles an hour." Peter Saltanis remembered the smell. "It was like a boiling vat of French Fries," he said. Nevertheless, the car arrived safely and without incident at C. W. Post (It. 43).

FIGURE 13.1. Professor Scott Carlin, Elisha Gibson, Peter Saltanis, and Kasey Jacobs with the "Veggie Car" they drove from Southampton to the C. W. Post campus. *Photo by Rita Langdon.*

The car expressed the essence of the Southampton historical experience. It was a collaborative effort, bringing together students, faculty, campus staff members, and the local community. The hope was that the car would be the symbolic centerpiece for an environmental consciousness that would transition to C. W. Post. They had planned to drive the car around campus, making regular recycling collections and promoting a student environmental organization similar to PEACE. Saltanis, Jacobs, and Gibson told the *Southampton Press* reporter that "they will use the car to educate other students about biodiesel and other environmentally-friendly fuels once they reach C. W. Post" (Sept. 15, 2005). To the disappointment of the "transitioning" PEACE members, there was only modest support for environmental programs on the Post campus. The administration ruled that the car was too dangerous to be driven on campus and locked it away behind a chain link fence, where it remained for the next three semesters. When the noble experiment was scheduled for demolition, Kasey Jacobs came to the rescue.

She contacted the department of Automotive Technology at Farmingdale State College and negotiated one last transition for the Veggie Car.

The car became a symbol for all that was lost in the transition from Southampton. The Marine Science program and the highly regarded Creative Writing program had already been absorbed into the SUNY system. The innovative new interdisciplinary curriculum, the successful run of student Fulbright awards, and the informal, interactive campus community culture that made so many of these things possible did not make the transition.

The Office of Transition, 2005–2008

During the summer of 2005, Dean Forestell moved from Southampton to the C. W. Post campus where he established the Office of Transition to provide oversight and support for the 240 "transitioning" students from Southampton. These students would follow the core requirements in the former Southampton College catalogue. Sixteen sections of Southampton classes were added to the C. W. Post 2005–06 academic schedule to accommodate these students. Most of these classes were taught by the thirty-five Southampton faculty members who relocated to Post. There were also twenty-five students from Southampton who chose to transfer into the C. W Post programs. At the C. W. Post commencement in May 2006, 150 undergraduate bachelor's and eighty graduate degrees were awarded to transitioning Southampton students. In 2007, ninety students graduated; among them was Peter Saltanis, the class valedictorian. On May 11, 2008, the last transitioning student class of twenty-four was recognized at a separate ceremony in the Interfaith Center during the C. W. Post graduation exercises.

Stony Brook's Piano, 2006–2011

In September 2005, Stony Brook's School of Marine and Atmospheric Sciences (SoMAS) did take over the Southampton undergraduate Marine Science program and the State University Board of Trustees unanimously approved the purchase of the Southampton campus based on the $35 million price set in the state budget allotment the previous spring. Forty Southampton Marine Science majors transferred to the newly established undergraduate major at Stony Brook. The students were shuttled from the Stony Brook campus to the Marine Science Station facility at Southampton. Three former Southampton faculty members, Joseph Warren, Chris Gobler, and Brad Peterson, were hired by Stony Brook, and provided a continuity for the transfer, which went well enough. Nevertheless, problems soon emerged.

In a five-year period the Southampton campus was shut down twice and reopened twice. This sad chain of events began with the departure of LIU, followed by the opening of Stony Brook, Southampton in the fall of 2006, only to be shut down in 2009 and reopened again in the fall of 2011. Pattison's analogy about Laurel and Hardy's piano was as apt for Stony Brook as it was for LIU. For the students, parents, faculty, and local administrators, however, there was nothing humorous about this unfortunate series of events. They saw themselves as the innocent victims of administrative failures well beyond their control.

Throwing up Roadblocks

SUNY Stony Brook was anxious to close the deal in order to begin developing a curriculum based on ecological sustainability and to recruit students for Fall 2006. Shirley Kenny hoped to have an enrollment of two thousand students by the fall of 2007. "I am in awe at how quickly Stony Brook gets things done," Harry Marmion told a reporter for the *Southampton Press*, adding that he hoped LIU doesn't throw up any roadblocks (Sept. 22, 2005). Paola Curcio-Kleinman declined to comment on the negotiations, saying only that "we are moving in a positive direction." Relationships between the two universities, which had never been very warm, soured over the next few months. When LIU transferred the prestigious Masters of Fine Arts in Creative Writing to Brooklyn, the two prominent faculty members, Roger Rosenblatt and Robert Reeves refused to leave the Hamptons. In February 2006, Reeves told a *Southampton Press* reporter that the MFA program had been designed to take advantage of the cultural richness of the Hamptons. "To some extent," said Reeves, "LIU abandoned the playing field" (Feb. 9, 2006). President Kenny lost no time in hiring both of them and establishing an MFA program at Southampton.

After four months of negotiations and lobbying by the SCS, LIU finally agreed in March 2006 to sell the campus to Stony Brook for the $35 million originally allotted in the state budget. The contract stipulated that the buildings on the campus would be empty and "broom clean" for the new occupants. The months of procrastination by LIU forced Stony Brook to limit its fall offerings to undergraduate Marine Science majors and the master's program in Creative Writing. Paola Curcio-Kleinman refused to explain the reasons for the delay, saying only that negotiations were ongoing and progress was being made. Nevertheless, all parties were enthusiastic about what they thought was the final closing of the deal. The *Southampton Press* led with a headline proclaiming, the "Deal is Done" (March 30, 2006) and wrote about the anticipated boon to local businesses following the arrival of students for the fall classes. Unfortunately for Stony Brook University and for the Southampton business community, LIU did throw up roadblocks delaying the transfer of the campus, "broom clean," to Stony Brook.

On May 18, 2006 President Steinberg, sent a letter to Luis G. Pedraja, the executive director of the Middle States Commission on Higher Education, in response to a request for a progress report on the transfer of academic programs to C. W. Post. Steinberg assured Pedraja that "[f]rom every perspective, the relocation process had unfolded far better than any of us could have conceived two years ago" (SCC Archives B-IV, d, Steinberg to Pedraja May 18, 2006). He cited the work of Paul Forestell's transition team and the efforts of Associate Provost Jennifer Browne in inventorying the classroom and administrative furniture and equipment and creating a database to be used in distributing these materials to other parts of campus where there was a need. Their efforts were certainly worthy of praise, but LIU badly mishandled other crucial aspects of the transaction.

LIU apparently hoped that Stony Brook would take responsibility for cleaning the buildings and disposing of broken and damaged furniture, discarded library books, office files, outdated equipment, and other debris from the campus buildings. At the end of the Spring 2005 semester, however, many staff members were given little or no instructions about closing their offices. The HEOP staff, for example, simply closed the doors and walked out. The college library staff were uncertain about what to do with the books. Conrad Schoeffling, the director of special collections at the B. Davis Schwartz Memorial Library at C. W. Post, came out to Southampton to select books for transfer to the Post library, but there were several hundred books left behind with no specific instructions about what should be done with them. The author, working informally with Pamela Greinke, a member of the library staff, contacted the Southampton Historical Society and arranged for them to receive books and journals they wanted for their collection. We also invited representatives from the Shinnecock Indian museum to come and salvage any books related to Native American topics. The author, on his way to retrieve files from the Faculty Union office a month or so after the last commencement, saw several empty offices with computers still running and message lights on the phones still blinking. It was a very eerie feeling, something like a scene in a post-Apocalypse science fiction film where humans have suddenly disappeared leaving behind machines that continue to perform tasks that no longer have a purpose.

The Stony Brook Southampton campus did open in September 2006 with eight faculty members and about 150 students. The delay in implementing the other programs, said Donna Brannon, a spokesperson for Stony Brook, was because they were not able to take full ownership of the campus. Paola Curcio-Kleinman responded to repeated questions from the press about the reasons for the delay following the "done deal," signed in March, with an evasive comment. "We are in a holding pattern," she said, "due to the size and complexity of the deal and the large amount of supporting paperwork that has to be completed" (*Southampton Press* Sept. 7, 2006). State Assemblyman Fred Thiele sharply dismissed her explanation. The reason, he said, was a failure by LIU to clear a $7 million encumbrance for construction costs on Chancellor's Hall. LIU had been reluctant to acknowledge yet another example of poor planning and questionable managerial decisions. Thiele

FIGURE 13.2. Official opening of Stony Brook Southampton. (Left to right) New York State Assemblyman Fred Thiele, Stony Brook University President Shirley Kenny, and New York State Senator Kenneth LaValle. *Photo by author.*

was furious. "It's frustrating," he said, "because clearly this is something LIU has known about for some time." They should have taken care of this, he continued, voicing a frustration shared by many local elected officials and by the Southampton business community. The fault, said an editorial in the *Southampton Press,* falls squarely on the shoulders of the LIU executives (Sept. 24, 2006). The editor further charged LIU with stalling until Thiele forced their hand by going public. Many suspected that LIU had hoped to pass along the bond encumbrance to Stony Brook. During the month of September, LIU scrambled hastily to remove the debt on Chancellor's Hall.

There was, however, another unresolved "roadblock." The campus buildings remained cluttered with debris. In frustration, Stony Brook officials confronted LIU with an ultimatum. Unless the buildings were cleaned prior to the scheduled formal opening on October 4, 2006, Stony Brook would hire their own crew to clean the buildings and deduct an estimated $30,000 fee from the $35 million purchase price. LIU scrambled to find a crew, only to discover that there was no single removal company capable of the task in such a short time. According to Burke Irwin, the associate director of the Southampton physical plant, they finally had to hire several firms to do a rush job (Irwin, pers. comm. 2006). The result was a chaotic operation still in the last stages of completion when the opening ceremony took place. President Shirley Kenny, flanked by State Senator Kenneth LaValle, Congressman Tim Bishop, State Assemblyman Fred Thiele, Southampton town supervisor Patrick Heaney, and Martin Schoonen, the newly appointed dean of Stony Brook Southampton, officially announced the opening of the new college. Her comments were made against the rumbling of trucks in the background carting away the broken remains of Southampton College. Later that day, I walked past a pile of desks and lounge furniture on the lawn of the Fine Arts building awaiting to be loaded onto the trucks. I was reminded again of Bob Patterson's analogy of Laurel and Hardy's piano. The piano had rolled down the hill for the last time and now lay broken and discarded.

Stony Brook Southampton: Beginning Again with the Piano

In its first full year of operation (2007–08) the new college offered only undergraduate majors in Marine Science and Marine Vertebrate Biology and the graduate program in Creative Writing. Most of the Marine Science majors were Southampton College transfers. President Kenny appointed Martin Schoonen, the current director of the Sustainability Studies program at Stony Brook, to serve as the interim dean. The total enrollment of about two hundred students increased to nearly 350 the following year. Schoonen developed an innovative interdisciplinary undergraduate major in Sustainability Studies that was similar in many ways to the curriculum developed by the Southampton faculty in 2003–04. Students integrated the concept of sustainability into the study of literature, economics, architecture, and statistics. The program included five sustainability majors: Ecosystems and Human Impact, Environmental Design, Policy and Planning, Coastal Environmental Studies, Sustainability Studies, and Environmental Studies. Recognizing that the emphasis on the environment and the importance of alternative energy sources was symbolized by the campus windmill, President Kenny continued the annual ceremony marked by the tradition of lighting the windmill at the end of the year.

The approach was highly praised in an article in the *New York Times*'s "Education Life" (July 27, 2008). The author, Anthony DePalma, noted that the Southampton program was part of a growing movement that included Dartmouth, the College of the Atlantic in Maine, and Arizona State University. "We can't just engineer ourselves out of these problems,"

FIGURE 13.3. Annual Christmas Windmill lighting, 1995. *Photo © Gary Mamay 2012.*

said Schoonen, adding that complex contemporary issues require "system thinking." A lot of campuses, he continued, have courses in sustainability, but here we have a campus that is going to develop around the idea. The small cohort of students were most enthusiastic about being a part of the experimental program. They were given a chance to have an important role in shaping the curriculum and planning the campus physical plant. According to Schoonen, the students would be involved in the design and construction of a stormwater collection facility (DePalma,2008, 29). The Stony Brook undergraduate majors also included Marine Science and Marine Vertebrate Biology, and the graduate programs in Marine Science and Creative Writing.

Extensive work on the campus facilities began immediately. Stony Brook spent an estimated $43 million beyond the $35 million purchase price in an effort to improve the deteriorating campus structures. The partially completed library building was taken out of mothballs. It had begun to deteriorate and an expensive renovation was required. Six of the dormitories were renovated and equipped with air conditioning. There were plans to tear down the remaining dorms and replace them with a state of the art

LEED (Leadership in Energy and Environmental Design) standard three hundred bed dorm. The Marine Science Station, the Student Center, the old library building, the iconic Southampton College windmill, and the Fine Arts Theater also underwent costly renovations. Plans were being developed for a new marine science station on Fort Pond Bay. The new library, the centerpiece of the campus makeover, was designed to meet the LEED criteria. The library, scheduled to open in 2009, would have a geothermal system for heating and water, a rooftop collector for rainwater to be used in the bathrooms, and large windows positioned to make effective use of the sun for heat and light (DePlama 2008, 29). The Stony Brook staff reported that Pratt Hall, the venerable historic Claflin building dating back to the nineteenth century, was contaminated with a potentially toxic fungus and presented a danger to health (*Southampton Press* July 12, 2007). The building was closed and has never been reopened.

In February 2009, President Kenny announced that after an intensive international and national search she was thrilled to appoint Dr. Mary Pearl as dean of the Stony Brook Southampton campus. Pearl came with impressive credentials. She had a PhD in Physical Anthropology from Yale and was the current president of the Wildlife Trust, a global organization dedicated to innovative conservation science. She had been elected by her peers to the Association for the Advancement of Science and had co-founded the Center for Environmental Research and Conservation at Columbia University, where she was an adjunct research scientist. She had published several scientific papers and was the on editorial board of the journal *Conservation in Practice*. Dean Pearl stressed a commitment to the concept of sustainability and the importance of an outreach to the diverse communities of eastern Long Island.

In July 2009, Kenny retired after serving as SUNY Stony Brook president for fifteen years. Her successor, Dr. Samuel Stanley, who had been vice chancellor for research at Washington University in St. Louis, was a prominent biomedical researcher with extensive publications in his field. His primary concerns focused on medical research and on solidifying the university's position among the nation's top research institutions. He did not share Kenny's enthusiasm for the development of the Southampton campus nor for the focus on sustainability. Concerns about the emphasis on sustainability were also raised by the university admissions staff who had examined the marketability of the major. They warned that such a narrow offering would have great difficulty attracting a large enough "critical mass" of undergraduate students. Stanley had the misfortune to assume the presidency in the midst of a national economic downturn. When the state legislature made substantial cuts in the budget allocations for Stony Brook University, Samuels was quick to target his predecessor's pet project.

Recruitment for the Fall 2009 semester did not go as well as expected. Only sixty-one of the 373 graduate and undergraduate students elected to take one of the Sustainability majors. Nevertheless, the enthusiasm among the students in the Sustainability programs was palpable. The author spoke informally with many of the students who described their courses and their projects with great excitement, but they also expressed concern about the future of these programs under the Stanley administration.

Dean Pearl also reached out to connect with the local communities and environmental organizations in Suffolk County. She recognized the historical and cultural significance of the Native American reservations on Long Island and sought to establish ties with them. I was directly involved with one of Dean Pearl's initiatives. In the fall of 2009, she met with Unkechaug chief Harry Wallace and Lance Gumbs, one of the Shinnecock tribal trustees, and established the Algonquian Language Initiative (ALI). Their goal was the reclamation of native dialects spoken by the two Long Island Indian nations. The organization included representatives from the Unkechaug and Shinnecock nations, Dr. Robert Hoberman from the Stony Brook Linguistics department, Dr. Carol Peabody from the School of Social Work

FIGURE 13.4. Algonquian Language Revitalization Project. Stony Brook Southampton Dean Mary Pearl (center), Unkechaug Nation Chief Harry Wallace (left), and Shinnecock Nation Trustee Lance Gumbs (right). *Photo by author.*

at Stony Brook, and Howard Treadwell, an Unkechaug who had recently graduated from the Hoberman's department, and myself. Dean Pearl provided us with a dedicated room in the new library for a distance learning Internet workshop led by Stephanie Fielding, a Mohegan linguist. Fielding shared with the group a language learning program she had developed for the Mohegan Nation.

Closing Time Again, April 2010

The spring semester began with what appeared to be many good omens. The new library was opened and other renovations were either complete or nearly so. In January, the university appointed a highly qualified community relations specialist, Valerie Scopaz, to develop relationships with all levels of local government, nonprofit environmental organizations, and the Shinnecock and Unkechaug Indian reservations. There were 373 full-time students on campus and more than one hundred part-time students, making up a cohort that was expected to grow significantly over the next few years. Ironically, the mood was similar to the one reflected in the comments made by Dean Hitchcock at the 2003 Southampton Commencement when he said that he had never felt so positive about the future of the college.

The piano, however, never made it to the top of the hill. On Tuesday evening, April 6, Dean Pearl was informed that the campus would close at the end of the spring semester. "It was a complete shock," Pearl told the author. "There was no consultation, no warning." President Stanley came to Southampton the next day to address the campus community. Ironically, Stanley's address closely paralleled the statements made by David Steinberg in June 2004. This has been a very difficult decision for us, said Stanley, we thought about it long and carefully. "The campus is not closing," he said, "we are simply moving the sustainability majors to the Stony Brook campus" (*Southampton Press* April 15, 2010). The graduate program in Marine and Atmospheric Science and the Master of Fine Arts in Creative Writing would remain in operation on the campus, but there would be no students in residence.

The Southampton campus, continued Stanley "drains about $10 million a year from the university budget. . . . We can save about $6 million a year by closing Southampton." The response from students, the press, and the local elected officials also had close parallels with June 2004. The meeting with Stanley quickly turned ugly as students vented their anger. There were raucous appeals to keep the campus open and accusations charging the university with purposely keeping the students in the dark until it was too late to mount a challenge.

LaValle and Thiele described Stony Brook's actions as "deceptive acts and practices," and threatened legal action against the university. The legislators met with their attorneys to discuss the preparation of an injunction preventing Stony Brook from closing the campus pending a further investigation of the matter. Thiele pledged to head a movement to take the campus away from Stony Brook and establish an independent four-year college. Stony Brook doesn't believe in Southampton, said Thiele. President Stanley, in response, made it clear that Stony Brook had no intention of giving up the campus. He said that he welcomed discussions about the future of the campus and was currently considering plans for the best utilization of the facility.

At the same time, six students from the new campus, Katherine Osiecki, Nicole Altimari, Tara Linton, Dean Tarulli, Kathleen Furey, and Martha Weller, with the help of the SCS, led at this time by V. Anthony (Vam) Maggipinto, Bob Martin, and Joan DiPaolo Tutt, filed a suit in the New York State Supreme Court charging Stony Brook with taking this drastic action without the approval of a university advisory committee. Joan Tutt used her Web site to keep the SCS members in regular communications with Osiecki and her supporters. A strong feeling based on a love of the campus and a common sense of betrayal united the two groups. The decision to close the campus, they argued, was illegal. The plaintiffs alleged that President Stanley "made the decision behind closed doors in order to bypass the students, public, and the press, and to shield an improper process from public scrutiny" (*Osiecki v. Stanley* 2010). Editorials in the *Southampton Press* excoriated Stony Brook as vigorously as they had done in their attacks on LIU. Karl Grossman, a regular columnist for the *Press*, accused Stony Brook of making "an outrageous decision," and the editorial page denounced the action as baffling and most cruel to the students and "brutal" for the Southampton business community. The appalling, abrupt decision, continued the editor, pulled the new college up by the roots. The editor compared it to the decision of Civil War surgeons who amputated a leg rather than seeking a cure capable of saving a life.

LaValle and Thiele again suggested the possibility of establishing an independent state-supported college at Southampton. The state university officials quickly rejected this suggestion. The student legal action was, to the surprise of many, quite successful. In August 2010, State Supreme Court Justice Paul J. Baisley ruled in favor of the six Southampton students and the SCS. The Stony Brook administration, said Baisley, had erred by closing the campus without approval of the ten-member Stony Brook council. The decision was not sufficient to force the reopening of the sustainability programs, but it did put pressure on the university administration to expand some of the academic programs. That same month The Garrison Institute, an internationally recognized foundation committed to environmentally friendly solutions to global problems, appointed Mary Pearl to serve as their new CEO.

Opening Time Again, 2011–2012

In March 2011, Stony Brook announced their plans to reintroduce residential housing and to establish a "Semester by the Sea: Marine Sciences" program open to undergraduate Stony Brook students and visitors from other colleges and universities. According to university spokesperson Lauren Sheprow, these limited offerings would not require costly administrative services. The Masters in Fine Arts in Creative Writing would be expanded in the fall of 2012 to include Literature, Theater, Film, and Visual Arts. The new master's program would offer seminars and workshops in fiction, screenwriting, film criticism, poetry, arts administration, and publishing. The courses would be taught by professional artists and writers, most of whom lived or summered in the Hamptons.

In the fall of 2011, SoMAS lauched the undergraduate Semester by the Sea program. A small cohort of about twenty students took a full semester of fifteen credits in courses including Long Island Marine Habitats, Maritime Traditions of New England, and Coastal Culture Experience. During the summer of 2012, a summer course in Oceanography was offered to a small class of twelve high school students. The students were able to earn college credits for the course. The class will be opened to a larger number of participants next year. In the fall of 2012 the enrollment doubled and a small support and planning staff was added to the program. Some of the students were full-time residents in one of the federal dorms on campus. Kurt Bretsch, a member of the SoMAS faculty, heralded these developments as a good beginning for the expansion of the program in the future (pers. comm. Sept. 11, 2012).

In January 2012, a winter conference schedule of graduate writing programs was introduced. Students traveled to Kenya where they participated in a writing workshop held in the Turkana Basin Institute. A second workshop was held in Italy at the Florence University of the Arts. These workshops will be offered every January. In July, an ambitious schedule of thirty-five workshops was offered in two summer sessions. These concurrent workshops would focus on such themes as fiction, poetry, nonfiction, playwriting children's literature, screenwriting, film production, directing, acting, and visual arts.

In spite of these ambitious programs, suspicions still lingered in the minds of Thiele and LaValee about the long-term commitment of Stony Brook to the Southampton campus facility. There were rumors once again that the campus might be sold to developers. Southampton Town Supervisor Anna Throne-Holst cited "recent talks suggesting that the campus should be sold and developed." Although spokespersons for Stony Brook stated emphatically that they were committed to maintaining the campus for educational purposes, the town rezoned the eighty-two acre area to a "U-25" designation limiting any future development to nonprofit educational or other public uses. Senator LaValle endorsed the action, saying that "[t]he Town's action will cement the state's vision" (*Southampton Press* April 12, 2012). The state's vision was further cemented a month later with the groundbreaking ceremony for an $8.3 million Marine Science facility on the site of the existing marine station on Fort Pond Bay. President Stanley, Assemblyman Thiele, and Senator LaValle attended the ceremony. LaValle praised the project, but Thiele made it clear that he had not given up on his goal to have an independent residential SUNY campus at Southampton (*Southampton Press*, May 21, 2012).

The SoMAS program celebrated another important achievement at the end of the summer. The gradual deterioration of Shinnecock Bay had been monitored for the last decade by Dr. Chris Gobler and the SoMAS faculty. This data was presented in an application to the Laurie Landreau and Simons Foundations for funds necessary to restore the water quality. They received a $3 million grant to fund a five-year program to reverse the decline of the bay. Dr. Chris Gobler and the SoMAS faculty at Southampton believe that they now have a solid foundation for the future growth of the Southampton facility.

The most recent development involving the campus was announced in October, 2012. A letter of intent was signed by the Southampton Hospital president Robert Chaloner and the Stony Brook University Medical Center to build a 125 bed teaching hospital on the Southampton campus. As this book goes to press the two parties have entered into a "due diligence phase," exchanging financial, business, and legal information. Assemblyman Thiele and Congressman Bishop welcomed the project as another building block in the revitalization of the campus.

The Peconic Bay Sustainability Institute

The vision of a four-year Southampton campus was at the heart of a project initiated by Thiele and LaValle in the fall of 2011. The two legislators, with the support of the SCS and several of the former Southampton-Stony Brook Sustainability majors began efforts to establish a not-for-profit Peconic Bay Region Sustainability Institute. The institute would sponsor research, education programs, and policy discussions related to sustainability issues on eastern Long Island (Thiele press release August 12, 2011). The two legislators acknowledged that the necessary "startup" funds would be a considerable challenge. They would approach foundations, and seek government grants and private donors. There was hope that this first step would eventually lead to the development of a four-year undergraduate program

FIGURE 13.5. Deserted western section of Southampton campus. *Photo by author.*

on the Southampton Campus. Thiele repeated his support for the institute at a press conference called in April 2012 to announce the town's action rezoning the campus. The institute, said Thiele, would link Southampton with other Long Island research institutes such as Brookhaven Lab, Hofstra University, and Cold Spring Harbor. "Unless we establish our own centers of higher education excellence, the East End will be left at the gate. This proposal is a major step to insure that we are a part of Long Island's future and not an economic backwater" (*Southampton Press* April 12, 2012).

At present, however, many of the campus facilities, including the library, the gym, the Peconic and the Montauk dorms, and the dining hall are shuttered and empty. Deer are often seen grazing around the Peconic dorms and flocks of Canadian geese have made a home on the athletic field. The northwestern section of the campus has the eerie feeling of a ghost town.

Notes

Chapter One. Long Island University

1. Syracuse University worked steadily throughout the 1930s to reduce Jewish enrollment. The admissions director in 1932 stated that students had complained to him about the number of Jewish students at the university and argued, therefore, that it was in the best interests of the university to reduce the percentage of Jewish from 12 percent to 5 percent and to impose a permanent cap on that figure. "This would be one of our strongest factors,: he said," in securing the type of student which we desire (Clark, Leslie, and O'Brien 2010, 30–31).

2. University publications and internal memos referred to Metcalfe as "Doctor Metcalfe." *The Alumni Review,* most press releases, and even a commencement address Metcalfe gave at Roslyn High School identified him with the fraudulent title (LIUABCL Archives, Box 1 Metcalfe file).

3. Although Conolly's staunch conservatism brought him favor among the wealthy Gold Coast residents, it undoubtedly played a role in a major miscalculation in 1959 when he approved the hiring of Edward Sittler to teach in the humanities department at C. W. Post. Conolly and Hoxie carefully and quietly reviewed Sittler's background because of his involvement in the Nazi government during World War II. Sittler went to Germany shortly before the war and apparently became enamored with the Nazi cause, although he said later that he had been "misled." He was so enthusiastic about Nazism that he renounced his U. S. citizenship in 1940 to become a German citizen and took a job as a news commentator for the Nazis. He returned to the United States after the war and earned a doctorate in English Literature. Sittler taught briefly in two or three places, but his past followed him wherever he went, leading to his dismissal. He applied to teach at C. W. Post in 1959. Conolly and Hoxie approved of his hiring, arguing that since he was no longer a threat to the United States, as would be the case if he were a member of the Communist Party, there was no reason to question his employment at

C. W. Post. Although the American Civil Liberties Union supported Sittler, and the faculty, led by Dr. Kenneth Cosgrove, supported Sittler's hiring in a faculty review hearing (*New York Times* Dec. 15, 1959, 10), the public outcry was so heated that Conolly backed down reluctantly and asked for Sittler's resignation at the end of the fall 1959 semester. Sittler promptly complied, but the damage to LIU's image was already done (*New York Times* Dec. 16, 1959; Dec. 17, 1959; Nov. 2, 1960, 20). In 1960, Sittler tried to get his citizenship restored but was rejected by the courts (*New York Times* Sept. 2, 1960).

Chapter Two. Southampton

1. The completion of the South Shore Railroad line in 1870 connecting New York City to Sag Harbor brought an increasing number of authors, artists, and wealthy summer visitors to the East End (Goddard 2011, 205). The area already had a well-established reputation as a refuge for creative intellectuals. James Fenimore Cooper wrote his first novel, *Precaution,* in 1820 while he was staying in a Sag Harbor hotel (Harrison and Denne 2002, 26–28). Cooper drew on his experience among the whalers who came in and out of the busy whaling port to develop the nautical themes in his early novels.

2. One of the first artists who found his way by rail to the Hamptons was Winslow Homer. In 1874 he spent most of the summer in East Hampton ("Art Notes," *New York Evening Post* July 25, 1874) where he completed several paintings. One of them was a portrait of David Pharaoh, the aging chief of the Montaukett Indians. Shortly after Homer had "discovered" the Hamptons, Thomas Moran arrived in East Hampton (Long 2005, 11–19). Moran, who had traveled to Europe and the American West in search of subjects to paint, was inspired by the ocean and the landscape and the on eastern Long Island. A few years after his brief visit, Homer joined William Merritt Chase and a few of their colleagues in founding an informal group called the "Tile Club." These artists painted decorative tiles for what they hoped would be a lucrative market, which would pay their bills while they painted their more serious works. It may have been Homer who encouraged the club members to experience the *plein air* of the Hamptons (Harrison and Denne 2002, 40).

3. A year after the Hoyts built their cottage, the developers turned their full attention to the Shinnecock Hills. They anticipated that the railroad would bring an increasing number of rich vacationers to the area. A group of wealthy entrepreneurs led by Austin Corbin, the president of the Long Island Railroad, bought plots of land in the hills and sold them to summer visitors. By 1905 there were eighteen summer cottages where visitors lived from July until Labor Day (Wetterau 1991, 26–27). Janette Hoyt became a prominent member of this small elite community. She was one of the founders of the Shinnecock Hills Golf Club and her daughter, Trixie, played in several of the first tournaments.

Chapter Three. Getting Started

1. Enrollment figures are almost impossible to cite with precision. The head-count changes until a month or so after the college opens. Figures given to the press in early September are seldom accurate because there are always late enrollments

and "no-shows." Even the mid-fall headcounts can be off by a small number. The ten-year plan published in 1967, for example, listed the 1963 enrollment at 249 while other sources cited figures as high as 313. The figures cited in this book, therefore, are general estimates, but they are a fairly reliable indicator of shifting patterns.

Chapter Four. LIU in Crisis

1. The 1964 Middle States Report noted the "insufficient educational know-how at the top," and called for the appointment of a well-qualified and experienced Vice Chancellor for Academic Affairs (LIUABCL, RG 3:2, Middle States, Report 1964, 12–16; also quoted in Gatner 1974, 603). This report calling into question Pell's leadership undoubtedly played a role in the LIU Board of Trustees' decision to find a chancellor with experience in educational administration. Ironically, they were later to discover that experience alone does not guarantee success.

2. Hoxie wanted to buy a helicopter for use by the chancellor's office, but he backed down when his proposal met with a storm of criticism. (Friedheim 1967, 4).

3. The partial transcript of the Hoxie meeting, taken by Walter Doyle, a *Windmill* staff member, appeared in the November 17, 1966, edition of the *Windmill*.

4. Ten Year Plan included several chapters describing the history of the university and plans for the future. The references to the future were very general, citing plans to establish a school of law at C. W. Post, and a health center, but giving no specifics about financing, market research, or a construction schedule. In chapter 8, entitled "The University Tomorrow," the report stated that the university was committed to providing access to all qualified students regardless of their ability to pay and to ensuring that qualified faculty would not have to make a financial sacrifice to teach in a private university. This would be accomplished by aggressive fundraising in the private sector to fund scholarships and faculty salaries. In spite of this goal, the fundraising task was left to the public relations officer without the help of a consultant. The two outside critics, Margaret Kelly, the dean for academic development at St. John's and Deane Malott, president emeritus at Cornell, criticized the lack of a specific timetable and organizational structure for a fundraising campaign. They also urged the university to strengthen existing programs before undertaking expensive expansion. The ten-year plan, said Malott "is either going to be a living document or an historic oddity." He warned that raising money for scholarships and faculty salaries is much more difficult than funding a building or a new program

5. William Birenbaum went on to become a very successful and highly regarded university administrator. He served as president of Staten Island Community College from 1968 to 1976 and assumed the presidency of Antioch College in 1976, at that time the college was in serious financial trouble. Birenbaum instituted a program of stringent austerity measures, which resulted in a recovery by 1980. He later served as the dean of the New School for Social Research. In sharp contrast, Hoxie's image was so negative that when his successor, George Stoddard, discovered that the university catalogue for 1969–70 still listed Hoxie as chancellor and included his photo and brief introduction, he was furious. He ordered the catalogues to be withdrawn and reprinted without any reference to Hoxie. Unfortunately about 5,000 of an 11,000 run were already distributed. Stoddard ordered those remaining to be destroyed. The revision cost $8,000, but Stoddard insisted that it was necessary.

Chapter Five. Drift and Uncertainty 1968–1972

1. The 1973 report to Middle States repeated the goal to "improve the quality of the students recruited and to retain a higher proportion of the better students for a longer period." The SAT scores had improved slightly since 1963, but the median combined math and verbal scores remained below 1,000. Meinhart's critique was validated by the statistics in the report, but ignored once again in the statement of goals. The Middle States evaluation team, however, made no mention of this in their report. The 1980 Long Range Plan (1980–85) noted that the college was unable to provide adequate remedial services for weak students, but that that problem would be resolved, as "a selectivity process designed to lessen the demand on these resources has just begun." The 1982 Middle States Report evaluation, however, noted "only 1–2% of the students who complete their applications are normally rejected." The median SAT scores remained below 1,000. Clearly, the 1973 and 1980 goal to raise admissions standards had not been met. The first official recognition that Meinhart was right about the disconnect between reality and the goal of higher admission standards came in Tim Bishop's remarkably candid report to the Board of Trustees in 1987. Bishop told the trustees that while the minimum standards for admission called for a 75 percent high school average and an 800 combined SAT score, nearly one-third of the 1986 entering freshman class were below those minimal standards. This was not going to change, he continued, because the students in the moderate to high end of the academic scale make up a minority of college-bound students each year, and that number has been shrinking. In 1982 the national pool of college-bound students included about 76,000 students with combined SAT scores above 1,100. By 1987, that number was down to 67,000. All of these students are heavily recruited by the top universities in the nation. We can not successfully recruit from that particular niche, concluded Bishop. In the 1989 Comprehensive Development Plan, the candid approach continued. "Our shadow attempts at increased admissions selectivity were misguided." The typical Southampton student had a combined SAT score of 903. "All of the information cited results in a series of inescapable conclusions: our students are weak and appear to be getting somewhat weaker; despite our efforts to remediate they perform poorly." The 1992 self-study prepared for the 1993 Middle States evaluation acknowledged the reality of our enrollment pattern, by stating that the mission of the college was to provide an opportunity for students of disparate levels of academic preparation. The 2003 report to Middle States restated that mission.

2. The scholarship required that students be enrolled full time. Graduates included David Silva, Nelson Cause (1988), Lanette Cooke (1996), Caprice Crippen (1998), Danielle Hopson (1994), Michael Hunter (1992), Lynne Marshall (1996), Lauryn Randall (1990), Ella Smith (1992), Gordell Wright (1996), Ray Clendenin (2002), and Tohonash Tarrent (2002). Among the part-time students were: Rueben Valdez, Peter Smith, Margo Thunderbird, John Perry, Michelle Johnson, Benjamin Silva, Michael Smith Jr., Guy Reddick, and Diane Bess.

3. The first recipient of the scholarship was Ronald Darden, from Southampton High School. Darden, a business major and captain of the wrestling team, graduated and went on to have a successful career in business.

4. One of the professors, Richard Cummings, charged that this was a purge of faculty members who opposed the war in Vietnam. His position was disputed by

two professors, Robert J. Cooke, the chair of the Humanities Division, and William Burke chair of the Natural Science Division, who were active opponents of the war (*Windmill* April 5, 1971). Although Burke did not support Cummings's accusations, he did protest the dismissal of faculty, "merely for financial needs related solely to survival" (*Windmill* Oct. 7, 1971).

5. LIU sold the parcel over the protests of a neighborhood organization and The Group for the South Fork, a local environmental organization. There had been no consultation with the natural science faculty about the sale. The donor testified in an affidavit that LIU had assured him that the property would be preserved for a science facility (*Southampton Press* Oct. 6, 1983, 6).

6. At a halftime ceremony in February 2000, Ron Gargill's number 22 was retired (*Windmill* Feb. 23, 2000).

Chapter Six. Great Potential amid Continuing Deficits 1972–1978

1. President Glanz had prepared a Long Range Plan (1971–1980) for the Middle States College Development Committee in the spring of 1972, which called for an architectural consulting firm to assist them. The Warner, Burns, Toan, and Lunde plan drew heavily from the work done by Glanz, Professor Nate Stevens, chair of the Student-Faculty Assembly, and the college Academic Planning Council.

2. In the fall of 1974, an ad hoc committee led by Richard Czerniak, Barbara Severns, Kathy Matz and Wayne Penello, the Student Assembly president, stormed unannounced into a meeting between Chancellor Bush-Brown and President Marmion with a list of demands that included an extensive refurbishing of the dorms (*Windmill* Nov. 1, 1974). Taken by surprise, the two men assured the students that they were aware of the problem, but Marmion did not change his priorities.

3. Dean Burke had listed the closing of the college as one of the three options for the college in a memo to President Marmion on Sept. 26, 1974, but he clearly intended it as an "attention getter" at the time. Nevertheless, the shadow of closure was ever present throughout the history of the college.

4. It is interesting, but not at all surprising given the parochial nature of the three campuses, that no consideration was given to the possibility of forming a common university-wide union, even though it would have provided the faculty with a much stronger bargaining base. Ironically, the university proposed this (*University Bulletin* March 1974) but it was rejected by the three campuses. The Post and Brooklyn faculties believed that too often any surpluses generated by their campuses would be shifted to offset Southampton's annual deficit. Post also complained that they were financing Brooklyn as well. These concerns undermined any effort to cooperate at the university level. About a month after Southampton's union election, The C. W. Post faculty voted to investigate the possibility of seceding from Long Island University, recalling former chancellor Ferguson's recommendations (*Newsday* Nov. 20, 1973). There was a serious effort to establish an independent C. W. Post University. Faculty, administrators, and students sent many appeals to Marjorie Post asking for a multimillion dollar gift. Some were Hoxie supporters who wanted him vindicated (see ch. 3). She declined and cut off all communication with LIU. The previous spring C. W. Post president Robert Payton had resigned in protest over what

he deemed the loss of autonomy under Chancellor Bush-Brown (*Windmill* March 29, 1973). Foreshadowing 2005, the Post faculty were also concerned about the possibility that they would have to absorb faculty from Southampton and Brooklyn if those campuses were closed. Chancellor Bush-Brown sharply opposed the secessionist move and promised that no money would be siphoned off from Post and sent to Brooklyn or Southampton. The movement faded after that, but the episode clearly demonstrated once again that the university remained deeply fragmented.

5. The idea for a special scholarship based entirely on merit came from Edward Glanz in his last semester. Marmion renamed it and gave it his full support.

6. The college had insufficient funds to hire an experienced remedial educator or to provide a secretarial staff that could create a structure designed to integrate the SAS with the relevant areas of the campus community. Undeterred by these limitations, Hitchcock decided to proceed on a shoestring just to get something in place that could be expanded and developed in the future. This is another example of the pattern described later by Tim Bishop wherein creative and energetic, but relatively inexperienced, people working at low wages served the college well. The college hired Julia Ludmer to serve as a part-time director with two tutorial instructors. The program was innovative and well intended, but served few students because there were no procedures established for referring the students. As Hitchcock had hoped, the program did expand and develop a structured connection with the faculty, admissions, and student counseling services. Jack Kenneally, a member of the English faculty became part-time director in 1977. The SAS now coordinated a testing program to determine remedial needs and established remedial courses in reading, social science, math, and science. In 1979 the SAS became the Study Center and in 1980 had a full-time director, Pamela Topping, and an experienced remedial reading specialist.

Chapter Seven. High Hopes and Hard Realities

1. The Seventh Day Adventist Church had its roots in the Millerite movement whose founder, William Miller, believed that the second coming (advent) of Christ would occur on Oct. 22, 1844. Many devout followers gathered in prayer to prepare for the great day of judgment when the world would end. When that day passed in what Millerites called "the great disappointment," many of them went back to their Methodist, Baptist, Presbyterian, or other Protestant churches. A Millerite woman named Ellen G. White, however, claimed to have had a vision soon after "the great disappointment" which revealed to her that Christ had gone into a "special place in heaven" in 1844 to investigate the souls of the dead in preparation for the final day of judgment when he would make his second advent at an unspecified time in the future. White soon had a following from among the former Millerites that grew over the next two decades. In 1863, White's followers formed the Seventh Day Adventist Church, which today has about fifteen million members. They believe that the Sabbath comes on Saturday, the seventh day, not on Sunday. The failure to observe the Sabbath on Saturday was one reason, White believed, that Christ did not make a physical appearance in 1844. See Alice Felt Tyler, *Freedom's Ferment: Phases of American Social History from the Colonial Period to the Outbreak of the Civil War* (New York: Harper and Brothers, 1944), 68–85; Whitney R. Cross, *The Burned*

Over District: The Social and Intellectual History of Enthusiastic Religion in Western New York, 1800–1850 (New York: Harper Torchbooks, 1950), ch. 17).

2. The university had rented a house only a few doors away on the same street for President Marmion with the same hope. It should have been evident by this time that the wealthy summer elites would never give substantial funds to the college.

3. Danziger was familiar with Co-op because he had earned his PhD at Northeastern University in Boston, where the program had become the signature focus of the university. He had discussed the possibility of developing a somewhat similar program at Southampton with Dean Burke. Burke liked the idea and urged President Wilson to give it consideration. P.

4. President David Steinberg, who most frequently referred to Southampton as the jewel in the crown, shifted to the albatross metaphor when he addressed the C. W. Post faculty after Southampton closed. The Southampton albatross, he said, has now been removed from our necks (Forestell, pers. comm. 2006).

5. When asked about the causes of the tension between the chancellor and President Wilson, Tim Bishop and Kevin Coveney said that they believed that it was Bush-Brown's "broken promises" (Coveney, pers. comm. Sept. 24, 2007; Bishop, pers. comm. Sept. 13, 2007).

6. In 1980, Bob Miller studied Geochemistry in France. That same year, Elizabeth McKenna received a Fulbright for a research project in Switzerland that, unfortunately, was canceled by the laboratory at the last moment. Instead, she went to SUNY Stony Brook where she earned her doctorate in Biochemistry. In 1983, Martyn Botfield studied the ecology of giant clams on the Great Barrier Reef in Australia. The following year, Jeff Riegel studied at the Institute for Genetic Research in Cologne, West Germany. That same year, Beatrice Chasse studied Paleobiology and the History of Science in Belgium. In 1986, Norris Armstrong studied antifreeze proteins in the blood sera of fish at the University of Keil in West Germany.

7. Newspaper clippings mentioning the arts festival can be found in the Wilson papers, SCC Archive B. The *Windmill* front page Sept. 24, 1981, illustrated the contradictions on college campuses. Half of the page featured a biography and a photo of Ms. Salerno-Sonnenberg and the other half reported the arrest of a student who had been growing marijuana in his dorm room.

8. Kenneth Simsarian's contract ran until the end of August,1983. When he was terminated in May he was furious. "I could have been writing grants all summer," he told a reporter (*East Hampton Star* Aug. 15, 1983).

9. The damage was reported by Cy Madison, the director for public relations and development affairs, who had an office in the building. In November 1969, Madison, a very fastidious fellow, requested that the Zeta Beta Tau fraternity be prohibited from having any more parties in the building because they had left litter and alcohol stains on the chairs and the kitchen counters and had burned some holes in the hallway rug. A few months later, he again sent an angry, detailed memo to Provost Glanz about a party sponsored by the Sigma Alpha Mu fraternity which lasted most of a Saturday night. Madison came in on Sunday and was so upset that he photographed the condition of the building and sent a detailed memo to Provost Glanz. The living room was strewn with empty beer, wine, and vodka bottles, pretzels, cooked green beans, silverware, and patties of butter. The kitchen was littered with food, and there was a large garbage can full of more empty beer, wine, and

vodka bottles amid the litter. Cigarette ashes had been ground into the bedsheets and several chairs had been stained. The evidence of smoking was of particular concern because the wooden building was a firetrap at the time. It was out of compliance with the fire code. There was no fire alarm system, no fire extinguishers, and the nearest fire hydrant was a half-mile away.

10. Pellicane owned one lot and three C. W. Post alumni, Daniel Fruitbine, Gary Herman, and Barry Weiner, owned the other. The three alumni agreed to donate their plot to the college.

11. Unfortunately, the Environmental Studies major was not integrated with the existing Environmental Science major. The rigid academic boundaries separating the Natural Science and the Social Science divisions made it very difficult to develop an interdisciplinary approach. There were also constant conflicts over the distribution of funds and faculty lines in the two divisions, as well as personality conflicts, making compromise and cooperation nearly impossible. As a result, the two environmental majors went their own separate ways until the 1990s when a new generation of faculty became involved.

Chapter Eight. A Decade to Build

1. One such alumnus was North Fork Bank chairman John Kanas, class of 1968. He had taken over as manager of the Mattituck branch of the bank in 1971 and became acting president of the North Fork Bank in 1975. He expanded the bank's branches into Western Suffolk and Nassau counties (*New York Times* Feb. 29, 2004). By 2004, he was reputed to be earning about $8 million a year. Kanas had joined the Board of Trustees in the 1970s, but was unhappy with the inactivity of his fellow board members. He was encouraged by Bishop to rejoin the board in 1996 and pledged $100,000 for the construction of Chancellor's Hall in 1998. This was the largest gift that ever came from any college alumnus/a (*Southampton Press* Feb, 5, 1998). The $10 million building was under construction at the time. In 2001 Kanas and his wife gave an additional $35,000 unrestricted gift for a scholarship fund.

2. There were, however, many faculty who felt that the prevailing pattern was still a "top-down" style of management. A year after the implementation of the LIU Plan, the faculties of the three main centers sent a letter to the Board of Trustees with a copy to Steinberg asking for a change from his old pattern to "A New Partnership of Faculty, Administration and Trustees" (April 10, 1989). The faculties asked for full voting representation on the board. They wanted the faculty representatives to make up one-third of the board membership. This, of course, never happened, but the board did agree eventually to invite faculty and student representatives to attend open board meetings, but they had no vote and were not allowed in closed sessions.

Chapter Nine. A Decade of Treading Water 1993–2002

1. The entertainers who performed at the concerts are as follows; Crosby, Stills and Nash (1992), Tina Turner (1993), the Doobie Brothers (1994), Tony Bennett (1995), The Allman Brothers Band (1996), Jimmy Buffett (1996), James Taylor (1997), Rod Stewart (1998), Tom Petty (1999), Jimmy Buffett (2000), Paul

Simon (2001), Bob Dylan (2002), Jimmy Buffett (2003). The last concert featured Rod Stewart (Aug. 29, 2004).

2. For a review of Dolgan's book see Richard Welch, *Long Island Historical Journal* 18, no. 1–2 (2006): 170–71.

3. In January 1996, Tom Lloyd the newly appointed fundraiser, sent a memo to Steinberg and Kleinman noting that several members of the LIU board had voiced considerable skepticism about Sillerman's pledge and about his role in the fundraising campaign. Lloyd was also concerned and urged that Sillerman be told that his inactivity was hurting the college. Sillerman responded to these concerns, apologizing to Bishop for his inactivity on the capital campaign and agreeing to "cultivate" three of his fellow trustees and two wealthy prospective donors. His efforts, however, were only partially successful. In September, Bishop notified Sillerman that the "challenge" pledges came to $368,000 of which only $143,700 had actually been paid into the LIU coffers. Bishop appealed to Sillerman to begin making some payments on his million dollar challenge even though the trustees had fallen far short of the goal. Sillerman agreed, sending a check to Mary Lai for $71,850 in accordance with his "2 for 1" gift challenge.

4. Mario Sengco (1994–95) studied the ecology of plankton at the University of Konstanz in Germany. Sandra Melloy (1994–95) studied the same subject in Tasmania, Australia. Trina Filan (1995–96) studied rainforest ecology at the Smithsonian Tropical Research Institution in Panama. Matt Stutz (1995–96) studied coastal geology in Australia. Kelly Ryder (1996–97) studied at the University of Melbourne. Stephanie Burkhart (1996–97) studied at the University of Otago in New Zealand. Jennifer Melnyk (1996–97) studied at the Laval University in Canada. In one remarkable year (1997–98), seven Southampton students received Fulbright awards. Bethanie Carney studied Baltic salmon at the University of Goteborg in Sweden. Meredith Clinton had a Fulbright to study endangered loggerhead turtles in Greece but the facilities became unavailable. She then attended the Virginia Institute of Marine Science. Farrell Hochmuth helped develop sustainable agriculture techniques at the University of Zimbabwe. Allison Dwileski studied sea urchins at the Smithsonian Tropical Research Institution in Panama. Toni Ferrara studied fish parasites along the Great Barrier Reef at the University of Queensland in Australia. Kristen Schultz, an English major, studied the effects of the United States military base on the women of Okinawa. Matt Sullivan did his research on bacteria in seaweed at Queen's University of Belfast, in Northern Ireland. The following year, three more Southampton students received Fulbrights: Paul Cancellieri had a Fulbright to study at the Max Planck Institute in Germany, but decided to begin his doctoral studies at North Carolina State University instead; Liberty Trimarchi, a Psychobiology major, documented the sounds of beluga whale mothers and calves at Dalhousie University in Canada; Brian Wysor studied marine flora at the Smithsonian Tropical Research Institute in Panama. In 1999, Josh Newton studied water resource management in Bolivia.

5. The election was a major upset for the long-established Republican Party. It also brought to the surface the growing tensions between Roger Tilles, who was chairman of the Board of Trustees at the time, and Robert Sillerman. Tilles, although a lifelong Democrat, at first supported the Republican incumbent, Felix Grucci, because he expected that Grucci would easily defeat Bishop. Tilles argued that LIU

should have some influence with Grucci to better protect the university's interests. Sillerman, who had urged Bishop to run and had provided considerable financial support, had little patience for that argument. In a dramatic twist, Tilles turned against Grucci when the Republican incumbent attempted to smear Bishop, charging him covering up an alleged rape on campus when he was provost. Tilles denounced Grucci and brought a libel suit for $6 million against him on behalf of LIU, charging that Grucci had slandered the university and had caused "material damage. Grucci was one of only two Republican congressional candidates to lose in 2002.

References

Altbach, P. G., R. O. Berdahl, and P. J. Gumport, eds. 2005. *American higher education in the twenty-first century: Social, political, and economic challenges*. Baltimore: Johns Hopkins University Press.

Anderson, T. 2002. *This fine piece of water: An environmental history of Long Island Sound*. New Haven: Yale University Press.

Austin, A. W., et al. 1974. *The American freshman: National norms for Fall 1974*. Berkeley: University of California Graduate School of Education and the American Council on Education.

Birenbaum, R., and P. D. Eckel. 2005. The dilemma of presidential leadership. In *American higher education in the twentieth century: Social, political, and economic challenges*, ed. P. G. Altbach, R. O. Berdahl, and P. J. Gumport, 340–65. Baltimore: Johns Hopkins University Press.

Bowen, H. R. 1980. *The costs of higher education*, San Francisco: Jossey-Bass.

———, and J. W. Minter. 1975. *Private higher education*. Washington, DC: Association of American Colleges.

Bowen, W. G. 1968. *The economies of major private universities*. New York; McGraw-Hill.

Carlin, S. 2005. *Greenprint: A 10-year legacy in sustainability*. Unpublished manuscript, Southampton Town Historians Office, Southampton, NY.

Carden, M. L., and S. E. Dinan, eds. 2001. A history: The struggle for access. In *Long Island University: 75 years of access and excellence*, ed. C. Corey, 55–91. Brookville, NY: Long Island University.

Carnegie Commission on Higher Education. 1973. *Higher education; Who pays? Who benefits? Who should pay?* New York: McGraw-Hill.

Celebrating the 25th Anniversary of C. W. Post Center, 1954–79. September 1979. C. W. Post Archives.

Chambers, M. M. 1970. *Higher education in the fifty states*. Danvillle, IL: The Interstate Printers and Publishers.

Clark, J. B., W. B. Leslie, and K. P. O'Brien. 2010. *SUNY at sixty: The promise of the State University of New York*. Albany: State University of New York Press.

Creager, J. A. 1968. *National norms for entering college freshmen Fall 1968. ACE Research Reports* 3, no. 1. Washington, DC: American Council on Education. 1968.

DeBenedetti, C. 1990. *An American ordeal: The antiwar movement of the Vietnam era*. Syracuse: Syracuse University Press.

Dolgon, C. 2005. *The end of the Hamptons: Scenes from the class struggle in America's paradise*. New York: New York University Press.

Douglas, L. E. 2006. The origins of Adelphi Suffolk College: The Port Jefferson and Stony Brook initiatives: 1953–1956, *Long Island Historical Journal* 18, no. 1–2: 92–109.

———. 2007. The origins of Adelphi Suffolk College: The Sayville and Southampton initiatives 1957–1958, *Long Island Historical Journal* 19, no. 1–2: 81–97.

El Khawas, E. H. 1976. *Public and private higher education: Differences in role, character, and clientele*. (Policy Analysis Service Reports). Washington, DC: American Council on Education.

Friedheim, W. 1967. LIU: University in crisis. *Newsday* Special Edition, Nov. 25.

Gabriel, R. 1921 *The evolution of Long Island: A story of land and sea*. Port Washington, NY: Ira Friedman Press (reprint 1968).

Gatner, E., S.M. 1974. Long Island University: The history of a relevant and responsible university, 1926–1968. Doctor of Education dissertation, Columbia Teacher's College. Ann Arbor: University Microfilms.

Glanz, E. 1969. *The story of the college windmill: An affectionate history*. Southampton, NY: Steamboat Press.

———. 1970. A five year dilemma and a call for a new college look. Summarized in the *Christmas Camel* 1, no. 8. In file "Models of Southampton College Future" along with a detailed draft of six models, dated Oct. 16, 1970.

Goddard, D. 2011. *Colonizing Southampton: The transformation of a Long Island community, 1870–1900*. Albany: State University of New York Press.

Gregory, D. 2003. History of the environmental movement at Southampton College. Unpublished Senior Honors Thesis, SCC Archive B, Environmental file, Misc. Box 6.

Gwaltney, C. 1967. Many private colleges facing financial crisis, *The Chronicle of Higher Education* 1: 1.

Hammond, M. F. 1984. Survival of small private colleges: Three case studies, *Journal of Higher Education* 55 (May/June): 360–88.

Handler, J. 1973. Windmill remembrances. Mimeo, SCC Archive B Misc Box 6, 30 pp.

Harrison, H., and C. A. Denne. 2002. *Hamptons Bohemia: Two centuries of artists and writers on the beach*. New York: Chronicle Books.

Howlett, C. F. 1995. The Anti–Vietnam War movement on Long Island, Part two: The high schools, the October 1969 moratorium, and Kent State (1970), *Long Island Historical Journal* 8, no. 1: 56–75.

Jenny, H., and G. R. Wynn. 1970. *The golden years: A study of expenditure, growth, and distribution of 48 private four year liberal arts colleges, 1960–1968*. Wooster, OH: College of Wooster.

Horowitz, M. 1981. *Brooklyn College: The first half century*. Brooklyn: Brooklyn College Press.

Keiser, A. 1952. *College names: Their origin and significance*. New York: Bookman Associates.

Kenkel, C. 2004. Closing time: You don't have to go home, but you can't stay here. *Windmill*, Sept.

Kurkowsk, J. 1987. LIU status report on preliminary marketing research findings and marketing recommendations. LIUABCL, Nov. 2, Records Group 3:1, Box 3.

Lai, M. 1970. Recommendations for the organization and structure of Long Island University. Typewritten Manuscript in LIUABCL, 27 pp.

Landes, J. 2004. College closing blamed on debt, poor enrollment. *East Hampton Star*, June 24.

Lee, E. C., and F. M. Bowen. 1971. *The multicampus university: A study in academic governance*. New York: McGraw-Hill.

Long, R. 2005. *De Kooning's bicycle: Artists and writers in the Hamptons*. New York: Farrar, Straus, and Giroux.

Magali, P. 1970. The rationale for Long Island University, A rebuttal of Chancellor Glenn Ferguson's report to the Board of Trustees dated September 29, 1969. 20pp. LIUABCL R.G 2.

Marmion, H. 1975. A report to the community, 1974–75. *Southampton Press*, Aug. 28.

———. 1976. A report to the community, 1975–76. *Southampton Press*, Sept. 2.

———. 1977. A report to the community, 1976–77. *News Review of Riverhead*, Sept. 1.

———. 1978 A report to the community: 1977–78, *Southampton Press*, Aug. 31.

Massy, W. 1990. *Endowment: Perspectives, policies, and management*. Washington, DC: Association of Governing Boards of Universities and Colleges.

Marshall, G. J. 1995. The survival of colleges in America: A census of four-year colleges in the United States, 1636–1973. Stanford University PhD dissertation, School of Education. Ann Arbor: UMI Dissertation Services.

Murphy, J. L. 1989. *The reluctant radicals: Jacob L. Beilhart and the Spirit Fruit Society*. New York: University Press of America.

Murphy, R. C. 1991 *Fish-shaped Paumanok: Nature and man on Long Island*. Great Falls VA: Waterline Books.

Paul, D. A. 2008. *When the pot boils: The decline and turnabout of Drexel University*. Albany: State University of New York Press.

Pisano, R. G. 2010. *William Merritt Chase*. New Haven: Yale University Press.

Rather, J. 2004. Anger and angst at Southampton College. *New York Times*, June 27.

Rice, H. K. 1965. Admissions practices of Long Island University: A comparative study. Unpublished EdD thesis Rutgers The State University of New Jersey, New Brunswick. Ann Arbor: University Microfilms.

Rosen, C. 1978. *The scandals of 1951: How the gamblers almost killed basketball*. New York: Holt, Rinehart, and Winston.

Rothfeld, M., and O. Winslow. 2004. The little college that couldn't. *Newsday*, July 18.

Royer, J. T., and J. A. Creager. 1976. *A profile of 1968 college freshmen in 1972*. ACE *Research Reports* 10, no. 2. Washington, DC: American Council on Education.

Sale, K. 1973. *SDS: The rise and development of the Students for a Democratic Society.* New York: Random House.
Sartor, L. 1968. A student profile for use in the evaluation of needs and programming at The Southampton College of Long Island University. SCC Archive A I, K.
Thelin, J. R. 2004. *A history of American higher education.* Baltimore: Johns Hopkins University Press.
Turner, R. 2005. A subjective review of Core 101: Introduction to interdisciplinary studies. Unpublished paper in SCC Archive B.
Wettereau, H. 1991. *Shinnecock Hills long ago.* East Patchogue, NY:
Winerip, M. 1998. The blue collar millionaire. *New York Times Magazine*, June 7, 72–76.
Winslow, O. 2005. College's faculty rip LIU chief. *Newsday*, March 12, 2005, A12.
Wormley, W. M. 1978. Factors related to the ability of certain small private liberal arts colleges to cope with the new depression in higher education. PhD dissertation, Stanford University. Ann Arbor: University Microfilms.
Wynn, G. R. 1974 (April). *At the crossroads: A report on the financial condition of the 48 liberal arts colleges previously studied in "The golden years: The turning point."* Ann Arbor: Center For the Study of Higher Education.
Zeckendorf, W., and E. McCreary. 1970. *Autobiography of William Zeckendorf.* New York: Rinehart and Winston.

Primary Documents

LIUABCL, LIU Archives, Brooklyn Center Library.
SCC Archives A and B are located in the B. Davis Schwartz Memorial Library, Special Collections.
Windmill and *The Christmas Camel*, Southampton College newspapers, on file in the B. Davis Schwartz Memorial Library Special Collections and in the Southampton Town Historians Office, Southampton, New York, 11968.

It. 1–64. Interviews. Oral History Interviews 1–53 on DVD; 54–65 on Cassette.

1. Alumni interviews #1. June 4, 2005. Michael Director ('68), Andrew Lowe ('81), David Reed ('82), Beth Magazzo ('81).

2. Alumni Interviews #2. June 4, 2005. Jenifer Auger ('82), John Bedford ('76), Kenneth Murphy ('77), Linda Murphy-Melter ('77), Tara Fucci ('99), Elisa Rattiner ('00), Chris LaPorta ('80), Robert Farace ('82).

3. John Agria. June 1, 2005. Dean of Southampton College 1980–84.

4. Anne Hickey Algieri. May 24 2005. Instructor of English, Director of CORE program 1996–2005.

5. Mae Ann Anderson. June 17, 2005. Custodian 1968–2005.

6. Don Baker. April 5, 2005. Professor of Social Science, Social Science Division Director.

7. Baker, second interview (1964–2005). June 2, 2005.

8. Kathy Bess. May 26, 2005. Library staff 1995–2005.

9. Tim Bishop. April 17, 2003. Environmental programs.

10. John Bolog. May 26, 2005. Entered Sept. 1963, graduated May, 2005.

11. Jennifer Browne. June 14, 2005. Associate Provost 1998–2005.

12. Scott Carlin. March 3, 2003. Associate Professor of Environmental Studies and Geography.

13. Carlin, second interview. June 13, 2005.

14. Jennifer Cohen. June 6, 2005. Class of 2008.

15. John Cousin ('05) and Gash Kidane ('06), May 15, 2005.

16. Robert Danziger, second interview (first interview 2001, on cassette). April 29, 2005. Professor of Chemistry 1966–2005.

17. Bob DeLuca. March 6, 2003. Pres. of Group for the East End and adjunct prof. in Social Science Department.

18. Michael Disher. June 7, 2005. Director of Fine Arts Theater 1984–89, 1996–2005.

19. Alice Flynn. May 26 2005. Administration 1974–2005.

20. Paul Forestell. May 12, 2005. Professor of Psychology, Acting Dean of Undergraduate Programs.

21. Daniel F. Gearon, BME, MMS, PE. May 25, 2005. Director of Physical Plant 1993–2006.

22. Robert Gerbereux. April 28, 2005. Director of the Library 1966–2005.

23. Carol Gilbert. May 9, 2005. Director of Alumni Relations 1975–2005.

24. Art Goldberg, second interview. May 19, 2005. Professor of Chemistry 1973–2005; Travel courses to Australia, Peru 1973–2005.

25. Elizabeth Granitz. May 17, 2005. Associate Professor of Economics 1985–2005.

26. Thomas Haresign. Jan. 18, 2001. Professor of Biology 1966–2005.

27. Kenneth Haar (mislabeled Maar on DVD). June 3, 2005. Class of 1970.

28. Charles Hitchcock. May 3, 2005. 1967–2005: Associate Professor of Sociology; Social Science Division Director; Dean of College 2002–04; Dean of Graduate Studies 2004–05.

29. Wayne Hudson. June 13, 2005. Custodian 1987–2005.

30. Eric Kruh. April 29, 2005. Professor Emeritus of European Literature and Modern Languages.

31. Mary Lai. June 16, 2005. Director of University Finances 1945–2003.

32. James L. Larocca. May 11, 2005. Keyspan Distinguished Professor of Public Policy.

33. Larry Liddle (with Howard Riesman). April 26, 2005. Professor of Biology and Marine Science; travel courses to Caribbean, Israel, South Pacific 1969–2005.

34. Harry Marmion, second interview (first interview Oct. 12, 1999). May 26, 2005. President of Southampton Center.

35. John McCrudden. May 24, 2005. Director of Cooperative Education, Career Development, and Internships 1978–2005.

35A. Kathleen Modrowski. 2005. Director of the Friends World North American Center.

36. Sanjeeva Nayak. Feb. 19, 2003. Associate Professor of Political Science; Environmental Studies at Southampton.

37. Roy W. Nicholson. May 16, 2005. Associate Professor of Art 1986–2005.

38. Robert Pattison. June 1, 2005. Professor of English 1978–2005.

39. Nancy J. S. Peters. May 10, 2005. Professor of Chemistry 1982–2005.

40. William Peterson. May 20, 2005. Professor Emeritus of English.

41. Daniel Rodas. May 4, 2005. Provost May 2003–05.

42. Daniel Rodas, second interview. June 7, 2005.

43. Peter Saltanis. April 20, 2005. Orphans of Southampton Class of 2007.

44. Herbert Sherman. May 23, 2005. Associate Professor of Management 1996–2005.

45. Alvin Siegel. May 2, 2005. Professor of Chemistry and Marine Science 1968–2005; Dean 1989–1995.

46. David J. Steinberg. May 27, 2005. President of Long Island University 1985–2005.

47. Stephen T. Tettelbach. May 4, 2005. Associate Professor of Biology and Marine Science; Travel to South Pacific 1986–2005.

48. Fred Thiele. May 12, 2006. New York State Assemblyman; Class of 1976.

49. Mary Topping. May 24, 2005. Director of Physical Education and Athletics 1980–2005.

50. Robert Turner. May 11, 2005. Assistant Professor of Marine and Environmental Sciences 1999–2005.

51. Joyce Tuttle. May 19, 2005. Friends World Director of Enrollment 1998–2005.

52. Amy Urquhart. June 8 2005. Associate Dean of Students.

53. Ral Welker. Southampton College's Marine Science Program: A Memoir, Oct. 21, 2004 (CD with Interviews).

54. John Andrews. Jan. 21, 2003. Origins of the Environmental Science major.

55. Alan Braveman. Aug. 27, 2005. Class of 1969.

56. Richard Brown. July 2005. Class of 1968.

57. Bill Burke. Sept. 22, 1999. Professor of Biology; Natural Science Division Director; Dean under Harry Marmion.

58. Robert Danziger, first interview (second interview 2005 on DVD #16). Jan. 24, 2001. Professor of Chemistry.

59. Nora Detwiller (with Joan Tutt). June 3, 2005. Class of 2005.

60. Arthur Goldberg, first interview (second interview 2005 on DVD #24). Feb. 10, 2003. Professor of Chemistry and Environmental Sciences; Director of the Environmental Science program.

61. Harry Marmion, first interview(second interview 2005 on DVD #34). Oct. 12, 1999. President of Southampton College.

62. Isaura Marshall. July 26, 2001. Secretary in Social Science Dept. and Dean's office.

63 Michael Rosch. July 2005. Adjunct Professor of Fine Arts.

64. Joan Tutt (with Nora Detwiler). June 3, 2005. Class of 1969.

65. L. Joan Zimmer. Nov, 2, 1999. Personnel Coordinator.

Oral Interviews: Typewritten Notes: On file in the Southampton Town Historians Office, Southampton, N.Y.

1. Tim Bishop. May 15, 2005. U.S. Congressman, Former Provost of Southampton College.

2. Alan Braveman (phone). Fall 2005.
3. Peter Dosch. May 31, 2005. Custodian 1991–2005.
4. Paul Forestell. Nov. 29, 2005.
5. Carol Gilbert. Summer 2005.
6. Jarron Jewel. Sept. 22, 2005. Archives secretary, Local #3948 union official.
7. Mary Lai (phone). Aug. 24, 2004.
8. Pekka Paavonpera. Aug. 29, 2005.
9. Mary Peterson. May 23, 2005. Student Advising Office Director.
10. Red Owl. Dec. 1, 2005.
11. Kenneth Thompson. June 8, 2005. Custodian 1990–2005.
12. Susan Ulrich. July 2005. Enrollment Services, COOP 1987–2005.

Index

Illustrations are indicated by an *italic* page number.

AAUP (American Association of University Professors), 69, 70, 102
Abruzzo, Matthew T. (judge), 6
Achuthan, Radh, 102, *103*, 122
Adamczyk, Henry, 265
Adelphi-Suffolk College (now Dowling College), 16–17, 89, 98, 147, 164, 199
Agria, John, 131, 136, 140, 144–45, 154
Akindle, Jacob, 91
Alfred, Randy, 91
Allen, James, 65
All For The Sea (concert series), 174, 204, 222, 247–48
Aloia, Vincent, *7*, 51, 117, 118, 121
Altholz, Robert, 227, 231, 259
Altimari, Nicole, 276
Alvarez, Alfonso, 92
American Association of University Professors (AAUP), 69, 70, 102
Anderson, Mae, 181
Andrews, John, 91, 92, 98, 108
Arch-Walton, Melissa, 85–86, 184
Arons, Michael, 180, 193, 199
Arroyo, Cassie, coach who led team to win ECAC title, 261
Arter, Rhetta M., 21
"Ashley Montana Goes Ashore in the Caicos" (Rosenblatt)," 231–32
Athletic programs for women, 133–34, 192, 231
Atterbury, Grosvenor, 20
Atwood, Chase, 22, 37
Auger, Jenifer, 109, *147*
Avenoso, Ellen, 162
Avram, Michael, 196

Bahnsen, Alvin, 9
Bairdi, John, 66
Baisley, Paul J., 276
Baker, Donald
  call for resignation of Hoxie, 59–60, 70
  concern on funds allocated to Natural Science, 104
  and curriculum planning group, 43
  on Glanz's duress in office, 84
  and internship for Thiele, 107
  and joint statement in *Windmill* on minority presence on campus, 114
  and LIU administration as inept, 227

Baker, Donald *(continued)*
on military draft and core requirements, 44
and objection to Kane's unilateral imposition, 208
recruited by Glanz as director of Social Science division, 27–28
and SCS founding, 246
testimony on Brooklyn Center sale, 63–64
and Women's Studies program, 186
Bales, Andrew, 51
Banahan, Susan, 124
Bane, Gil, 90, 91
Barneau, Katherine, 171
Barry, Glenn, 93
Barton, Jay, 26, 36
Basketball scandal (1950s) at LIU, 5, 8–9
Beach, Herb, 145
Beavers, Russell Jr., 85
Bee, Claire, 5, 8–9
Berger, Gretchen, 48
Berger, Harold, 124
Berger, Thomas, 111
Bergman, Richard
dean of students, *32*
on drug use by students, 42–43
praise for Marmion, 99–100
Berkebile, Alan, 101, 104–105, 121
Bernatzky, Robert, 107
Bernstein, Bonnie, 193
Bertuglia, Robert, 181
Bess, Henry, 87
Bess, Kathleen, 86
Beville, Mel, 38
Birenbaum, William M.
and Brooklyn strike, 59
dismissal by Hoxie upheld by Board, 58–59
Hoxie's dislike of, 62, 70
Hoxie's expansion plans predicted by, 55, 67
praised in press, 60
Bishop, Tim
on the commitment of Southhampton College people, 36
denial of racism in custodian outsourcing, 184
departure of, 202
as "everywhere man," 131
hired by Marmion to the admissions staff, 101
and "kitchen cabinet," 166–67, 174
leave of absence to run for Congress, 202, 289n5
named provost at Southampton, 157–58
photos of, *106*, *174*, *179*
questions to chancellor after merger, 151–52
on "Southampton College" at last graduation, 263
on Southampton's undercapitalized history, 242
at Stony Brook Southampton opening, 271
on "Wilson's reality," 140
See also Bishop-Steinberg era
Bishop-Burke Learning Center, 238
Bishop-Steinberg era, 157–171
Al Siegel deanship, 163–64
Bishop named provost at Southampton, 158
Bishop's "kitchen cabinet," 166–67, 174
Friends World College merger (1991), 164–65
Friends World Program, 165–66, 171, 175, 184, 193
Long Island University Plan, 161–63
Merger collapse (1986–1988), 158–161
Bishop's assessment of Southampton, 159–160
"Decade to Build" and, 159, 288n1
and enrollment drop, 159
negative profile of LIU student, 160
and outstanding students, 160–61
and planning committee, 159, 288n2

Middle States (1993–1994), 167–171
and database establishment, 168–69
and fall evaluation, 170–71
and mission statement, 167
negative image of LIU in *Newsday*, 171, 175
and outcomes assessment, 169–170
Murphy named dean of continuing education, 158
Steinberg chosen for presidency of LIU, 157
See also Bishop, Tim; Middle States Association; Steinberg, David
Black Artists Festival, 113
Black Students Alliance (BSA), 89–90, 112–14
Blakelock, Chester, 16, 21
Blue, Richard, 93
Bolog, John, 36, 38
Bolotowsky, Ilya, 36, 93, 111, 141–42
Bonal, Dennis, 262
Borde, Arvind, 208, 211–12, 227
Bottomly, William, 53
Bowden, Christa, 212
Bowen, H. R., 66
Bowen, Lisa, 86
Brackett, Lorna, 114
Bradshaw, Peter, 42
Braun, Kevin, 48
Braveman, Alan
as editor of *Windmill* showed concern for campus, 63
on gym campaign, 71
on LIU's negative reputation, 54
and paternalism, 59
and SCS founding, 246
successful graduate, 36, 37
Breivaite, Rita, 192
Brennan, Edward, 17
Bretsch, Kurt, 277
Bridge, John, 144, 178
Bright, Donelle, 262
Brill, Bob, 99
Brill, Joan, 37
Bromberger, David, 48
Brophy, Michael, 189, 199
Brown, Richard, 36–37, 40, 54
Browne, Jennifer, 235, 239, 254–55
Bruce, Mrs. Ailsa Mellon, 24
BSA (Black Students Alliance), 89–90, 112–14
"Buffalo T." (Terry Jones)., 154–55
Buffett, Jimmy, 222
Burke, Tim, 109
Burke, William
Agria as replacement for, 135–36
antiwar stance of, 47
and Bishop-Burke Learning Center, 238
and chancellor's unsympathetic phone calls, 100
concern if Brooklyn faculty joined Southampton, 65
efforts to ban *The Christmas Camel*, 124
environmental concerns focus of, 91, 92
and Glanz resignation request, 119
goals set for, 126
on Kenny Haar's tent city, 41
and Marmion's resignation request by Bush-Brown, 126
named dean of college, 98
photo of, *100*
and registering student in TAP, 125
replaced by Agria, 136
Burns, Kevin, 96
Bush-Brown, Albert
accusations in faculty resolution, 155–56
background of, 82
and Brooklyn strike of 1979, 135
complaints on Southampton to Glanz by, 83
condescension toward Middle States team, 148
criticisms of Marmion, 100
death of, 156
delays on Simonson sale by, 144
demeaning comments about Southampton College, 148–49
and "double suicide," 155
drinking problems of, 82

Bush-Brown, Albert *(continued)*
enthusiasm for Wilson, 130
Ferguson's successor in spring 1971, 79, 81
and First LIU Southampton College Federation of Teacher's agreement, *103*
Krasnoff's disillusionment with, 150–51
Little Neck Road parcel sold by, 92
loss of confidence by trustees, 150
messy exit of, 155–56
report to Marmion on fragile state of university, 97
signing labor agreement, *146*
Southampton urged to cut costs by, 89
thirteen-year tenure of, 81–82
title changed from chancellor back to president, 152
and union movement, 101
and Wilson administration tension, 135–36
Butler, Nicholas Murray, 2

Camberis, Van, 48, 71, 115
Campus for sale (Brooklyn Center). *See under* Hoxie Administration
Canis (dog), *103*
Carbone, Joseph, 139, 140
Cargill, Ronald, 93, 285n6
Carlin, Scott
and environmental programs, 178
and fear of developers, 246
and new course, 229
and SCS founding, 246–47
and sign *Save Southampton's College*, 249–250
and Veggie Car, 265–66
Carr, Elroy, 145
Cause, Nelson, 86
Chancellors Hall, 192
Characteristics of Excellence in Higher Education, 168
Charles, Harold, 283n4
Chase, William Merritt, 26–27
Chesis, Linda, 138
Childs, Cathy, 96
Chisholm, Shirley, 93
Chorst, Gary, 99
Christmas Camel, The (underground newspaper)
Burke's efforts to ban, 124
close watch on Marmion, 95
on Glanz, 79, 84
on Marmion, 95
origin of, 123
on Ratti, 117
on Social Science on deathbed, 104–105
See also Underground press
Ciabocchi, Elizabeth, 213
City University of New York (CUNY), 61–62, 63, 66, 67, 117
Claflin, Arthur B., 20
Clark, Edward, 135
Clarke, Dorothy, *133*
"Closing Time" (song), 261–62
Coalition for Justice, 184
Cobb, Irving S., 27
Cockenoe, 24–25
Coderre, Jeffery, *106–107*
Coffey, Richard, 124
Colclough, James, 93
Collado, Emilio, 76–77, 79
"College within a college," 245
Commencement 2003, 221–23
Conference Center building, damage to, 142, 287n9
Conolly, Richard Lansing (admiral)
authoritarian behavior of, 10, 12
background of, 10
death of, 21, 53
decision not to open college in fall of 1962, 18–19
market research on Southamption expansion conducted for, 21
souring of relationship with Hoxie, 12
Conroy, Jean, and student contact on college closing, 239–240
Cook, Edward, 151
Cooke, Robert, 47, 50
Co-op career development program, 132, 191
Cooper, William, 22

Cooperative education program (Co-op), 132, 191
Co-op program, and Danziger, 132, 144, 162, 287n3
Core curriculum committee members, 212
Corwith, Cindy, *133*
Cosgrove, Bob, 99
Crippen, Annette, 192
Crippen, Caprice, 192
Cristal, Robert, 101
Cultural diversity at Southampton. *See under* LIU-Southampton uncertainty, 1968–1972
CUNY (City University of New York), 61, 63, 66, 67, 117
Curcio-Kleinman, Paola
  evasive comments on opening of Stony Brook Southampton, 269
  losing struggle to counter negative publicity, 252
  and no comment, 248, 250, 268
  and publications nightmare, 241, 246
  and welcomes the moratorium on sale of Southampton, 254
Cutler, Sara, 138
C. W. Post (Brookville)
  background of, 281n3
  commencement, May 2006, 267
  confusion caused by name of, 12–13
  Hoxie named president (1955), 12
  named after Mrs. Davies's father, 12–13
  purchase of Post estate by Metcalf (1947), 8
  success of, 13–14, 17
  See also under Epilogue; Final Days; Wilson and the merger
C. W. Post Graduate Education Department, 125–26
Czerniak, Richard, 124

Dailey, James, 34, *35*
Dalmeda, Josephine, 89
Danziger, Robert
  blunt assessment of new curriculum, 242
  and Co-op program, 132, 144, 162, 287n3
  as "everywhere man," 131–32
  and faculty poker game, 34, *35*
  Faculty Union representative, *103*
  and Fulbright awards, 137, 171
  and honors program, 154
  internship programs of, 108, 162
  and student-centered programs, 91, 107
Davies, Marjorie Merriweather Post, 8, 12–13
Dawson, Edward, 101
Decade of treading water, 1993–2002, 173–202
  "dollar a year" chancellor, 173–180
    "The Capital Campaign" and, 176–77
    faculty salary freeze and, 177
    and growing deficit, 175
    improving the product, 175–76
    lead programs designated, 178
    and Red Owl hired, 179–180
    sabbatical for Siegel, 178
    Sillerman as chancellor, 173–75
  end of an era, 202–3
  Larocca's 240 days (Sept. 2001–May 2002), 199–202
    Hitchcock, as interim dean, 200
    poor fit for Southampton, 199–200
    positive happenings during, 200
    resignation of, 200
  Margaret Madden's 700 days (1999–2001), 194–98
    optimism in fall of 1999, 194–96
    recruitment strategy change, 196–97
  outsourcing the custodians (1997–1998), 180–85
    close campus community, 180
    and Coalition for Justice, 184
    custodians' part of college family, 181
    and FWP, 184
    Laro given custodial contract, 181–82

Decade of treading water, 1993–2002 *(continued)*
and meeting with author and others, 182–83, 184
staff inefficiency disputed, 182
termination of Laro contract, 184–85
Southampton Five Year Success Initiative (1998–2003), 188–194
and 40 percent graduation rate, 193
challenge of fundraising, 188–89
and competition in Marine Science, 193
and good omens, 189–190. *See also* Larocca, James; Madden, Margaret
and increasing deficits, 188
Wayne Miller's seven hundred days (1996–1998), 180, 185–88
ambitious plans, 186
and lapses in management, 186–87
"State of the University" memo from Steinberg, 185
Decade to build. *See* Bishop Steinberg era
"Decade to Build," announcement of (1986), 158
DeCerbo, Brett, *224*
DeCerbo, Vinnie, 145, *224*
DelliGatti, Mike, 99
DeLuca, Robert, 178, *179*, 251
De Mayo, Thomas, 37
Denny, Julia, *224*
Despalji, Walter, 138
Detweiler, Nora, 246, 253
Dewey, Mrs. Lloyd, 21
Director, Michael, 43, 246
Directory of American Colleges, The, 152
Dolgon, Corey, 175, 184
d'Oronzio, Joseph, 84
Dosch, Peter, 181–82
Douglas, Joanne, 262, *262*
Dowling College (formerly Adelphi-Suffolk College), 16–17, 89, 98, 147, 164, 199
Downes-Vogel, Hillary, *191*
Doyle, Walter, 43
Dress code and other administration policies, 40–41
Drexel, Michael, 212
Drift and uncertainty, 1968–1972. *See* LIU-Southampton uncertainty, 1968–1972
Druckenmiller, Jamie, 192
Drug use at Southampton, 42–43, 120, 121
Duberman, Daniel, 34, *35*, 101, 102, 104, 121
DuFrane, Harold, 15
Dugan, James, 109
Duke, Angier Biddle, 15, *154*, 159, 173
Dylan, Bob, 204
Dzintarnieks, Pat, *133*

East End Environment (newsletter), 91
East End Guidance Association, 17
Easton, Rene, *103*
ECAC Basketball championships, 192, 261
Eddy, Paul, 16
Eliot, John, 24
End of the Hamptons, The (Dolgon), 175
Environmental Science major, 145, 288n11
Epilogue: transition to Stony Brook, 265–279
beginning again (with piano), 271–75
Dean Pearl's initiative for Kenny, 274–75
facility improvements by Stony Brook, 272–73
Pearl appointed dean, 273
Schoonen appointed interim dean, 271
Stanley as replacement for Kenny, 273
Sustainability Studies program, 271–72
windmill lighting at Christmas, 271–72

closing time again, April 2010, 275–76
good omens in spring, 275
parallels with June 2004, 275–76
and Pearl's surprise notification of closing, 275
press in support of students, 276
suit filed by students successful, 276
C.W. Post commencement, May 2006, 267
opening time again, 2011–2012, 277–78
grant received by SoMAS to reverse bay decline, 278
and limited offerings, 277
and rumors again, 277–78
Semester by the Sea program (SoMAS), 277
Peconic Bay Sustainability Institute, 278–79
and empty campus facilities, 279
and vision of four-year Southampton campus, 278
Stony Brook's piano, 267–68
transition office opened by Forestell, 2005–2008, 267
opening of Stony Brook Southhampton campus, 269–271
programs lost in transition, 265–66
SUNY occupation delayed by LIU, 268–69
Veggie Car project, symbol of programs lost in transition, 265–66
Erickson, Susan, 124
Ernst, Kelly, 192
Evan Frankel Foundation, 244
Ewing, Tom, 111

Faculty retreat, 2003, 213–14
Faculty student government (FSG) (1970–1973), 115–123
Fairbrother, Dean, 55, 56
Fearon, Edward, 13–14, 17, 19
Feeley, Kathleen, 212
Ferguson, Glenn W.
approach to job, 77–79
background of, 77
critique of LIU by, 77–78
later positions of, 81
resignation of, 79, 81
Ferren, Bran, 111
Festival of Life celebration, 91
Fielding, Stephanie, 275
Figlioa, Carl, 158
Final days, 2003–2004, 225–248
closing announced, June 16, 2004, 234–39
closure delayed until fall of 2005, 237
"consolidation" plan proposed, 235–36
emotional responses of staff and faculty, 236
Forestell's plea to board for delay, 236–37
rumors that emerged, 237–38
Sillerman's refusal to donate $5 million, 234
Steinberg's letter to community, 237
students ignored in closing strategy, 235–36
word of closing received impersonally, 238–39
"college within a college," 245
core curriculum development
challenge for Kane's small group, 225
and faculty depression, 227
faculty indifference to curriculum planning, 225
fine-tuning of, 229–230
Forestell's discussion items, 228–29
funding for conferences approved, 225–26
interdisciplinary education workshop held, 226
new curriculum accepted, 226–27
urgency of, 226
Forestell's appointment as dean, 245

Final days, 2003–2004 *(continued)*
mixed messages (April–May), 230–33
drop in enrollment predicted by Rodas, 233
high tuition discount rate, 231
positive news from admissions office, 233
search committee for new dean called off, 230
Sillerman's upbeat Q&A session, 233
successes of graduates, 232
unsustainable budget losses for 2004 reported, 231
upbeat discussion of capital campaign, 232
world-class performances to be brought to Avram Theater, 232
public relations nightmare
dimension of problem, 241
Halsey reception, 243
"just a new location," 242
Marmion's disparaging remarks, 242–44
media fires, 245–46
press release confirming suspicions of development, 246
requests for donation returns, 244
Steinberg's response to charge of incompetence, 242
Save the College at Southampton (SCS), 246–48
situation room, 239–241
Fincke, Mrs. Reginald, 22–23, 24
Fincke Fine Arts Theater, renaming of, 196
Fine Arts program, 92–93, 108–11, 136–37, 138, 186
improvements made by Marmon, 104
Finger, Allan, 113
Fitzgerald, F. Scott, 27
Flynn, Alice
on "consolidation" plan, 235, 236
on dean parade, 180
on "kitchen cabinet," 167, 174
and personal student contact on college closing, 239–240
on physical plant and recruitment, 73
on recruiting campaign, 230
on strategy for closing of college, 235, 236
transition team member, 254–55
Forbes, Michael, 189, 241
Forestell, Paul
address to board to delay August closing, 236–37
appointed dean to lead transition (2004), 245
background of, 178
chairman of faculty council, 207
and faculty poker game, 34, 35
and field trips, 200
and freshman orientation program (2004), 249
and interdisciplinary education workshop, 226
move to C. W. Post campus by, 267
and New Southampton meetings, 208
and Office of Transition, 2005–2008, 267
and Psychobiology program directed by, 194
and six discussion items, 228–29
and transition team, 254–55, 269
Fort Pond Bay, 90
Francis, Katherine McLane, 149
Frank, Harry, 24, 71
Franklin, Cheryl, 86
Frazier, Jon, *155*
Frederickson, Lisa, 160
Freeman, Shari, 114
Free Speech Movement at U.C. Berkeley, 46
Fresco, Robert, 170–71
Friends World College (FWC), 164–65
Friends World Program (FWP), 165–66, 171, 175, 184, 193
Friesman, Jim, 34
FSG (faculty student government) (1970–1973), 115–123
Fulbright, Harriet, *106*
Fulbright awards, 107, 137, 189–190, 232, 261, 287n6

Furey, Kathleen, 276
FWC (Friends World College), 164–65
FWP (Friends World Program), 165–66, 171, 175, 184, 193

Gallentine, Bonnie, 99
Gambacorta, Frank, 51
Gant, Thomas, 113
Gatti, Stacy Horstman, 212
Gearon, Dan, 181, 182, *183*
Gearon, Daniel, 33
Gee, Al, 89
Gerbereux, Robert, 111–12, 212, 238, 244, 263
Getz, Donald, on Welker, 90–91
Gibson, Elisha, 252, 253, 265–66
Gilbert, Carol
  on Bush-Brown, 131, 149
  as director of admissions, 159, 162
  introduction of Sillerman, 173–74
  on learning of merger from *Newsday*, 151
  on loss of identity with merger, 152
  on public relations, 220–21
  Sillerman's critics dismissed by, 175
  on Wilson, 130
Ginsberg, Allan, 40
Glanz, Edward C.
  Bush-Brown and, 83, 84
  dress code established by, 40
  and faculty cuts, 89, 284n4
  Fine Arts program as goal of, 138
  first provost of Southampton, 25–26
  frustrations of, 84
  interactions with diverse cultures of the East End, 26–27
  naive vision for college, 83–84
  and NCAA division title in 1972, 285n6
  and opening of college, 31, *32*
  policy council established by, 76
  vision for college, 284n1
  See also Glanz, Edward C., legacy of
Glanz, Edward C., legacy of
  Fine Arts program, 92–93
  Fort Pond Bay purchase, 90
  Marine Science program, 90, 91
  NCAA division title in 1972, 93
  nurturing college in early years, 93
  opening of gym in 1970, 93
  professional publications of, 93
  See also Glanz, Edward C.
Gobler, Chris, 194, *207*, 220, 267, 278
Goldberg, Arthur, 108, 200–*201*
Gonzalez, Julio, 34, *35*, 226
Goodhines, Edward, 195
Gordon, Lisa, 99
Gormley, William, 117, 118, 122
Granat, Michael, 51
Grand experiment (2003), 216–19
Granitz, Elizabeth ("Liz")
  academic steering committee (ASC) member, 207, *207*, 210–11
  on Carl Figlioa, 158
  core curriculum committee member, 226
  and faculty poker game, 34, *35*
  and new core, 229–230
  and new course, 229
  opposition to faculty wage freeze, 177
Green, Peter, 122
Greene, Helen, 158
Greenhouse fiasco, 142
Greenprint campus, 178–79
"Greenprint Campus," 178
Greenstein, Lewis, 165, 171, 193
Gregory, Daniela, 212, 213–14, 219
Grigo, James, *224*
Grodd, Barbara, 245
Grogan, Donna, 115–16, 117
Gronlund, Linda, 111
Grossman, Karl, 145
Guider, Joseph, 1–2
Guinness record for Frisbee Club, 144
Gumbs, Harriett Crippen, 85
Gumbs, Lance, 274
Gym campaign (1968–1970), 34, 71–73

Haar, Kenneth ("Kenny"), 41, 45
Haar, Susan, 42
Haile, Elizabeth (aka Chee Chee), 87
Halper, Jeff, 165
Halsey, John, 243

Handler, John, 48–49
Hardie, George Robert
appointed first dean of LIU, 3–5
borrowing policy of, 4, 29
Hardy, C. Douglas, 108, *110*
Haresign, Tomas, 26, *103*, 121, 130, 192
Harney, George, 181, 182, *183*
Harrison, Leigh, 55
Harvey Gamage (Seamester ship), 108–*109*
Hasbrouck, Emerson, 117, 118
Hassan, Frederick Childe, 27
Hayden, Juanita Jay, 113
Heald, Henry, 59, 62–63
Heald Hobson and Associates, 58
Heald Hobson Report (1968)
Hoxie's leadership called dictatorial, 68
Hoxie's plans deemed unrealistic, 67–68
LIU's future "is no assured," 69
need for centralization of LIU, 75
and reevaluation of Southampton called for, 68
reviewing of by trustees, 75–76
Southampton College policy council (1968) and, 76–77
and unaddressed problems, 69
Heany, Patrick, 241, 250, 271
Hehre, Ed, 90
Hemmingway, Ernest, 27
Hendrickson, Dorothea, 22
HEOP (Higher Education Opportunity Program)
beginning at Southampton, 88
and BSA, 112
Helen Smith as director of, *115*
Hitchcock as administrative director of (1974), 114, 202
and Jane Strong as founding member, 176
McCrudden as counselor for, 167
praise from Middle States team for, 148
and Southampton's lack of funds, 89, 90, 113
and Thornhill's praise for, 176
Herbert, Janet, 265
Herbert, Ralph, 144–46, 178
Herrick, Samuel, 22
Higa, Yoshi, 161, 195, *195*
Higher Education Opportunity Program. *See* HEOP
Hiltner, George, 131
Himmelblau, Ed, 212
Hirsch, Peter, 99
Hitchcock, Charles
appointed interim dean, 201–202
appointed permanent dean, 204
and appointment of Madden, 193
on Bush-Brown administration, 136
and Commencement 2003, 221, 275
counseling staff director, 120
on Dean Miller, 187
and decision on closing college, 205
faculty retreat ordered by, 208
HEOP administrative director, 114
on high discount rates, 231
Kane memo in honor of, 223–*24*
and news of closing, 234–36
as overseer of graduate programs, 245
Social Science division director, 125
in support of situation room, 239
university award to, 264
Hoberman, Robert, 274
Honeywell, Kate, 192
Hook, Sydney, 93
Hopson, Linda, 114
Horne, Edith, 89
Horstmann-Gatti, Stacy, 213
Howl (Ginsberg), 40
Hoxie, R. Gordon
appeal for support from AAUP, 70
architectural design of Glanz opposed by, 36
background of, 10
Baker's call for resignation of, 70
and board controversy between Birenbaum and Roth, 69–70
criticism from press on, 60
distance from reality of, 70
helicopter visit to Southampton by, 54, 283n2
lavish dinners of, 54, 55

letter to faculty asking for board support, 70
named president of C. W. Post center, 12
no-confidence vote by Brooklyn faculty, 59–60
ouster of by the board (Sept. 1968), 70–71
secret negotiations for sale of Brooklyn center to CUNY by, 61–62
Simonson estate purchased with funds earmarked for gym, 34
on successful LIU accreditation, 10–11
successor to Pell as chancellor (1964), 53, 283n1
Ten Year Development Plan and, 58, 63, 283n4
university leadership forever denied to, 71, 283n5
unpopularity of, 62
See also Hoxie administration (1964–1968)
Hoxie administration, 1964–1968, 53–74
campus for sale, 61–67
$32 million offer from CUNY, 66
and bad press for LIU, 67
and Brooklyn admissions office reopened, 66
and freeze on Brooklyn admissions, 64, 66
fundraising campaign shelved by trustees, 66
Heald Hobson Report (1968) cited by Hoxie, 62
Hoxie's secret negotiations for sale of Brooklyn center to CUNY, 61–62
LIU's offer officially declined, 67
LIU stonewalled on finance questions, 65
Mayor Lindsey's opposition to, 64, 67
opposition to sale, 62–63
SGA's support for Brooklyn Center, 63
Southampton concerns, 64–65
gym campaign (1968–1970), 71–73
cheap construction of, 72–73
first class graduated without gym, 71
gym construction delayed two years, 72
poor quality of physical plant hurt enrollment, 73
Heald Hobson Report (1968), 67–69
board disillusioned with Hoxie, 67
Hoxie deemed dictatorial, 68
Hoxie plans deemed unrealistic, 67
and low faculty morale, 68
success improbable for Southampton, 69
uncertainty expressed as to future of LIU, 69
Hoxie's "day of infamy," 58–61
Birenbaum's dismissal upheld by board by, 58–59
board members accused of conflict of interest, 60
Brooklyn students went on strike supported by faculty, 59–60
criticisms of Ten Development Plan and, 58
first graduation amidst turmoil, 61, *61*
further damage to LIU image problem, 60
and Zeckendorf's settlement with students, 60–61
Hoxie's untidy exit, 69–71
Hoxie baffled by controversy, 70
negative effect on LIU image, 70–71
public controversy over Hoxie's worth, 69–70
resignation requested September 1968, 70–71
identity and tuition protest, 53–58
See also Hoxie, R. Gordon
Hoyt, Janet, 20, 26–27, 282n3
Hoyt, William S., 19

Hudson, Wayne, 181, 182, 184
Hudson, William M. (acting LIU president), 9–10
Hull, Arthur, 22, 71, 72
Humanities division
  annual art festival organized by, 92–93
  Art majors placed in, 211
  improvements made by Marmon, 104, 111–12
  and lecture presentations, 37
  and master's degree programs, 186
  and rich local resources, 27, 36
  and tribal events, 97
  and Welt's course in Canary Islands, 109
  Willoughby as director of, 26
Hunter, Chris, 46
Hunter, Kenneth, 34, 71, 72

Identity and tuition protest (1964–1968), 53–58
  Hoxie's unpopularity major factor in protest, 55
  Hoxie unconvincing in speech to students, 55–56
  incompetent leadership blamed for financial troubles, 54, 58
  lack of consultation with students charged, 57
  sharp opposition from Birenbaum, 55
  students identified with individual school, 53, 54
  University-wide protest against tuition increase, 53
  See also Tuition at Southampton
International Prize winning Young Artists Series, 138–39, 287n7
Inventing a new college, 2002–2003, 203–24
  aggressive recruiting approach, 220–21
  commencement 2003
    pledges made but not honored, 222
    signs of hope, 223
    Sillerman's $60 million dollar promise, 221
  and grand experiment? (2003), 216–19
    enthusiastic response to new core, 219
    and linking of interdisciplinary courses, 217
    new core approved, 216–17
  honoring Dean Hitchcock, 223–24
  parallel universes of committees, 207–13
    class size increase and, 208, 210
    faculty committee ignored, 208
    Kane's "relevant considerations," 209–10
    Natural Science division and, 208, 211
    and secret meetings charged, 208–209
  Price Waterhouse Report, 203–6
    blunt assessments of, 204–205
    closing college opposed by Sillerman, 205
    goals set by trustees, 205–206
    "New Southampton" undertaken, 206
    PwC hired to study college, 203–204
  Rodas as new provost (2003), 219–220
  Turner's memorandum on ASC model, 215–16
  See also Rodas, Daniel; Sillerman, Robert F. X.; Turner, Robert
Irwin, Burke, 271
Isaacs, Charles, 57, 60

Jackson, Keith, 145
Jacobs, Kasey, 201, 252, 265–66
Jahn, Joseph, 21
Jaycox, David, 192
Jensen, Jill, 231
Ji, Jonathan, 160
Joel, Billy, 196
Johnson, Clarence, 114
Johnson, Lyndon B., 46, 47–48
Jonas, Ralph
  endowment fund established for LIU, 2

losses suffered in stock market collapse, 3
opposition to Jewish quotas, 2, 281n1
replaced on board by Zeckendorf, 6
"two-university" proposal of, 2
vision of, 161
Jones, Buffalo T (Terry), 154–55
Jones, J. Wilbert, 19, 21
Jones, Walter S., *115*, 158, 164, 165, 180
Jordan, Roy, 145
Jr., Russell Beavers, 84–85
Juidice, Charles, 99

Kamison, Barry, 50
Kanas, John, 57–58, 231
Kane, Jeffrey
accused of heavy-handed role, 212
and dissatisfaction among trustees, 231
faculty resentment of, 225, 229
memo honoring Dean Hitchcock, 223
monitoring of "New Southampton" by, 207
and New Southampton meetings, 208
radical new interdisciplinary curriculum urged by, 199, 209
raising class size a goal of, 210
Katalyn, Leila, 111
Kelly, Lee, 169, 204, 240
Kempton, Murray, 65
Kenkel, Carly, 253
Kenneally, Jack, 34, *35*, 123–24
Kenny, Shirley Strum, 242, 247, 260, 268, *270*, 271
Keyes, Sharon, 99
King, Martin Luther, 88
Kirkwood, Robert, 148
Kleinman, Jerry, 176
Koestner, Michele, 164–66, 178
Kohon, Harold, 93
Kooning, Willem de, 93, 111
Korn, Jonathan, 265
Kosman, Carol, 171, 261
Kotter, Joseph, 65
Krasnoff, Abraham, 141, 150–51, 153, 155
Krasnow, David, 149
Kratovil, Ted, 63
Kretzmann, Maria, 200, 220
Kron, Johan, 195, *224*
Kruh, Eric, 111, 121–22, 127
Kudder-Sullivan, Phyllis, 88, 216, *217*, 225–26
Kunnakkat, Saroj, 191
Kunzeman, Susan, 99
Kurkowski report, 160–61

Lai, Mary
bursar hired by Metcalf, 6
on Bush-Brown and Kirkwood, 148
confusion of C. W. Post name addressed by, 13
decentralization of LIU deplored by, 80–81
dismay at Ferguson's approach to job, 78–79
dormitory solution found by, 35
enthusiasm for college reported by, 21
Hoxie's accreditation account disputed by, 11
on Hoxie's likeability, 54
indispensable as chief financial officer, 6, 81
photo of, *7*
on promised pledges, 222
report to Marmion on expenditure freeze, 97
retirement of, 227
in support of sale of Brooklyn Center, 63
and warnings on fragility of university, 125
on Wilson, 130
LaMacchia, Armand, 42
Langhauser, Jim, 47
Langlois, Rebecca, 261
Lardner, Ring, 27

Larocca, James
  contract of, 199–200
  hired "to turn college around," 199
  and negotiations on Peconic Bay parcel, 223
  rebuffed at every turn, 200
  replacement for Maddon, 198
  resignation of, 200
  in Southampton whaleboat race (2001), *207*
Laro Service Systems, 181–82
LaSpina, John, 37
LaValle, Kenneth (state senator)
  and $35 million in state budget for Southampton purchase, 260
  and Peconic Bay Sustainability Institute, 278
  photos of, *179*, *270*
  reaction to closing of Stony Brook Southampton, 275–76
  state-supported college at Southampton suggested by, 276
  Stony Brook called "deceptive," 275
  Stony Brook move approved by, 242
  at Stony Brook opening, 271
  support for Greenprint, 178
  support for moratorium on development, 254
Lee, William, 86
Lenti, Robert, 57
Leonard, Courtney, 87, 88
Leonard, Craigh, 17
"Leon's Views" (Parks), 88–89
Lester, Nancy, 164
Levitt, Arthur III, 149
Lewis, Kerith, 192
Lewis, Marvin, 34, 84–85
Libert, Lorna, 161
Liddle, Larry, *103*, 104, 137, 154
Liebel, Andrea, 251–52, 253
Lindberg, Andres, *224*
Lindquist, Andres, *224*
Lindsey, Mayor, Mayor Lindsey's opposition to, 67
Linton, Tara, 276
Litchman, John, 48
Little Neck Road parcel, 92, 285n5
LIU Southampton College Federation of Teacher's agreement, First, *103*
LIU-Southampton uncertainty, 1968–1972, 75–93
 committees and policy councils (1968–1969), 75–77
  able leadership lacking after Hoxie's dismissal, 75
  centralization of administration lacked support, 76
  Ferguson appointed chancellor, 77
  Ferguson's critique of, 77–78
  Heald Hobson Report (1968) reviewed by board, 75–76
  models proposed for Southampton, 79–80
  policy council for Southampton established by Glanz, 76
  restructuring of, 76–77
  Stoddard named interim chancellor, 75
 cultural diversity at Southampton, 84–90
  black students encouraged, 88
  BSA and, 89, 90
  faculty cuts and, 89
  and HEOP, 88, 89, 90
  "Leon's Views" (Parks), 88
  Martin Luther King scholarship, 88
  minority concerns published in *Windmill* (1963), 84–85
  seminar on prehistoric pottery from Southwest, 87–88
  and Sherry Institute of Career Opportunity (SCIO), 86–87
  Shinnecock community and, 86–88
  Shinnecock Nation Cultural Coalition, 87
  Shinnecock students increased after 1973, 88
 Edward Glanz: successes of an orphan child, 82–84
 Glenn Ferguson chancellor for fall 1969, 77–81
  Bush-Brown as successor to Ferguson, 79, 81–82

decentralization of LIU deplored by Lai, 80–81
selection process of new chancellor challenged, 77
See also Bush-Brown, Albert; Ferguson, Glenn W.; Glanz, Edward C.; Meinhart, Charles; *specific names of participants*
Lloyd, Tom, 176, 189
Lombardi, Anita, 37
Long Goodbye, 2004–2005, 249–264
beginning of the end
freshman class protest, 251
good news on campus sale, 250
hostility of students, 249
no-confidence vote by faculty, 250, 254
last commencement, May 22, 2005
Chancellor Sillerman addressing, 263
"Closing Time" (song), 261–62
and expression of community by faculty, 264
honorary degrees awarded, 263
students expressed feelings on caps, *262*
meeting with students, 253
new core introduction
enthusiasm of faculty, 255–56
mock lemonade stand, 256–57
and student evaluations, 256
options 05 initiative, 254–55, 261
rescheduling nightmare for trustee meeting, 251–52
and Sillerman's role, 251
spring 2005
action proposals discussed by faculty, 259
legality of transition questioned, 258–59
and Steinberg sharply criticized by faculty, 259–260
Tilles defense of Steinberg, 260
Stony Brook solution, 260–61
student protest, 252–53
transition team appointed, 254–55
and twelve-month moratorium on development approved, 254
See also Orphans of LIU
Long Island University (LIU), 1–14
beginnings to bankruptcy (1926–1946)
Adelphi as women's college (1926), 2
Adelphi College Board of Trustees, 2
admissions office below standard, 3–4
bankruptcy of, 5–6
basketball scandal at (1950s), 5, 8–9
City College (CCNY) and, 1–2
closing of Southampton in (2004), 1
endowment fund established for, 2
endowment fund lacking, 5, 29
first commencement of, 4
founding of, 1
Hardie appointed as first dean, 3
identity crisis of, 29
lack of accreditation by Middle States, 4, 5
Metcalf's fiscal reorganization plan, 5, 29
nondiscrimination policy of, 2–3, 281n1
and "quality distress" of, 5, 29
quota systems on Jewish applicants, 2, 281n1
and stock market collapse, 3
G.I. bonanza and move to Brookville (1946–1953)
endowment fund lacking, 7
financial crisis ended by G.I. Bill, 6
and Hudson (acting president), 9–10
lack of accreditation by Middle States, 9
legal battle over zoning issues, 9
staffing problems of, 6
veterans' counselor hired, 6–7
negative image of, 8, 13, 54, 60, 171, 175, 250

Long Island University (LIU) *(continued)*
struggle for accreditation (1953–1955), 10–14
accreditation granted (1955), 12
admissions office below standard, 11
campus designations assigned by Board of Trustees, 13
Conolly replaced Hudson as president, 10
faculty morale low, 11, 14
and Hoxie appointment, 10
identity crisis of, 12–13, 14
recommendation to defer expansion ignored by trustees, 14
See also Conolly, Richard Lansing (admiral); Hardie, George Robert; Hoxie, R. Gordon; Hoxie administration, 1964–1968; Jonas, Ralph; Lai, Mary; Metcalfe, Tristram Walker; Zeckendorf, William
Long Island University Plan (Steinberg), 161–63
Loop, Kristin, 171
Lotito, Richard, 131
Love, Douglas, 107
Lozier, Greg, 204
Luntey, Eugene, 189

Macella, John, 48
MacNeil, Neil, 19–20
Madden, Margaret
authority undermined, 197
background of, 193–94
blindsided by firing, 198
hired at Potsdam, 198
photo of, *194*
replaced by Larocca, 198
transparent approach of, 196
Maggipinto, V. Anthony (Vam)
applauded BSA for urging more black students, 112
and opposition to Vietnam war, 51–52
poor leadership charged by, 250
on recruiting students, 122
and SCS founding, 246
SCS leader, 276
Malott, Deane W., 66
Mandel, Jill, 194
Mandush scholarship program, 88
Maniscalco, Peter, 201
Marine Science program
cap on major proposed, 136–38, 220
competitive edge lost, 203
and deficits, 208
and environmental programs, 108
and Evan Frankel Foundation, 244
and Fulbright awards, 137, 171
national reputation of, 174
and Natural Science progress, 108
positive report from Middle States, 106
and Seamester program, 108–*109*, 110, 137, 257
and Simonson estate, 105–106
Social Science affected by success of, 104–105
student success rate, 106–107
success of, 90–91, 104–105, 136–37
taken over as Stony Brook's SoMAS, 267
and transfers to Stony Brook, 242
transfer to Post impossible, 241, 242
wags the dog, 104–14
See also SoMAS program
Marmion, Harry, 125
accusation that closing was "land grab:, 243–44
career after Southampton, 126
continuing support for college, 188–89
at faculty retreat, 2003, 213
leader in Stony Brook purchase, 260
photo of, *103*
resignation requested by Bush-Brown, 125
and SCS movement, 246, 254
on Stony Brook's efficiency, 268
See also Marmion administration, 1972–1978

Marmion administration, 1972–1978, 95–127
Bush-Brown-Marmion relationship, 124–25
faculty union
and 5 percent pay hike for faculty, 101
AAUP and, 102
custodians first to form union, 101
and C. W. Post Union, 102, 284n4
Marmion sympathetic to unions, 102
NLRB and, 102
and relaxed climate, 104
and strike, 104
and union contracts, 102–103
Glenn Ferguson chancellor for fall 1969, 124–25
great potential, 95–101
academic programs first focus of, 97
competition from other schools and, 98
and continuing deficits, 101
criticisms from Bush-Brown, 100
and "day of discussion," 101, 285n4
Marmion's inauguration day speech, 95–96
master plan commissioned, 97–98, 285n1
praise for, 99 100
primary challenges of, 97
small successes in first year, 98
spring enrollment drop and, 98
Marine Science program wags dog, 104–14
McGregor's brief interlude, 126–27
student-faculty government (1970–1973)
creation of FSG, 115–16
demise of FSG, 122–23
drug problem addressed by, 120, 121
and Glanz came under attack, 119
and language requirement abolished, 120–21
negative view of FSG, 121
serious challenges faced by, 117–18
and student attendance, 119–120
and tuition and fee increase, 118–19
tutorial support recommended by, 120
underground press, 123–24
See also Bush-Brown, Albert; Marine Science program
Martin, Paul, 139
Martin, Robert, 38, 239, 246, 276
Martine, David, 87
Martin Luther King scholarship, 88, 284n3
Mason, George, 149
Mathews, Philip, 20
Matthiessen, Peter, 189
Matz, Catherine, 124
McCann, Lawrence, *194*
McCarty, Alexandra, 160
McCormick, Larry, 101
McCrudden, John, 167, 191
McEntire, Robert, 111
McEvoy, Kevin, 139
McGrath, John P., 60, 64, 77, 81
McGregor, David, 126–27, 167
McGunnigle, Patrick, 231, 261
McIntosh, Sandy, 40, 48
McIntyre, Richard, 237
McNamara, Robert, 46
Mead, Margaret, 93
Meinhart, Charles, 83
Melton, Linda, 99
Meltor, Robert, *103*
Merger collapse (1986–1988), 158–161
Metcalfe, Tristram Walker
death of, 9
fiscal reorganization plan of, 5, 29
Hardie replaced by, 5
Lai hired by, 6
Post estate purchased by, 7–8
replacement for Hardie despite lack of college degree, 281n2
Meyer, Melinda, 192
Meyers, Mark, 48–49

Meyers, Russell, 163
Michael, Joanne, 204
Middle States Association
  accreditation granted to LIU (1955), 10, 12
  Bush-Brown's condescension toward, 148
  concerns on LIU expressed by, 11–12, 14
  LIU denied accreditation by, 4, 5, 9
  positive report on Marine Science program, 106
  See also under Bishop-Steinberg era; Wilson and the Merger
Military Selective Service Act (June 1967), 46
Miller, Wayne
  and alcohol problems, 187
  background of, 180
  death of, 188
  lapses in management, 186–87
  LIU Board of Trustees resolution, 188
  termination of, 187
Mills, Joslyn, 262
Morehouse, Lisa, 107, 124
Moreland, Larry, 114
Moses, Robert, 15
Mudrowski, Kathleen, 165
Mullarkey, Tess, 208
Mullin, Fran, 131
Mulvey, Vicky, 167, 212
Mumford, Robert, 161
Murphy, Dennis, 154, 157–58
Murphy, Frank, 55
Murphy, Sara and Gerald, 27

Namuth, Hans, 93
National Labor Relations Board (NLRB), 102
Nayak, Sanjeeva, 108, 144–46
Neill, John, 191, *191*, 200
Newell, William, 226
Newsom, Carrol, 8
New Southampton. *See* Inventing a new college, 2002–2003
Newton, David, 104
New York Times, 60
Nixon, Richard M., 49, 51
Nyquist, Ewald, 12

Oatis, Susan, and new course, 229
O'Doherty, Kevin, 117–18
Office of Transition, 2005–2008, 267
Opportunities, lost, 141–42
Options 05 initiative, 254–55, 261
Ormsby, Diane, 96
Orndoff, Robert, 98
Orphans of LIU, 251, 256, 257, *258*, 260, 262
Orth, Peter, 138
Osborne, James, 19–20, 22, 23
Osei-Owusuh, Daniel, 166
Osiecki, Katherine, 276
Ossario, Alfonso, 93
Owens, Lester, 149

Pananan, Michele, 237
Parks, Leon, 88–89
Parrish, Samuel, 27
Pascarella, Vince, 163, 178
Pascucci, Michael, 223
Pataki, George, 260, 261
Patten, William, 98
Pattison, Robert
  background in humanities, 112
  on contrasting lifestyles of Bush-Brown and Wilson, 130
  course on science and literature relationship designed by, 218
  critical 1995 report from, 177
  and custodian outsourcing, 182–83
  and database establishment, 168–170
  and effect of closing on union contract, 240–41
  first Southampton recipient of TASA award, 112
  and Laurel and Hardy's piano analogy, 267–68
  and master's degree program in Fine Arts, 186
  memo after merger, 152–53
  report as chairman of faculty budget, 175
  and union contract under, 145–46

Patton, William, 109
Pawlukiewicz, Janet, 91
Pawlukiewicz, Michael, 91
Payette, Dennis, 168
Peabody, Carol, 274
PEACE (Protecting Every Aspect Concerning the Environment), 178, 194, 201, 265–66
Pearl, Mary
  and Algonquian Language Initiative (ALI), 274
  and Algonquian Language Revitalization Project, *274*
  appointed as CEO of Garrison Institute, 276
  as dean of Stony Brook Southampton, 272–73
  and notice of campus closing in April 2010, 275
  outreach initiatives of, 274
Peconic Bay Sustainability Institute, 278–79
Pell, John H. G.
  Conolly's replacement as chancellor, 21–22
  Glanz recruited by to serve as first provost, 25
  ineffective leadership style of, 32, 34–35, 69
  resignation of, 53, 283n1
Pellicane, Richard, 144–45, 288n10
Pelligrino, Charles, 107
Perl, Patrick, 171
Peters, Barbara, 87
Peters, Nancy, 227, 229–230
Peterson, Brad, 267
Peterson, Mary, 167
Peterson, William, 111
Phillip, Peter, 42, 57
Piano analogy (Laurel and Hardy), 75, 153, 267–68, 271, 275
Pierth, Jane, 47
Plaskow, Merrill, 109
Platt, William B., 15, 16
Poley, John, 50, 91
Pollock, Lee Krassner, 93
Porter, Fairfield, 93
Posmentier, Eric, *115*
Post, Charles William, 8
Post, C. W., 34
Post, James H., 2
Post, Steve, 107
Potter, Mrs. Cary, 24
Pratt, Edmund Jr., 189
Presidential Scholarship program, 108, 286n5
Price Waterhouse Cooper (PwC) report (2002–2003), 203–6
Primus, Pearl, 166

Quist, Brian, 184

Ratti, Joseph, 51, 117–18
Reagan, Ronald, cuts to education by, 145–46
Red Owl, 179–180, 205
Reed, Christopher, 124
Reeves, Robert, 268
Reisman, Howard, 90, *103*, 137, 192, 223
Remkis, Tisha, 39
Rice, Grantland, 27
Richard, Ronald, 86, 114
Richert, John, 261
Ridgeway, James, 60
Ringer, Bruce, 38
Rivers, Larry, 93, 111, 189
Roberson, Bill, 212, 240–41
Rodas, Daniel
  and "aggressive market strategy" planned, 232
  authored introduction to viewbook, 230
  background of, 219
  closing school as "done deal," 235
  concern for college deficit, 222–23
  drop in enrollment predicted by, 233
  installed as provost, 220
  and recruitment concerns, 225
  response to questions on speedy transfer of students to C. W. Post, 235–326
  response to request for return of gifts, 244–45

Rodas, Daniel *(continued)*
on Sillerman's meeting with trustees, 234
Rodriguez, Juan, 145
Rosenblatt, Roger, 185, 186, 189, 231–32, 236, 268
Rosentreter, Richard, 192
Roth, Arthur T., 64, 69–70
Rover, Frank, 113
Ruffino, Betty, 104–105
Rydell, Freddie, *224*

Sabin, Andrew, 244
Sale, Kirkpatrick, 49
Salerno-Sonnenberg, Nadja, 138
Saltanis, Peter
on 2004 meeting with Steinberg, 249
class valedictorian, 2006, 267
on learning of college closing, 239
and meeting with Steinberg, 252–53
and mock lemonade stand, 257, *257*
and Orphans of Long Island University, 251
and Veggie Car, 265–66
Sargent, Lindsy, 252
Sartor, Larry, 44
Save the College at Southampton (SCS), 246–48, 254, 256, 258, 260–61
Savio, Mario, 46, 123
Schilling, Peter, 117, 118, 123
Schmidt, Maithili, 154
Schoeffling, Conrad, 269
Schoonen, Martin, 271–72
Schwartz, Jack, 124
Schwerin, Warren, 232, 233
Scopaz, Valerie, 275
SCS (Save the College at Southampton), 246–48, 254, 256, 258, 260–61
Scudder, Tracy, 112
SDS (Students for a Democratic Society), 48–49
Seamester program, 108–*109*, 110, 137, 192
Selander, Mats, *224*
Selective Guide to Colleges, 145
Serafy, Keith, *103*, *207*, 223
Seventh Day Adventist church, 129, 286n1
Severns, Barbara, 124
Shaffer-Walsh, Rory
aggressive approach to recruiting by, 220–21
anger at closing announcement, 235–36
background of, 204
enrollment increase predicted by, 233
on one student's notification of closing, 239
and student contact on college closing, 239–240
and transition team, 254–55
Sherman, Herbert, 227, 240
Sherman-Smith, Jackie, *217*
Sherry Institute of Career Opportunity (SICO), 86–87
Sherter, Sidney, 117, 119, 158
Shinnecock (research vessel), 38
Shinnecock Hills, 19–20, 254
Shinnecock Indian Nation, 28
Shinnecock Nation Cultural Coalition, 87
Shinnecock Nation Museum and Cultural Coalition, 87
Shinnecock Oyster Hatchery, 87, 136–37
Shumway, Sandra
background of, 107
and focus on environmental concerns, 91
internship program arranged by, 194
and memo stating Marine Science could fall behind, 193
TASA recipient, 190, *190*
and "Women in Science" conference, 154
Shurberg, Deborah, 160
Siebert, Muriel, 176–77
Siegel, Alvin ("Al"), 47, 90–91, *103*, 163–64, 178
Sillerman, Laura (Mrs. Robert F. X. Sillerman), 173–74, 221

Sillerman, Robert F. X.
addressing last graduation ceremony, *263*, 264
criticisms of by Dolgon, 175
inadequate academic credentials of, 225
monitoring of "New Southampton" by, 207
and opening of Chancellors Hall, 192
opposition to closing college, 205
partial payment of pledge by, 204
pledge as matching donation, 222, 231
pledges made by, 177, 189, 194, 196, 289n3
pressure on trustees for matching funds, 233, 234
promise of $60 million from, 221–22
refusal to donate doomed college, 234
replacement for Duke as chancellor, 173–74
resignation as chancellor requested, 247
Silva, Peter, 85, 87
Simonson, Helen, 92
Simonson, Henry, 92
Simonson estate
proposed selling of, 105–106
purchase of, 34, 92
selling of, 141–44
Simsarian, Kenneth, 138–39, 140
Singh, Aatisha, 201
Sklare, Arnold, 103
Skoniezny, Christina, 111
Smith, Charles, 87
Smith, Helen, 114, *115*
Smith, Josephine, 87
Smith, Lamont, 87
Smith, Linda, 89
Smith, Ro-Ann, 114
Smith, Ronald, 123–24
Smith, Shedrick, 20
Smyth, Russell, 22
Snyder, Roger, 139
Social Science division
budget decline of, 91
"on deathbed," 104–105
Environmental Science major developed for, 108, 145, 208n11
faculty decline of, 104
focus of, 44, 87
Hitchcock as director of, 125
SoMAS program, 267, 277, 278
Sommer, Elliot, 71, 72
Soupios, Michael, 158
Southampton: a magical place, 15–30
Adelphi's considerations for Southampton campus, 15–17
Adelphi-Suffolk (now Dowling College) prospered, 17
Chisholm Estate purchase negotiations and, 16
excitement faded as potential problems arose, 16
location removed from population centers, 16
plan prepared for prospective college, 15
Sayville, N.Y. became ultimate choice, 16–17
Southampton College committee (1961–1963), 17–25
Adelphi experience unknown to, 21
expansion and renaming of, 19
fundraising campaign after Tucker Mill option, 22–24, 29
fundraising committee established, 17
growth of support for, 29
lack of support from wealthy residents, 24
market research positive on expansion, 21
Mayor Brennan's proposal, 17
Merrill estate under consideration by, 17
need for college endorsed by community, 25
opening set for September 1963, 25
residents in opposition to plans of, 17–18
Swartz estate purchased by, 20
Tucker Mill Inn property agreed on by, 19–20, 22

Southampton: a magical place *(continued)*
unique culture and geography of, 25–30
and art school founded by Chase, 26–27
basic studies program in response to veterans' needs, 25
curriculum focus on unique culture and geography, 26, 29
established as refuge for creative individuals, 26–27, 282ch2n2
and interdisciplinary humanities program under Willoughby, 26
Marine Science program potential and, 26
New York elites drawn to, 26, 282n2
Shinnecock Indian Nation and, 28
Southampton College: getting started, 1963–1968, 31–52
beginning in fall of 1963, 31–32, 282ch3n1
on birth of college, 32–33
curriculum evolution of (1963–1970)
core replaced by 1970 with liberal arts distribution requirement, 45
core seminars in major divisions, 44
criticisms of core growing, 44
decline in morale, 45
degree requirements, 43–44
faculty objections to, 44–45
student profile study on, 44–45
inaugural year at Southampton College (1963–1964)
Bergman's recollections of, 33
and cheaply built dormitories, 35–36
first graduation of, *61*
and inadequate planning, 32–33
and John Kennedy assassination, 38–39
and resourcefulness of creative faculty and staff during, 33, 36
and socializing of faculty, 34, *35*
and student activities, 39–40
and student profile, 36–39
and student protests over inadequate facilities, 34–35
student culture shift (1963–1968), 40–43
administration policy of *in loco parentis*, 41
and drug experimentation, 42–43
letter to *Windmill protesting* policy of *in loco parentis*, 42
mild protests by first two classes, 40
refusal of subsequent classes to follow rules, 40–41
Vietnam protests, 46–52
ad calling for protest march on Washington in *Windmill*, 47
boycotts following Cambodian invasion and, 51
concerns more focused after draft enacted, 46
descriptions of march on Washington, 50
Glanz in support of "creative protest," 49
Glanz supported protests with Nixon telegram, 51
last major demonstration of, 51–52
SDS on campus and, 48–49
support for eroding after Tet Offensive, 47
varying levels of interest in by students, 46
Southampton College policy council (1968), 76
Southampton culture and geography, New York elites drawn to, 26, 282n2
Southampton seventh grade, donation of, 23
Southampton Student Government Association (SGA), in support of Brooklyn Center, 63
Southampton Village College Committee, 17–18
Spitzer, Randy, 265
Spitzer, Wayne, 46, 47

Stafford, Bill, 99
Stanchfield, Ronald, 48
Stanley, Lee, 180, 181, 278
Stanley, Samuel, 273–76
Stansbury, Gregory, 113
Stansbury, Roland, 34, 84, 85
"State of the University" memo from Steinberg (July 1996), 185
State University of New York (SUNY), 21
Steinbeck, Elaine (Mrs. John Steinbeck), 111
Steinbeck Room, 111–12, 139
Steinberg, David
  chosen for presidency 1985, 157
  on Commencement Day 2003, 221
  greeted by silence at last graduation, 264
  letter to community on closing of college, 237
  photo of, *174*
  photos of, *110*
  refusal to take student calls after closing announcement, 240
  response to author on closing strategy, 236
  response to incompetence charge, 242
  and Sillerman, 234
  Southampton referred to as "jewel in the crown" of LIU, 287n4
  spring 2005, sharp criticisms from faculty, 259–260
  and student protest (2004), 253
  as student target in closing of school, 253–54
  and upbeat comments missing at commencement, 234
  visit upon Bush-Brown's departure, 156
  See also Bishop-Steinberg era
Stewart, Rod, 247–48
Stock market collapse, endowment fund wiped out, 3
Stoddard, George, interim chancellor after Hoxie's dismissal, 75
Stone, Hallie, 166
Stony Brook Southhampton official opening, Sept. 2006, *270*
Stony Brook's School of Marine and Atmospheric Sciences (SoMAS), 267, 277, 278
Storrer, William, 111
Strong, Jane, 114, 176
Strong, John A. (author)
  and Algonquian Language Initiative (ALI), 274–75
  conference on prehistoric pottery attended by, 225–26
  custodian outsourcing and, 181–84
  and faculty poker game, 34
  field trip to Guatemala (1974) and, 99
  Fulbright and TASA received by, 190, *190*
  in History department at Southampton for more than thirty years, 78
  interview with Larocca on Madden by, 198
  and joint statement in *Windmill* on minority presence on campus, 114
  Miller incident and, 187
  native garden project and, 87
  and new course, 229
  out of retirement to teach anthropology class, 217–18
  and Pearl's shock at closing of school, 275
  query to Steinberg on rapid closing, 236
  Windmill article on racism concerns and, 84–85
Students for a Democratic Society (SDS), 48–49
Stutz, Matt, 261
Sudak, Valerie, 201
Sullivan, Francis, 23
Sullivan, Joe, 91
Sustainability programs
  in danger, 273–74
  Dean Pearl's commitment to, 273
  majors included in, 271
  majors to be moved to Stony Brook, 275

Sustainability programs *(continued)*
and Peconic Bay Sustainability Institute, 278
and Schoonen's enthusiasm for, 271–72
Stanley's lack of commitment to, 273
Stony Brook eager to begin curriculum of, 268
Sutton, George, 240
Suzdak, Valerie, 219
Svensson, Roger, *224*
Swan, William, 23
Swartz, Florence (Mrs. Thomas Tucker), 20
Swartz, Thomas Tucker, 20
Systak, Valerie, 213–14

TAP (New York State Tuition Assistance Program), 125
Tarulli, Dean, 276
TASA (Trustees Award for Scholarly Achievement), 112, *190*
Taylor, Carol, 160–61
Ten Year Development Plan (1967), 58, 63, 283n4
Tettelbach, Steve, 212, 220
Thiele, Fred
angry reaction to news of Southampton closing, 241
best known Southampton graduate, 107–108
endorsement of Southampton closing by, 242
at founding of Greenprint, *179*
good news on sale of campus, 250
"Greenprint campus" approved by, 178
Long Island University Plan, 163
opening ceremony of Stony Brook Southampton and, 271
and Peconic Bay Sustainability Institute, 278
reaction to closing of Stony Brook Southampton, 275–76
and SCS founding, 246
Thompson, Kenneth, 86
Thompson family greenhouse, 142
Thornhill, Mary, 176
Throne-Holst, Anna, 277
Till, Emmett, 88
Tilles, Roger
ambiguous press release of, 246
clashes with Sillerman, 175, 231
defense of Steinberg by, 260
honorary degree awarded to, 263
pledge made to college, 177–78
PwC hired to study college by, 203
Tolkoff, Todd, 99, *99*
Tooker, William Wallace, 24
Topping, Mary
on closing the college, 238
ECAC Basketball championships, 192, 261
milestone in women's athletics, 133–34
photo of, *133*
Trakis, Louis, 93
Travaglianti, Edward, 208, 210, 247
Treadwell, Howard, 274
Trustees Award for Scholarly Achievement (TASA), 112, *190*
Tucker Mill Inn property, 19–20
Tuition at Southampton, 54–58
discount rates, 108, 203, 231
disproportionately high, 203
increase contested by students, 54–58, 118–19
and TAP, 125
Tunnell, Arthur W., 24
Turner, Robert
chair of C. W. Post union, 102
on core curriculum committee, 212, 213
as course coordinator for new core, 255–56
faculty in whaleboat race, *207*
grant won by, 194
on ignored recommendations, 207–208
memo of, 215–16
and Peconic Estuary Program, 230
and report on Peconic Bay property, 223
strike called by, 104
Tutt, Joan, 41

Tutt, Joan DiPaola, 246, 276
Twomey, Tom, 92
Tyson, Brady, 57
Tytel, Judith, 143

Ulrich, Susan, 13, 264
Underground press, 123–24
  See also *Christmas Camel, The* (underground newspaper)
Uris, Leon, 189
Urquart, Amy, 239–240

Valerio, Joseph, 139
VanDerzee, Robert ("Bob"), 42, 61
Veggie Car project, 265–66
Victor, Terry, 48
Vietnam protests. *See under* Southampton College: getting started, 1963–1968
Viewbook, 221, 230
Volpe, Kimberly, 241

Walker, Jimmy, 2
Wallace, Harry (Unkechaug chief), 274, *274*
Wanamaker, Mrs. Rodney, 18
Ward, Richard C., 92
Warren, Joseph, 34, *35*, 267
Weathermen, 49
Weber, Richard, *110*, 116
Weinstein, Arnold, 45
Welker, John R. ("Ral")
  founder of Marine Science program, 38, 90–91
  honorary degree awarded to, 263
  photo at retirement ceremony, *39*
  photo of, *106*
  and Shinnecock tribal oyster hatchery facility, 87, 136–37
Welker, Mary, *174*
Weller, Martha, 276
Wells, Peter, 167
Welt, Elly, 109
Wendell, Nancy, 244
Whinnie, John Mac, 111
Wilbur, Ray Lyman, 4
Williams, Victoria, 86
Willoughby, John
  arts festival organized by, 92–93
  background of, 26
  and core curriculum developed (1964), 43
  and cultivation of local artists, 36
  and solutions to attendance, 122
  and sponsored lecture presentations, 37
Wilson, Donald
  background of, 129–130, 286n1
  and Bush-Brown relationship, 135–36, 148–49
  death of, 150
  disconnect between "Wilson's reality" and real world, 140
  and endorsement by Bush-Brown, 130
  and enthusiasm for new job, 131
  goals set for, 132
  house rented for, 130, 287n2
  personality of, 130–31
  photo of, *146*, *147*
  See also Wilson and the merger
Wilson, Lanford, 111
Wilson and the merger, 1979–1985, 129–156
  background and reception of Wilson
    and dedicated staff, 131
    endorsement by Bush-Brown, 130
    enthusiasm for new job, 131
    personality of, 129–130
  capping Marine Science program in 1980, 136–37
  cooperative education program (Co-op), 132
  merger implementation (1983–1985), 153–56
    and "double suicide" (Krasnoff and Bush-Brown), 155
    honors program initiated, 154
    leadership concerns of trustees, 153–54
    and messy exit of Bush-Brown, 155–56
    new university-wide structure announced, 154
    and piano analogy, 153

Wilson and the merger, 1979–1985 *(continued)*
merger with C. W. Post, Feb 2, 1983, 150–53
after Middle States briefing, 150–51
and attempts to mollify union members, 152–53
and concerns on, 153
and faculty discontent, 152
LIU accreditation not renewed, 151
unanticipated problems, 152
perfect storm, 144–150
and distinguished alumni, 149
and Middle States' evaluation, 148, 149–150
other factors contributing to, 147
positive accomplishments of administration, 145
and Reagan's cuts to education, 145–47
and Wilson's firing, 150
Wilson's optimistic message of fall 1982, 144–45
Performing Arts Festival (1981–1983), 138–141, 287n7
failed festival cancelled in 1983, 140, 287n8
fundraising campaign for new library, 140
inadequate resources for sustaining, 141
International Prize winning Young Artists Series, 138–39, 287n7
and money removed from Marine Science account, 140–41
radio station WPBX and classical music, 139
problems encountered, 134–35
attrition rate high, 134
and costly strike, 134, 135
improvements made, 134–35
lack of financial support from LIU, 136
and "Master Plan," 135
tension between Wilson and Bush-Brown, 135–36
and Reagan's cuts in federal education aid, 145–46
Simonson estate sale
and Bridge's research project, 144
and donated land exchange, 143–44
marketing of property, 142–43
money lacking for donated works, 141–42
Southampton referred to as "jewel in the crown" of LIU, 135, 287n4
Topping's college athletics program, 133–34
See also Marine Science program; Wilson, Donald
Windmill, The (campus newspaper)
ad calling for protest march on Washington in *Windmill*, 47
awards won by, 192–93
Bergman's recollections in, 33
on BSA demands, 90
establishment of, 40
on last Vietnam protest demonstration on campus, 52
"Leon's Views" (Parks), 88
on SGA's concern about Brooklyn Center sale, 63
student protest against classical music on radio, 139
in support of Birenbaum, 60
Wilson's optimistic message of fall 1982, 144
Windmill lighting ceremony, 271–72
Winfield, Richard, 89
Winslow, Olivia, 260
Winter session, 90
Winthrop, John, 87
Wise, Walter Sr., 86
Women's sports, success of, 133–34, 192, 195, 231
Women's Studies program, 186
Wood, Chester, 22, 23, 32
Woodhull, Kim, 233
Wright, Allison, 194–95

Wright, Gordell, 85, 86

Zak, Andrew, 40, 48
Zeckendorf, William
  bankruptcy of, 69
  Conolly hired by, 10
  elected as chairman of board, 6
  intervention in Birenbaum's
    dismissal, 60
  McGrath succeeded, 64
  resignation of, 62–63, 64
  and search committee, 155
Zellner, Bob, 184
Zwirn, Ben, 246